The Soviets:
The Russian Workers, Peasants, and Soldiers Councils, 1905–1921

The Soviets:
The Russian Workers, Peasants, and Soldiers Councils,

1905–1921

OSKAR ANWEILER

Translated from the German by Ruth Hein

Pantheon Books
A Division of Random House, New York

Library of Congress Cataloging in Publication Data
Anweiler, Oskar.
    The Soviets.
Translation of *Die Rätebewegung in Russland, 1905–1921.*
    Bibliography: pp. 309–24.
    1. Soviets. 2. Socialism in Russia—History.
3. Russia—Politics and government—1894–1917.
4. Russian—Politics and government—1917–1936
I. Title.
HX313.A713   329′.07   74–4769
ISBN 0–394–47105–9

Design by Fran Gazze

Publisher's Note

The publisher gratefully acknowledges the collaboration of Susan G. Morrow and Wolfgang Sauerlander in the translation of this volume.

Contents

Preface to the American Edition

The translation of an unrevised edition of this study of the council movement in Russia, written more than ten years ago, may certainly be considered questionable. When I first dealt with the subject, I found myself on almost virgin soil. Since then—especially on the occasion of the fiftieth anniversary of the October Revolution of 1917—numerous publications in the Soviet Union and in the West have treated development of the Russian soviets, drawing on source material unknown or unavailable at the time I wrote. In the introduction to my book, I mentioned a hope that further study of special features of soviets in the Russian revolution would expand or even modify my attempt at an overall picture; that hope has proved to be justified.

Nevertheless, incorporating into a new edition details of recent investigations would not have changed essentially either the book's overall conception or its most important conclusions. The framework first developed here remains valid, especially that dealing with historic roots of the Russian soviets, their establishment during the Revolution of 1905, the attitude of Lenin and the Bolsheviks toward the councils, their effectiveness during the Revolution of 1917, and the demise of the council movement in the Kronstadt mutiny. To help the critical reader learn of progress in scholarly research, however, a list of the most important recent literature on the subject, especially of documentary sources, has been added to the bibliography.

Oskar Anweiler

Bochum, July 1971

Preface

I first became interested in undertaking this study in a seminar held by Professor Fritz Fischer (Hamburg) on "Revolution and Reform in European Socialism." After finishing my university studies I continued to be fascinated by the Russian councils—their origins, development, and effects—and pursued my investigations. Extensive professional commitments, however, delayed completion of the work.

The editors of *Studien zur Geschichte Osteuropas* were kind enough to include the book in their series. My thanks go first of all to Dr. Peter Scheibert (Cologne) for his initiative and for much expert advice. Dr. Dietrich Geyer (Tübingen) readily allowed me access to rare source materials. Professor Gotthold Rhode (Mainz) has for years shown friendly interest in my work's progress. In procuring materials, I have had the help of the State and University Library in Hamburg, the library of the Institut für Auswärtige Politik and the library of Auer-Verlag (both in Hamburg), as well as the Westdeutsche Bibliothek in Marburg. A grant from the Research Program on the History of the CPSU of Columbia University in New York enabled me to spend several weeks at the university library in Helsinki.

My deepest thanks to all who have been involved in this project, not least my wife, who watched over the book's creation with patience and encouragement and who helped me digest the source material and type the manuscript.

Oskar Anweiler

Reinbek bei Hamburg
August 1958

Introduction

The constitution of contemporary Russia, the Union of Socialist Soviet Republics, is formally based on a system of councils or soviets.[1] Consequently everyday speech treats the terms "soviets" and "Bolshevism" as virtually identical, usage which may correctly reflect the political situation today, but which is not justified historically. On the contrary, a closer look at the origins of the Bolshevik state shows that the councils developed independently. It was only at a particular stage in their development that they combined with a second element, Lenin's theory of revolution and government and the Bolshevik practice of party and government, to form a new entity—the Bolshevik council system.

This work's purpose is to trace that historical process, from the origins of the councils through their various activities to their transformation in the Bolshevik state—the process I call the council movement.

So far no such attempt has been undertaken—rather surprisingly since the councils are a central theme of the Russian revolution and Bolshevism and, beyond this, a political and social phenomenon whose significance transcends the unique historical event. As such, the soviet movement certainly should tempt study from the most varied viewpoints. The revolutionary events in Hungary and Poland during the autumn of 1956 dramatized unexpectedly the pertinence of the council issue, just as the Yugoslav system of workers councils had earlier elicited attention.

These examples show a wider intellectual and social historical context that has the Russian revolution at its core. Lenin's slogan of 1917, "All power to the soviets," sent out shock waves that were felt beyond Russia's borders long after the councils had played out their roles in Bolshevik Russia herself. A council myth developed that became basic to the history of the European labor movement and of socialism; tracing its various manifestations would be a fruitful research project. In Germany, for example, from 1918 through 1920 passionate discussion of the councils ranged from idealized glorification to rigid rejection and produced a great many theoretical models.[2] More recently, in the short-lived revolutionary councils in Hungary and especially in the workers councils in Polish factories, the example of democracy that councils embody was the driving intellectual force behind the workers' revolution.[3]

These references to the Russian council movement's continuing attraction as an ideal also serve to stake out the boundaries of this investigation. Its purpose is to describe and analyze the soviets' origins in the Russian revolution, their practical work and political role in 1905 and 1917, with the theoretical and tactical positions taken toward the soviets by the Bolsheviks and the other socialist parties, and finally the soviets' transformation from revolutionary organs into pillars of state power in the new "soviet" state. The work ends with the year 1921, the turning point for the soviet movement: suppression of the Kronstadt mutiny means a forced end to the soviet idea in Russia and at the same time its drastic transformation. While in Bolshevik Russia the soviets solidified into administrative agencies of the state, the battle cry of Kronstadt, "Free Soviets," became the symbol of the "third revolution" directed against Communist usurpers of the council concept. From the sailors' mutiny in March 1921 in Kronstadt, through June 17, 1953, in East Germany, and on through October 1956 in Hungary and Poland, the revolutionary rebirth of the councils in a struggle against Bolshevik dictatorship runs its course.

As mentioned earlier, the Russian council movement as a whole has never been researched and accounted for. Either the soviets have been treated with other events in studies of the Russian revolution, or it was thought sufficient to point out the legal peculiarities of the council system in examining the Soviet Union's constitution, without reference to the councils' historic roots. Only the works of Artur Rosenberg and Martin Buber,[4] though they deal with a much larger field, touch upon development of the Russian councils—naturally without investigating details.

A word here about sources, which were more readily available than I had anticipated when I began research. I was able to use numerous collections of documents covering the Revolutions of 1905 and 1917 and subsequent years, the writings of Lenin, Trotsky, and other participants in the revolution, as well as various memoirs, brochures, and pamphlets, and the most relevant newspapers. The materials, however, were widely dispersed geographically and not all accessible to the same degree. Nor could I examine all the documents and treatises of a local character which had been published in the Soviet Union—not to mention, of course, the unpublished source material still existing in central and local archives. A presentation of all regional developments and peculiarities was neither possible nor intended. Better relations with Soviet historians, however, would open a fruitful field for monographic studies on this subject.

Note on Transliteration

The linguistic system of transliteration of Russian, used in the original German edition, has been observed here with this exception: in the text, the spelling of names of persons and places follows the most common American usage, on the basis of standard biographical dictionaries, encyclopedias, and recent British and American works. Notes and bibliography have been retained in their original form to facilitate their accessibility to scholars.

The Soviets:
The Russian Workers, Peasants, and Soldiers Councils, 1905–1921

CHAPTER ONE

Antecedents
of the Russian Councils

---

1. THE COUNCIL CONCEPT

In standard usage, "council" is understood to be an assembly of representatives, a congress or committee which exists for the purpose of "counseling" and which may perform various tasks and functions —as, for example, a municipal council, a privy council, a factory committee, or a board of directors. As a specific historical-political concept, however, the word is applied to representative organs that most often came into existence in revolutionary situations to represent the lower levels of society, such as soldiers, artisans, or workers.[1]

This concept, the only relevant one for our purpose, is often used rather loosely to include numerous historical manifestations that are assumed to emanate from one basic type of "council." Rosenberg reduces to a common denominator the "urban communes of the middle ages, the Swiss peasant cantons, the original collective settlements in North America, the Paris Commune of 1871, and the Russian soviets."[2] Another writer goes so far as to detect the first historical instance of the council idea in the Roman lex Hortensia of 287 B.C., which recognized plebeian associations as legal institutions

of the Roman state.[3] Still other authors restrict the concept to certain
well-defined manifestations in more recent history—such as the
English soldiers councils of the seventeenth century, and the Paris
Communes of the French Revolution and of 1871—but they too
fail to provide a consistent criterion for "council" in a historical
context. This lack of terminological clarity stems chiefly from
efforts to find historical antecedents and models for a unique
historic phenomenon—the Russian soviets. In this search for models,
historians discovered the soviets' organizational principles and revolutionary tendencies in similar institutions of the past, which
thereupon were classified as "councils." In this way the council concept was extended beyond its single concrete manifestation in Russia
—and later during the German Revolution of 1918—to stand for
a basic constitutional form that recurs in different historical epochs.

There can be a difference of opinion about the usefulness of such
a sweeping concept of councils. When applying the concept, one must,
however, consider that thereby various individual occurrences are
isolated from the manifold historical conditions that produced them,
and reduced to a few, often purely formal, common characteristics
that make up the prototype. Such a process can be meaningful only
when one deals with a period of continuous development, which in
the present case means leaving aside obvious examples provided by
ancient and medieval history.

Accepting this limitation, the following general characteristics of
the council concept may be noted:

1) its connection with a particular dependent or oppressed social
stratum;

2) radical democracy as its form;

3) a revolutionary origin.

The inherent tendency of such councils, which may be called "the
council idea," is the striving toward the most direct, far-reaching,
and unrestricted participation of the individual in public life. When
applied to the collective, it becomes the idea of self-government of
the masses, combined with the will to revolutionary transformation.

The council idea became effective "whenever the masses wished
to overcome a feudal or centralized power,"[4] as, for example, during
the rise of the bourgeoisie in its struggle against feudalism or later
in the proletariat's struggle for social emancipation.

Among such councils three basic forms can be distinguished:

1) Council = commune = "the people" organized to exercise state power. (Example: the Paris Commune of 1871.)
2) Council = revolutionary committee = organ for directing the revolutionary struggle for a limited time. (Example: the soldiers councils of the English Revolution.)
3) Council = workers committee = representation of proletarian interests. (Example: the Luxembourg Commission of 1848.)

But the boundaries are frequently fluid. It will be seen that none of these forms alone is characteristic of the Russian councils; rather, they underwent a development that encompassed all three types—council as workers and revolutionary committee and as state power.

No conscious connection with any historical models can be proved for the creation of the soviets in the Russian Revolution. Therefore the various organs commonly named as antecedents are of only limited interest for the history of the soviets. If some of them are considered here, it is solely to show that in similar situations, emerging social groups arrived at similar experiments in communal organization—that, in other words, the council idea before 1917 is not informed by any continuous historical tradition, although historical parallels and analogous organizational forms did exist.[5]

An understanding of the councils' characteristic qualities can more readily be gained by knowing their respective concrete political, social, and socio-psychological circumstances than through references to historical models. Even so, the councils as they actually existed must be clearly distinguished from the ideology that was subsequently developed. This ideology tries to construct an ideal council system that tends to leave reality far behind. Karl Marx, in his interpretation of the Commune, and especially Lenin, in his theory of the soviet state, drew such an idealized picture, which stands in sharp contrast to reality. One aim of the present study is to call attention to this contradiction and to compare the actual histories of the council movement and its accompanying ideology.

2. HISTORICAL ANTECEDENTS

In all three Western European revolutions of modern times—the English Revolution of the seventeenth century; the French Revolution of 1789; and the Revolution of 1848—we encounter revolutionary organs that exhibit the characteristics of the council prototypes described above.

A kind of soldiers council was formed by the notorious "agitators" of the English Revolution.[6] In the spring of 1647 the soldiers of Cromwell's army, reacting to parliament's intention to dissolve, named spokesmen—agitators—to represent the interests of the common soldier. A "General Council of the Army" was created, composed of two elected soldiers or noncommissioned officers and two appointed officers for each regiment; in a manifesto issued on Newmarket Heath on June 4, 1647, this council declared itself as representing the interests of the army "of free men of England." The agitators were an expression of democratic tendencies within the English army, and were close to the radical popular leader John Lilburne. In their negotiations with the army high command, the agitators sought to urge it forward on a revolutionary course. Conflicts soon arose, however, and after an unsuccessful army mutiny in November 1647, the General Council was disbanded in January 1648 and the system of representation abolished. Thus, the attempt at forming "a government of revolutionary dictatorship"[7]—if it can be called that at all—was quickly crushed.

The Paris Commune during the French Revolution—"the purest manifestation along class lines"[8] of the bourgeois revolutionary movement against feudalism in the years 1789–1794—was the political organization of the revolutionary French bourgeoisie and petit bourgeoisie. During the nineteenth century the Commune not only served as a model to the radical democratic movements, but some of its traits justified its consideration as a precursor of the councils.[9]

The commune movement during the French Revolution began in the 60 Paris districts (primary districts) that had been established for elections to the national assembly. These districts constituted themselves into self-governing bodies of the third estate, and from their midst elected a revolutionary municipal council, the Commune. From Paris, communes spread quickly throughout France. Everywhere revolutionary municipal councils sprang up. At the beginning the propertied bourgeoisie (voting citizens) was in the vanguard, but under pressure from the nonvoting citizens, the municipal councils grew increasingly radical. In April 1790 the Paris districts were replaced by 48 sections, whose spokesmen formed the general assembly of the Paris Commune.

Along with the political clubs and the citizens' committees, the sections became the actual centers of revolutionary activity. They introduced universal suffrage on their own, had their own police, and assumed economic functions (supplying uniforms to the army, establishing workshops)—in short, they were the actual representatives of the people's sovereignty. At the same time they were in continuous session as permanent agitating revolutionary assemblies. On August 10, 1792, a coup prepared by the Jacobins overthrew the old Paris Commune and replaced it with the Revolutionary Commune, composed of spokesmen for the radical sections.

With the establishment of Jacobin rule in 1793 the sections, through the committees set up by the government and directly answerable to it, were more and more transformed into organs of the central power and tools of the Terror, "thus obliterating the sections and the revolutionary municipal administration."[10] After the assassination of Robespierre, and with a growing reaction setting in, the sections, and the Commune based on them, increasingly lost significance.

The Paris sections were expressions of a direct radical democracy; the delegates chosen by universal suffrage were held permanently answerable and could be recalled. Though modified by immediate political and strategic needs, direct democracy as embodied in the Commune nevertheless remained the central principle of a continuing revolutionary tradition.

The "Commission du gouvernement pour les travailleurs" (also called "Commission du Luxembourg" after its headquarters in the Palais Luxembourg) belongs to the type of council classified as a "workers committee." It was founded in Paris during the February Revolution of 1848, by governmental decree in response to pressure from the workers,[11] and consisted of a commission and a parliament. It included not only delegates elected by the workers clubs, but also employer delegates and socialist theoreticians (foremost among them Louis Blanc). Despite its creation by government decree and its nominal composition of workers and employers, the latter's absence and a continuing revolutionary ferment made the Luxembourg Commission the spokesmen for political and social reform desired by Parisian workers. After the insurrection of June the Commission was dissolved.

Although without practical effect (the government regulation fixing the working day at ten hours in Paris and eleven hours in the provinces was rescinded), the Commission was historically significant for the labor movement. Karl Marx was highly critical of the Luxembourg Commission's activities, but nevertheless credited it with "having revealed from a European platform the secret of nineteenth-century revolution: the emancipation of the proletariat."[12]

3. THEORETICAL FORERUNNERS

What has been said about historic antecedents of the Russian councils applies in greater measure to their theoretical forerunners. The political and revolutionary conceptions and social blueprints advocated by leading nineteenth-century socialist and anarchist thinkers, Russian as well as non-Russian, reveal many elements of the council idea, though there is no direct historical connection. Ideas that seem to foreshadow the Bolshevik system of councils erected after 1917, or the "pure" theory of councils developed by its opponents, come quite naturally to people who are committed to social reform or a "restructuring" of society, as Martin Buber put it. Release from the state's tutelage, self-government by cooperative producer groups, autonomy of local communes, were basic concerns of European socialism, from the so-called "utopian socialists" of the early nineteenth century, to Proudhon, Bakunin, Marx, Engels, and Kropotkin, to all kinds of syndicalism and the organized socialist parties in many countries.[13] Often there are striking parallels in form and structure with the later council system, but their significance must not be overestimated.

The ideas of only two figures from this group will be discussed here: Proudhon and Bakunin. Proudhon, though Marx's antithesis, was next to him the most creative socialist of the nineteenth century. Proudhon's views are often directly associated with the Russian councils, and sometimes even held decisive for their establishment.[14] Bakunin must be mentioned because he, much more than Proudhon, linked anarchist principles directly to revolutionary action, thus arriving at remarkable insights into the revolutionary process that contribute to an understanding of later events in Russia.

The prodigious writings of Pierre-Joseph Proudhon (1809–1865) contain—as recent scholarship demonstrated[15]—a "kernel of anti-authoritarianism," and his anarchist thinking is "the expression of a basic human attitude"[16] that is not limited to any particular historical period. Proudhon's libertarian position determined his political and economic views. He believed in private property, and in a "just" social order founded on producer associations. With the disappearance of rent and money, the bases of class exploitation, state authority, with its attendant bureaucracy and police, will collapse, and natural economic groups can legislate and govern for themselves.

In 1863 Proudhon declared that the proper form of government consists of a maximum number of small groups with extensive autonomy. "All my economic ideas as developed over twenty-five years can be summed up in the words: agricultural-industrial federation. All my political ideas boil down to a similar formula: political federation or decentralization."[17]

Thus Proudhon consciously opposes Marx, whose communist centralization of the society of the future he criticized as a variation on the old absolutism.[18] The confrontation between Marxism and Proudhonism, which led to the division and dissolution of the First International, was reenacted fifty years later in Russia. Proudhon's concept of a self-governing state founded on producers' corporations, is certainly related to the idea of "a democracy of producers" which emerged in the factory soviets. To this extent Proudhon can be regarded as an ideological precursor of the councils. But his direct influence on the establishment of the soviets cannot be proved. Conversely, Lenin's centralization of both state and economy, which robbed the soviet system of its inherent strength, was Marx's belated answer to Proudhon.[19]

The thought and action of Mikhail Bakunin (1814–1876) centers on passionate rejection of any principle of authority and of the state that embodies it.[20] "The revolution as we understand it must, from the first day, basically and completely destroy the state and all state institutions. . . . Every payment of duties and every levy of direct and indirect taxes will cease; the army, the bureaucracy, the police, and the clergy will dissolve; the judiciary, the established law, and the exercise of that law will disappear"—so wrote Bakunin in 1868 in the program of the Alliance of International Brothers.[21] Bakunin dreamed of a huge peasant rising in Russia and of a Western European revolution carried to the countryside by urban workers. Although he believed in spontaneous action by the masses, he nevertheless expected a secret "revolutionary general staff" to mediate between the people's unformulated instincts and the revolutionary idea. He suggested the formation of revolutionary committees with representatives from the barricades, the streets, and the city districts, who would be given binding mandates, held accountable to the masses, and subject to recall. These revolutionary deputies were to form the "federation of the barricades," organized as a revolutionary commune to immediately unite with other centers of rebellion.[22] In the villages revolutionary peasants' committees, composed of the most active men, would replace the legal village administration. The revolution would produce the "new revolutionary state," no longer a state in the accepted sense, but "developed from the bottom upward by revolutionary delegations encompassing all countries with uprisings based on the same principles, disregarding previous borders and differences in nationality"; its purpose would be "administration of public services, not regimentation of the people."[23]

Bakunin proposed the formation of revolutionary committees to elect communal councils, and a pyramidal organization of society "through free federation from the bottom upward, the association of workers in industry and agriculture—first in the communities, then through federation of communities into districts, districts into nations, and nations into international brotherhood."[24] These proposals are indeed strikingly similar to the structure of the subsequent Russian system of councils, and also anticipate its claim to universal validity.

The extent of Bakunin's influence on the theory and practice of Bolshevism is moot. As loyal followers of Marx, the Bolsheviks continued his battle against Bakunin and denied any kinship with anarchism. The question is not so simply decided, however. Lenin's Revolution of 1917 and the development of the soviet state bring Bakunin's role into a double focus. On the one hand Bakunin recognized very clearly in Marx's authoritarian and centralist principles the danger of a future dictatorship of "the leaders of the Communist Party" who will "begin to free [the people] in their own way,"[25] whereby abolition of the state, though promised by the Marxists, would be postponed indefinitely. On the other hand, Bakunin's practical program for revolution is obviously connected with the tactics followed by Lenin and the Bolsheviks during the Russian Revolution. Bakunin called for radicalization of peasants by urban workers and propaganda divisions—armed if necessary—and despite his fundamental mistrust of authoritarian principles of leadership, he expressly admitted that spontaneous mass risings must be led by a small minority of revolutionary conspirators. His frequent assertion that the revolution must remove—"smash"—all existing institutions became a constant formula in Lenin's revolutionary vocabulary of 1917. Bakunin's ideas about spontaneous development of the revolution and the masses' capacity for elementary organization undoubtedly were echoed in part by the subsequent soviet movement. But an immediate intellectual connection cannot be demonstrated. Because Bakunin—unlike Marx—was always very close to the reality of the social struggle, he was able to foresee concrete aspects of the revolution. The council movement during the Russian Revolution, though not a result of Bakunin's theories, often corresponded in form and progress to his revolutionary concepts and predictions. In turn, Lenin's anarchist leanings in 1917 resulted from his accommodation to tendencies embodied in the councils. Thus in the council movement the fundamental difference between Lenin and Bakunin is temporarily concealed by their apparent connection and kinship.

4. KARL MARX AND THE PARIS COMMUNE OF 1871

The Paris Commune of 1871 and its interpretation by Karl Marx have a special place among antecedents of the Russian councils, though like those discussed above, the Commune too had no direct influence on the formation and early activity of the soviets. Nevertheless, it formed the point of departure for the Bolshevik theory of soviets. The Commune marks the beginning of the dual development mentioned at the outset: the concrete historical phenomenon of the councils, as opposed to the ideology that appropriated them. And it was precisely Marx's picture of the Commune, though it coincided only partially with reality, that became historically effective. It was the bridge Lenin crossed when he sought to incorporate the Russian soviets into the Marxist theory of state and revolution.

The Paris Commune of 1871 originated in the wake of France's defeat in the war with Germany and in the context of the republican and revolutionary tradition of Paris.[26] The central committee of the National Guard, which headed a system of soldiers councils, took the initiative in proclaiming the Commune. The battalion clubs, as the lowest elements, elected a legion council, each of which sent three representatives to the sixty-member central committee. In addition, provisions were made for a general assembly of delegates from the companies, which was intended to meet once a month. All delegates could be recalled at any time.[27]

A clash between the troops of Thiers' government, sitting in Versailles, and the National Guard on March 18, 1871, ended in victory for the latter. The central committee found itself in power in the capital and moved to the city hall. Since the committee thought of itself as a provisional body, it hastily passed on responsibility to what it considered the legal government—the Commune. For some time the various political clubs had agitated for a commune formed by revolutionary means in the tradition of the Great Revolution. Thus the ground was prepared for the elections to the Commune announced for March 26, 1871. About 230,000 persons (47 percent of the enfranchised inhabitants) took part; for the most part they were workers and members of the petit bourgeoisie, whereas the bourgeoisie in part abstained. Among the elected communards, 25 workers and 7 clerks faced 30 members of the intelligentsia (doctors, lawyers, journalists); the remainder were small merchants, artisans, and the like.[28] Of the 25 workers, only 13 were members of the First International, and most of these were adherents of the teachings of Proudhon.[29]

The political grouping within the Commune depended hardly at all on the social standing of its members. On key questions the workers were split just as much as their colleagues. In the first days the Commune split into a "socialist" minority, consisting predominantly of members of the International and followers of Proudhon, and a "Blanquist-Jacobin" majority, whose main support came from the revolutionary clubs and the central committee of the National Guard.[30] While the minority advocated a federation of free communes in the political sphere and an association of producers in the economic area, the majority adhered to the centralist traditions of Jacobin rule. These ideologic differences found expression in the Commune's proclamations, which were often obscure and full of contradictions; in its practical dealings the pressure of external conditions enforced a certain middle course of action.

It is difficult to reconstruct something like a program of the Commune from the various currents, legislative measures, propaganda pronouncements, and practical steps. Most evident was the call for municipal republican self-government as a basis of the new state organization. In order to cloak the natural antagonism—particularly acute in France—between the capital and the provinces, which might harm the cause of the Commune, and to allay provincial mistrust, the Commune called for free confederation of all French communes with Paris in one national organization.[31] Another principle voiced equally frequently was the replacement of the civil service bureaucracy with elected people's delegates, subject to recall. "The members of the municipal assembly, who are permanently controlled, supervised, and criticized by public opinion, can be recalled and are responsible and accountable."[32] Social questions, however, were only rarely and rather vaguely considered in the proclamations. The decrees that introduced a few social reforms (such as abolition of night work by bakers' apprentices, or prohibition of money fines in factories) or that were intended to realize earlier socialist ideas (such as transfer to workers corporations of workshops and factories abandoned by their owners did not originate in any clear socialist program and were far more often dictated by immediate need.

The Commune of Paris lasted a bare two months. The capital remained isolated, for uprisings in several provincial cities were put down as early as the beginning of April. On May 21, 1871, the government troops began their offensive; the bloody street fighting lasted until May 28. The high losses and numerous prison and death sentences represented a heavy setback for the French workers' movement. Nevertheless, the significance of the Paris Commune rests not primarily in French history, but with the international socialist workers' movement. It created a commune myth, which in the end had very little in common with reality. "The struggle of the working class against the capitalist class and its state has entered a new phase with the struggle in Paris. Whatever the immediate results may be, a new point of departure of world-historic importance has been gained," wrote Karl Marx even before the collapse of the Commune.[33] That his prediction came true is due primarily to Marx himself.

It is difficult to speak of Marx's theory of state and revolution as a progressive, coherent development. His remarks, especially about the future form of a socialist society, were in response to immediate political circumstances, and often incidentally fulfilled tactical purposes.[34] Lenin's attempt, in *State and Revolution*, to erect a complete theoretic structure upon disparate sources ranging from the young Marx of 1847 to Engels in his old age, is an over-simplification that was intended mainly to support his own new theory. It is therefore wrong simply to count Marx and Engels among the legitimate forerunners of the soviets and of the Bolshevik council system, as is constantly done in Soviet theory of the state.

The *Communist Manifesto* of 1848 states the tasks of the proletariat during the revolution as follows: "The proletariat will use its political supremacy to wrest, by degrees, all capital from the bourgeoisie, to centralize all instruments of production in the hands of the state, i.e., of the proletariat organized as the ruling class."[35] Two years later, after the defeat of the revolution, Marx—filled with hope for a new revolutionary rising—wrote: "It is our concern and our task to make the revolution permanent, until all more or less propertied classes are ousted from supremacy, until supreme power has been captured, and the association of the proletariat—not only in one country, but in all the ruling nations of the world—has progressed to the point that . . . at least the main productive energies are concentrated in the hands of the proletariat."[36] Marx's revolutionary optimism during the years 1848–1850 led him to discern socialist production methods in the still incipient capitalism and leadership for the social revolution in the as yet weak working class. By taking political power and "by means of despotic inroads on the rights of property, and on the conditions of bourgeois production"[37] a new society was to be formed.

In the course of the "permanent revolution" proclaimed by Marx[38] the relationship of the proletariat and the workers' party to "bourgeois democrats" plays a decisive role. In his "Address of the Central Authority to the Communist League" of March 1850, Marx projected the basic revolutionary tactics that represent his first contribution to the council idea. The essay states: "During the struggle and after the struggle the workers must at every opportunity advance their own demands alongside the demands of the bourgeois democrats. . . . Alongside the new official governments they must simultaneously erect their own revolutionary workers governments, whether in the form of municipal executives and municipal councils, or of workers clubs and workers committees—so that the bourgeois democratic governments not only lose the backing of the workers, but also from the very beginning find themselves watched and threatened by institutions behind which stand the entire mass of workers." Marx further called for arming the workers and for the formation of a proletarian guard "with elected leaders and a general staff of their own" and "under orders, not of the state, but of the revolutionary municipal councils established by the workers."[39]

The municipal councils, workers clubs, and similar organizations called for by Marx are really revolutionary committees intended to make the revolution "permanent" and to set up a kind of "dyarchy" alongside the bourgeois government. This is indeed a striking anticipation of the role of the workers and soldiers councils after the February Revolution of 1917, which confronted the Provisional Government with their own claim to rule, and pursued an independent course of revolutionary politics. Marx's revolutionary program of 1850 is interesting for still another reason. By calling for revolutionary municipal councils in opposition to the central bourgeois government, he seemingly becomes an advocate of local self-government in opposition to the centralized state. This obvious interpretation, however, was vigorously rejected by Marx himself. In the same address, he stressed the necessity for a central organization of the workers clubs in the Communist League. He held that a cardinal point of the program had to read: against the democratic slogan of federated republics; for a strong central power. "The workers must strive . . . for a clear-cut centralization of power in the hands of the state authority. They must not let themselves be led astray by democratic talk of communal liberties, self-government, and the like."[40] Marx considers the revolutionary municipal councils as nothing more than temporary organs in the political struggle to advance the revolution, not as the germs of a radical transformation of society, which can only be achieved from above, through the centralized power of the proletarian state. Nevertheless, the contradiction remains between the localized revolutionary organs recommended for tactical reasons, and the demand for proletarian centralism, a contradiction Marx did not attempt to resolve; perhaps he was not aware of it. He faced the same problem concerning the Commune of 1871 as did Lenin in 1917.

Marx had neither foreseen nor prepared for the Commune insurrection. After proclamation of the republic in September 1870 he warned the French workers against overthrowing the new regime and "establishing the Commune of Paris," since to do so would be "desperate folly."[41] But when the revolution broke out, Marx placed himself unreservedly on the side of the Commune. After its collapse he prevailed upon the general council of the International to release an "Address Concerning the Civil War in France" on May 30, 1871, which he himself wrote, and in which the International declared the cause of the Paris Commune to be the concern of the international proletariat. "In this way Marx annexed for himself the Commune of 1871. An odd historical procedure, since the Commune rebellion was neither politically nor theoretically Marx's work," was Artur Rosenberg's justified comment.[42]

The main ideas of the 1871 "Address" and of the subsequent statements by Marx and Engels referring to it may be summarized as follows:

1) In a victorious revolution the proletariat must destroy the old state machinery, the instrument of the ruling class. "One thing especially was proved by the Commune, viz., 'that the working class cannot simply lay hold of the ready-made state machinery, and wield it for its own purposes,' " wrote Marx in the preface to a new edition of the *Communist Manifesto* in 1872.[43]

2) The armed forces, the police, and the civil service must be replaced by an armed people's militia and by self-government of the working masses by means of deputies who may be removed from office at any time, and who are held accountable.

3) From these premises follows the rejection of parliamentarianism and of division of powers. Their place is taken by a corporate entity that exercises the legislative, executive, and judicial functions all in one. "Rather than deciding once every three or six years which member of the ruling class will represent and repress the people in parliament, universal suffrage should serve the people organized into communes, just as individual suffrage serves any other employer to choose workers, supervisors, and bookkeepers for his business. . . . The Commune is to be, not a parliamentary, but a working body, executive and legislative at the same time."[44]

4) A Commune-type state is based on far-reaching local self-government of the separate municipalities, which, however, are united in pyramid-like fashion, into a confederation. "As soon as the Commune regime was introduced in Paris and the secondary centers,

the old central government should have given way even in the provinces of the self-government of the producers. . . . The simple existence of the Commune brought with it as a matter of course local self-government, but no longer directed against the power of the state, which had been rendered superfluous. . . . The unity of the nation was not to be destroyed; on the contrary, it was to be organized by means of the Commune constitution."[45]

5) The Commune state represents the transition to communism, the classless society, in that it abolishes private property, socializes the means of production, and regulates the economy according to a general plan—in short, it realizes the socialism that has been nascent in capitalist society. In 1875 Marx wrote: "Between capitalist and communist society lies the period of revolutionary transformation of one into the other. There is a corresponding period of political transition, during which the state can be nothing but the revolutionary dictatorship of the proletariat."[46] After Marx's death, Engels concluded the foreword to a new edition of the "Address," to commemorate the twentieth anniversary of the Commune, with the following statement: "The German philistine has lately again experienced a salutary shock at the phrase 'dictatorship of the proletariat.' Very well, gentlemen, do you want to know what this dictatorship looks like? Look at the Paris Commune. That was the dictatorship of the proletariat."[47] These words by Engels are virtually the formula to which Marxism reduced the essence of the Paris Commune. A state modeled on the Paris Commune was, as Marx wrote in the "Address" of 1871, "the political structure, finally discovered, under which the economic liberation of work can take place";[48] it was the concrete historical form of the dictatorship of the proletariat, of the transitional stage toward the classless society and toward the final "withering away of the state."

Even a superficial comparison of the actual history of the Paris Commune with Marx's description shows that his picture of the Commune coincides only in part with reality. By stressing certain traits of the Commune and bypassing or reinterpreting others to support his thesis, Marx created an idealized "Marxist Commune" that was to fit his conception of history and revolution. Marx was accused even in his lifetime of having "usurped" the Commune. Bakunin, most notably, pointed out that Marx was forced by the powerful impression of the revolutionary events to adopt the Commune's program as his own, contrary to his previous views, in order to maintain his position in the Socialist International.[49] Indeed, it is not easy to reconcile the picture of the revolution painted in the "Address" with Marx's earlier political theories. That Marx himself was surely aware of the contradiction is shown, for example, by his attempt to combine the Commune's basic federalist tendency—which he could hardly deny—with his own centralist concept of the state.[50] He resolved the antithesis, as it were, by declaring that "self-government of the producers" rendered the old state power superfluous and that the new "unity of the nation" did not admit of conflict between centralism and self-government.

To draw attention away as much as possible from the Commune's anticentralist nature, Marx and Engels—and later Lenin, even more pronouncedly—chiefly stressed the negative aspects of the Commune: its "destruction" of the existing bourgeois state and its difference from conventional parliamentarianism. By over-emphasizing formal characteristics of the Commune (such as abolition of the bureaucracy, voters' right to recall delegates), Marx laid the groundwork for sanctioning of the Commune and later the council as the only form of proletarian class dictatorship. Only after 1945 was a variant of this form—in the guise of "people's democracies"—admitted, and after the CPSU Twentieth Party Congress in 1956 other "paths to socialism" were recognized—without, however, relinquishing the soviets as the model.

Marx's interpretation of the Commune had no ideological significance for the socialist parties of the Second International. It came to the fore only with the Bolshevik Revolution of 1917, the establishment of the soviet state, and the Bolshevik ideologic struggle against the socialist parties. On the one hand Marx's view was the strongest argument for the Leninist theory and practice of government; on the other hand it was utilized by the anti-Bolshevik Marxists to prove the perversion of genuine Marxism by the Bolsheviks. The extensive controversial literature[51] centers on the question: What did Marx mean when he called the Commune the prototype of the dictatorship of the proletariat? While the Bolsheviks overwhelmingly understood him to be referring to the unlimited power of the proletarian regime against class enemies, reformist socialists emphasized the Commune's democratic nature, derived from universal and egalitarian elections.

Trotsky was undoubtedly correct when he wrote in his polemic against Kautsky that Marx had emphasized, not the Commune's general democratic nature, but its class content (that is, as a workers' government).[52] Contrarily, it is equally correct to say that Marx equated the dictatorship of the proletariat, at least in theory, with the rule of the great majority of the people over the minority of the "exploiters."[53] The deciding factor in this ideological conflict in the Marxist camp was the reality of the Bolshevik soviet state, which claimed to be the legitimate heir of the Paris Commune of 1871.

CHAPTER TWO

The Soviets and
the Russian Revolution of 1905

The year 1905 marks the birth of the Russian councils. The concept and form of the soviets, the "councils of workers deputies" (sovety rabočich deputatov) originated in the first Russian revolution. Indeed, the 1905 soviets turned out to be of world-historic significance as the beginning of the Bolshevik council system and Russia's present government. The council concept in its Leninist form or in any form outside Russia falls back on the model of the 1905 soviets. Quite apart from that, the soviets of 1905 are of interest as an attempt at establishing a political organization within a revolution, and as a first step toward a radical democracy. As self-governing bodies of Russian workers and as committees serving the revolutionary struggle, the soviets of 1905 were new, having traits which were specifically Russian but also useful outside Russia and typical of revolutionary and sociopolitical conditions later repeated elsewhere.

As bases for the Bolshevik council system and as organizational models for the revolution, the 1905 soviets were only precursors of the 1917 soviets. During their relatively brief existence, much remained embryonic and tentative, wide open to development in one direction or another. Soviet historians see a straight line of development from the first soviets of 1905 to Bolshevik governmental institutions after the October Revolution of 1917. But this work holds that the more realistic view is that the soviets of 1905 and those of 1917 for a long time developed independently of the Bolshevik party and its ideology, and that their aim initially was not the seizure of state power. Only Lenin's 1917 theory of state and revolution established the logical sequence—Paris Commune of 1871, to soviets of 1905, to soviets of 1917—as the basis of state power. In the first Russian revolution practical considerations more or less shaped the soviets; more ambitious aims developed only gradually, and a full-fledged council ideology was the final step.

1. THE RUSSIAN LABOR MOVEMENT BEFORE THE 1905 REVOLUTION

a) Early Forms of the Russian Labor Movement

The soviets evolved with the Russian labor movement and were rooted in Russian life.

Crucial to Russia's modern history is her inclusion in the capitalist development of Western Europe in the second half of the nineteenth century. The introduction of modern industrial forms into a country that for a long time to come was to remain predominantly agrarian carried with it many social and political problems. These were intensified by the absence of constitutional mechanisms which might have favored an evolutionary compromise among conflicting interests. Russia remained a semifeudal state under an autocracy, while new social alignments began to take shape and almost all of the intellectual leadership opposed czarism. Russia was the first to face a "revolution of underdeveloped nations"—the major problem of the second half of the twentieth century.[1]

Russian industrial workers—numbering a scant three million on the eve of the first revolution[2]—had their roots predominantly in the villages. Even after the Emancipation Act of 1861, the Russian factory worker was an "economic amphibian"[3]: at first he worked in the factory seasonally, returning to the village only to set out again to find factory work, perhaps in another area. He continued to be a member of the village community, the mir; he received a parcel of land which was cultivated by his family; and even in the legal sense he was considered a peasant.[4] The shifts from place to place discouraged the emergence of a skilled, culturally advanced working class, conscious of its place in society. Nevertheless, by the end of the nineteenth century a new industrial worker had emerged: a proletarian who was born in the city, or who retained only weak ties with the mir, except for formal police registration there. Differences in area and branch of industry were important in the development of the new class. Textile workers in the central regions around Moscow and miners in the Ural Mountains remained more closely connected with the countryside than were metalworkers in the giant factories of St. Petersburg, who had largely freed themselves from their native soil.[5]

Workers who had only just escaped from slave labor and serfdom were exposed in the new factory environment to a dependence no less strict. Just as Russian industry, beginning in the 1870s, exhibited all the traits of an era of ruthless expansion, so Russian workers encountered conditions paralleling the early capitalist stages which had been outgrown by them in Central and Western Europe. The clash between Western rationalized industrial management and the traditions of Russian life was particularly violent within the confines of the factory. The workday was nowhere less than eleven hours; wages were low and sometimes reduced even further by punitive fines; there was no protection against dismissal, and no insurance covering accidents, illness, or retirement. At the end of the nineteenth century certain leading groups of workers, such as the printers and some metalworkers and dockers, achieved better conditions, and in the 1880s a few protective laws were passed (prohibition of nightwork for children, adolescents, and women, and introduction of factory inspections). But for the working masses the harsh social conditions remained until the eve of the 1905 Revolution.[6]

In this soil grew the first incidents of labor unrest, as yet unorganized and only local. Statistics show 176 strikes in the decade from 1870 to 1879, and 165 from 1880 to 1890, most of them carried out by textile workers.[7] Often workers' hostility turned directly against the site of their exploitation, the factory; demolition and other excesses occurred. The strikes of this period were typical of beginning labor movements in other countries.

The 1870s witnessed the first short-lived attempts at political organization of workers, initiated by the Narodniks.[8] However, neither the leaders nor their semirural followers had a "proletarian class consciousness" as yet. A political movement among Russian workers began only at the end of the 1890s, when small revolutionary circles of the Marxist intelligentsia extended their activities to the working class. Until that time, and for long thereafter, the workers' daily economic struggle and the intelligentsia's revolutionary activities ran on separate tracks, though they increasingly converged. With the second wave of industrialization in Russia, during Witte's era in the mid-1890s, the labor movement began to change significantly. The spontaneous strike movement increased greatly, and the workers tried to create organizations to assist and sustain their economic struggle. In 1896 and 1897 St. Petersburg and other cities experienced several strikes that can be called the first mass strikes of Russian workers. Their eruption was spontaneous, but many workers had no doubt been intellectually prepared through the socialists' revolutionary agitation.[9]

In the first attempts at self-organization of this spontaneous movement two principal forms appeared: 1) strike funds or strike committees; 2) workers relief funds (mutual-aid societies).

The first were illegal organizations by workers of a single enterprise, with establishment of a strike fund as immediate goal. Starting in the early 1890s, the funds first gained ground among Jewish workers of western Russia, and even formed the basis for the Social Democratic Jewish Workers Party, the Bund. During the mass strikes of 1896 and 1897, such committees also emerged within Russia proper. Beyond their primary goal, these strike fund committees inevitably became a rallying point for workers of a particular enterprise. The committees tried to direct and discipline the chaotic strike movement, and by mobilizing the most capable and alert workers they provided a link with revolutionary political groups. In this atmosphere, the tendency called "economism" within Russian social democracy developed around 1900. The strike committees stubbornly survived despite police repression and numerous dissolutions. Until the 1905 Revolution they were the sole trade-union-type organizations in Russia, and in some cases were direct precursors of later trade unions.[10]

The only workers organizations that were legal before the Revolution of 1905, the relief funds, cannot be considered genuine union action groups. They did not conduct strikes or support strikers financially. They never participated in politics, but were still subject to stringent surveillance by the authorities and to constant intervention in their affairs.[11]

Apart from these two important workers organizations—leaving political parties aside for now—a third, at the lowest level of the social struggle, is particularly interesting in our context. Reports even of early strikes in the 1870s and 1880s noted that workers selected deputies from their group to negotiate with management and authorities. In February 1885 a strike broke out in Morozov's large textile plant in Tver, where the management, and later the police chief, called on the workers to elect deputies, since negotiation with all workers was impossible. Seven delegates were immediately chosen, with this number increased to sixteen two days later by order of the governor, who had come to the factory. During negotiations the workers began to demolish buildings. When the strike ended, most of the elected delegates were fired.[12] Similar incidents occurred ten years later during a textile workers strike in Ivanovo Voznesensk. Here too the strikers were asked to select spokesmen to present workers demands to the governor. The twenty-five deputies included several women. Negotiations proved fruitless, however, and the next day some of the spokesmen were arrested.[13]

Workers deputies in various factories were also mentioned in a ministerial report to the czar about labor unrest in St. Petersburg in May 1901. Deputies of a large steel foundry included in their demands a pointed request for a permanent delegation to transmit workers complaints to management.[14]

As these examples show, deputations grew primarily because industrialists and authorities needed a negotiating partner from the opposite camp. As soon as immediate need for such spokesmen passed—as when a strike ended—factory owners quickly got rid of the delegations. Also, frequent firings and arrests of elected deputies made moderate and experienced workers hesitate to appear as deputies, while younger, more radical workers stepped into the foreground. The lack of any freedom of association, the prohibition against collective bargaining, and the penalties for striking made the best possible seedbed for revolutionizing the Russian working class.

b) The Government and the Working Class

For a long time the czarist government assumed that in Russia there was no "labor question" such as existed in Europe. The patriarchal conditions of the countryside, frequently idealized, were simply applied to the new domain of the factory. Further, the government had to consider the interests of employers, who resisted all reforms protecting workers. The ministry of the interior, opposing the ministry of finance which favored employers, claimed that domestic security might be endangered by labor unrest and strikes; and it tended therefore to make economic concessions in order to eliminate revolutionaries' influence on the workers. On the whole, there was no constructive sociopolitical policy; minor concessions and repression appeared in alternation.[15]

The growth of the labor movement around the turn of the century, and the necessity of dealing with authorized workers representatives, finally did induce the government to intervene more actively in the affairs of industry. The ministerial report of May 1901, referred to above, already recommended permanent delegations so that workers could negotiate legally with industrial managements and governmental factory inspectors. After deliberations carried on by a commission for more than two years, a law was passed on June 10, 1903, creating factory elders (starosti) in industry. With the employers' permission, workers could nominate candidates from their midst; out of this group management could select one for each department as starost. At the nominating conventions only questions and complaints falling within established regulations could be discussed, not demands for changes of these regulations. Factory elders enjoyed no immunity; they could be fired like any other worker, and the governor too could remove them.

Although the law on factory elders represents only modest progress toward modern shop stewards, it engendered the hostility of employers, who had the power to permit or refuse election of the starosti. The ministry of finance found that the majority of employers did not adhere to the law. Only rarely and briefly did a few factory inspectors succeed in making factory elders effective mediators between workers and employers.[16]

The workers too, on the whole, reacted with skepticism or rejected the factory elders. Limitations of the elders' authority prevented effective initiative and visible success. The strike fund committees, which had existed secretly for some time, or the deputies spontaneously elected during strikes, enjoyed far greater prestige than did the starosti. The socialists' political propaganda sought to discredit elders altogether. A Social Democratic proclamation of 1905 contains the words: "Comrades! We need no starosti and no lackeys of our masters; what we need are workers organizations and workers societies. You see how they fooled us with the starosti. . . . We need freedom of association, of assembly, of speech, and of the press."[17]

The law on factory elders was issued by the government when the labor movement had reached its greatest momentum. In 1902–1903 southern Russia was swept by a strike wave in which an estimated 225,000 workers participated.[18] During these strikes socialist agitation became more effective as the struggle for economic reform turned to political demands. In several places strikes developed into mass demonstrations and bloody clashes with police and army. This prelude to 1905 was interrupted temporarily by the outbreak of the Russo-Japanese War in February 1904.

Quite separate from this revolutionary trend within the labor movement stood the remarkable attempt by Sergei Zubatov and his circle to solve the labor problem within the traditional patriarchal-bureaucratic system.[19] "Zubatovščina," or "police socialism," was based on separation of the economic struggle from revolutionary political action. The plan was that the government, by supporting such workers demands as were considered justified, would keep control and steer workers away from the influence of the revolutionary intelligentsia. The experiment's success, however, depended on a modicum of genuine political concessions toward workers self-government and on effective social legislation. Since the czarist government was not prepared to allow either, Zubatov's plan was bound to fail in the end.

Nevertheless, his Society for Mutual Aid for Workers in Mechanical Industries, founded in Moscow in 1901, attracted a great many members. Similar societies in other cities—such as Odessa, Kharkov, Kiev, and Minsk—were equally successful, proving Russian workers had a strong desire to organize as broadly and openly as possible. Educated workers especially thought the society would enable them legally to fight for their interests against employers, without being drawn into revolutionary struggle against the government. Zubatov's plan provided for the exercise of personal initiative through the election of factory-wide workers committees that joined into district associations and were able to act as recognized workers representatives. The first steps in this direction were taken in Moscow:

chairmen were chosen by workers assemblies in many sections of the city, and these met regularly and formed a "council (sovet) of the workers in mechanical industries." This council was the highest level to which workers could turn with problems and grievances; it monitored compliance with legal regulations in factories and, if necessary, negotiated with factory inspectors.[20] After liquidation of Zubatov's society at the end of 1903, activity of the soviet stopped as well; some of its members were active in 1905 in establishing trade unions.

c) Marxism and the Workers

The Russian workers movement before 1905 described so far sprang from the workers' daily social struggle and their natural need for alliance. Action was directed against individual factory owners, and economic goals were sought on a case-by-case basis. The groups were indigenous, growing directly out of individual factory conditions, and sustained by the workers themselves. As a consequence, their horizons were limited; they did not develop extensive political goals and were not really revolutionary. Only in the mid-1890s when the labor movement, born spontaneously of economic hardship, encountered the Marxist intelligentsia and its theory, did a political and revolutionary "proletarian" movement develop. This was the Social Democratic Party. The meeting of these two currents is the principal theme of the Russian labor movement until the Revolution of 1917.

The flow of Marxism into Russia and its reception by the Russian intelligentsia has often been described and analyzed.[21] Of chief importance here is the almost simultaneous arrival in Russia of industrial capitalism and Marxism.[22] "Marx shows what capitalism will be like before it arrives on the scene. Marx, who studied the early stages of capitalism in Western Europe, becomes the gospel for Eastern Europe before capitalism arrives there, or at the same time, while Western European capitalism undergoes profound changes. . . . The Russian intelligentsia can consciously welcome and experience the first storm signals of Russian capitalism, and at the same time use Marxism to overthrow a bourgeois social order at the first—the very first—moment."[23] The nascent Russian labor movement became totally dominated by the Marxist intelligentsia, which assigned to the proletariat the messianic role of redeemer in its revolutionary scheme of salvation. Following the young Marx, the intelligentsia denied that the Russian working class could independently develop a "social consciousness"; therefore subordination to the intelligentsia was justified. Trotsky, who knew the situation from the inside, wrote in 1909 of the intelligentsia's influence: "By joining the workers party they [the socialist intelligentsia] introduced into the party all their social traits: a sectarian spirit, intellectual individualism, and ideological fetishism; to suit these peculiarities they adapted and distorted Marxism. Thus for the Russian intelligentsia, Marxism became the means to carry every bias to an extreme."[24] As a result, the socialist labor movement in Russia was marked from its inception by innumerable splits into warring groups and factions. Their ideological hairsplitting and political feuds took place behind the workers' backs and above their daily struggles. Recognizing this difference is essential for understanding the Russian council movement. The soviets' fate under Bolshevism after 1917 is proof that the revolutionary intellectuals triumphed over the working masses.

After Plekhanov and the Geneva group, Liberation of Labor (Osvoboždenie truda), had prepared the ground, the first significant Marxist circles appeared in Russia itself in the late 1880s. The upswing of the spontaneous labor movement in the mid-1890s gave revolutionary students a chance to follow up their fervent perusal of Marxist literature by direct contact with the workers. In St. Petersburg in 1895 existing groups first organized a coalition, the League of the Struggle for Liberation of the Working Class (Sojuz bor'by za osvoboždenie rabočego klassa), in which Lenin and Martov played leading roles.[25] Other such leagues sprang up in the country during the next few years.[26] On the whole, they were groups of intellectuals, numbering only a few workers in their ranks.[27] The first attempt to unite existing Social Democratic organizations was at the so-called First Party Congress of the Russian Social Democratic Workers Party (RSDWP: Rossijskaja social'-demokratičeskaja rabočaja partija) in Minsk in early March 1898.[28] The effort failed because the participants were arrested soon afterward. Again typical for the undeveloped character of the Social Democratic "workers" movement in Russia, the second attempt had to be made from the outside, by a group of emigré Russian intellectuals. This was the purpose of the Marxist newspaper *Iskra* (*The Spark*), founded in late 1900 under Lenin's direction.

Lenin's entry into the socialist workers movement in Russia[29] at once aggravated its basic problem: the relationship between intelligentsia and working class. With one-sided passion Lenin plunged into the battle of the late 1890s between "economists" and "politicians" within the Russian Social Democratic Party; the dispute raised questions that later became the focus of severe factional struggles between Bolsheviks and Mensheviks. Economism reflected the workers' increasing consciousness and organization in mutual-aid societies as discussed above, and their indifference or hostility toward the political ideas of the revolutionaries. A number of Russian Marxists considered economism a revisionist trend directed against Plekhanov and his adherents, which was related to a similar controversy within Western European socialism. The economists attached equal importance if not priority to the Social Democratic Party's day-by-day efforts to improve working conditions through strikes, while the orthodox stressed political action and organization. The economists were closer to labor's daily grievances and emphasized action from below. They felt that for the time being political struggle against the czarist regime should be left to the liberal opposition and that the Social Democratic workers movement was still too feeble to be an independent political force.[30]

Around 1900 the economists had achieved predominance in most of the local party organizations. Against this situation Lenin now directed his vehement and embittered attacks in *Iskra*. His pamphlet written in 1902, *What Is to Be Done?*, opposed economism and laid down the theoretical basis of Bolshevism long before the existence of a separate group or party. In the pamphlet, the practical revolutionary experience and ideological tenets of the nineteenth-century pro-Marxist Russian revolutionary movement were blended with basic Marxist ideas about revolution and the dictatorship of the proletariat. By its belligerence toward the economists, Lenin's pamphlet early and unmistakably shows the basically dictatorial and militant traits of Bolshevism; though obscured at times, they have never been abandoned.

For the development of the Russian workers movement, the most important result of *What Is to Be Done?* was its radical rejection of the purely economic trade-unionist struggle carried on by Russian Social Democrats. Lenin strengthened and extended Plekhanov's thesis of the primacy of political action: "The basic economic in-

terests of the proletariat can be served only by a political revolution
which would replace the dictatorship of the bourgeoisie with the
dictatorship of the proletariat."[31] The principal aim of the Social
Democratic Party, Lenin declared, must be the overthrow of czarism as the precondition for socialism. The economist concept of a
"spontaneous development" of the labor movement, to which the
party must adapt itself, could at best lead to "trade unionism," Lenin
said. Opposing that concept, he stressed the leading role of "consciousness," of revolutionary theory. Both these convictions—that
the "proletariat" must be the protagonist in the revolution, and that
the intelligentsia must implant "revolutionary consciousness" in the
working masses—demanded an organization of professional revolutionaries, small in number and conspiratorial in nature, to assume
leadership of the revolution.

Despite existing differences between Lenin and Plekhanov, no
criticism of Lenin's theses was heard from any of the collaborators
in *Iskra* until the split in 1903. Vera Zasulich, for example, stated
almost word for word the same views as Lenin in an article in *Die
Neue Zeit*, the organ of the German Social Democratic Party.[32]
Nevertheless, what Lenin considered an absolute principle for Social
Democratic organization appeared to others a temporary manifestation of the party's adolescence, to be left behind as soon as possible.[33]
During those years when he gradually developed the practice and
theory of Russian Social Democracy, Lenin's later opponents—Martov and his followers—probably did not yet recognize the implications of Lenin's ideas, since there was agreement on fundamental
questions of Marxism. The party split during the Second Congress
of the Russian Social Democrats in the summer of 1903, therefore,
came as a complete surprise to most participants. The debate over
paragraph 1 of the party's organization statute was the first indication of a deep-seated difference of opinion. Lenin's draft was consistent with his views on organization as laid down in *What Is to Be
Done?* For him there was no possible doubt that only professional
revolutionaries (as signified by the phrase "personal collaboration
within a party organization," as against Martov's wording, "under
the leadership") constituted the core of the party and had the right
to deliberate and decide. Martov's wish: "We should be pleased if
each striker, each demonstrator accountable for his actions, could
declare himself a party member,"[34] was countered by Lenin's: "It

is better that ten comrades who are workers do not call themselves party members . . . than that one loudmouth have the right and opportunity to be a party member."[35]

Lenin and his followers, the later Bolsheviks, envisaged an elitist organization of revolutionaries that would have a tight grip on leading the masses but not merge with them, an active revolutionary core able to prepare and execute a revolutionary master plan. Martov and the Mensheviks, on the other hand, stood in principle for a broadly based socialist *workers* party representing the proletariat's special interests within society—in practice they too were obliged to conspire with a small circle of professional revolutionaries. While the Mensheviks aimed their work among the proletariat at the striker who declared himself for the party, Lenin's ideal was the popular leader of the masses in an assault on absolutism.[36]

The split at the Second Congress had other causes,[37] but its basic origin lay in these differences of principle that suddenly came to light. In the next few months additional points of contention arose, and the split spread to local committees in Russia itself. Lenin left *Iskra* and lived in almost total isolation abroad. Literary polemics of former allies took on ever more abrasive tones. The workers, whose future welfare was supposedly at issue, felt repelled by the ideological bickering and the personal calumnies traded among their "leaders." A letter by a worker and party member to the Central Committee states the case: "The battle now being waged by the majority and the minority is totally incomprehensible to me, and a great many of us do not think it is right. . . . Is it really normal to expend all one's energies and travel from committee to committee only to talk about the majority and the minority? . . . Is the question really so important that we should devote all our strength to it and confront one another almost as enemies? . . . Already workers circles are getting dissatisfied with the intelligentsia, which forgets the workers over its internal quarrels; the more eager are about to give up because they do not know what they should do."[38]

Significantly, the nascent Russian labor movement, despite workers' disgust at the intelligentsia's feuding on theory, could not do without the intelligentsia's leadership and remained dependent on it intellectually and politically. In spite of loud Bolshevik protests, Axelrod, a founder of Russian Marxism, was correct when he stated at the Fifth Party Congress in 1907: "The mass of the proletarians re-

ceived into the party exists within it as a sort of plebeian class, while
the intelligentsia plays the role of the aristocracy that controls internal and external affairs of our party state and shields the plebeian
against all corrupting influences from outside."[39]

Before the Revolution of 1905 the intelligentsia succeeded in
familiarizing with Marxist ideas a thin layer of the working class and
gained a foothold within the proletariat. The majority of Russian
workers, however, had not yet been reached by the Social Democratic Party, and the labor movement was primarily dedicated to
economic struggles, carried out in numerous independent strikes.
Most workers' political consciousness was still minimal, and only a
very few recognized the necessity of a direct attack on czarism. Their
socially depressed status and lack of political rights, however, made
the working masses a factor of considerable revolutionary potential
that was decisive in 1905.

2. THE FORMATION OF THE SOVIETS

a) The Labor Movement in 1905

On the eve of the first revolution the Russian labor movement lay
embedded in a broad stream of revolutionary opposition that embraced various social and political groups without, however, being
homogeneous or like-minded. Anarchic localized peasant disturbances,
terrorist assassinations which flared up anew, reform demands by
liberal aristocratic and bourgeois opposition, and efforts toward autonomy and separatism of the non-Russian peoples in the border-
land—all these ran parallel to the labor movement and touched it
only occasionally. The outbreak and luckless course of the Russo-
Japanese War intensified the various revolutionary and oppositional
stirrings after the fall of 1904, and Czar Nicholas II and his government confronted these without a constructive program of their own.[40]

The Revolution of 1905 was triggered by an event that symbolizes
the changes in direction from old Russia toward the revolution. The
mass march of workers on the Winter Palace on January 9 (22),
1905, with Father Gapon at its head, with icons and portraits of the
czar—a procession rather than a demonstration—was a last appeal
to the czar of the patriarchally minded Russian worker before he
turned into a modern proletarian and a revolutionary. The ante-

cedents of "Bloody Sunday" in St. Petersburg—from Gapon's Union of Russian Factory Workers, a Zubatovščina offshoot, to the strike in the Putilov Works and the petition drawn up by left liberal intellectuals—clearly show a mix of different levels of political consciousness and development in the Russian labor movement at the beginning of the century. Even among workers of the capital the almost mystical faith in the Czar-Protector still prevailed, nourished by the religious ecstasy emanating from Gapon; socialist revolutionary groups were in effect excluded from the movement. But contrary to plans of participants, the criminal carelessness of court and government officials turned the peaceful demonstration into a bloodbath, and made "Bloody Sunday" a signal for revolution. During its course, naturally, the Russian workers' "patriarchal illusions" very soon dissipated and were replaced by radical revolutionary slogans.[41]

The January events in St. Petersburg released a revolutionary wave that soon engulfed the entire Russian empire and peaked in October and December 1905. It offers a confusing juxtaposition of differing political and social trends and isolated revolutionary actions, ranging from liberal petitions and deputations, labor strikes and demonstrations, peasant disturbances, and navy mutinies, to armed uprisings of entire localities and regions. Just once—during the general strike in October—was there a united revolutionary front; it resulted in the issuance of the "October Manifesto" with its constitutional concessions which did not, however, fundamentally change Russia's political and social structure. Radicalization of the revolution, most acutely evinced during the December insurrection in Moscow, provoked harsh counter-measures by conservatives, thereby killing all hope for a free parliamentary system in 1906-1907. With this, the Revolution of 1905 changed from a "chance" for Russia to "assimilate to Europe" politically and constitutionally—as was the case in the economic area, through industrialization—into a "dress rehearsal" for the Bolshevik Revolution of 1917, which would not have been possible without the "backward" conditions in old Russia.

Immediate consequences of "Bloody Sunday" were by no means confined to the labor movement; rather, they brought about a general heightening of political activity in all social strata. The liberal opposition, centered around the organs of self-government, the zemstvos and the municipal dumas, and around the more radical Union of Liberation (Sojus osvoboždenija), intensified its criticism of the

regime. Existing professional associations formed the starting point
for the professional-political organization of the Russian intelligentsia.
In early May, the separate groups joined together in the Union of
Unions (Sojuz sojuzov), which through the spring and summer became increasingly radical.[42] A similar coalition of politically conscious
peasants was sponsored by the All-Russian Peasant Union (Vserossijskij krest'janskij sojuz), which held its first congress at the beginning of August.[43] The socialist parties, emerging from underground
into semilegitimacy, increased their activity, and new political parties
in the liberal and monarchist camps began to be formed. Organizational activity encompassed all segments of the population. The revolution and the concomitant relaxation of government restrictions for
the first time made possible public participation in Russian politics;
passionately aroused and torn between extremes, Russians were seeking stable outlets for political activity.

The strike movement represented the most dynamic force among
the various currents of the first Russian revolution. There is a kernel
of truth in Rosa Luxemburg's conscious exaggeration: "The history
of the Russian general strike is the history of the Russian revolution."[44] Equally apt is her characterization that "The general strike,
as the Russian revolution has shown us, is so adaptable a phenomenon
that it mirrors all phases of the political and economic struggle, all
stages and moments of the revolution. . . . Political and economic
strikes, general strikes and partial strikes, demonstration strikes and
militant strikes, general strikes of single trades and in individual cities,
quiet struggles over wages and street fights, battles on the barricades
—all these go on together, side by side, cross each other, flow into
each other."[45] Only the dramatic battles stand out from the vast
total of small, limited, often unreported strikes.[46] They are both
highlights of the revolution and cradles of the soviets.

At the peak of the January movement in St. Petersburg, about
150,000 workers were on strike.[47] Reverberations of "Bloody Sunday" were felt in almost all large cities and industrial centers, and the
number of workers on strike during January and February 1905
was greater than the total for the ten years preceding.[48] At first
the Russian borderlands with non-Russian populations (Poland, the
Baltic, the Caucasus) led; in these regions the movement became politicized much more rapidly because of ethnic differences.[49] The strike
movement within Russia until October 1905, on the other hand, was

largely motivated by economic considerations; political objectives developed only gradually. The impetus of the St. Petersburg events first of all brought about a general awareness of the "proletarian situation." The next goal was immediate improvement of working and living conditions; political slogans generally found only feeble response among workers or were rejected outright.[50] This held true particularly for proletarian groups still closely connected with the land, such as miners and metalworkers in the Ural region and, to a lesser extent, textile workers in the central area. Metalworkers of the large St. Petersburg factories and dockers in Black Sea ports, on the other hand, more quickly and more consciously adopted the anticzarist battlecries.[51] The nucleus of metalworkers and textile workers, who could look back on years of strike activity, was joined after January 1905 by new groups of semiproletarian workers, who were now striking for the first time. Bakers, longshoremen, sales people, clerks, and municipal employees (streetcar conductors, sewer workers, lamplighters, and others) all raised their demands and chiefly succeeded in reducing the workday to ten, nine, or sometimes even eight hours.[52]

The rail strikes were of special importance.[53] In southern Russia thirteen major rail lines went on strike during the first half of February. The strike was directed by elected strike committees, and management was forced to negotiate with them. The railroaders' principal demands were: establishment of an elected body to work out the strikers' demands, freedom of assembly to discuss all labor questions, various wage demands, and the eight-hour workday. Considering the war's course, the government at first thought it wise to make promises: on all rail lines the workday was to be reduced to nine hours, and the workers associations would be granted a voice. But when the strikes continued, all railroad workers were made subject to the mobilization laws, and strikes were prohibited under pain of severe penalties. During the following months the rail workers launched intensive organizing activities, culminating in April in the establishment of an All-Russian Union of Railroad Workers, which joined the Union of Unions and played a significant part in the preparations for the October strike.[54]

In view of the strike wave set in motion by "Bloody Sunday," the government felt constrained to take steps to restore the St. Petersburg workers' shattered faith in the czar and to attest official interest in helping them. Two commissions were established, one under Senator Shidlovsky, to determine "the causes of dissatisfaction of St. Petersburg factory workers and formulate proposals tor their eradication," and the other, under Minister of Finance Kokovcev personally, to study German labor legislation.[55] Elected workers representatives were to take part in the first commission. They were to be chosen in indirect elections from among the workers, who were divided into nine electoral divisions grouped by trades.[56]

Although the whole experiment lasted a scant two weeks and ended in failure, the Shidlovsky Commission marked an important step in the labor movement during 1905; to some extent it provided the groundwork for the St. Petersburg soviet of workers deputies, and helped revolutionize the working class.

Its practical effect was doubtful from the beginning, but it did have considerable organizational and agitational value. The socialist parties themselves saw the commission and the elections as helpful.[57] Here for the first time was a concrete though limited example of the differences between Bolsheviks and Mensheviks concerning revolutionary tactics. Both factions emphasized the elections' usefulness for propaganda, since they allowed Social Democrats to appear more openly than before and to be active at election meetings in the factories. But while the Bolsheviks never expected the commission to succeed and did not even want it to,[58] the Mensheviks wanted to use the commission as a platform from which to address the entire Russian proletariat. In *Iskra* Martov pointed out that the commission must include elected representatives of all Russian workers, and that in St. Petersburg close ties could be established between delegates and factory workers by utilizing the legally authorized factory elders. In this way the commission could become a public advisory and propaganda center of Russian workers.[59]

On February 17, 1905, 400 electors met; of these, 20 percent were organized Social Democrats, 40 percent were radicalized workers, and the remainder consisted of "economist" workers and uncommitted elements.[60] Because some of their colleagues had been arrested, the assembly was in a revolutionary mood. Influenced by the Bolsheviks, the membership submitted to Senator Shidlovsky the following nonnegotiable demands: freedom of assembly and speech for the election of delegates to the commission; unhampered exercise of delegates' responsibilities, including free speech and discussion during primary elections; and release of the arrested electors.[61] On the following day, when election of commission members had been scheduled, the government refused the demands, and the electors decided to boycott the commission. Their appeal set forth reasons for the boycott and called on the workers to unite for the struggle for an eight-hour day, state insurance benefits, representation of the people in the government, and an end to the war.[62] Dissolution of the commission on February 20 ended the czarist government's sole attempt in 1905 to solve the labor question through legal channels. The real significance of the Shidlovsky Commission lay in another area: by electing deputies in the factories, it prepared the way for the soviets to represent the metropolitan working class.

b) Workers Committees

The strike movement beginning in 1905 did not rely on trade-union or political organizations. Unions emerged only during the revolution and indeed because of the strikes, and the revolutionary parties were too limited in their scope. The strike movement was spontaneous in the true sense of the word—that is, the strikes flared up out of some local incident or other, lasted for a few days or at most weeks, and burned themselves out after certain concessions had been achieved or labor's resources were exhausted. Leadership of these spontaneous strikes lay with workers committees of various factories. As was shown above,[63] such committees had appeared at the beginning of the Russian workers movement; their intent was to bring unity and leadership to a chaotic movement. Outbreak of the revolution gave new impetus to the spontaneous organizational efforts. Where the 1903 law concerning factory elders was in effect, the workers no longer adhered to the provisions for age, length of service, or rights of the starosti. Elsewhere—the majority of cases—the workers on their own initiative elected representatives who were increasingly recognized by management as the workers' spokesmen in charge of negotiations. These committees carried various labels: assembly of delegates or deputies (delegatskoe, deputatskoe sobranie), workers commission (komissija rabočich), commission of electors (komissija vybornych), council of factory elders (sovet starost), council of authorized representatives (sovet upolnomočennych), strike committee (stačečnyj komitet), and the like—or simply deputies (deputaty) and authorized representatives (upolnomočennye). In rare instances they were already called councils of workers deputies (sovet rabočich deputatov).

In the strike at the Putilov Works, which began on January 3, 1905, and in which Gapon's association participated, a deputation of 37 was elected to negotiate with the factory management.[64] Among the workers' demands was a request for a standing commission of such workers representatives.[65] When the strike resumed in late January, new deputies were elected, who also went to other factories to enlist support for the Putilov workers. In consequence, the management granted election of factory elders according to the law of 1903. The 56 elected starosti drew up 22 demands, which they presented to management. The directors rejected the more important demands and forbade the starosti to assemble. The next few weeks saw increasingly violent clashes between both sides, until the deputies resigned.[66] During a strike in June a number of workers were fired. An assembly of unemployed elected a commission of 26 deputies who established relief measures, among which were four soup kitchens.[67] Workers committees—some temporary, others permanent—were organized in many large enterprises in St. Petersburg during January and February.[68] Reports about similar deputies committees are available from numerous Russian cities.[69] In the Ukraine alone over 30 deputies assemblies could be traced, the most significant those in the Brjansk metals factory in Ekaterinoslav, the locomotive shops in Kharkov, the South Russian Machine Factory in Kiev, and the shipyard in Nikolaev. Usually these committees functioned only during strikes and were disbanded when the strikes ended, at which time the most active members were often jailed or fired. In a few cases the strikers won the right to maintain a permanent representation of deputies.[70] In the spring of 1905 deputies committees were also established in a few mining enterprises and foundries in the Ural region, among them the Naděždinskij factory, where the name "soviet of workers deputies" was used.[71]

In all these cases we are dealing with elected workers committees in individual enterprises, with little contact among them. They resemble the later factory committees (fabrično-zavodskie komitety), though only rarely did they have precisely defined functions. A further step toward a trade union was taken when several factory committees representing a trade amalgamated. Such delegates councils were formed chiefly in Moscow and Kharkov, among workers in the printing, textile, metal, and tobacco trades.[72] The most significant trade-wide council was the Council of Printers in Moscow (sovet deputatov ot tipolitografij Moskvy), which appeared in late September at the center of a general strike in Moscow. It included 264 delegates from 110 plants, had an executive council of 15 members, and held 10 sessions in all.[73] It considered its task "to call general and sectional meetings of printing-trade workers, to prepare questions for discussion, to submit to the meetings resolutions adopted by the soviet, to implement the resolutions, to distribute funds received for support of the strike, to negotiate with printing-plant owners."[74] The delegates council survived even after the strike ended, and resolved to draw up trade-union statutes. Subsequently one of Russia's most significant trade unions grew out of this group.[75]

Workers committees in factories and trade-based delegates councils were in many cases the nuclei of trade unions which sprang up in Moscow, St. Petersburg, and other major cities in the spring and summer of 1905.[76] Another development, however, also became possible: during the revolution when strikes included several factories and often several branches of an industry, a need for unified local leadership grew acute. Thus representatives of separate factories joined in a city-wide strike committee. Whenever such a strike committee—for running a single action, for a limited time—turned into a permanent elected delegation with much broader aims, then we have before us a council (soviet) of workers deputies.

A clear-cut distinction between strike committee and soviet cannot be made for the early phase of the council movement in 1905, however, as the genesis of various soviets will show. Nor can a distinction between functions of the two organizations be maintained. The historical facts contradict some Soviet historians who see the principal difference between soviets and other workers organizations—such as strike committees and trade unions—in that soviets were essentially militant political organs of the proletariat, aimed at revolutionary seizure of power.[77] Various factors determined whether a soviet that had started as a strike committee turned militant or devoted itself to workers' economic concerns. In any case it is the fusion of economic and political struggle that characterizes the soviets. Their genesis in the 1905 Revolution unequivocally shows that they represented workers' interests on the factory level. The first soviets were founded because workers desired unity and leadership in their splintered struggle, and not because they wanted to seize political power.

c) The First Soviets—Summer of 1905

The first soviet of the Russian revolution appeared in mid-May 1905 in Ivanovo Voznesensk in the Moscow textile district.[78] Around this time the central Russian industrial region, which until then had reacted rather mildly to the events in St. Petersburg, became the arena of violent strikes, the duration and tenacity of which were unprecedented. The working and living conditions in this "Russian Manchester," as the city was called, were particularly bad. In the previous year many smaller strikes had already taken place, and the Social Democrats had propagandized among the workers for some time. It was they who initiated the strike in May. At a workers meeting on May 9, 26 demands were made and were circulated among the workers in the next three days. Almost without exception, the demands concerned questions of economic and working conditions, such as abolition of nightwork and overtime, a monthly minimal wage, and abolition of the "factory police" that existed in some plants. Only one point demanded "the right to assemble freely and discuss hardships, and freely to write about the workers' hardships in the newspapers—that is, freedom of speech and assembly,"[79] in short, was of a political nature.

The strike began May 12; within a few days about 40,000 workers were participating.[80] The following day a huge crowd assembled before the city hall and handed the hectographed demands to the factory inspector of the province. He suggested that deputies be elected from individual factories and that they should deal with owners through factory inspectors. The workers agreed but asked for guarantees that no deputy would be arrested. When this demand was granted, elections to the deputies council took place both on the spot and, on the following day, outside the city.

On May 15 the Ivanovo Voznesensk Council of Representatives (Ivanovo-Voznesenskii sovet upolnomočennych) was constituted at a session in the city hall at which the factory inspector of Vladimir province took part. He recognized the assembled deputies as the authorized workers representatives and cautioned them to restrict their demands to economic improvement and not to pursue political or revolutionary aims. On May 17 a prohibition was issued against assembling in the streets, town squares, and city hall. The soviet thereupon moved to the shores of the Talka River, where for the next few weeks it held its sessions among the striking workers, who were camping there.[81]

The soviet numbered 110 deputies[82] and a presidium of several people. Although most strikers were textile workers, the presidium included mechanics and engravers—a fact that reflected the low cultural level of the textile workers. The soviet declared its task to be: 1) to conduct the strike; 2) to prevent separate actions and negotiations; 3) to assure the orderly and organized behavior of the workers; 4) to resume work only on order of the soviet.[83]

In the first three weeks the strike ran its course quietly and undisturbed. The soviet conducted numerous meetings, where the first political demands were made, including that for a constituent assembly. But in general the strikers' mood was peaceful and averse to revolutionary solutions.[84] After the factory owners rejected labor's demands, the soviet turned to the minister of the interior with a list of requests that extended from legal regulation of workers pensions to a parliament based on general, universal suffrage elections.[85]

On June 3 military intervention brought about bloody clashes with the strikers, which with increasing famine led to a radical⋯on expressed in looting of stores and in arson on June 24 and 2⋯ hese reactions were a significant relapse into the spontaneous, vengeful chaos of earlier strikes, and not even the soviet could control them. On the contrary, the soviet had to declare in advance that it could no longer assure maintenance of order. The authority of this self-elected organ was not yet strong enough to subordinate the striking workers to its leadership, but it could prevent collapse of the strike movement, threatened by the workers' growing exhaustion. The soviet decided to resume work on July 1. When the employers demanded a declaration from every worker that he would return to work under the old conditions, the strike dragged on until July 18. On that day the deputies—several leading members having by then been arrested —asked factory inspectors to negotiate resumption of work under the old conditions. The soviet disbanded. In the following weeks and months the former soviet deputies continued to act as spokesmen for workers in various factories during negotiations and conflicts with management.

Although the workers had gained no material advantages, the Ivanovo Voznesensk strike left a lasting impression on Russian public opinion by its unprecedented solidarity and its long duration. The chief credit for this undoubtedly goes to the soviet. Formed as a strike committee, it grew rapidly into the first open city-wide representation of the proletariat's interests. Its authority among the workers allowed the soviet to become the recognized spokesman for the entire work force, even in the eyes of the mill owners and the government. If a revolutionary seizure of power was completely foreign to the soviet, and if it restricted itself to achievement of practical economic demands and proclamation of a few general political points, the reason lay in the undeveloped political consciousness of most workers and in the general situation, which in the summer of 1905 was not yet dominated by the militant revolutionary fervor of October. As an elected city-wide organ of the workers, however, the soviet represented a newer, higher form of workers organization, which in the coming months shaped the revolutionary labor movement.

Under influence of the Ivanovo Voznesensk strike, a strike of about 10,000 workers also broke out in early July 1905 in the neighboring city of Kostroma. On July 6 a factory meeting was attended by delegates from other striking plants. On the following day a "deputies assembly of strikers" (deputatskoe sobranie bastujuščich) of 108 members was formed. It elected from its midst a 12-man executive commission (strike commission) and a finance commission. Together with the Social Democratic Party committee, the strike commission issued a *Bulletin* reporting the most important events during the strike. The provincial factory inspector treated the soviet as legal representative of the striking workers but demanded removal from it of all persons not connected with the factories or under twenty-five years of age. This would have eliminated socialist agitators who had been crucially involved in the soviet's creation. The soviet refused and continued in its original form. The owners tried to circumvent the soviet by refusing to negotiate with it; they tried instead to deal separately with representatives of individual concerns. After three weeks, the deputies council decided to end the strike, since the manufacturers had agreed to shorten the workday by an hour and the workers were exhausted. Unlike the Ivanovo Voznesensk strike, that in Kostroma ended in an organized manner, with a proclamation. Bolshevik propaganda in favor of an armed rising, however, went unheeded.[86]

Both the Ivanovo Voznesensk and Kostroma soviets and the above-mentioned council of Moscow printers, had only local impact, despite their importance and success. Like the strike movement which since January 1905 had splintered into numerous local and partial strikes, these workers organizations could affect solely their immediate area. Only the general October strike in St. Petersburg evolved an organization capable of directing an all-Russian worker revolution: the St. Petersburg Soviet of Workers Deputies.

d) The October Strike
and the Formation of the St. Petersburg Soviet

In the late summer of 1905 the first revolutionary wave, sparked by January events in St. Petersburg, had subsided.[87] Publication on August 6 of the manifesto creating the Imperial Duma and granting a limited franchise, as well as the conclusion of peace with Japan on August 23 (September 5), 1905, seemed to stabilize Russia's domestic situation, without significant successes for the revolution. The internal atmosphere, however, was still far from calm, even without such dramatic events as the mutiny of the battleship *Potemkin* in May. It needed only a new impulse to express the population's widespread dissatisfaction and latent readiness for revolution.

Events leading to the great October strike began with the printing-trade workers strike in Moscow,[88] followed on September 27 by a general work stoppage. After a few days the Moscow movement seemed to die out, but the spark flashed across to St. Petersburg, where on October 3 the printers began a sympathy strike. This wave too subsided, but on October 6 the workers of several railroad shops in Moscow began a walkout. In recent months a general railroad strike plan had been much discussed by the All-Russian Union of Railroad Workers. In late September the government called a conference of delegates of railroad employees and workers, who met in St. Petersburg to discuss pension statutes.[89] The central bureau of the Union of Railroad Workers had called for a boycott of the delegates election, but the railroad workers sent their representatives to the congress, since they hoped for far-reaching resolutions from it, and pictured its activities in the "most revolutionary colors."[90] Because of the railroad workers' excitement, the central bureau set the strike in Moscow for October 4. On that day, everything remained calm. Then a rumor spread like wildfire: participants in the St. Peters-

burg conference had been arrested. Now the strike—rescheduled for
October 6—was fully successful; railway workers of the Moscow-
Kazan line walked out, and within two or three days the strike paralyzed all lines leading into Moscow.[91] Though the rumor about arrest
of conference members was soon proven false, there was no stopping
the movement, once it started. On October 9 the conference announced support of the strikers and raised a series of political demands. Starting October 10 the strike spread to other rail lines, and
by October 13 almost all Russian lines were on strike, with the sole
exception of Finland. On October 16 the Finnish trains too came
to a halt. Strike committees formed at all stations, and acted in
concert to block rail traffic. By October 10 factory workers struck
and on October 12 the strike became general, joined by postal workers, telephone and telegraph workers, service employees, both public
and private, and professional workers.[92] Moscow and St. Petersburg
led the way, all other major cities followed, and even a number of the
smaller towns were engulfed by the strike wave.[93]

From the first day, the October strike had a political character. The
fight for inviolability of the railway workers congress became over-
night a struggle for personal and civil liberties, a constitution, political
amnesty, and similar reforms. The dominant rallying cry was: constituent assembly based on a universal, impartial, direct, and secret
ballot. Widespread participation by nonproletarian groups turned
the October strike into a political protest against the czarist system.
At this same time (October 12-18) the Constitutional Democratic
Party was founded at a congress in St. Petersburg, which expressed
solidarity with the strikers and demanded convocation of a national
assembly.[94] The Union of Unions helped organize the strike of employees and professionals. Numerous industrialists allowed workers
to hold meetings in factories, paid full or partial wages on strike
days, and did not dismiss a single worker because of the strike.[95]
The municipal dumas sympathized with the strike or at least remained neutral: they gave financial support to strikers, took workers
delegates into their ranks, and pleaded for restraint by authorities
and troops.[96]

Since October 14 the capital of the Russian Empire had been
without rail connection, without streetcars, electricity, telephones, or
newspapers, and often without open shops.[97] In view of this desperate
situation, Czar Nicholas II sought Witte's aid and named him presi-

dent of the council of ministers. At Witte's suggestion the czar issued on October 17 (30), 1905, the now famous October Manifesto, which guaranteed civil liberties, extended suffrage for elections to the Duma to previously excluded segments of the population, and conceded the Duma's right to enact laws, in place of its purely advisory functions.[98] In the eyes of the majority of the Russian people this meant nothing less than the end of autocracy and the dawn of a constitutional parliamentary era. The masses responded accordingly; rail traffic resumed on October 19, industrial strikes ended, the united front of the revolutionary forces began to crumble.

The St. Petersburg Soviet of Workers Deputies emerged in the Russian capital at the peak of the October strike. Metropolitan workers had long been familiar with the idea of a workers representation chosen in the plants. Beginning with the January strike deputies committees were formed in a number of factories. The elections to the Shidlovsky Commission for the first time aimed at workers representation for the entire city.[99] After failure of that commission, the electors chosen in the factories continued to function as worker representatives in dealings with managements.[100] Alongside these practical preliminaries some theoretical preparation existed among St. Petersburg workers, thanks to the concept—spread by the Mensheviks in the spring and summer of 1905—of "revolutionary self-government" and of a "workers congress" that was to include factory delegates.[101] However, a concrete revolutionary impetus was needed before the St. Petersburg soviet sprang from these beginnings. When the strike wave spread from Moscow to St. Petersburg on October 11, the workers spontaneously reached out for concerted action. Deputies (starosti) were elected in several factories, including the Putilov and Obukhov Works; a number of deputies had earlier been members of strike committees or electors to the Shidlovsky Commission.[102] On October 10 a session of the Menshevik "Group" (of St. Petersburg) proposed founding a city-wide "workers committee" to lead the general strike, and to begin propaganda for its election. Next day about fifty agitators began circulating among workers an appeal proposing election of one deputy for each 500 workers, a procedure used for election to the Shidlovsky Commission.[103] When Trotsky, who was considering a similar plan, came to St. Petersburg, he learned that the Mensheviks had already initiated it.[104] On October 12 at a workers meeting Chrustalev-Nosar, subsequently chairman of the soviet, reported on the Moscow council of printing-trade workers of September and advocated formation of a similar council as core of the strike movement.[105]

Thus the St. Petersburg soviet grew from three separate roots:

1) the representatives spontaneously elected in the plants;
2) propaganda by the Mensheviks, who saw the soviet as a link in their campaign for "revolutionary self-government";
3) the example of the Moscow council of printing-trade workers.

On the evening of October 13 the St. Petersburg soviet first met at the Technological Institute; about 40 people took part. Some had been delegates to the Shidlovsky Commission, some were deputies chosen in factories at the beginning of the strike, and 15 had been especially elected to the soviet.[106] Zborovskij, a Menshevik, presided at the first session. The participants issued this appeal to St. Petersburg workers for election of delegates: "The assembly of deputies from all factories and workshops will form a general workers committee in St. Petersburg. The committee will strengthen and unify our movement, represent the St. Petersburg workers to the public, and decide actions during the strike, as well as its termination."[107]

The appeal shows clearly that the new soviet set itself a limited goal: unified direction of the strike. Mikhail Pokrovski therefore rightly noted that initially the soviet was a strike committee similar to the Ivanovo Voznesensk soviet.[108] At first workers and press quite naturally referred to the soviet as a "strike commission," "strike committee," "workers association," etc.[109]

Responding to the appeal, workers elected deputies during the following days, and the soviet took shape. At the second meeting on October 14 there were already 80 to 90 delegates from 40 large plants; at the third, on the following day, 226 representatives from 96 factories and workshops and 5 trade unions were present. At this session, too, the 3 socialist parties (Menshevik, Bolshevik, and Social Revolutionary), with 3 representatives each were officially admitted. They had only advisory powers in the executive committee. Chrustalev-Nosar was elected permanent chairman of the soviet.[110] At the next meeting on October 17, in the building of tl e Free Economic Society, the soviet constituted itself definitively: it named itself Sovet rabočich deputatov (Council of Workers Deputies), elected a provisional executive committee of 22 members (2 each from 7 boroughs of the city, 2 each from the 4 largest trade unions), and decided to issue its own newspaper, *Izvestija soveta rabočich deputatov* (News of the Council of Workers Deputies).[111] The workers of St. Petersburg gave their pilot organization the name that became the symbol of the Russian revolution, as the same hour when the czar issued the October Manifesto.

Organized to lead the October strike, the St. Petersburg soviet a few days after the strike had started turned into a general political organ representing all workers, and the revolutionary movement in the capital. Its functions rapidly grew beyond those of a mere strike committee; it became a "workers parliament" that had to take a stand on a great many questions and a mass organization of the St. Petersburg working class such as had not existed heretofore. When the St. Petersburg workers council continued after the strike's end, it had definitely changed from a simple strike committee into a general militant revolutionary body. This transformation was neither intentional nor conscious: the revolutionary movement, which at its zenith had produced the soviet, had not yet ebbed and continued on its stormy course, and the organ it created had to go along. During the "freedom days," the St. Petersburg soviet took on the character that made it the model for other councils in 1905 and later in 1917.

e) Formation of Workers Councils in the Provinces

The mere existence of the St. Petersburg soviet and the authority it enjoyed among workers in the capital popularized the soviet idea far beyond St. Petersburg, so that workers councils were formed everywhere in Russia's larger and smaller industrial cities from October to December 1905.[112] All told, about forty to fifty councils of workers deputies can be traced, to which can be added several soldiers and peasants councils.[113] Some were modeled on older organizations such as strike committees and deputies assemblies; others were formed directly, initiated by Social Democratic Party organizations, which then exercised considerable influence in the soviet. Frequently boundaries between a simple strike committee and a fully developed council of workers deputies were fluid, and only in the main revolutionary centers with considerable concentrations of workers—such as (apart from St. Petersburg) Moscow, Odessa, Novorossiysk, and the Donets Basin—were the councils thoroughly organized.

It was remarkably late when the Moscow Council of Workers

Deputies was formed: after the St. Petersburg council the Moscow soviet was the most important in Russia and it played a leading role in the December insurrection.[114] Initiated by the local Bolshevik organization, which on October 2 appealed for election of deputies to conduct the strike,[115] and modeled on the council of printing-trade workers, an assembly of representatives from five trades, meeting in early October, recommended formation of deputies councils by trades, to be united into a city-wide soviet.[116] It never came to that, however; rather, on October 10 a municipal strike committee, mainly composed of members of the professions and including only a few workers, was formed and became the organizational center of the October strike in Moscow. The chairman of the railroad workers strike committee, a Menshevik, became chairman of the municipal strike committee, which included official representatives of the socialist parties. The strike committee was not exclusively proletarian but represented a coalition of all revolutionary forces. Because the Bolshevik Party's Central Committee had a negative attitude toward the St. Petersburg soviet,[117] the Moscow Bolshevik committee hesitated for a long time before reviving the original idea of a pure workers council. At the beginning of November the joint committee of the RSDWP, including Mensheviks as well as Bolsheviks, decided to go to the factories and agitate for the election of workers deputies. It was emphasized that these deputies should have nothing in common with the earlier factory elders (starosti) but that they were to lead the workers' struggle against the employers and give needed unity to the labor movement. Finally, on November 21, the first session of the Moscow soviet was held; some 180 deputies participated, representing roughly 80,000 workers.[118] From that point on the Moscow soviet developed rapidly into a militant revolutionary organ of the workers movement which became an armed insurrection in early December 1905.

As the movement gained momentum in December, several soviets —especially in the mining communities of the Urals and in the Donets Basin—prepared to lead the armed struggle. Relatively little is known about their brief existence.[119] The Bolsheviks gave them the highest mark: that they had aimed at revolutionary seizure of power through insurrection. In reality these short-lived, partially developed soviets were ad hoc committees fighting for the revolution, rather than broad proletarian representations like the St. Petersburg council.

Soviets roughly corresponded geographically to workers and strike movements. By far the greatest number of soviets arose in the Moscow industrial region, in the Donets Basin, in the Urals, and along the Black Sea coast. With the exception of Poland, the provinces with the highest number of strikers and the greatest concentration of strikes were also the areas where soviets were most active.[120]

f) Soldiers Councils and Peasants Councils

Along with soviets of workers deputies, the Revolution of 1905 already saw isolated instances of soldiers and peasants councils, such as became widespread in 1917.[121] In general, we have even less information about their establishment and activities than for workers councils. The soldiers' unrest in 1905 and 1906 sprang from fortuitous causes (inadequate food and clothing, rough treatment by officers, cancelation of leaves, and the like), and only rarely was there evidence of a conscious revolutionary attitude. Not until after the October Manifesto did soldiers garrisoned in large cities come into closer contact with political life and with revolutionary organizations seeking entry into the barracks to agitate and to form political cells. The government faced a critical situation in the Manchurian army which, when demobilized after the peace treaty with Japan, encountered striking railroad workers during the soldiers' difficult and frequently interrupted homeward journey on the Siberian railway.[122] Soldiers councils were formed during November and December 1905 in several cities along the Siberian railway line, the most significant in Krasnoyarsk and Chita.[123] In Krasnoyarsk a railway workers committee founded during the October strike and then expanded into a general "workers commission," and a soldiers committee of the railroad battalion established at the beginning of December, united and proclaimed a workers and soldiers council on December 9, consisting of 80 workers and 40 soldiers deputies. In Chita a council of soldiers and cossacks was organized in November, in addition to the workers council. In both cities the councils exercised a number of revolutionary powers until they were suppressed in late December 1905 and early January 1906. A far smaller role was played by a 20-man soldiers committee formed in Moscow on December 2 in the regiment of Rostovskij Grenadiers. The committee issued an appeal to all soldiers in Moscow to elect deputies from their midst "for common consideration of all matters of interest to soldiers."[124] On the following day numerous representatives of other regiments and battalions took part in a committee session, but no general council of the Moscow garrison was organized when the mutiny was suppressed on December 4. In Sevastopol, where a sailors council had been formed November 12 during a sailors mutiny, they could not induce the artillery and infantry units to join them and send delegates.[125] In Kiev, finally, during the soldiers demonstrations in mid-November, matters went no further than an appeal by the RSDWP's military organization to elect deputies to a soldiers council in all units.[126]

For the soldiers the words *strike* and *soviet* were symbols of the revolution and their organizations were modeled on the workers soviets; similarly the workers councils occasionally exerted a revolutionary influence on local peasants. In four volosts of Tver province, as well as in the vicinity of Novorossiysk and Rostov, peasants committees or peasant councils (the designations vary) appeared in November and December 1905 in direct collaboration with workers from those cities. Sometimes these were nothing more than the usual village assemblies (schody) in revolutionary guise.[127] Some of the deputies councils formed in the spring of 1905 in Urals mines and factories were de facto workers and peasants councils, since many members were peasants who worked in factories, but lived in villages.[128] Independent forms of the peasants revolution were exhibited by the peasants committees in Gurev, the site of violent peasant disturbances since early 1905. The elected revolutionary community representatives refused to pay taxes and rents and deposed the local authorities. Here the movement was strongly influenced and led by Menshevik party organizations, which saw peasant committees as organs of "revolutionary self-government."[129] However, the few peasant soviets modeled on workers councils were not significant for the course of the revolution or for organizing the peasantry. Even in 1917 soviets prevailed only slowly in the countryside. In 1905 the agrarian revolution lagged behind the urban workers movement and proceeded with even less unity and organization than the latter. With minor exceptions, the year 1905 did not bring about "revolutionary solidarity" in the form of soviets of workers, soldiers, and peasants deputies.

3. THE NATURE AND ACTIVITY
OF THE 1905 SOVIETS

a) Councils as Organs of Proletarian Self-Government

Trotsky, at the age of twenty-six one of the leading minds of the St. Petersburg Soviet of Workers Deputies, in his history of the Revolution of 1905[130] aptly characterized the factors that determined the soviets' rise: "The soviet of workers deputies emerged in fulfillment of an objective need—generated by the course of events—for an organization that would represent authority without containing tradition, for an organization ready to encompass the scattered masses numbering hundreds of thousands without imposing on them many organizational restraints; for an organization that would unite revolutionary currents within the proletariat, that could take the initiative and automatically control itself; and, most importantly, for an organization that could be created within twenty-four hours."[131]

The Russian working class lacked even the limited opportunity enjoyed by the liberal bourgeoisie in the zemstvo and municipal dumas, to organize legally. Revolutionary parties could function only as conspiratorial circles and workers were forbidden to form trade unions to aid the economic struggle. In other words, at the moment of revolution the workers possessed no existing organizations that could have unified and led the movement. Lack of a strong class organization fostered spontaneous self-help in the form of soviets and the absence of semiproletarian organizations (unions, parties) enabled the soviets to become associations of the entire proletariat.[132] To what extent the tradition of the old Russian village peasant commune (obščina) had an influence on workers councils is hard to determine. Certainly many Russian factory workers were still familiar with the "democratic" customs and common deliberations of village meetings, just as the "factory elder" is linked to the peasant "starost." These experiences may have contributed to the ease with which soviets caught hold of the working masses, who discussed their concerns and elected deputies in open meetings. The proverbial cooperative spirit of Russian peasants and workers—though this concept should not be stretched too far—as manifested, for example, in the "production cooperative" of the artel', probably also favored their joining in soviets.

The natural soil in which these organizations grew was the place of work, the factory. It determined the worker's economic and social status; here class antagonism was a daily experience. Here, too, was the lever by which the worker could improve his position: through organization and through federation with workers in other enterprises. Thus it was here that the Russian worker became politicized. Excluded from all participation in the state—even in elections to existing self-governing bodies—and ignorant of the rules of the parliamentary system of representation, the worker performed an act of practical democracy through the soviets. General election of deputies in factories, with the possibility of their continuing accountability and recall at any time, gave the workers the feeling of genuine and effective participation in an organ elected by them.[133]

The St. Petersburg workers council and the provincial soviets were the first freely elected proletarian mass organizations. No matter how informally elections were carried out—through open voting by show of hands at general meetings—and no matter how fortuitous the outcome might have seemed at times, the councils' power and authority rested primarily in the free election of deputies.[134] This was not true of party organizations; under existing conditions of illegality there could be no thought of building a democratic organization. The parties were, in Trotsky's words, "organizations *within* the proletariat . . . , but the soviet at once rose to be the organization *of* the proletariat."[135]

Most workers were revolutionary, but not aligned with any particular party. The nonpartisan stance of the St. Petersburg soviet, as well as most others, enabled even workers who were cautious in politics and distrustful of parties to regard the soviets as "their" institutions, "where all matters are decided by workers, and not by intellectuals."[136] When participation by representatives of the socialist parties was first raised at the second session of the St. Petersburg soviet, the unaffiliated delegates grew heated and shouted that no "polemic" was needed, that the assembly was for dealing with "general labor matters" and not concerned with "polemics."[137] The initiators of the St. Petersburg soviet took into account these feelings of the workers, and avoided every appearance of subordinating the soviet to any one of the socialist parties. The choice of chairman, the independent attorney Chrustalev-Nosar, affirmed the over-all proletarian position of the St. Petersburg soviet, rising above factional quarrels. The soviets' neutrality toward partisan politics was the condition of their popularity among the masses. Equal representation of the three socialist parties (Mensheviks, Bolsheviks, and Social Revolutionaries) in executive committees of the soviets in St. Petersburg and most other cities seemed to the workers to be a fair solution.

The declared nonpartisanship of the soviets, on the other hand, did not prevent the Social Democrats, knowledgeable in theory and experienced in revolutionary struggle, from gaining intellectual leadership of most soviets, as the resolutions, appeals, and slogans clearly show.[138] For all Russia, Menshevik and Bolshevik influence on the soviets remained more or less equal; in St. Petersburg, Odessa, Baku, Kiev, and a number of other cities, especially in the south of Russia, the Mensheviks prevailed, whereas in Moscow, Kostroma, Tver, and various cities in the Donets Basin the Bolsheviks predominated. The Social Revolutionaries and some ethnic socialist parties (for example, the Jewish Bund) were in the minority everywhere.

The soviets had no standard voting procedure or representation ratio; accordingly, their numerical strength fluctuated widely. In St. Petersburg the proportion of one delegate for each 500 workers was adopted from the Shidlovsky Commission. In Moscow, plants with 400 workers could send one delegate to the soviet; smaller ones were told to band together so they could elect one delegate for each 500 workers. In cities with fewer workers, the pro rata representation was lower; for example, in Odessa it was one to 100, in Tver one to 50, in Kostroma one to 25. In other places (such as Novorossiysk, Ekaterinoslav) no fixed proportions were set.[139] The St. Petersburg soviet was the largest; by the end of November it reached the peak figure of 562 deputies.[140] The Moscow soviet had 204 delegates, the Kostroma soviet (in November) 135, the Novorossiysk soviet 72, the Odessa soviet 153.

In St. Petersburg, Moscow, and Odessa there were borough councils in addition to the city-wide workers soviets.[141] In St. Petersburg formation of borough soviets occurred only later, but in Moscow and Odessa they emerged before the city-wide soviet, which was based on them.[142] There was no sharp separation of functions. Usually the basic and important political questions were decided in the general council, and borough councils executed the decisions. In Moscow, during the December insurrection after the central soviet's

elimination, the borough soviets attained independent significance
as centers of the armed rising.

Just as election methods were far from clear-cut or uniformly
established, the soviets' organizational structure was provisional and
based on expediency. Nevertheless there were a few common traits, at
least among the larger and more fully developed councils. As a rule
the soviets were headed by an executive committee of several members (Ispolnitel'nyj komitet or Ispolnitel'naja komissija), which took
care of the day-to-day business. As against the general assembly of
deputies, the "parliament," the executive embodied the "government,"
as it were. After its expansion during late November, the Executive
Committee of the St. Petersburg soviet consisted of 35 voting and 15
nonvoting members. On their shoulders rested the chief burden of
the daily affairs that came before the soviet. The rush of events required quick decisions by the Executive Committee, which then
sought approval from the soviet after the fact. The Executive Committee of the St. Petersburg soviet also composed proclamations and
appeals—usually by Trotsky's pen—which were then ratified and
proclaimed at soviet plenary sessions. Sessions of the soviet itself
proceeded in a heated revolutionary atmosphere and often under
turbulent conditions; voting was public by show of hands.[143]

Some soviets formed special commissions to accomplish particular
tasks, for example, to administer moneys and establish a strike fund,
to assist the unemployed, to procure weapons, to publish proclamations and a newspaper. The last—*Izvestija soveta rabočich deputatov*
—was published in St. Petersburg, Moscow, Odessa, Baku, Novorossiysk, Kostroma, Taganrog, and a few other places of which we have
no detailed information.[144] Much activity of the St. Petersburg soviet
and the provincial soviets concerned workers' everyday social and
economic problems. In this the soviets were a substitute for non-
existent or beginning trade unions. The Baku soviet, for example,
was predominantly concerned with settlement of conflicts between employers and workers and with peaceful struggle for higher
wages, which later gained for it the name of a "typically trade-
unionist organization" from the Bolsheviks.[145] In Kiev the soviet
originally was a combination of strike committee and trade union; it
called itself "Sojuz rabočich g. Kieva" and even considered joining
the "sojuz sojuzov," the professional political association of left-wing
intelligentsia.[146] Boundaries between trade unions, as professional

associations within various industries, and the soviets, as representing the entire proletariat, were still fluid during these weeks. Between the two there were reciprocal relations; at the end of November 54 official representatives from 16 unions sat in the St. Petersburg soviet; further, a number of deputies were also leading union members. The St. Petersburg printers union supported the soviet in bringing out *Izvestija*, which the printers produced on their own authority in various shops.[147] Conversely, the soviet called on the workers to establish trade unions, supported those already established, and rendered material aid during strikes. The associations of railroad workers and of postal and telegraph employees, which extended beyond St. Petersburg, sent official representatives to the soviet and recommended that their locals cooperate with the workers councils.[148] In mid-November the St. Petersburg soviet appealed for delegates to an all-Russian workers congress planned for December, in which the soviets, the trade unions, and the parties would participate. Because of the defeat in December 1905, however, the plan could not be realized.[149]

b) Councils as Organs of the Revolution

The St. Petersburg soviet arose, in the words of its founding manifesto, to represent "the interests of the St. Petersburg workers vis-à-vis the rest of society," but this happened at a time when Russia was experiencing the revolution's high point and when the St. Petersburg workers stood at the revolution's center. The same was true for other soviets formed during the "freedom days." Their role was therefore necessarily dual: on the one hand they were autonomous organizations representing working class interests; on the other hand they were militant political organizations aimed at revolutionary overthrow. These are two aspects of the same thing, the workers' economic struggle against the employers and the political struggle against the regime, which were irrevocably connected in the 1905 revolution.

Various factors combined to let one or the other emerge more strongly. There was the general psychological state of the workers, their greater or lesser political consciousness and revolutionary readiness for the struggle; there was the degree of influence revolutionary parties had in a soviet; and not last came the power of the local government authorities. If the St. Petersburg soviet was able to function openly and almost without interference for 50 days, it was only because of unsettled conditions then, which made the government hesitate to arouse the workers by dissolving the soviet—an action that at the time the workers would hardly have tolerated calmly. "The revolutionary activity of the working masses not only serves as the basis for the formation of such organizations as the soviets, but it also secures the 'legality' essential to their functioning."[150] The strength of the soviets lay in this revolutionary mood of the masses, in the capital's bellicose atmosphere, and in the regime's insecurity. During the political euphoria of the "freedom days" the working class readily responded to the appeal of its elected organ; as soon as the mood waned and gave way to exhaustion and disillusion, the soviets lost some of their influence and authority. To direct events, the soviets depended greatly on the masses' revolutionary temper and the opposition's actions. "The soviet," Trotsky wrote, "from the moment of its inception to the instant of its downfall was subject to the mighty pressure of the revolutionary groundswell, which relentlessly outpaced the work done by political consciousness. Every step of the workers movement was determined beforehand, and the 'tactics' were a matter of course."[151]

This situation became particularly evident in the struggle in the capital for the eight-hour day, at the end of October 1905, laying bare the economic roots of labor's revolution. On October 26 and 27 the workers and deputies of a number of large concerns decided on their own initiative to introduce the eight-hour day. When the question was debated at a plenary session of the soviet on October 29, only isolated voices (including Viktor Chernov, the chairman of the Social Revolutionary Party) opposed this "syndicalist deviation"[152] and declared, for example: "We are not yet done with absolutism, and you want to take on the bourgeoisie."[153] The political parties in the soviet dared not resist this spontaneous tide. They saw themselves forced to support the movement in their appeals and speeches. Trotsky stated specifically that the politically farsighted element in the soviet had no choice but to endorse the resolution called for by the majority, to take matters into their own hands and introduce the eight-hour day in all factories beginning on October 31. "If it [the soviet] had shouted 'Halt' to the masses, from considerations of 'realpolitik,' they simply would not have complied and would have rebelled against it. The struggle would still have broken out, but without its leadership."[154]

The struggle for the eight-hour day was unsuccessful. Private employers and the state-operated services locked the workers out until work resumed under the old conditions, and they summarily fired 19,000 workers.[155] In a dramatic session on November 12 the St. Petersburg soviet, due to the faint response in the provinces, came to an ambivalent decision: they abandoned their plan to introduce a universal eight-hour day, but made it optional for workers of individual factories to return to work under former conditions.[156] By this maneuver the soviet divested itself of its greatest strength: the unified leadership of the workers movement. The struggle fizzled, and almost everywhere the workers were finally forced to submit to the old working conditions. The large number of unemployed thereafter was one of the soviet's principal problems; the soviet could solve it only partially, by forming an unemployment commission and by soliciting contributions from the public.[157]

The St. Petersburg soviet did not confine its revolutionary struggle to the economic sector, as for the eight-hour day. The political October strike, during which it was formed, made the soviet the political spokesman for Russian workers. On this level, more than in the direct struggle in the factories, came the ideological leadership by political parties—above all by the Social Democrats. In answer to the czar's October Manifesto, the St. Petersburg soviet on October 18 adopted a resolution that basically contained the Social Democratic political program for the 1905 Revolution. The resolution read in part: "The struggling revolutionary proletariat cannot lay down its arms until the political rights of the Russian people are put on a solid footing, until a democratic republic is established which represents the best way for the proletariat's continued struggle for socialism." Therefore the soviet asked the government to remove the military and the police from the city, to grant full amnesty to all political prisoners, to raise the state of war or siege everywhere in Russia, and finally to convoke a constituent assembly on the basis of a general, equal, direct, and secret ballot.[158] "Constituent assembly" and "eight-hour day" were the two recurring demands in the progress of most provincial soviets.

Between the October strike and the December insurrection the revolutionary parties and the workers succeeded almost everywhere in gaining de facto freedom of assembly; the best example is the open existence of the soviet in St. Petersburg and many other cities, almost unhampered by government or police. Depending on local conditions, the workers were successful to a greater or lesser degree in their demands for delegates' admission to municipal dumas, the use of public halls, applications for financial support of the unemployed, and the like. Beyond this, the weakness and occasional disorganization of the governmental apparatus even enabled the St. Petersburg soviet and some provincial councils to usurp certain governmental functions and—in the words of the chief of the St. Petersburg secret police—to behave like a "second government."[159] The St. Petersburg soviet, for example, on October 19 decreed "freedom of the press"— that is, it prohibited newspaper editors from submitting their papers to the censor, and the printers made sure that only newspapers carrying the notice "uncensored" appeared.[160] During the October strike, and later during the political November strike, the soviet gave instructions to the post office and the railroads; it negotiated with the municipal duma, with the captain of the militia, and once even with Witte; it showered government departments with inquiries, and in many instances received answers; its own militia gave orders to policemen. Even nonworkers turned to the soviet for advice and assistance. A major part of the Executive Committee's activity was devoted to such matters of revolutionary everyday life, and this conferred on the soviet its prestige and authority in the eyes of the masses.

Beginning in mid-November, the St. Petersburg soviet also sent special delegates to Moscow, southern Russia, and the Volga district, to establish relations with local workers organizations. In return, delegates from other cities, especially in the St. Petersburg area, and even several peasants, came to the St. Petersburg soviet.[161] When in early November the St. Petersburg soviet championed the imprisoned Kronstadt mutineers with a political demonstration strike,[162] it won adherents also among the soldiers. These turned to the soviet with various requests and inquiries, and the soviet for its part addressed a special appeal to the soldiers.[163] The St. Petersburg soviet maintained constant contact with the association of railroad workers and the postal and telegraph association, as well as with the All-Russian Peasant Union. In this way it increasingly developed into the potential center of the revolution throughout Russia.

Editorials in *Izvestija*, numerous resolutions and appeals, and deputies' speeches more and more strongly emphasized the inevitability of armed struggle against the czarist regime. The soviet, however, as a public mass organization, was not in a position to carry through practical preparations for that struggle. Nor did the majority of members believe in the success of an isolated action by the capital's proletariat; others, again, saw the general strike as a sufficiently effective weapon. The soviet's propaganda was intended first of all to prepare the workers psychologically for the moment when part of the troops would go over to the revolution and help the workers initiate the revolt. Arming the deputies only served self-defense. The socialist parties organized their own shock troops; they were intended to be the cadres of the proletarian army in case of revolt.[164] On November 19 the conservative newspaper *Novoe Vremja* wrote: "Possibly we find ourselves on the eve of a monstrous insurrection. Even the government is already declaring that the proletariat commands a whole division of armed mutineers.[165] . . . The party advocating open revolt is by no means small. This party behaves as if it were the ultimate power, and each day more people believe it. The revolutionary regime [the soviet] already acts like another assembly, sends its commissars to the provinces and speaks openly of armed struggle. This is no longer an underground activity; rather the reverse: it is the work of the established power that seems to be going underground."[166]

The czarist regime was not of a mind to give the soviet enough time to prepare a revolt. At the end of November 1905 the government decided to regain the initiative lost in the October strike and to take up the struggle against the revolution. On November 26 the chairman of the soviet of workers deputies, Chrustalev-Nosar, was placed under arrest. The following day the full meeting elected a new three-man presidium, among them Trotsky (using the pseudonym Yanovsky). In answer to the arrest of the chairman, many deputies demanded a strike and others called for a mass demonstration,[167] but on the whole the workers' reaction was mild. The soviet therefore abstained from any protest action and decided to continue preparations for the uprising.[168] A fatalistic atmosphere hung over the soviet's last days, with everyone knowing that the critical clash with the regime was inevitable but that the soviet's forces were too weak. All hopes centered on revolutionizing the peasants and the army, but this could be done only through intensive propaganda. For this reason the St. Petersburg soviet used its last days to issue still another revolutionary appeal to the public. With the peasant union and the socialist parties, the soviet on December 2 issued the so-called Finance Manifesto, which called on the population to refuse to pay taxes to the state, to withdraw all funds from savings accounts, and to accept payment only in gold and foreign currency.[169] The regime's countermeasure was taken at once: on the very same day strikes by railroad, postal, and telegraph workers were prohibited under severe penalties. On December 3, the Executive Committee and about 200 deputies were finally arrested before the soviet session could begin.[170] Thus a crucial chapter in the Russian Revolution of 1905 came to an end.

Immediately after the arrests, a second soviet was formed from delegates who had accidentally escaped arrest, previously elected alternates, and newly elected delegates; the new Executive Committee was headed by Parvus (Aleksander Helphand).[171] On December 6 this soviet called for a political general strike throughout Russia.[172] But now the deputies had to meet in secret, and a plenary session was held only once. Nor did the soviet continue to enjoy the popularity of its predecessor; the workers were exhausted; the strike movement in St. Petersburg became fragmented and had to be abandoned on December 19. On January 2, 1906, the Executive Committee was placed under arrest, as were additional deputies in the following days and weeks. The official end to the history of the St. Petersburg Soviet of Workers Deputies of 1905 came in October 1906 in the trial of 52 members of the soviet, among them Chrustalev-Nosar and Trotsky; but its revolutionary legacy remained alive.[173]

The center of gravity of the revolution had shifted to Moscow early in December 1905; there the general strike turned into an armed insurrection.[174] In Moscow the soviet became, in Lenin's words, "an organ of the insurrection," but it had no over-all plan and was incapable of leading the movement. The soviet did not use the favorable moment of unrest in the Moscow garrison. Only because of the events in St. Petersburg did the Moscow soviet decide on the evening of December 6 to call for a general strike, with the express proviso that an attempt would be made to turn the strike into an insurrection.[175] No one, however, had any clear idea of how this was to be done. The Social Democratic joint committee (Bolsheviks and Mensheviks), the actual center of leadership, had been arrested the night of December

8, and thereafter the soviet's executive council transferred leadership of the strike to the various borough soviets. During the following few days communications between boroughs were severed, so that battles took place independently. The first armed clashes were more accidental than planned. The military, contrary to expectation, did not join the revolution, and the resulting disappointment exploded in separate "partisan actions." Bitterness increased gradually, and barricade skirmishes took place. Since the Moscow garrison was undependable, troops of guards had to be brought from St. Petersburg; by December 18 they had broken the resistance of the fighting groups.

During the ten-day strike and insurrection, the Moscow soviet and some borough councils acted as revolutionary organs of power. They issued a number of directives—for example, for regulating the water supply, keeping essential stores open, postponing rent payments for workers—which presupposed general authority. Nevertheless, the designation "revolutionary government," which soviet historians love to apply, is exaggerated. The various measures grew out of immediate needs, not from any comprehensive political program; and the soviets' sphere of action was limited. But the predominance of Bolsheviks in the Moscow soviet and its role in the armed rising made it for Bolshevik historians the "classic revolutionary proletarian organization"[176] and a model for all other councils.

The strike call of the St. Petersburg soviet and the Moscow events had a strong resonance in the provinces. The number of strikers came close to the October totals.[177] In various localities, especially the Donets Basin, armed battles erupted,[178] in which the soviets, some formed in direct connection with the December strike,[179] were important. The Novorossiysk soviet captured power in the city on December 9 and proclaimed the Novorossiysk republic; the governor and chief of police fled the city, the municipal duma and mayor submitted to the soviet, and garrison troops refused to fire on workers. The Novorossiysk soviet proclaimed as goals: 1) continuation of the political strike; 2) establishment of a people's self-government and a people's court; 3) struggle against the propertied classes; 4) organization of trade unions and political associations; 5) immediate relief for the unemployed; 6) preparations for the armed rising.[180] This program, with its mixture of economics and politics, basic and secondary questions, generalities and practical measures, genuinely reflects what the workers expected from their soviet: not a complete ready-made program for revolutionary reconstruction of the state, but mastery of practical tasks resulting from the revolution.

Similar revolutionary power was exercised for a time by the workers and soldiers councils in Chita and Krasnoyarsk in Siberia.[181] Supported by soldiers of the Manchurian army who had been infected with revolutionary feelings, the soviets dismissed local administrations in December and formed their own administrative departments. In Chita, furthermore, railroads, postal and telegraph systems, and state lands were declared communal property. Not until punitive expeditions were sent to Siberia in late December 1905 and early January 1906 could the regime's authority be reestablished.

Defeat of the revolution then also meant the end of the soviets. A number of the most active deputies were arrested or went into hiding while others remained in the factories as representatives and spokesmen of the workers. How close and tenacious the tie between deputies and workers in St. Petersburg was, even after the soviets' dissolution, was shown during preparations for the trial of the accused deputies. The workers supported the prisoners by numerous protest assemblies and resolutions, in hearings of witnesses, and through financial contributions.[182] Hope revived for a rebirth of the soviet when the council of unemployed was formed in the spring of 1906.[183] This council grew out of the soviet's earlier commission on the unemployed and reached almost 20,000 jobless St. Petersburg workers with soup kitchens. With backing from the municipal duma, which arranged relief work for the unemployed, the council led a semilegal existence. Seeking to extend its activities to the factories, it agitated for revival of the general workers council. Among the 300-odd deputies, several were factory delegates. While the Social Revolutionaries supported agitation for a new soviet of workers deputies, Lenin decidedly rejected it.[184] At the close of 1906 radicals dominated the council of unemployed, demanding a mass demonstration of the jobless, but resulting conflicts split the council in the summer of 1907.

Councils of unemployed were also formed in Moscow, Kharkov, Kiev, Poltava, Ekaterinoslav, Baku, Batum, Rostov, and Kronstadt; as in St. Petersburg, they raised political demands along with furnishing material aid to the unemployed.[185] During a Moscow strike in July 1906 formation of city-wide soviet and district councils was attempted. About 150 deputies met and elected an executive committee to lead the strike. After a few days, the strike had to be ended, and with it the soviet.[186] A document which as late as May 1907 was signed "Soviet of Workers Deputies" has come down to us from the Nadeždinskij factory in the Ural region, where a deputies council had been formed in May 1905.[187] These last flickers of the council movement in 1906–1907 could not survive the changing political situation. Soviets were organs of the revolution, which in 1906 turned into parliamentary battles. As limited class representation of a particular proletarian group, such as the councils of unemployed, they lacked the mass appeal of the 1905 soviets. Attempts at reviving the soviets nevertheless proved that the form and idea had taken firm hold among Russian workers, and that the memory of the great days of the Revolution of 1905 endured.

c) Significance of the 1905 Soviets

The question arises here whether the soviets of 1905, as organizations of proletarian self-government and revolutionary struggle, thought of establishing a government patterned on themselves—that is, a soviet republic—if the revolution succeeded. Bolshevik historians favor this view, and pointing to statements by Lenin on the soviets as "nuclei of the new revolutionary power,"[188] they assert that the soviets aimed to capture political power.[189] However, their contentions lack evidence. The basic political proclamations always demand a constituent assembly and a democratic republic. The soviets did not consider it their job to replace the constituent assembly, but to convene it. No one then in Russia would have proclaimed a soviet system in place of some kind of parliamentary-democratic republic, even though, as will be shown, a few revolutionary groups and personalities had recognized the soviets' great significance and had predicted for them an important future role. For the workers who looked to the soviets for practical organization and leadership, such an idea was remote.

It is therefore idle to speculate whether, had the revolution succeeded, the soviets would have played a role similar to 1917, when they supplanted the existing regime. In their brief existence during the first Russian revolution, they were never fully developed; tendencies to supplant governmental machinery with revolutionary organs were vague; and the soviets' evolution toward a workers and peasants democracy or trade-unionist organizations was still wide open.

The 1905 soviets are nevertheless very significant for the history of the Russian revolution. In the soviets the Russian workers created an instrument of democratic self-government, well-suited to represent the revolutionary demands of the oppressed masses. The soviets of 1905, and especially the St. Petersburg Soviet of Workers Deputies, created a revolutionary tradition of lasting impact. The instant revival of the Petrograd soviet in the February Revolution of 1917 and the upsurge of workers and soldiers councils all over Russia expressed a living memory of the revolutionary role of the soviets of 1905 and proved that these organizations could adapt instantly to widespread needs in a new revolutionary rising.

In contrast to 1917, the soviets' effect outside Russia during the first revolution was minimal. While events of 1905 found a lively echo in the international labor movement (among the German Social Democrats, for example, during the debate on the mass strike where the Russian experience gave greater prominence to the left wing led by Rosa Luxemburg and Karl Liebknecht), the uniqueness of the soviets went all but unnoticed. Only a few socialists, such as the Dutchman Pannekoek in his critique of the parliamentary system and bourgeois state, came close to the later council idea as advocated by the Bolsheviks starting in 1917.[190]

The significance of the 1905 soviets can be compared to that of the Paris Commune of 1871. Both gained historical importance primarily from later events: the Paris Commune from its inclusion in the theory of the state articulated by Marx and later by Lenin; the soviets of 1905 as precursors of the 1917 soviets. From the combination of the two—the interpretation of the Commune by Marx and Lenin and the soviets—emerged the theory and practice of the Bolshevik soviet system.

4. THE SOCIALIST PARTIES AND THE SOVIETS

The 1905 soviets had a tremendous impact on the socialist parties, which had not decreed or foreseen the coming of these new organizations but now had to reconcile them with socialist principles. The revolutionary programs of the different socialist factions naturally resulted in different positions on the soviets. Divergent views about methods and aims of the workers movement surfaced again, even though the lower party ranks had successfully cooperated in the soviets. The two Social Democratic factions of Mensheviks and Bolsheviks, the lone wolf Trotsky, and the Social Revolutionary groups, all developed their own ideas, which to some extent determined their attitudes to the 1917 soviets.

a) The Mensheviks

Outbreak of the revolution in January 1905 caught the Social Democratic Party poorly prepared, both practically and theoretically. After the split in 1903 its energy had gone into factional quarrels, and organizational questions dominated ideological argument. When attempts to reunite the party failed in early 1905, Bolsheviks and Mensheviks took separate positions on the urgent questions, and developed their revolutionary programs in the spring and summer of 1905. Although immediate pressures brought the two factions closer together in the practical struggle, theoretical controversies about the revolution's nature and about party tactics retained fundamental importance. The differences exposed the full extent of the 1903 split, which could never again be healed, and simultaneously established the principles that guided both wings of Russian Marxism until the Revolution of 1917.

Bolsheviks and Mensheviks started out with Plekhanov's old program: the coming Russian revolution would be "bourgeois" and the proletariat must fight for and win a democratic republic. Given the agrarian and semifeudal conditions in Russia, with little industry and a weak working class, the building of socialism would remain the task of the second phase. Controversy set in when this model— ultimately derived from Marx's schema of 1848[191]—was applied to concrete sociopolitical action in the Russia of 1905.

The Mensheviks concluded that the decisive social force in this revolution, according to the objective laws of social development taught by Marx—would be the bourgeoisie, which therefore would assume leadership during and after the revolution. In his attack on Lenin on the eve of the revolution, Martynov formulated this idea:[192] "The proletariat can attain neither complete nor partial control of the state so long as it has not made the social revolution. . . . If this is true, then clearly the forthcoming revolution cannot create any political forms against the will of the bourgeoisie, for it will rule tomorrow. . . . The proletariat can influence the bourgeois revolution's course and outcome only by exerting revolutionary pressure on the will of the liberal and radical bourgeoisie. . . . In any case the proletariat will present the bourgeoisie with the dilemma: either to go back to oppressive absolutism, which will suffocate it, or to go forward with the people."[193] In March 1905 Martov reaffirmed that even after the January 9 events the character of the revolution and the party's tasks had not changed, and that the primary goals were "unification of the proletariat as a class" and "building and consolidation of its class party."[194] A programmatic article, in the Menshevik newspaper *Načalo*, finally spelled out the tasks of the working class and of the Social Democratic Party: to support the bourgeoisie's struggle against czarism, to help it achieve victory, and to "enlarge the bourgeois revolution by advancing the proletariat's interests within this framework and by creating within the bourgeois constitution itself the broadest possible base for the revolutionary transformation of society."[195]

According to the Menshevik view, a bourgeois regime, emerging from the victorious revolution, would have to carry out democratic and social reforms. The socialists would have no part of such a government; responsibility for capitalism's drawbacks would have to remain with the bourgeoisie. Parliamentary struggle within the democratic constitution would strengthen Social Democracy and raise the political consciousness of Russian workers. Also, Russia's economic conditions would have changed so much by then that when the socialist revolution began in the advanced countries of western and central Europe, it could spark across to Russia.[196]

The Menshevik revolutionary program stemmed from recognition of Russia's economic backwardness and reacted to conditions in the rest of Europe. For the Mensheviks, socialist revolution and the proletariat taking of power only completed a chain of economic changes. Their fundamentally democratic attitude, which grew even stronger in the next few years, saved the Mensheviks from the temptation of a dictatorship of the minority when a "dictatorship of the majority" (in the true sense of Marx's dictatorship of the proletariat) was not yet possible in Russia, and stood in sharp contrast to the "Jacobin" revolutionary path pursued by Lenin.[197]

Based on this evaluation of the Russian revolution, the Mensheviks saw the chief practical tasks of the party as: "building a strong Social Democratic organization by merging the old conspiratorial apparatus with the new mass organizations and development of trade unions."[198] The spontaneous and widespread awakening of the working class made the Social Democrats' most urgent task that of winning and organizing the masses into a political force. In this way, the argument went, the Social Democratic Party program would apply to the problems arising during the revolution.[199]

The Mensheviks smarted under their party committee's isolation and negligible influence among the workers; both resulted from the party's illegal status, the chasm between intelligentsia and workers, and the feud with the Bolsheviks. From January 1905, the Mensheviks had their first opportunity to exert broad influence, given the heightened revolutionary sensitivity of the masses and simultaneous relaxation of police surveillance. Elections in February 1905[200] to the Shidlovsky Commission, which the Mensheviks envisioned as a potential propaganda center of the Russian workers movement, brought a similar plan by the St. Petersburg group. The workers were to elect deputies in the factories (as had been done for the Commission), form a council of deputies in each particular city, and their representatives in turn would meet in an all-Russian workers congress.[201] Thus the Mensheviks hoped to draw into the revolutionary movement those workers still outside political life, and to transform the Social Democratic Party from an illegal conspiratorial band into a public mass party. During the spring and summer of 1905 Axelrod in particular defended in a number of articles this proposal for a workers congress.[202] One Menshevik group combined the project with concurrent efforts for an alliance of existing workers welfare associations.[203] Others, such as Parvus, pointed out that there were associations of all other social classes in the zemstvos, the municipal dumas, the Union of Unions, and the like, and that a working-class forum was needed.[204]

Growing out of and paralleling the plan of a workers congress, the Mensheviks developed as their principal tactical line the idea of "revolutionary self-government," the counterpart to the Bolsheviks' "provisional revolutionary government" (to be discussed below). These slogans perfectly illustrate the contrast between the two factions. In practice the concept of revolutionary self-government— propounded particularly by Martov—attempted to disrupt the czarist bureaucratic apparatus through a democratic change "from below," and thus to force constitutional concessions by the government. Workers and all other population sectors excluded from voting for the "Bulygin Duma" were to initiate "people's propaganda committees." "They should set as their goal election of authorized revolutionary deputies outside the legal framework. They should call on the peasants to send their freely elected deputies into the cities to consult with the urban population on what is to be done. As this tactic succeeds, we will cover the country with a network of revolutionary self-government organs. The all-Russian association of this self-government will also function as the political all-Russian forum that we need so urgently."[205] The goal of this Menshevik campaign was exertion of revolutionary pressure on the duma that was to meet in the autumn of 1905, and if necessary, convocation of a constituent assembly outside the legal framework. "Organizing such self-government and its open operation everywhere is the way to liquidate the autocracy which refuses to inaugurate the constitutional era."[206]

The Menshevik concept of revolutionary self-government owes certain of its traits to historical memories of the French Revolution of 1789 and especially of the Paris Commune of 1871. The Menshevik conference of April 1905 alluded directly to "formation of revolutionary communes in one city or another, in one district or another . . . in the interest of spreading insurrection and disorganizing the government."[207] Martov tried to tell Lenin—who called the plea for communes an "empty revolutionary phrase"[208]—that Marx and Engels had expressly approved voluntary union of communities as the revolutionary program of the Commune and that "revolutionary self-government" in Russia accorded with this idea.[209] Significantly, the Paris Commune, later the basis of Lenin's theory of the state and of the Bolshevik system of soviets, was introduced into the Marxist program of revolution in Russia, not by the Bolsheviks, but by the Mensheviks. Nevertheless it is not clear what relationship was envisaged between the essentially proletarian-peasant organs of revolutionary self-government (the local "communes") and the bourgeois government postulated by the Mensheviks. This contradiction in the Menshevik program of revolution, which Lenin forcefully pointed out, grew out of the discrepancy between the belief, held by the Mensheviks, in the "objective" course of social and political developments and their practical revolutionary activity, which went beyond the limits they themselves had set. Had the campaign for revolutionary self-government succeeded, perhaps its organs were meant to be a kind of lower authority controlling the bourgeois-democratic government at the top, as happened in 1917 in the relationship of the soviets to the Provisional Government. Such considerations were far from the Mensheviks' minds in 1905; nevertheless their plan of revolutionary self-government, with its structure from the bottom up and uniting workers and peasants in a deputies organization, remains remarkable. If we can speak at all of a theoretical forerunner of the 1905 soviets, then it is the Menshevik concept of revolutionary self-government, even though it never existed in the form envisaged by them. Instead of an election campaign to produce the local propaganda committees, a general strike broke out in October 1905 and fostered the St. Petersburg soviet. The Mensheviks saw it as substantially realizing their concept of revolutionary self-government. The earlier projects on paper for a "workers congress," for "communes," and the like, now took on living shape. It was easy for the Mensheviks to include the new soviet organizations in their revolutionary program; in a way they had been ready for the soviets since the onset of the revolution.

The local Menshevik organization had actively participated in forming the St. Petersburg Soviet of Workers Deputies in October 1905.[210] The St. Petersburg Mensheviks had the idea that the "workers committee"—that is, the soviet—would prove to be the "very best instrument for education and propaganda, an instrument preparing a nationwide revolutionary organization" such as had been described in *Iskra*.[211] When Martov returned from abroad to St. Petersburg at the end of October 1905, the soviet struck him as the "embodiment of our concept of revolutionary self-government."[212] In practical matters too the Mensheviks' earlier policies enabled them to relate to the soviets more quickly than did the Bolsheviks. The Mensheviks realized that the workers looked to the soviets as their own organizations that represented their interests, much more than to the parties; the Mensheviks adapted themselves to the will of the majority of the unaffiliated deputies by refraining from exerting any official influence in the soviets.

It would, however, be wrong to assume that the Mensheviks saw the soviets both as the fruition of their own work among the prole-

tariat and as their actual goal. Rather, they explained the soviets
by the absence of a strong Social Democratic workers party in Russia, which forced the masses to create substitute organizations
through spontaneous self-help. Martynov, a leading Menshevik during
these years, put it quite plainly: "The coexistence of two independent
proletarian organizations—a Social Democratic Party organization
and another one that is officially nonpartisan, though influenced by
the Social Democrats—is an abnormal phenomenon that must disappear sooner or later. When we recommended the creation of
organs of the revolutionary self-government of the proletariat, we
considered this form of organization as something provisional and
temporary."[213] He went on to suggest that the Social Democrats
direct all their efforts to transforming their illegal party organization
into a broadly based open workers party "that is wide enough to
include or to render superfluous organizations on the pattern of
soviets of workers deputies."[214] Thus for the Mensheviks the soviets
were primarily organizations that should unite the broad masses of
workers who had heretofore not been reached by the party, lead them
in the revolutionary struggle, and not least, win them over to Social
Democracy. The soviets, in Martov's words, were to be an "arena
where the cadres of a broadly based mass party can be formed."[215]
The Mensheviks therefore supported the efforts of the soviets to
summon all existing proletarian organizations to an all-Russian
workers congress.[216]

The defeat of the revolution in December 1905 effected a revision
of Menshevik revolutionary tactics. Under the influence of the mighty
revolutionary wave during the "freedom days" the Mensheviks had
abandoned their policy of conditional support of the liberal opposition and drawn appreciably nearer to the Bolshevik conception of
the counterrevolutionary role of the bourgeoisie. But now the right
wing subjected the tactics of radical overthrow to sharp criticism:
the December defeat of the workers was the result of the workers'
isolation from the other democratic forces; the December rising had
been "artificially" brought about, without first having strengthened
the party by sufficiently widespread propaganda and organization;
finally, instead of concentrating on the elections to the duma, the
party's powers had been dissipated by precipitate actions.[217] The
Social Democrats would now have to suffer the consequences of the
altered situation and take a realistic view of the duma convening at

the end of April 1906. To transform it into a revolutionary people's parliament and the focal point of the struggle against czarism should be the party's immediate goal.[218]

In the election campaign to the duma that was supported by the Mensheviks (the Bolsheviks and Social Revolutionaries refused to take part in the elections), they fell back on the original concept of revolutionary self-government as framed by Martov and Dan in the spring and summer of 1905. The Mensheviks advocated assemblies of authorized representatives and electors—the elections were indirect—which, united on a nationwide basis and joined by representatives of other revolutionary classes, would form a "revolutionary parliament" and serve as a counterpart to the czarist duma.[219] Significantly, Dan, who first proposed this idea, considered these organizations as superior because they were better suited to developing the workers' political consciousness and to strengthening the Social Democrats' influence than the frequently nonpolitical soviets, to which the workers had elected their deputies regardless of party membership.[220] In spite of the Mensheviks' efforts on behalf of such assemblies of representatives and electors, especially during the election campaign for the Second Duma in the winter of 1906–1907, these organizations found acceptance only in the Donets Basin.[221] It was their primary purpose to establish close revolutionary ties between the working masses and the Social Democratic delegates to the duma and to raise the duma's prestige among the workers.

At the Fourth Party Congress of the RSDWP in Stockholm in April 1906 the Mensheviks, still fresh with impression of the soviets' activities in the autumn of 1905, introduced a resolution calling on the party "not only to support spontaneously nonpartisan proletarian organizations on the pattern of the soviets of workers deputies, but also to participate in their formation at the moment of a revolutionary upswing and to aid them in fulfilling their tasks."[222] Here the Mensheviks differed from the Bolsheviks, who at this time advocated only very conditional support of such "nonpartisan" organizations.[223] But on the whole even the Mensheviks placed the soviets more and more in the background. The idea of an all-Russian workers congress was revived in the summer of 1906 to give the Social Democratic Party the broad base it so urgently needed. The proposal brought tendencies to light that had also been present in the soviets: the desire to escape the dominating influence of the intelligentsia, all too prone in its factional quarrels to forget about the workers plight, and the readiness if need be to risk a break with the Social Democratic Party.[224] In April 1907 Chrustalev-Nosar, the former chairman of the St. Petersburg soviet, developed a complete scheme for the workers congress; it was to be structured like a pyramid, with the factory committees as the bottom cells, municipal committees in the middle, and finally the general workers congress, made up of representatives from the unions, cooperatives, relief societies, and elected factory deputies.[225] In the Menshevik view, this type of mass organization would at least have enabled the Social Democratic Party to rid itself of the shackles of illegality and "sectarianism" and to transform itself into a "European" workers party. To create such a well-organized proletarian mass party on the pattern of the German Social Democratic Party was the Mensheviks' immediate goal. On the way to its accomplishment valuable services could be rendered by nonpartisan organizations such as the soviets or the projected workers congress. The Mensheviks assigned no further and certainly no permanent tasks to the soviets. They considered them stopgap organizations and substitutes for the still-lacking broadly based workers political party and the nascent trade unions; once party and unions were formed, the soviets would have to relinquish their functions to the new organizations. As instruments of revolution and as temporary bodies for proletarian self-government, the soviets of 1905 were supported by the Mensheviks, but permanent establishment of the soviets as new organs of government was not considered. In 1917 the Mensheviks found themselves in the same position, which now became fatal for them: on the one hand they were the leading party in the soviets and champions of "soviet democracy"; on the other hand, since they were convinced of the "bourgeois" nature of the revolution, they did not envisage any future for the soviets, and therefore were outmaneuvered by the Bolsheviks.

b) The Bolsheviks

Lenin's revolutionary tactics in 1905 followed from his class analysis of social forces. At this time Lenin, too, believed that Russia must first finish its "bourgeois" revolution and that achieving a democratic republic was the most immediate task. But Lenin's formulas were different from those of the Mensheviks. Lenin argued that he was following Marx, who in 1848 had said the proletariat should assume leadership in the struggle for a democratic republic and propel the revolution right up to the gates of socialism with the support of the petit bourgeoisie (which in Russia would mean primarily the peasantry).[226] The Russian peasants—"who at present are not so much interested in the absolute protection of private property as in the expropriation of the landowners' holdings"—were, according to Lenin, capable of "becoming the most committed and radical followers of the democratic revolution."[227]

The goal Lenin set for this specifically Russian form of European "bourgeois" revolution was "revolutionary-democratic dictatorship of the proletariat and peasantry." In practical terms, Lenin pictured the revolution's development in this way: "The workers movement conquers in the democratic revolution through the liberals' passive temporizing and with the active support of the peasantry, the radical republican intelligentsia, and the corresponding strata of the urban petit bourgeoisie. The peasant rising succeeds; the power of the landowners is broken."[228]

The political form of the revolutionary-democratic dictatorship of the proletariat and peasantry (a formula reflecting the social power structure) was to be the "provisional revolutionary government." It was to emerge from the victorious popular uprising, from which it would draw support and which it would lead until the established powers were totally defeated. Lenin took for granted participation of the Social Democrats in such a government. "Provisional revolutionary government" meant a coalition of Social Democrats, Social Revolutionaries, and possibly other radical-democratic parties.[229] Although Lenin's writings are not very revealing in this respect, there can be no doubt that even then Lenin's "last secret thought" was that he would emerge from the victorious revolution as "sole leader of the democratic republic."[230]

The revolutionary government was to have dictatorial powers and initiate radical social change, and thus, Lenin thought, encourage the socialist revolution which the proletariat alone, possibly with the help of the rural poor, would carry out against the bourgeoisie and the rich peasants: "Immediately after the democratic revolution, and with all our power we will . . . start upon the transition to the socialist revolution. We are for the permanent revolution. We will not stop halfway," Lenin wrote in the autumn of 1905.[231] Here Lenin was employing the same term used by Marx in 1850 and elaborated by Trotsky during the first Russian revolution into his theory of "permanent revolution." Here too begins Lenin's theory of the changeover from bourgeois to socialist revolution, announced in April 1917 and the basis for his agreement with Trotsky. This theory was closely connected with expectation of a proletarian revolution in Europe: even in 1905 Lenin hoped that the victorious revolution in Russia would "signal . . . the onset of the socialist revolution in Europe. . . . The European workers will show us 'how to do it' and then with them we will carry out the socialist revolution."[232]

On the other hand Lenin was realistic enough, even during the revolution's high points, to allow for a "half" victory. He attempted to clarify for himself the revolution's probable outcome by careful analysis of the pros and cons of the question, "Have we been given a revolution of the 1789 type or of the 1848 type?"[233] (The year 1789 stood for the total overthrow of czarism and the introduction of a republic, 1848 for the compromise of a constitutional monarchy.) In spite of such sober, comprehensive evaluation, his driving revolutionary ambition led him to passionate appeals for an uprising against czarism and an organization to implement it.

As early as 1902, in *What Is to Be Done?*, Lenin had proclaimed the primary goal of the Social Democratic Party to be preparation, initiation, and execution of a general people's rising.[234] And after January 1905, the Bolsheviks had no doubt that an armed uprising was imperative. The Third Party Congress of the RSDWP of April 1905, to which only the Bolsheviks sent delegates, advised the various party organizations to propagandize and agitate for uprising, to arm the workers, to form special cadres, and to plan for rebellion.[235] Here the close connection between Lenin's ideal of a party of professional revolutionaries and the Bolshevik claim to leadership becomes evident: only a small, determined, and disciplined troop of revolutionary fighters could organize the insurrection and seize power. The sympathizing masses lent the movement the necessary thrust, but the conspiratorial minority gave it direction and goal.

In order to revolutionize the masses and prepare the rebellion, Lenin proposed formation of special revolutionary committees. Shortly after "Bloody Sunday" he wrote: "The slogans of the struggle for freedom will spread further and further among the urban poor, the millions of peasants. In every factory, in every quarter of every city, in every sizable village revolutionary committees will form. The rebelling population will work to overthrow all governmental institutions of czarist absolutism and to proclaim immediate convocation of the constituent assembly."[236] After that Lenin primarily promoted establishment of revolutionary committees in the countryside because, as he noted, few organizational cells of any kind existed there, and because making peasants rebellious was the most urgent task. The peasant committees were to take charge of democratic reforms in the countryside and to constitute the local organs of insurrection.[237] But their task could be enlarged: "The peasant committees are an elastic institution as useful under today's conditions as, let us say, under the provisional revolutionary government, where the committees would become instruments of government."[238] They would be composed of Social Democrats as a tight political group with other revolutionary parties and nonpartisan groups; they would incorporate in a microcosm "the revolutionary-democratic dictatorship of proletariat and peasantry."

The urban and rural revolutionary committees advocated by Lenin had nothing in common with the Menshevik idea of revolutionary self-government. In contrast to the Menshevik concept of revolution as a "spontaneous process" without advance organization Lenin stated: "An insurrection can be arranged if those who arrange it are influential with the masses and are able to assess the moment correctly."[239] The Menshevik campaign for revolutionary self-government was described by Lenin as a "completely childish idea," since it ignored the real power relationships and the government's military superiority. "In the revolution it is first of all important to win—even if only in a single city—and to establish a provisional revolutionary government, so that this government, acting as an instrument of the insurrection and as recognized leader of the revolutionary people, can undertake to organize revolutionary self-government. . . . Organization of revolutionary self-government and election of the people's delegates are not the prologue but the epilogue of the insurrection."[240] While the Mensheviks believed convocation of a sovereign constituent national assembly to be a primary goal of the revolution, such an assembly—though constantly included in the Bolshevik battlecries—was subordinate among the Bolsheviks as early as 1905. The decisive measures of the revolutionary government were to be taken before a possible meeting of a constituent assembly. "We will demand of the constituent assembly . . . that it sanction changes that will have been effected by the provisional government with the help of the rebelling people," Stalin wrote in this connection.[241]

The Bolshevik revolutionary program was based on the party's leading role. After the revolutionary tidal wave of 1905 the Bolsheviks repeatedly confronted the problem of how to combine the party's absolute demand for leadership with the spontaneous progress of the labor movement. Their strength in numbers was small; even among the St. Petersburg workers the party had fewer than 1,000 members during the first half of 1905.[242] Most party committees had, to use Lenin's words, "become frozen in illegality"[243] and were in no position to attract the politically awakened levels of the working class. At the party congress of April 1905 Lenin demanded that the party committees heretofore dominated by the intelligentsia be expanded by including workers from the factories, but he was resisted by professional revolutionaries on the committees, who maintained that no suitable workers were available.[244] This is an early instance of the "bureaucratization" of the party—a problem that occupied Lenin until his death, but which in the final analysis stemmed from his conception of an elite party and his suspicion of "spontaneity."

The Bolsheviks' mistrust of labor organizations that were independent of the party was most strongly expressed in their relations with the soviets. The view of the Stalinist rewriters of history, widely accepted even abroad, that the Bolsheviks were instrumental in the founding of the soviets in 1905, is opposed by the sober truth that the Bolsheviks did not play godfather to the soviets, and that originally there was no room in Bolshevism for the soviet idea. Notwithstanding participation of many Bolshevik workers in the soviets, the basic position of Bolshevik executive groups wavered between overt rejection and half-reluctant recognition of these "foreign bodies" within the revolution. Their attitude toward the soviets at this time varied from place to place and underwent certain alterations. Lenin himself never reached a final verdict on the soviets, though he was the only Bolshevik who attempted to analyze this new revolutionary phenomenon and to incorporate it into his theory and tactics of revolution.

Workers with a Bolshevik orientation, like all other workers, participated in the founding of the St. Petersburg soviet during the October strike. The party committee—which, unlike the Mensheviks, had not originally advocated election of deputies—sent its official representatives to the Executive Committee; among them was Knuniants (Radin), who later became the leading Bolshevik in the soviet. During the first few days of the soviet's existence, when it functioned as a strike committee and no one knew exactly what its future role would be, the Bolsheviks were quite favorably disposed toward it. This changed, however, when after the October strike ended the soviet began developing into an instrument of political leadership for the metropolitan working class. From then on a majority of St. Petersburg Bolsheviks were hostile toward the soviet.[245] The Bolsheviks got the joint committee representing both factions of the RSDWP to pass a resolution demanding that the soviet officially accept the Social Democratic program, since nonpartisan organizations such as the soviet could not steer a specifically proletarian course and were therefore harmful.[246] The party's Central Committee published the resolution on October 27, thereby making it the binding directive for all other Bolshevik organizations. In St. Petersburg itself Bolshevik agitators began to promote it among workers and soviet deputies. In a few plants they successfully persuaded workers to accept a declaration concurring with the joint committee's resolution.[247] In the meantime, however, the Mensheviks had dissociated themselves from these radical tactics, and the Social Revolutionaries introduced a counterdeclaration at the soviet plenary session, expressing strong opposition to the Social Democratic Party's claim to be the sole representative of proletarian interests.[248] After Lenin's arrival in St. Petersburg, the Bolsheviks stopped their open attacks against the soviet.

Discussion in the columns of their newspaper, *Novaja Žizn'*, turned primarily on the relationship of the soviet, as a "nonpartisan organization," to the Social Democratic Party. Bolshevik criticism was mainly directed against the soviet's effort to act as the proletariat's political organization, standing above parties. The St. Petersburg Bolsheviks were convinced that "only a strong party along class lines can guide the proletarian political movement and preserve the integrity of its program, rather than a political mixture of this kind, an indeterminate and vacillating political organization such as the workers council represents and cannot help but represent."[249] The consensus was that parallel existence of the soviet and the party was in the long run impossible. For a group of Bolshevik agitators and propagandists, P.

Mendeleev demanded unequivocally: "The soviet of workers deputies has no right to exist as a political organization, and the Social Democrats must resign from it, since its existence damages development of the Social Democratic movement. The soviet may either exist as a trade-union organization or it should not exist at all. As a trade-union organization it can be of great significance, inasmuch as it unites all workers into a single organization, agitates in the factories for the formation of trade-union war chests, and functions as a strike committee during the strike." Accordingly, the writer proposed that the party adopt a three-pronged procedure toward the soviet: 1) the Bolsheviks should attempt to induce the soviet to limit itself to trade-union functions; 2) should this fail, the soviet was to issue a declaration on principle accepting its subordination to the leadership of the RSDWP; 3) the soviet was then to be dissolved forthwith, since its continued existence as a Social Democratic organization alongside the party would be superfluous.[250]

The question, "Soviet or Party?" was also posed by Radin in an article bearing that title, which was later used by Lenin to develop his own concept of the soviets. Radin admitted the need for an organization that could call and lead a strike of the working masses, since the political parties alone were not in a position to do so. The soviet could in no way replace the party, however. "It can only direct specific actions of the proletariat, stand at the head of particular mass actions. It is able to set concrete tasks that unite the entire proletariat, but its task is not to guide class politics." Radin, too, concluded that the soviet should "reveal its political profile" and state "which political party it recognizes as leader and which political program it follows. The proletariat should know exactly what banner its chosen organization marches under and which party's program and directives it will act on."[251]

The negative attitude of the St. Petersburg Bolsheviks toward the soviet arose from fear that the elected workers organization might push aside the party committee and thus lead to "subordination of consciousness to spontaneity."[252] The St. Petersburg Bolsheviks still remembered vividly the great success of Father Gapon's workmen's society and the powerful spontaneous movement of January, during which the party circles kept aloof. They saw in the soviet of workers deputies the danger of a new "Gaponovščina"—all the more so as the deputies included several one-time adherents of Gapon.[253] In the efforts of many Mensheviks to use the workers soviet as the starting point for an internal reorganization of the Social Democratic Party, the Bolsheviks saw symptoms of the dissolution of the "avant-garde of the proletariat" and its tight organization. Finally, they feared that under the colors of nonpartisanship "the rotten goods of bourgeois ideology" might be introduced among the workers.[254]

The attitude of the metropolitan Bolsheviks influenced that of the provincial party committees toward the soviets. This was particularly evident in Moscow. In connection with the printing-trades employees strike and the printers council,[255] the Bolshevik party committee on October 2, 1905, exhorted the Moscow workers to elect deputies in the factories to lead the general strike. "Let the deputies of all factories and workshops come together in a general soviet of deputies from all Moscow," the appeal read. "Such a general soviet of deputies will unite the proletariat of all Moscow. It will give the workers the unity and organization needed for the struggle against their enemies—both the autocracy and the bourgeoisie."[256] This proclamation is an isolated instance of Bolshevik initiative in formation of the soviets in 1905. The appeal had no practical consequences. Influenced by the negative attitude of the party's St. Petersburg and central committees, the Moscow Bolsheviks waited a long time, even after the October strike, before establishing a workers council in late November.[257] The opening day of the Moscow soviet, a congress of the northern committees of the RSDWP passed the following resolution: "A council of workers deputies should be established only in places where the party organization has no other means of directing the proletariat's revolutionary action or where it is necessary to free the masses from the influence of the bourgeois parties. The soviet of workers deputies must be a technical instrument of the party for the purpose of giving political leadership to the masses through the RSDWP. It is therefore imperative to gain control of the soviet and prevail upon it to recognize the program and political leadership of the RSDWP."[258]

These "sectarian tendencies"[259] in numerous Bolshevik party committees, which saw undesirable rivals in the soviets, partly explain the belated formation of many provincial soviets. In Saratov, for example, the Bolsheviks opposed the founding of a deputies council as late as November 20. When a soviet was nevertheless elected, the Bolsheviks demanded acceptance of the Social Democratic Party program at the first session. The majority—Mensheviks and un-

affiliated—objected, however, and the soviet decided not to tie itself
to any particular party program but to be "a nonpartisan instrument
of leadership of the working masses, the majority of whom are unaffiliated."[260] On the other hand, the Bolsheviks in Tver persuaded the
soviet deputies to accept the party program almost unanimously.[261]

The views concerning the soviets which Lenin developed during
1905–1907 had little influence on the practical relationship of the
party to the soviets, but they are of considerable theoretical significance, especially for the Revolution of 1917. Lenin hit on the soviet
concept that was to be fruitful in the future; next to Trotsky's
analysis of the soviets, drawn from direct experience, Lenin's view is
among the most important theoretical results of the 1905 revolution.
His experiences with the soviets of 1905 had a significant impact on
his revolutionary program in 1917.

Lenin's earliest statement about the soviets in 1905 already contains in embryo all the ideas he later varied or expanded. It appears in
a letter to the editors of *Novaja Žizn'*, written in Stockholm during
the first days of November (o.s.), which bore the title "Our Tasks
and the Soviet of Workers Deputies"; it was not printed at the time
and was not published until 1940.[262] In the letter Lenin rejected the
alternative stated by Radin in the fifth issue of *Novaja Žizn'*—"Soviet
or Party?"—which he considered too narrow. It was an error, he
claimed, to demand that the soviet declare itself for a particular party
program; it inherently represented a militant alliance between Social
Democrats and revolutionary bourgeois democrats. What was needed
was an expansion not a contraction of its membership: deputies of
sailors and soldiers, peasants, and the revolutionary intelligentsia
ought to be admitted. "The soviet should elect a core-group to constitute the provisional revolutionary government and augment it with
representatives of all revolutionary parties and all revolutionary
democrats. We are not afraid of such breadth and variety of membership; rather, we desire it, since complete success of the great
Russian revolution is not possible without an alliance of proletariat
and peasantry, or without the collaboration of Social Democrats and
revolutionary democrats."[263] "Possibly I am mistaken," Lenin states
further, "but it seems to me that politically the soviet of workers
deputies must be viewed as the nucleus of the provisional revolutionary government, and that the soviet should as soon as possible
declare itself to be the provisional revolutionary government of all

Russia or (the same thing in another form) bring about the pro-visional revolutionary government."[264] Such a government, founded by the soviet, would be an instrument of the impending armed insurrection, give it a clear political program, and call on the people to overthrow czarism.

During the first revolution, Lenin only rarely stated, in such unequivocal and incisive terms, his faith in the soviet. After his return to Russia his remarks on the St. Petersburg soviet became much more guarded. Although he rejected the "boycott tactics" of the St. Petersburg Bolsheviks, he sided in principle with those who saw in the soviet the danger of an amorphous nonpartisan organization. "We can, and under certain circumstances we must, . . . go along with the unpoliticized proletarians [!], but on no account and at no time should we jeopardize the tight unity of our party, on no account and at no time should we forget that animosity among the proletariat toward the Social Democrats is a remnant of bourgeois attitudes. . . . Participation in unaffiliated organizations can be permitted to social-ists only as an exception, . . . only if the independence of the workers party is guaranteed and if within unaffiliated organizations or soviets individual delegates or party groups are subject to unconditional con-trol and guidance by the party executive."[265] Although Lenin took part in several sessions of the Executive Committee and once ad-dressed the plenum, he played no major role in the St. Petersburg soviet.[266] Lunacharski later reported that Lenin "stood with a certain helplessness before the imperfections of this apparatus, which was neutral and was not at our disposal."[267] Lenin's element was the party, not the forum of a mass organization; his job was at head-quarters, not on the battlefield of the revolution.

Opposing the Menshevik interpretation of the soviets as organs of revolutionary self-government, Lenin repeated his earlier thesis that only a victorious insurrection could prepare the ground for self-government. "The soviet of workers deputies is not a workers parlia-ment nor an instrument of proletarian self-government, nor indeed an instrument of any self-government, but a militant organization for the attainment of specific goals."[268] In January 1906, after forcible dissolution of the soviets, Lenin wrote that events had shown "how untenable 'revolutionary self-government' is without the victory of the revolutionary forces, how inadequate a temporary nonpartisan organization is, which at best may supplement a stable and durable militant organization of a party, but can never replace it. The metropolitan soviets of workers deputies collapsed because they lacked firm backing by a militant proletarian organization."[269] From now on he saw the soviets primarily in connection with armed revolt. Lenin welcomed development of the soviets into instruments of revolt, as had most clearly happened in Moscow, and at the same time he objected to senseless and harmful attempts to revive the soviets during a declining phase of the revolution. A resolution on the councils of workers deputies that he submitted to the Fourth Party Congress of the RSDWP in April 1906 reads in part: "that insofar as the soviets represent cells of revolutionary power, their strength and significance depend entirely on the vigor and success of the insurrection." And again: "Such institutions are inevitably doomed to failure if they do not base themselves on the revolutionary army and overthrow the government powers (that is, transform them into a provisional revolutionary government).[270]

Thus Lenin saw the soviets as organs of revolution which, as he had written in the spring of 1905, "even if only in one city, . . . must inevitably (if only provisionally, partially, intermittently) carry out *all* government business."[271] The soviets would act on behalf of the revolutionary people's government and institute a series of revolutionary reforms. Carried away by the vision of the revolution's triumph, ignoring its momentary setback, Lenin celebrated the "revolutionary genius of the people" and its power which "recognized no other force or law, from whatever source. Power that is unlimited, that is beyond legal constraints, that is based on force in the true sense of the word—this is dictatorship. . . . By its sociopolitical nature, this is the source of popular revolutionary dictatorship. . . . This force is based on the masses of the people. This was the fundamental difference between the new power and all previous power. The latter was minority power above the people, above the masses of workers and peasants. The former is popular power of workers and peasants above a minority, above a handful of oppressors, above a bunch of privileged nobles and officials. . . . The new power exercised by the dictatorship of the vast majority could and did maintain itself exclusively with the help and the confidence of the vast masses, exclusively through letting the entire mass share in the power in the freest, broadest, and strongest manner. . . . Are you a worker? Do you want to fight for the liberation of Russia from a handful of police oppressors? You are our comrade. Elect your deputy, we will gladly and happily welcome him as a fully qualified member of our soviet of workers deputies, the peasant committee, the soviet of soldiers deputies, and the like. . . . That was the face of the new power—or rather its germinal form, since the victory of the old power destroyed the young shoots very early on."[272]

Here Lenin approaches most closely the ideas subsequently developed in the spring of 1917 of the soviets as instruments of revolutionary workers and peasants power and (beginning in the summer of 1917) the dictatorship of the proletariat. Notwithstanding his evaluation—outstripping the realities of 1905—of the soviets as pillars of revolutionary state power, a status they achieved only in a few places and incompletely, Lenin here laid the groundwork for his theory of the soviets of 1917. At the same time there are already elements of an idealization of the soviets as an expression of the "people's creative genius" and of mass democracy; these ideas were carried over into the official myth of the soviets and are used to this day to prove the superiority of Soviet democracy over "bourgeois" democracy. Plekhanov—that sober, intellectual, and materialist Marxist—could feel only scorn and rejection for such irrational notions; he characterized Lenin's phrase of "the people's creative genius" (narodnoe tvorčestvo) as an obsolete and romantic heritage from the Narodniks. Lenin countered this reproach with the comment that the Revolution of 1905 had demonstrated the strength of spontaneous revolutionary forces and the growth of new instruments of power in the soviets and other revolutionary organizations.[273] But fundamentally Plekhanov was not in error: it was no accident that Lenin's paean of praise for the revolutionary genius of the Russian people as evidenced in the soviets coincided with the vocabulary of the Narodniks, Social Revolutionaries, and anarchists. During the revolutionary struggle Lenin was always closer to Russia's revolutionary tradition with its belief in the "people," its idealistic élan, and its anarchic undertone, than to the determinist doctrine of Western Marxism embraced by the Mensheviks. Lenin thought that in the soviets he could detect the people's long-suppressed powers which could be creative as well as destructive and which were now bursting forth in the revolution, powers which Bakunin and others had long hoped would be victorious in the revolution. Lenin was still hesitant in 1905, and saw these powers only as ideas without practical implications, but he was also determined to master them and to guide them toward the goal he desired. Thus the relationship between party and soviets became the central problem of Lenin's council theory and of the Bolshevik council system.

While between November 1905 and the summer of 1906 Lenin incorporated the soviets into his program as "instruments of insurrection" and "cells of the new revolutionary power," he continued to remain very cautious about the soviets as agencies of proletarian self-government. When Menshevik agitation for an all-Russian workers congress was revived in the second half of 1906,[274] his aversion to interpretation of the soviets as "above parties" and "nonpartisan" proletarian organizations deepened. Lenin went so far as to considerably modify his earlier view of the soviets as organs of the coming revolutionary power. In the spring of 1907 he wrote: "During a new upsurge of the struggle, during the transition into this phase (of the insurrection), such organizations (the soviets) are certainly necessary and desirable. But their historical development should not consist of a schematic expansion of the local soviets into an all-Russian workers congress, but a metamorphosis of the embryonic instruments of revolutionary power (these were above all the soviets) into central instruments of the victorious revolutionary power, into the revolutionary provisional government. The soviets of workers deputies and their union are essential to the victory of the insurrection. The victorious insurrection will of necessity create other instruments."[275] The last sentence shows that the future form of the revolutionary regime still took a subordinate place in Lenin's thinking and that he had not yet adopted the soviet system of state power. At the same time the difference between the Menshevik and Bolshevik approaches to the soviets becomes once again apparent. For the Mensheviks, the soviets were important because they could spawn a broad proletarian class party; for the Bolsheviks, the soviets were tactically useful in the power struggle.

Lenin strictly maintained the Marxist party's claim to power within the workers movement as against all nonpartisan workers organizations of the soviet type. In March 1907 he wrote a draft resolution for the Fifth Party Congress of the RSDWP, giving it the characteristic title, "On the Unaffiliated Workers Organizations in Relation to the Anarcho-Syndicalist Tendencies Among the Proletariat." In this work he condemned all efforts within and outside the party toward a workers congress and declared "that the participation by organizations of the Social Democratic Party in all-party councils of workers spokesmen and deputies and in congresses of their representatives, as well as the creation of such bodies, is permissible if need be, on the condition that party interests are strictly preserved and the Social Democratic Workers Party is strengthened and consolidated." Elsewhere in the resolution he states that "such bodies (the soviets of workers deputies) can actually prove superfluous if the Social Democratic Party understands how to organize its work among the proletarian masses properly, efficiently, and sweepingly."[276]

The "revolutionary genius" of the people, which Lenin had mentioned and which was present in the soviets, constantly harbored the danger of "anarcho-syndicalist tendencies" that Lenin fought against all his life. He detected this danger early in the development of the soviets and hoped to subdue it by subordinating the soviets to the party. The drawback of the new "soviet democracy" hailed by Lenin in 1906 is that he could envisage the soviets only as *controlled* organizations; for him they were instruments by which the party controlled the working masses, rather than true forms of a workers democracy. The basic contradiction of the Bolshevik soviet system—which purports to be a democracy of all working people but in reality recognizes only the rule of one party—is already contained in Lenin's interpretation of the soviets during the first Russian revolution.

In the period 1907–1916 Lenin did not further elaborate his concept of soviets. In an occasional comment he emphasizes their revolutionary and militant character. In the fourth of his important theses of October 1915, for example, he says: "Soviets of workers deputies and similar institutions must be considered instruments of the insurrection and of revolutionary power. These institutions can be of definite usefulness only in spreading the political mass strike and an insurrection, depending on the degree of preparation, development, and progress."[277] In a covering letter to the theses Lenin explicitly warned against formation of soviets unless these conditions were present. A soviet without an insurrection, he claimed, was nothing but a marvelous opportunity to arrest a few dozen workers' leaders.[278]

Lenin's followers remained oblivious to these beginnings of a council theory. In 1922, when the Bolshevik role in the founding of the soviets was beginning to be eulogized, Karl Radek wrote: "That the soviets were not only organizations fighting the bourgeois government but cells of the future organization of proletarian power was not recognized by the Russian Marxists, let alone those in Europe."[279] The decisive turning came only with Lenin's theses of April 1917. Stalin's writings of 1905, for example, contain not a word about the soviets, which later led Trotsky to the biting remark that therefore "essentially, he stood with his back to the Revolution itself. . . ."[280] Lenin's 1905 conception of the soviets was treated much the same way as his theory of the transition of the bourgeois revolution into the socialist revolution.[281] In both cases it was a matter of perspectives running ahead of events, perspectives that Lenin ventured from his analysis of the revolutionary situation and the social balance of power in Russia. For the practical politics of his party and the immediate concerns of his followers, these theoretical excursions into a realm that was still far distant were at most of literary interest. But they gained extreme practicality during the 1917 revolution when Lenin pursued these perspectives and steered his resisting party toward the new goal—the socialist soviet republic.

c) Trotsky

Trotsky was the only well-known Marxist and revolutionary to play an important part in the 1905 soviets. His membership in the Executive Committee and, after Chrustalev-Nosar's arrest, in the presidium of the St. Petersburg soviet placed him in the front ranks of the socialist leadership and accounted for his popularity among the masses, which in turn benefited him in October 1917. His 1905–1906 ideas on the course of the Russian revolution, which he synthesized in the theory of "permanent revolution," and his practical experiences in the soviet, developed into what was probably the most significant and farsighted concept of the soviets during the first Russian revolution.

When the RSDWP split in 1903, Trotsky first allied himself with the Mensheviks and attacked Lenin with unusual vehemence, accusing him—in words that had a prophetic ring—of ultracentralism and "dictatorship over the proletariat."[282] He could not, however, agree with the Menshevik program of revolution, which granted the working class only second place, after the bourgeoisie. From the end of

1904, therefore, he became disaffected with the Menshevik leaders in the emigration, and until summer 1917 he stood somewhere between the two warring factions. Trotsky's personal vitality and revolutionary drive, and his international perspective on the revolution, were built into his theory of "permanent revolution," which enlarged on similar ideas of his literary ally, Parvus.[283] Trotsky's formulation was as follows:

"The Russian revolution, whose immediate goals are bourgeois, can under no circumstances stop there. These immediate bourgeois tasks can be solved only through seizure of power by the proletariat, which can not thereafter limit itself to the bourgeois framework. On the contrary, the proletarian avant-garde must secure victory by the deepest inroads not only into feudal but also into bourgeois property. Therefore the proletariat will clash with all bourgeois groups and with the peasantry who helped to establish proletarian power. Contradictions in the position of the workers government, in a backward country with an overwhelming peasant majority, can be solved only on an international scale, in the arena of proletarian revolution."[284]

Trotsky shared Lenin's disbelief in the revolutionary power of the bourgeoisie, on which the Mensheviks counted. But while Lenin included the peasantry as a significant factor in his alliance of democratic forces, Trotsky saw only the narrow stratum of urban proletariat as the agent of the revolution. Lenin's theory of the transition into socialist revolution depended on an interim "revolutionary-democratic dictatorship of the proletariat and peasantry" of indefinite duration. For Trotsky, the "dictatorship of the proletariat" would follow the czarist regime; the boundaries between the "minimum" and "maximum" program would disappear.

From 1905 until spring 1917 Lenin rejected both Trotsky's theory of permanent revolution and the dictatorship of the proletariat for Russia, because the peasantry's importance seemed to be ignored.[285] In preparing for the October Revolution, however, Lenin adopted Trotsky's view and steered the same course toward socialist revolution.

With the outbreak of the revolution Trotsky's tactical views were much closer to the Bolsheviks than to the Mensheviks. Even before January 9, 1905, he had seen the political general strike as a next step in the revolutionary struggle, and after "Bloody Sunday" he, like Lenin, advocated preparations for the armed insurrection and a "simultaneous action of the proletariat of all Russia."[286] In March he called for a provisional government, in which the Social Democrats would inevitably play the leading part. As if he had a premonition of the Bolshevik seizure of power in October 1917, Trotsky writes that "in a decisive victory of the revolution, those who led the proletariat will be awarded the power."[287] In the same "Political Letter" to *Iskra* Trotsky gives an example of how a provisional government might emerge from the revolution: "The recent elections to the Shidlovsky Commission voted in roughly 400 representatives of the St. Petersburg proletariat. Among these 400 are 10 or more of the most influential and most popular workers of St. Petersburg. The elections led to a strike that could develop into a general strike. The strike can lead to a victorious uprising and to the formation of a provisional government. The Social Democratic workers who are members of the Commission might find themselves in the provisional government. What demands will the party make upon them? That they refuse to join the government or, if they join, that they take orders from the bourgeois radicals? No, the party must demand, first, that they secure a majority and, second, that they submit to its authority."[288]

Although Trotsky had largely cut his ties to the emigré leaders, he was considered the chief spokesman for the Mensheviks in the St. Petersburg soviet, to which he belonged from the beginning. During the power struggles after Lenin's death, this fact was held against Trotsky as proof of his "treacherous" past. In reality, of course, the metropolitan Mensheviks were much more radical than their emigré fellows, because of Trotsky's influence and their immediate revolutionary experiences. In the soviet Trotsky often spoke for Bolsheviks and Mensheviks; factional differences dissolved in the common struggle. To Trotsky such transcendence of factionalism was both a function and an accomplishment of the soviet.

Trotsky's detailed evaluation of the 1905 soviets, in his history of the revolution,[289] combines Menshevik and Bolshevik views. Trotsky calls the soviets' most prominent feature the spontaneity with which they arose from an elemental revolutionary need in the masses, rather than from conspiracy among professional revolutionaries. This is a distinct slap at the Bolsheviks' conspiratorial tactics, against which Trotsky and the Mensheviks had polemicized since 1903. "Proletarian representation" and "revolutionary groups of self-governing workers"[290] were, in Trotsky's eyes, not "assemblies of political hot air and mutual instruction" but "means of struggle."[291] The revolution's course prompted the soviets to become the instruments of insurrection of which Lenin had spoken. Addressing the tribunal that had indicted the St. Petersburg soviet for preparing an armed uprising, Trotsky attempted in sophisticated words to clear the soviet of direct, technical preparation of a rebellion, without abandoning his basic conviction that there would be an inevitable violent upheaval. However much expediency dictated his choice of words, they nevertheless reflect soviet tactics aimed at conquering the enemy psychologically, especially by winning army support. "To prepare ourselves for the inevitable rising . . . for us that means chiefly to raise the consciousness of the people, to explain that open conflict is inevitable . . . that only might can defend right, that a powerful organization of the revolutionary masses is necessary."[292] The latter was the chief task of the soviet: to "unify the revolutionary struggle of the proletariat"[293] and to fuse the various proletarian strata and political groups.

Trotsky emphasized, more strongly than Lenin, the St. Petersburg soviet's form of direct, genuine democracy. "In the guise of the soviet, for the first time there appears to us on the soil of modern Russian history a democratic power, the power of the masses themselves over their component parts. This is truly genuine unadulterated democracy, without a two-chamber system, without a professional bureaucracy, with the right of the voters to recall their deputies whenever they choose."[294] This formulation suggests that Trotsky was thinking of Marx's description of the Paris Commune of 1871 and applying Marx's interpretation to the Russian soviets, although he did not specifically refer to *The Civil War in France*. Like Lenin, in 1905 Trotsky did not yet view the soviets as sequels and heirs of the Paris Commune.

According to Trotsky's theory of revolution, the principal confrontation occurs between the urban proletariat and czarism. In the soviet, the proletariat had created an organization "capable of establishing revolutionary power."[295] Soviets were already "the nucleus of revolutionary power," and it would have been "utopian to try to make the soviets coexist with the old regime."[296] Here Trotsky once again agrees with Lenin, who also recognized in the soviets the embryonic revolutionary government. Trotsky, again like Lenin,

does not yet draw the ultimate conclusion and does not advocate a
republic patterned on the soviets but he definitely approaches this
idea. His theory of "permanent revolution" does, after all, contain
the sentence: "The revolution can solve its most immediate, bourgeois
tasks in no other way than through the seizure of power by the
proletariat. But once the proletariat has seized power, it cannot limit
itself to the bourgeois framework of the revolution."[297] The proletarian seizure of power would, in the light of Trotsky's experiences in
1905, most probably happen through the soviets. Thus the soviets
would become instruments of the dictatorship of the proletariat and
spontaneously transform themselves into pillars of the new socialist
state. In 1906 Parvus wrote: "The St. Petersburg Soviet of Workers
Deputies had a genuinely creative potential. One could feel a power
that might expand and completely transform the state."[298] Instruments of revolution, the soviets become instruments of government—
that is the essence of Lenin's slogan, "All power to the soviets."

Dictatorship of the proletariat in the form of the soviets, the idea
on which Lenin based the Bolshevik theory of the state in 1917, was
thus already expressed by Trotsky and Parvus in 1905, though they
did not develop the concept further. In an extraordinary forecast
written in 1907, Trotsky largely anticipated even the soviets' actual
development during the revolution of 1917: "Without doubt the
revolution's next new assault will bring in its wake everywhere the
establishment of workers councils. The general all-Russian workers
council, organized by a nationwide workers assembly, will then
assume direction of locally elected organizations." Trotsky outlined
the program for the councils during the new revolution: "Revolutionary cooperation with the army, the peasantry, and the plebeian
segments of the urban bourgeoisie. Abolition of absolutism. Destruction of its material structure: partly reform, partly immediate dissolution of the army, annihilation of the police and bureaucracy.
The eight-hour day. Arming the populace and especially the proletariat. Transformation of public authorities into agencies of municipal
self-government. Establishment of peasants councils as local carriers
of the agrarian revolution. Organization of elections to the constituent
assembly and of election campaigns based on a definite program of
the workers."[299]

Basically this list covers the call for soviet power as promulgated
by the Bolsheviks in 1917. If the soviets were to carry out all these

measures in a coming revolution, they would be the sole revolutionary power in the country. In that case the last point in the program— organization of elections to the constituent assembly—would not matter much. A national assembly, meeting after the revolution and wholly dependent on the soviets, can only sanction what has already taken place, or stand by helplessly. Trotsky's retention of the constituent assembly in his 1907 program, as in the Bolshevik slogans of 1917, is only a leftover from traditional revolutionary demands. As far as he was concerned the future belonged to the new organizations of the revolution, the soviets.

d) Social Revolutionaries and Anarchists

Within the Russian revolutionary movement the Social Revolutionaries could rightly claim to be the heirs of Russia's revolutionary tradition as it existed before Western European Marxism penetrated the country, and to be the successor of the earliest revolutionary party, the Narodniks.[300] Scattered groups of the Narodnaja volja (the People's Will) which had survived the smashing of their movement in the 1880s, or had emigrated, and a few more recent organizations in various parts of Russia founded the new party of Social Revolutionaries (SR) in late 1901.[301] At this time Marxism and Social Democracy already exerted a strong intellectual and organizational influence. The program of the Social Revolutionaries[302] contains Marxist ideas about the development of capitalism and the leading role of the urban proletariat alongside older views on the agrarian question and the role of terror. While the Social Revolutionaries recognized the significance and strength of the nascent Russian labor movement, they continued to look to the village for the broadly-based revolution. To them the Russian peasant would bring to life a fundamental socialism, best manifested in rural cooperatives. Opposing the Marxists' sharp class distinctions, the Social Revolutionaries adopted the concept of "the working people." They addressed themselves equally to peasantry, working class, and intelligentsia, and had, especially among students, far more followers than did the Social Democrats. Their part in the revolutionary movement before 1905, as in the revolution itself, equaled that of the Bolsheviks and Mensheviks; among the peasants and in various associations of the intelligentsia they were dominant.

The Social Revolutionaries' program on the eve of the first Russian revolution contained a number of points that were important for their position within the revolutionary front and their relationship with the Bolsheviks. Although like the Marxists they distinguished between two phases of the revolution—the first leading to the overthrow of czarism, the second resulting in the socialist transformation of society—they hoped to achieve the transition from the first to the second stage as smoothly and directly as possible. Already in 1903 the party paper, *Revoljucionnaja Rossija*, anticipated almost word for word Trotsky's subsequent theory of "permanent revolution" and Lenin's allusions to the concept.[303] After "Bloody Sunday" the Social Revolutionaries developed these ideas further. The urban proletariat, they suggested, would have to direct the agrarian movement; workers and peasants would seize power and establish a democratic republic; the land would belong to the village community and its usufruct would be proportionately allotted to individual peasants. This "socialization" of the soil was to create the precedents for fully developed socialism, which in Russia could largely bypass the negative aspects of the capitalist period.

In their emphasis on the peasantry's revolutionary role and in their distrust of the bourgeoisie's progressive role, the Social Revolutionaries were rather close to Lenin, who counted on the Social Revolutionary Party as a partner in the "revolutionary-democratic dictatorship of the proletariat and peasantry." The Bolsheviks and Social Revolutionaries also saw eye to eye on tactics, the Social Revolutionaries generally recommending more radical methods. Though Lenin rejected the assassination of various government figures by party militants since the turn of the century, there was basic agreement on strikes and especially on armed rebellion. As early as 1904 *Revoljucionnaja Rossija* stated that armed uprising, combining proletarian strikes, peasant revolts, and individual acts of terrorism, would bring about the downfall of czarism.[304] In 1905 and 1906 the Social Revolutionaries expanded their militant groups; students, workers, and even isolated officers joined their ranks to take part in revolutionary actions.

On the whole, though, the Social Revolutionaries were considerably weaker than the two Social Democratic factions within the labor movement, as evidenced by the workers councils. Though they had followers in all the soviets, they nowhere gained decisive influence.

In most of the executive committees the official party delegates had the same rights as the Mensheviks and Bolsheviks—the workers considered this the fairest solution.

In the St. Petersburg soviet the Social Revolutionaries succeeded in forestalling the Bolshevik attempt to make the soviet subscribe to the Social Democratic program.[305] Avksentiev in 1917 was head of the All-Russian Soviet of Peasants Deputies and was chief representative of the Social Revolutionaries in the Executive Committee. Chernov, the party's chief theoretician, gave only one address to the plenum in which he warned the workers against acting independently to introduce the eight-hour day in factories.[306] In contrast to most other party members, Chernov took a very sober view of the revolution and feared that aggressive tactics would result in government repression before the revolution could conquer the countryside.

After the defeat of December 1905, the First Party Congress of the Social Revolutionary Party was held at the turn of the year. It is worth noting that discussion at this congress never touched on the soviets.[307] One might conclude that the Social Revolutionaries— unlike Lenin, for example—were unaware of the soviets' importance during the first revolution. This is not so, however, as may be seen from an appeal of the party's Central Committee after dissolution of the First Duma in June 1906, in which local party organizations were urged to form "unaffiliated armed soviets of workers deputies to lead the struggles of the urban working population. . . . The soviets must conduct the general strike and, whenever possible, steer it toward armed revolt. The soviets should give special attention to insuring that the urban working population does not act separately from the peasantry and the army, thus fragmenting the revolutionary forces."[308] In this appeal the soviets appear—as they do with Lenin— as agencies both of revolt and of unification of the revolutionary forces. This view was also expressed by a delegate to the Second Party Congress in February 1907, where the soviets were mentioned in connection with party tactics and elections to the Second Duma. A left-wing duma would "form an organizational center for the masses and enormously facilitate the parties' organizational work, which must be energetically pursued during the duma's session. Workers, peasants, and soldiers councils must be established everywhere, with close ties between them and left-wing duma members. This organization of the masses in connection with the duma will insure that the future inevitable dissolution of the duma will become a genuine call to armed revolt."[309] Aside from tactical coupling of the soviets to the duma's activity, this is the first time that the trinity of workers, peasants, and soldiers soviets was used in a slogan, which became a standard formula after 1917.

This Social Revolutionary origin of the name by which the soviets were to be known in Bolshevik Russia is symptomatic. Although the Social Revolutionary Party did not officially adopt the slogan before the Revolution of 1917 or see the soviets as more than militant organizations, numerous threads connect the Social Revolutionary ideas with the subsequent Bolshevik slogan of soviet power. Within the Social Revolutionary Party a radical left wing took shape almost from the beginning, and in 1906 it split from the party. These Social Revolutionary Maximalists, together with the anarchists, espoused views that corresponded almost word for word with Lenin's April 1917 program of "All power to the soviets." The Maximalists rejected the "minimal programs" of the socialist parties and aimed to establish a "republic of working people" based on universal economic equality. In the words of the newspaper *Kommuna*, first published in December 1905, "Social revolution will lead us toward economic equality through the forced expropriation of land, factories, and workshops. We hold that there exists in contemporary Russian life a basic tendency pressing forward in this direction."[310] If the revolution succeeded, the peasants would reapportion the land and cultivate it for common use; workers in the cities would themselves manage the factories. Russian workers, they claimed, were still so closely connected with the villages that the idea of solidarity, of joint deliberation and decision, even in economic matters, was alive enough to be applied to factory management. Russia would not need to repeat the West's murderous capitalism. On the contrary, the "proclamation of the working people's republic [trudovaja respublika] in one country will carry in its wake the world-wide uprising of labor against capital. The workers of the West expect to hear from us history's battlecry, which is: a republic of working people!"[311]

Alone among revolutionary parties in 1905 the "Revolutionary Socialists," forerunners of the Maximalists, called for a commune. They claimed that the revolution's goal was not the democratic republic, a façade for supremacy of the bourgeoisie, as sought by the Social Democrats and most Social Revolutionaries, but rather a com-

mune modeled on the Paris Commune of 1871, as proclaimed by
Marx, Engels, and the Russian social theoretician Lavrov. In an
article entitled "How Should the Revolutionary Commune Be Organized?" *Kommuna* projected a detailed plan for "kommunal'nyj
sovet," a communal council that bore a striking resemblance to the
soviets organized during the 1917 revolution. Composed of various
divisions—for example, public safety, supply, arming the workers—
this municipal council was intended to exercise "the highest super-
vision over the life of the community [obščina]" and in doing so
"proclaim the dictatorship of the proletariat," and "organize the
provisional revolutionary government." This group's battlecry was:
"Comrades, workers, prepare yourselves for the proclamation of the
commune in the cities!" The rejection of parliamentarianism followed,
since the example of the Western European socialist parties had
shown that it would lead to alienation of the leaders from the masses
and would nourish the petit bourgeois tendencies within the working
class. Russia, therefore, required not a constituent assembly but the
federation of revolutionary communes.

Similar ideas were espoused by the anarchists, who were close to
the Maximalists. They formed small groups in various Russian cities
and published several newspapers.[312] A conference held in October
1906 and directed by the leading anarchist Kropotkin, stated that
the Russian revolution would lead, not to parliamentarianism on the
Western model, but to a far-reaching economic and political reorganization of the country in the form of local "independent communities,
production groups, and other associations and confederations."[313]
Kropotkin was convinced that "bureaucratic centralization is so foreign
to Russian life and the Russian mentality," while "the anarchist concept of political relations is so suited to them, that in this respect a
mighty task lies before us."[314] Exactly like the Maximalists, the
anarchists demanded the transfer of factories, coal mines, and railroads, "not to a ministry of labor, but to the workers who work in
them and who organize themselves in free associations."[315] Both
groups clearly show the influence of European syndicalism,[316] which
was manifested, for example, in the Maximalist program for the
general strike, which "may at any moment change into an armed uprising to seize the factories."[317] The anarchists differ from the socialists, with whom they agreed as to the ultimate goal, precisely in that
they hoped to bring about the revolution not by taking over state

power, but by "removing the state's military, judicial, and police pillars,"[318] through mass action from below.

Very little information is available concerning the attitude of the Left Social Revolutionaries and the anarchists toward the soviets during the 1905 revolution. The St. Petersburg soviet refused to admit the anarchists' official representatives to its Executive Committee—an action that Lenin explicitly approved.[319] Nor were anarchists represented in the Executive Committees of most provincial soviets. An exception was Bialystok, where the anarchists were supported by a majority of the workers council. The anarchists and Maximalists, remaining in separate groups, could not prevail against Social Democratic preponderance. In times of crisis, however, their influence increased in some places among the unaffiliated workers, as happened in 1906, when workers were exposed to renewed economic pressure from entrepreneurs. Lenin's previously mentioned resolution condemning the "anarcho-syndicalist tendencies among the proletariat"[320] was directed against the disturbing influence of the anarchists in Moscow and Odessa.

Without a doubt the anarchists had to see that the workers councils resembled the free proletarian work-based societies which they had advocated. They were likely to recognize in the soviets both the democratic principle of the free "obščina" and a suitable form for workers' management of the factories. In any case, Left Social Revolutionary and anarchist demands were well suited to furnishing the existing soviets with an ideology of their own. Lenin accomplished this at the outbreak of the 1917 Revolution with ingenious unconcern for the partial recantation of his previous principles. The aims of the revolutionary far left in 1905—a state on the model of the commune; transfer of the factories to the workers; destruction of the bureaucracy, army, and police; proclamation of world revolution from the East—all these Lenin combined in his call for soviet power, when he apparently assimilated the anarchist program to secure the support of the masses for the Bolsheviks.

CHAPTER THREE

The Soviets and the Russian Revolution of 1917

1. THE OUTBREAK OF REVOLUTION

a) The Russian Labor Movement during the War

After the 1905 revolution, the Russian labor movement underwent a phase of decline and decay beginning in 1907. The modest political rights (limited franchise and partial legalization of trade unions) gained during the revolution were impeded or curtailed by the authorities. Most of the workers' economic gains (shortening of the workday, pay raises, wage agreements) were rescinded. Because of the workers' exhaustion, the strike movement subsided and reached its nadir in 1910.[1]

With the dissolution of the Second Duma in June 1907, the revolutionary parties were forced once again to go underground or to conceal their activities behind innocuous societies, cooperatives and trade unions. Partial legalization of the working-class economic struggle led to new rifts within Russian Social Democracy. The so-called liquidators favored adaptation by avoiding all revolutionary action and concentrating on the practical immediate tasks. In contrast, the Bolsheviks and some Mensheviks and Social Revolutionaries sought to salvage from the crumbling party organizations the illegal cells and revolutionary core, to combat the apathy of the masses and create a new revolutionary surge at the earliest possible moment.

During this period Bolshevism achieved its definitive character. Collapse of the party under reactionary persecutions produced a small but tested nucleus of militants. Hardened by sacrifice, welded together by conviction and discipline, entirely free of moral obligations to the rest of society, these men almost completely embodied Lenin's ideal of the professional revolutionary. The formal division in 1912 into Bolsheviks and Mensheviks came when the Bolshevik Party found its own organizational form, in line with principles laid down by Lenin in 1902. When the labor movement took an upward turn in 1912,[2] the Bolsheviks' influence grew concurrently. In most unions in St. Petersburg and Moscow the Bolsheviks commanded a majority just before the First World War.[3] During the first half of 1914 the number of striking workers in Russia corresponded roughly with that of 1905. Russia seemed once again on the verge of a revolutionary crisis.

Outbreak of the First World War dealt this development a blow. The working class had to bow to the exigencies of war and was partially gripped by patriotic fervor. There were also structural changes: many experienced industrial workers were inducted into the army, while new workers, among them many women, streamed from villages to factories. Stagnation in the labor movement lasted only a short time. In the summer of 1915, with Russian reverses at the front and domestic opposition, strikes flared up anew. Workers' demands were caused primarily by acute economic privation, but as early as 1916 political issues were surfacing in demands for cessation of the war.[4] The number of strikers again reached a dangerous level: 113,866 in September 1915, 128,450 in January 1916, and 187,134 in October 1916.[5]

For the Russian socialist parties the outbreak of war meant a decisive turning point in their history. They faced the same dilemma as their European counterparts: continuation of the class struggle under the banner of international solidarity, or a "truce" with the bourgeois parties, that is, recognition that national interests took precedence over internationalism.[6] The socialist camp in Russia split into three main groups: the "national defenders" (oboroncy), the "internationalists," and furthest to the left, the Bolsheviks, who advocated "transformation of the imperialist war into a civil war."[7] Plekhanov and many Social Revolutionaries endorsed defensive war; the majority of the Mensheviks, whether emigrants, exiles, or duma members, wished for peace without annexations or indemnities but opposed any revolutionary action while the war lasted. Debates over the war intensified old differences and prepared the ground for new alliances that were to mature during the revolution.

Socialists who had remained in Russia thought they saw a new opportunity to organize the workers movement through participation in the war-industries committees during the summer of 1915. As "social self-help organizations" these committees were intended to increase and free production from the fetters of czarist bureaucracy. Leadership was assumed by the Constitutional Democrats and the Octobrists, who constituted the "progressive bloc" in the duma. The workers got a special section in the central war-industries committee in [Petrograd] and in the local commissions. As with the Shidlovsky Commission of 1905, factory workers were to vote for electors, who in turn would elect delegates to the "workers groups" of the war-industries committees.[8]

The question of workers' participation in the committees forced difficult decisions on the socialists. The right-wing Mensheviks favored participation. The majority of the Internationalists agreed with them but emphasized a tactical consideration: they thought workers groups in the committees offered an excellent opportunity to bring back centers of the workers movement that had been lost by the war. They hoped to use the committees to call an all-Russian workers congress of the chief industrial cities, trade unions, medical-insurance societies, and the like.[9] This is basically the 1905 Menshevik proposal for a general workers congress via the Shidlovsky Commission or the St. Petersburg soviet. As in 1905, the Bolsheviks opposed working-class participation in these "bourgeois" organizations. In October 1915 Lenin declared: "We oppose participation in war-industries commissions which further the imperialist, reactionary war. We favor participation in the first stage of elections, but only for the purposes of agitation and organization."[10]

At the beginning the Bolshevik boycott tactics were successful in Petrograd, for at the first meeting of electors there were 90 votes against joining the committee and 81 in favor. Since irregularities occurred during the polling, another meeting was held. This time the majority declared for joining and elected delegates to the workers group.[11] For the first time since the beginning of the war the election campaign offered a possibility for holding open meetings of workers, and political questions were often debated. The workers group members cultivated close contacts with unaffiliated workers. Though the groups were overwhelmingly composed of right-wing Mensheviks—the central group under Gvozdev exclusively so—they were the left wing of the bourgeois commissions. The workers groups dealt with a multitude of questions such as wage demands, complaints about rising prices and the housing shortage, and finding employment. Their written reports and public discussions made the rest of society aware of the workers' plight and promoted worker solidarity.[12]

The central group also tried to reactivate the factory elder (starost). Following a suggestion by the minister of commerce, the group produced a draft on the installation of factory elders, enlarging on the legal specifications of 1903, that was forwarded to local workers groups. In Kiev, this question was debated at several meetings. The local workers group stated that traditional "factory absolutism" must give way to "factory constitutionalism" and that elected workers councils must be given a voice in wage and personnel matters.[13] Before 1917 factory elders were introduced in several industrial cities, even though many workers were utterly opposed.

Factory-based election of electors was basically a continuation of the delegate system underlying the 1905 St. Petersburg soviet. It is not surprising, therefore, that the idea of a city-wide workers council was revived. In fact, this time the Bolsheviks seized on the idea. Earlier they had advocated formation of strike committees. Now they declared that the delegates should constitute themselves as a soviet of workers deputies in the event of a revolutionary upsurge. A report on party activity in Petrograd states that the workers' strong desire for an organization led the party committee to agitate for a workers parliament as counterpart of the various bourgeois organizations. "Representatives of factories and workshops, elected by proportional representation in all cities, should form an all-Russian soviet of workers deputies, in which we [i.e., the Bolsheviks] believe we would command a majority."[14] Lenin, in his theses of October 1915 and in a letter to Shliapnikov, stated his opposition to the establishment of soviets at this time.[15] Reactivation of the soviets never took place. However, the idea survived among workers and helped revive the Petrograd soviet during the February Revolution.[16]

At the end of 1916 the central workers group in Petrograd grew more revolutionary with the growing political unrest (the assassination of Rasputin, prorogation of the duma by the czar, workers demonstrations on the anniversary of "Bloody Sunday"). In an appeal which caused its members' arrest, the group advocated a mass demonstration by the Petrograd proletariat on the day the duma was to reconvene. The workers were to elect factory committees to consult and pool forces. "Radical elimination of autocracy and total democratization of the nation must now be realized without delay. . . . Only a provisional government organized from popular struggle can lead the country out of the current dead end and disastrous decay, and secure political freedom and a peace acceptable to the Russian proletariat and to the proletariat of other nations."[17] The night of January 26, 1917, the members of the central workers group were arrested, which led to events that provoked the revolution.

b) The February Revolution

Like the Revolution of 1905, the February Revolution began on February 18 with a strike by the workers of the Putilov Works in Petrograd and on February 22 spread to other factories. On February 24, 200,000 workers were out on strike, and by February 25 the strike was virtually general. The same day saw the first bloody clashes between demonstrators and army. The turning point came on February 27, when some troops went over to the revolutionary masses, sweeping along other units and thus robbing the government of its means of coercion.[18]

The revolutionary rising within a few days passed through all the stages of a revolution, from strike through street demonstrations to insurrection, and was "a movement without organizational leadership from above, bursting forth from the masses themselves."[19] There was no central leadership from any party or well-known figure. It is true that between February 23 and February 25 various secret meetings of socialist parties' representatives and left-wing duma delegates took place, but they were unable to influence the movement.[20] Even the Petrograd Bolsheviks played only a subordinate role. Of course Bolshevik workers and students participated in the demonstrations and street fights, as did supporters of other parties and the unaffiliated; but the Bolshevik Party as such did not direct this uprising, in contrast to the October Revolution and official Soviet legend.[21] Trotsky quotes Kaiurov, a leader of the solidly proletarian Vyborg district of the capital: "There was no sign of directives from party headquarters. . . . The representative of the Central Committee, Comrade Shliapnikov, was powerless to give instructions for the following day."[22] And Shliapnikov himself admitted, "None of us thought (on February 24) that the movement then under way would be the last and decisive battle with the czarist regime. We held no such belief."[23]

Only when the revolution's triumph was assured in the capital did two centers form almost simultaneously to impose organization on the spontaneous movement: the duma committee and the soviet. The former arose February 27, after the czar's dissolution decree, as a provisional committee of duma members (including Rodzianko, Miliukov, and Kerensky). Kerensky later characterized as "the greatest and worst blunder" the duma's failure to defy the dissolution decree and declare itself official center of the revolution and thereby its universally acknowledged leader.[24] Now, however, the "private" duma committee had no more legitimacy than the simultaneously established soviet, whose revolutionary origin immediately secured its greater popularity and authority among the masses.

However, for reasons discussed below, the soviet waived exclusive assumption of power and refused all participation in the new revolutionary government. But the duma committee's bourgeois majority needed moral support and recognition from the workers and soldiers council. Thus on March 1 (14), 1917, the duma committee and the Petrograd soviet agreed to form a Provisional Government. The soviet leaders did not join it (except Kerensky, who procured authorization for this step directly from the soviet membership) but gave it support under certain conditions.[25]

The Provisional Government's majority consisted of Constitutional Democrats and Octobrists, and its outstanding personalities were Foreign Minister Miliukov and Minister of War Aleksander Guchkov. Kerensky, as minister of justice, was the government's only representative of the left. On the evening of March 2 Czar Nicholas II, seeing the futility of resistance, abdicated in favor of his brother, Grand Duke Michael. On March 3 the grand duke also renounced the throne pending a final decision of the constituent assembly. Thus the czarist monarchy was overthrown. The first stage of the revolution had succeeded almost without a fight throughout Russia in the early days of March 1917.

"The Russian revolution broke out on the soil of war. To the revolutionary masses it represented a means of freeing themselves from war's privations, burdens, and suffering," wrote the Menshevik Dan, and spokesmen for all political ideologies agreed with this viewpoint.[26] Like the German Revolution of November 1918, the February Revolution resulted from Russia's military defeat and the ensuing internal disorganization. Hunger among urban workers and war weariness among the troops were at the root of the revolutionary disturbances in the capital. But the February Revolution had still another source in the outrage felt in patriotic circles over the defeats, which they blamed on the czarist court, and in their desire to rally all national forces to win the war. The revolution in the streets headed off a palace revolt that had been brewing for some time; now it was to be channeled into the wider national revolution, which was to combine domestic reforms along democratic lines with a vigorous pursuit of the war. The Provisional Government faced the difficult task of pursuing both these goals simultaneously. But after the first few weeks of a national orgy of unity and supreme confidence in a revolutionary victory, the longing for peace became so strong that the antagonism between various social and political forces that had lain dormant since the February Revolution came again into play until the October Revolution.

2. THE PETROGRAD WORKERS AND SOLDIERS COUNCIL

a) Formation of the Petrograd Council

Though existing only briefly, the soviets of 1905, especially the St. Petersburg Soviet of Workers Deputies, left behind a revolutionary tradition which became strongly ingrained in the working masses. Although, as already shown, the socialist parties had not incorporated into their programs the new concept of soviets, it emerged anew with a resurgence of the labor movement, as during the war in elections to the workers group of the war-industries committees.[27] Despite differing political tendencies among Russian workers, it was "as if the form of the organization itself [the soviet] stood above discussion."[28]

When revolutionary disturbances in Petrograd began in February 1917, therefore, the idea took hold of reestablishing the soviet, both in the striking factories and among the revolutionary intelligentsia. Eye-witnesses report that as early as February 24 spokesmen were elected in some factories to a projected soviet.[29] Between February 23 and 25, secret discussions took place among representatives of various socialist groups (leaders of illegal trade unions and labor associations, a few left-wing duma members, and party members). At one such meeting Cherevanin, a right-wing Menshevik, proposed elections to a workers soviet. The proposal was approved, with designation of meeting places for the deputies all over the city. The building housing the Petrograd Society of Workers Cooperatives was to be the city-wide center. However, that same night of February 25 most participants were arrested before their decisions on elections to the soviet could be communicated to the workers.[30] The deputies elected independently in various factories lacked central leadership and a meeting place. In the turbulent days of the revolution, whose outcome was uncertain until February 27, planned action was not to be thought of.

The decisive step in forming the Petrograd soviet was taken by members of the central workers group who were released from prison on February 27. Led by Gvozdev and accompanied by soldiers and the masses, they moved into the Tauride Palace, the seat of the duma. There they formed with several socialist duma members, among them the Menshevik Nikolai Chkheidze, and participants in the earlier secret conferences,[31] a "Provisional Executive Committee of the Soviet of Workers Deputies" on the afternoon of February 27 (March 12), 1917. The committee immediately appealed for the election of deputies, one for each 1,000 workers and one for each army company, and called the first session for 7:00 P.M.[32] When the meeting was called to order at 9:00 P.M., only 40 to 50 people were present; probably this number did not even include the delegates earlier elected in the factories, since they were still ignorant of the soviet's establishment.

The Provisional Executive Committee launched into feverish activity. The danger of revolutionary defeat still existed since troops loyal to the government might be sent to Petrograd. Therefore the Executive Committee organized a military staff of revolutionary soldiers and officers, which in swift raids occupied the capital's most important strategic points. At this first session it was resolved to send to the city's various areas commissars who were to establish revolutionary district committees and an armed workers militia. The Executive Committee was augmented with members of the socialist parties. Tasks were apportioned to various commissions, among them a commission for food supplies, one for literature, and a finance commission.[33]

The first issue of *Izvestija Petrogradskogo soveta rabočich i soldatskich deputatov* on the morning of February 28 carried the soviet's programmatic appeal to the population of Petrograd and all Russia: "In order to successfully conclude the struggle for democracy, the people must organize their power. Yesterday, on February 27, the Soviet of Workers Deputies was founded in the capital, consisting of elected representatives from factories, rebelling troop units, and democratic and socialist parties and groups. The Soviet of Workers Deputies . . . considers its basic function to be: organization of the people's forces in the struggle for political freedom and people's rule in Russia. . . . Let us, all together, fight . . . for the annihilation of the old regime and the convocation of a constituent national assembly, to be elected by universal, impartial, direct, and secret ballot."[34]

On February 28 most enterprises held elections for deputies. The plenary session at 1:00 P.M. was already attended by about 120 industrial delegates,[35] but there was still no check on credentials, and the meeting came to order without any agenda.[36] As before, decisions were made within the confines of the Executive Committee. On March 1 and 2 the committee rejected participation in the Provisional Government by a vote of 13 to 8.[37] Instead, the soviet representatives presented the duma committee with programmatic demands, as conditions for their support of the bourgeois government.[38] On March 2 the plenary of the Petrograd soviet overwhelmingly approved (with only 19 nays) the agreement between the soviet executive and the duma committee.[39] Thus the Petrograd soviet turned into a "controlling organ of revolutionary democracy" vis-à-vis the government, and this relationship became decisive in the revolution's further development.

The Petrograd soviet considered itself the heir of its 1905 predecessor,[40] but it differed markedly in the manner and circumstances of its formation. While the 1905 soviet grew directly out of a mass strike and continued to lead it, the new soviet was founded when the revolution had already gained ascendancy in the capital through the revolt of the regiments. The initiative for its establishment came, in contrast to 1905, chiefly from a few political leaders (among the workers groups and the duma delegates) who attempted to form a sort of "reserve and subgovernment" when the old regime collapsed.[41] Thus from the beginning the socialist intelligentsia decisively influenced the workers and soldiers deputies; of 42 members on the Executive Committee at the end of March only 7 were workers.[42] But the most important difference from 1905 is that the soviet of 1917 was a joint workers and soldiers council. The prominent role of rebelling troops in the revolution's victory was acknowledged by taking soldiers into the newly formed soviet. Some Mensheviks in the Provisional Executive Committee at first opposed the soldiers' admission since they wanted to preserve the council's proletarian purity and exclude the army from the political struggle, but the majority wanted to win over the military to the revolution by establishing a close connection between the soldiers and the soviet.[43] This was done by extending to the military the form of representation on which the workers council was based, and deputies were simply elected in regiments instead of factories. In this way, by using the adaptable soviet, 100,000 soldiers were quickly enlisted in the common revolutionary front. The soviet's authority among soldiers was officially secured on March 1 by Order No. 1, issued at the request of the military representatives in the soviet.[44] In it the soviet decreed the formation of elected soldiers committees in all military units from companies on up, the subordination of all units to the soviet in political questions, and finally civil liberties for all soldiers. The orders of the military commission established by the duma committee, which claimed supreme command over the garrison, were to be followed only if they did not contradict the decrees and resolutions of the soviet.[45] Thus the Petrograd Workers and Soldiers Council gained de facto power over the garrison.

b) Structure of the Petrograd Council

In the early weeks of its existence the Petrograd soviet resembled a huge permanent assembly of workers and soldiers. The number of delegates grew from day to day; in the first week of March it reached

1,200; by the second half of March it rose to almost 3,000.[46] Of this number, about 2,000 were soldiers and only 800 were workers, although at this time the total number of workers in Petrograd was two or three times that of the soldiers stationed in the garrison.[47] The reason for this disproportion was that each military unit, even the smallest company, sent its own delegate to the soviet. There was as yet no rigorous check of delegates' credentials, so that a number of outsiders found their way to the Tauride Palace.[48] Under such circumstances, even though all delegates were never present at any one time, the soviet's plenary sessions were poorly organized; they resembled demonstrations and rallies more than they did a working parliamentary institution. Aside from the plenaries, the worker and soldier deputies conferred in separate sections on particular problems. But even these specialized bodies were still numerically too large to carry out regular work. On March 18 and 19, therefore, both sections discussed various detailed proposals for a reorganization to reduce the number of deputies and increase efficiency. Several speakers pointed out that the soviet's composition was fortuitous and that new elections would have to be held to create a truly democratic basis. Others mentioned the revolutionary merit of the present body and thought it should not be dissolved. Without a formal resolution, approval was given in principle to the Executive Committee's suggestion for selecting a "little soviet" of 250 to 300 workers and soldiers each.[49] In mid-April a resolution of the Mensheviks and Social Revolutionaries was passed which proposed continuation of the existing workers and soldiers soviet. The credentials committee was asked to exclude random delegates and those from small groups. To deal with daily business, a small soviet of about 600 members was formed from the extant soviet. Workers and soldiers were to be equally represented in it.[50] Both sections had their own executives, which were called "executive commissions" to distinguish them from the joint Executive Committee.

Thanks to these oragnizational measures, the Petrograd soviet gradually gained some shape. Most practical activity, however, remained in the hands of the Executive Committee (Ispolnitel'nyj komitet), which maintained its preeminence dating from the first days of the revolution. The committee made the basic political decisions that were subsequently submitted to the plenary for approval. The countless daily tasks faced by the soviet[51] necessitated ever more detailed division of labor among members of the Executive Committee. In the very first days several commissions were formed, and their number increased steadily, finally to 12 to 15.[52] When a number of prominent revolutionaries returned from Siberian exile (among them the Menshevik Tseretelli, who soon became a leader in the Executive Committee, and the Bolsheviks Kamenev and Stalin), the Executive Committee was enlarged. By the end of March it consisted of 42 members, including the council chairman (Chkheidze) and the 2 vicechairmen (Skobelev and Kerensky).[53] In addition, representatives of the trade unions, members of the Social Democratic factions of the dumas, representatives of the district councils, the editorial board of *Izvestija*, and the commissars named by the soviet participated in the sessions as nonvoting members. A special "Bureau of the Executive Committee" with 7 members was formed in mid-March to deal with current business. On April 12 the Bureau was authorized to take independent political decisions in emergencies, with only retroactive confirmation by the Executive Committee required.[54] After the All-Russian Conference of Soviets in late March and early April 1917, 16 provincial representatives were taken into the Executive Committee. The Bureau was enlarged to 24 members; from then on it met daily, while the Executive Committee sat three times a week.[55]

In the course of about two months the Petrograd soviet thus changed from a provisional revolutionary organ into a well-organized administrative machine. The execution of its business required several hundred employees, most of them clerks in the various departments. The soviet's administrative expenditures from March to June ran to 800,000 rubles; during the same period it commanded an income of 3,512,000 rubles.[56] However, as the soviet worked more efficiently, it lost proportionately its direct contact with the masses. The plenary sessions, almost daily during the early weeks, were less frequent and only sparsely attended by the deputies.[57] The soviet Executive became increasingly independent, even though it remained subject to certain controls by the deputies, who had the right to discharge it. The thrust of this development and certain party traditions may have led to the concentration of power in small committees during the later Bolshevik soviet system. By that time, however—and here lies the definitive difference from the original soviet constitution—they were independent of genuine democratic control from below.

The official ratio of representation for the workers section in the soviet was one deputy for 1,000 workers; however, concerns employing fewer than 1,000 workers were also allowed to send one delegate. Thus large plants (with over 400 employees), accounting for 87 percent of all Petrograd workers, furnished 424 delegates, while concerns with fewer than 400 employees, accounting for 13 percent of all workers, had 422 delegates.[58] One could not, therefore, speak of equal suffrage; this failing was occasionally discussed in the soviet.[59]

Similar circumstances prevailed among the soldiers deputies. Each company, or any unit corresponding to a company, had the right to elect one deputy. No numerical norms were set, so that units of very different strengths could send equal numbers of deputies. The soldiers section repeatedly rejected proposals to adopt the one to 1,000 ratio.[60] This practice insured a close relationship between the soviet and the smallest military unit, but it also perpetuated the preponderance of soldiers over workers deputies. The soldiers deputies included relatively numerous "intellectuals": clerks, young ensigns with socialist or liberal leanings, medics, and the like. The masses of politically inexperienced and still partially illiterate "peasants in uniform" voted for those who were most overtly revolutionary.[61]

Borough soviets sprang up almost concurrently with the city-wide workers and soldiers soviet. In the working-class Vyborg quarter a workers and soldiers council was formed as early as February 28; by March 3, 4 other boroughs had soviets.[62] In the following weeks every quarter of the city organized its own council consisting of the district's deputies to the general soviet, and special deputies from plants too small to be represented in the Petrograd soviet. These borough soviets were intended to deal with borough problems specifically and to execute resolutions of the general soviet, but several borough soviets acted independently without even consulting higher soviet authorities.[63] Bolshevik influence rose much more rapidly in the borough councils than in the general soviet. The Bolsheviks constituted in June a conference of borough soviets (Meždurajonnoe soveščanie rajonnykh sovetov Petrograda) to counterbalance the Menshevik–Social Revolutionary control in the workers and soldiers council. The borough organization provided a base for the Bolsheviks after the July uprising.[64]

Unlike the 1905 soviet, the Petrograd soviet of 1917 from the beginning was heavily influenced by the socialist parties. The major posts on the Executive Committee and the editorial board of *Izvestija* were held by party intellectuals. The soldiers' numerical superiority was expressed in the Social Revolutionary Party's majority in the soviet. The SR revolutionary and democratic slogans and its tradition as the oldest liberation movement against czarism harking back to the Narodnaja volja, had won it popular support following the February Revolution. Because it lacked clear class lines (in contrast to the Bolsheviks and Mensheviks), the Social Revolutionary Party was the natural rallying point for the broad masses roused by the revolution.[65] Among the deputies, the Mensheviks were leading during the early months of the revolution. They had occupied strong positions in the wartime duma faction, in the workers group, and in the trade unions, which gave them an advantage now in the soviet. Their outstanding personalities were the soviet chairman, Chkheidze, and Tseretelli. Martov, returning from emigration with a group of Menshevik Internationalists, turned away from the party's official line. The Petrograd soviet also included representatives of several smaller groups which had no influence worth mentioning: the People's Socialists (narodnye socialisty) who were furthest to the right, the "Edinstvo" group around Plekhanov, the Social Democratic "Meždurajoncy" which joined the Bolsheviks after Trotsky's arrival, as well as the ethnic socialist parties which had delegates in the Executive Committee—the Jewish Bund and the Polish and Latvian Social Democrats.

The Bolsheviks' position in the Petrograd soviet during its first months was weak. The Bolshevik organization in Petrograd had been decimated by arrests and exile and demoralized by police informers; it took time to give the party a tight structure.[66] On March 9 an independent Bolshevik faction in the soviet was established. Of its 40 members, only 2 or 3 were soldiers,[67] a ridiculously tiny figure in view of the 2,000 to 3,000 deputies, most of whom, though not members of any party, supported the Mensheviks and Social Revolutionaries in political questions. After Lenin's return the Bolsheviks stepped up their efforts in the soviet. They agitated for new elections; when these occurred in May and June, they often got their candidates elected in the factories.[68] According to their own statements, by the July revolt they had captured about half the seats in the workers section and roughly one-fourth of the soldiers section.[69] In September, finally, came the breakthrough, and the Petrograd soviet became Bolshevik.[70]

3. GROWTH OF THE SOVIET MOVEMENT

a) General Characteristics of the 1917 Councils

After the February Revolution of 1917, the soviets became a mass phenomenon.[71] Spontaneously they mushroomed everywhere, without theoretical preparation, stimulated only by the immediate needs of the revolution. The council idea—that is, the idea of a revolutionary representative body that could be established simply, quickly, anywhere, and at any time—seemed to Russian workers and soldiers automatically the most suitable form of uniting along class lines at a time of political and social upheaval. Workers in the industrial cities and soldiers in the garrisons and at the front instinctively recognized the need for an independent organization corresponding to their numerical strength and capable of expressing their revolutionary energies. Workers were antagonistic toward bureaucrats, entrepreneurs, and the bourgeoisie, and the army's rank and file distrusted the old officers, thus creating sociopsychological conditions for the soviets' unique expansion. It was as important for the 1917 soviets as for the 1905 soviets that the Russian working class had no other strong organizations. Neither political parties, which had long since lost the temporary influence on the masses gained during the first revolution, nor trade unions, which also until 1917 led only a shadowy existence, were then in a position to organize and lead large masses of people. The soviets, therefore, were in many respects substitutes for absent or feeble unions and parties. A similar situation prevailed for the soldiers councils; to the soldiers the revolution brought sudden liberation from lack of political and frequently even human rights. For them the soviets were the first opportunity to enter a world of free political activity and to exercise their new rights as citizens. This circumstance explains the profound effect of Order No. 1 of the Petrograd Workers and Soldiers Soviet, which proclaimed the soldiers' freedoms.

Unlike the soviets of 1905, which developed into militant organizations struggling against the czarist system, the soviets of 1917 faced the task of political and social reconstruction of the country.

The debates in the soviets, therefore, concerned possible goals and the methods of achieving them. The 1905 soviets had been nonpartisan and revolutionary in a general way. The soviets of 1917 soon became the battleground for various political tendencies. In this way they became a substitute for barely developed local parliamentary institutions and a missing national parliament—while encompassing only part of the population. For the soviets, though internally democratic institutions and spokesmen of "revolutionary democracy," represented on a national scale only certain classes and not the whole nation.

The relationship between this proletarian-military (to a lesser extent peasant) class organization and general state institutions therefore became a central problem. The Bolsheviks recognized this question's significance and made it the starting point of their revolutionary tactics. Using the slogan "All power to the soviets," they hoped to make these the pillars of state power, which would naturally become a class dictatorship.

By their structure, however, the soviets were not intended or suited for administration. They were "purely militant organs, fitting in spirit and organization the extraordinary conditions of a revolutionary period,"[72] "instruments of revolutionary propaganda,"[73] "a permanent riot,"[74] without clear functions and without a firm constitution. But in many cases the collapse of the central government and local bureaucracies turned these instruments of revolution into governmental bodies that intervened in and arrogated to themselves administrative functions. Thus the soviets' actual development frequently came close to meeting Bolshevik demands for a soviet republic.

The soviets' strength was their close tie to the proletarian and military masses, for whom they spoke. Because of their flexible voting procedures (election of deputies in factories and military units, permanent recall and frequent elections), they were a sensitive barometer of the masses' changing moods. For the same reason, however, they were much more prone to political shifts than an organization with a fixed mandate and without controls from below. Their advantages were also a weakness. Radicalization of the masses during the revolution inevitably meant a radicalization of the soviets. If, however, soviet leadership was won by a group whose ultimate goals were at odds with the soviets' democratic purposes, then the only possible outcome was the demise of the soviet. This transpired with the Bolshevik victory during the October Revolution. The Russian soviet movement, which had begun as a democratic movement, became the trailblazer for Bolshevik dictatorship.

b) Workers and Soldiers Councils in the Provinces

The revolution's triumphal march through Russia, leading in only a few days to collapse of the czarist government and its administrative machinery, was accompanied by a wave of revolutionary organization among all levels of society, most strongly expressed in formation of soviets in all the cities of the nation, from Finland to the Pacific. The example set by the capital was decisive in this development. As the revolution's victory in Petrograd had carried the rest of the country, so formation of the Petrograd Workers and Soldiers Soviet spurred establishment of provincial soviets.

The soviet movement emanating from Petrograd first captured the large cities, the industrial towns with many workers, and cities housing large garrisons.[75] During March, soviets were formed in almost all these places. They emerged only later in cities having few workers and soldiers, in small district and country towns, and in remote localities. The spread attained by the soviet movement in the early weeks is clear from the following examples. At the Moscow District Conference of Soviets, held from March 25 to 27, 70 workers councils and 38 soldiers councils were represented.[76] A conference held in the Donets Basin in mid-March numbered 48 soviets. In April representatives of 80 soviets met at a district congress in Kiev.[77] The total number of workers, soldiers, and peasants councils in 1917 has never been exactly determined; it has been estimated that in May there may have been 400, in August 600, and in October 900.[78]

The first city to react to the revolutionary events in Petrograd was Moscow. The local bureau of the Bolshevik Central Committee called on workers to elect deputies to a workers soviet the night of February 27.[79] At the same time a provisional revolutionary committee was formed by left-wing members of the municipal duma, representatives of the zemstvo and the municipal union, the workers group in the war industry committees, and representatives of other public organizations. On February 28 this committee called on workers, soldiers, and employees to elect representatives to the soviet.[80] On March 1 elections were held in the factories, and the soviet met for its first session, at which a three-man Executive Committee was elected. On the following day the workers soviet received its final form; ratios for representatives were set, deputies to the Petrograd soviet were elected, and formation of a new Provisional Government was approved.[81] Unlike Petrograd, Moscow did not arrive at a joint workers and soldiers council; rather, on March 4 the soldiers formed a separate soviet that collaborated with the workers soviet but remained a fully independent organization.[82]

The Moscow Soviet of Workers Deputies was the second-largest in Russia, after Petrograd. On June 1, 700 deputies belonged to it, of whom 536 were factory workers, the rest employees and professionals. The Executive Committee had 75 members. By then the Bolsheviks were able to increase the number of their deputies to 205, from 51 when their faction was established on March 19. They nevertheless were in a minority against 172 Mensheviks, 34 United Social Democrats, 110 Social Revolutionaries, 54 unaffiliated members, and several small groups.[83] The Moscow soviet also had numerous commissions for specific functions, and as in Petrograd, its administrative apparatus soon swelled.[84] The various quarters of the city also set up borough soviets with executives and commissions of their own.[85] Here, too, the Bolsheviks won a majority in most borough soviets, even before capturing the general soviet.[86] Numerous irregular elections to the workers soviet—in May, for example, 167 delegates were elected anew—caused the council majority to pass a regulation assuring more orderly and controlled election methods.[87]

Local soviets were created directly by individual workers in factories, socialist party organizations, members of "workers groups," or garrison soldiers.[88] They were organized either on the Petrograd or on the Moscow model: as workers and soldiers councils (as in Krasnoyarsk, Saratov, and Kronstadt), or former workers soviets and soldiers soviets merged (as in Ekaterinoslav), or they remained separate (as in Kharkov, Odessa, and Kiev). Opinions often differed. Many deputies wanted to preserve their soviets' integrity along class lines and feared that the proletarian councils would be swamped by the rural soldiers, while the soldiers, mostly under the influence of their officers, often insisted on an independent soldiers council.[89]

Election procedures favored preponderance of soldiers in the united soviets in many places besides Petrograd. In Saratov, for example, 2 delegates were elected for each 350 workers and also 2 soldiers for each company (250 men); in Tula one delegate for each 500 workers and one for each company; in Ivanovo Voznesensk one delegate for each 500 to 1,000 workers and one for each additional 1,000, but among the soldiers again one delegate for each company.[90]

In elections of workers delegates small plants were usually favored over large ones, since even factories with few workers were eager to have a delegate in the soviet. In Moscow one deputy was elected for each 500 workers, but never more than 3 from a single factory. Thus a plant with 1,500 workers sent 3 delegates to the soviet, but so did one with 7,000 workers. In Samara factories and workshops of 20–100 workers elected one deputy, those of 200–300 had 2, those of 300–1,000 3, and those of 1,000–2,000 5 deputies.[91] At first the elections had been arbitrary and haphazard, but after a while the provincial soviets, too, made firm rules and issued specific regulations.[92] The soviets were nevertheless far from realizing the principle of equal representation among the masses of workers and soldiers.

The variable ratios of representation in election of deputies created equally wide differences among different soviets. Cities in the Moscow district, for example, showed the following variations: the number of deputies was 350 in Tula, 162 in Orel, 140 (for 20,000 workers) in Voronezh, 89 (for 35,000 workers) in Tver.[93] In April the workers and soldiers council of Krasnoyarsk numbered 320 deputies[94] and the workers council of Kiev, 444;[95] in May the workers, soldiers, and sailors council of the marine fortress Kronstadt had over 300 delegates.[96]

Even more than in Petrograd and Moscow, provincial soviets were politically undifferentiated during the early weeks and months of the revolution; party lines were blurred, and most deputies were unaffiliated or altogether apolitical. The workers elected first of all people they knew, without examining their specific political orientation. Usually it was enough if a candidate could identify himself as a "revolutionary," without needing a party card to prove it. Council members often belonged to a wide spectrum. Members came from socialist parties, trade unions, cooperatives, former "workers groups," medical insurance groups, and now and again even from higher administration.[97] At the beginning the soldiers councils often included officers. In Ekaterinburg, for example, 17 soldiers and 10 officers were elected to the executive committee; in Odessa the presidium of the soldiers and sailors soviet consisted of 4 officers, 2 ensigns, and

8 soldiers, the chairman being a sea captain.[98] During the first days of the revolution in Kursk a soviet of officers deputies was formed that was subsequently joined by soldiers representatives, after which it bore the name Soviet of Military Delegates.[99] In general, officers had the greatest influence in soldiers councils wherever these were independent and the working class weak. During the revolution, however, officers' influence in the soviets was gradually eliminated.

Most delegates were revolutionaries in general but not members of a particular party. Only gradually did the parties win sizable followings, and the number of registered party members in the soviets rose. Among the three leading socialist groups, Social Revolutionaries and Mensheviks normally enjoyed a majority over the Bolsheviks in the big cities. Thanks to their cooperation on basic political questions, they carried along the independent members, so that during the early months of the revolution the Bolshevik opposition found itself a hopeless minority. The Yuzovka council in the Donets Basin, established on March 5, had 20 Mensheviks and 4 Bolsheviks among 300 deputies; in Ekaterinoslav 14 Bolsheviks appeared at the first session; in Saratov there were 15 Bolsheviks in March; in Kiev before the new elections in September there were 62 Bolsheviks against 131 Mensheviks; in Baku 20–25 out of 300 deputies were Bolsheviks. Since Mensheviks and Bolsheviks belonged to the same organization in a number of cities until spring 1917, it was not until later that the Bolsheviks appeared as a separate faction in the soviets.[100] Only in a few naval bases on the Baltic, especially in Kronstadt, did the Bolsheviks relatively early exercise a stronger influence in the workers, sailors, and soldiers councils, thanks to their propaganda among the already radicalized sailors. In May the Kronstadt soviet consisted of 112 Social Revolutionaries, 107 Bolsheviks, 97 unaffiliated members, and 30 Mensheviks.[101]

The local workers and soldiers soviets throughout Russia were the backbone of the revolution. They helped it sweep the country with the speed of wind; their mere existence was apt to frustrate or prevent any attempt at reaction. The soviets were a marketplace for revolutionary ideas, mediating points between the simple masses and the revolutionary intelligentsia. Increasingly they changed from purely revolutionary mass organizations into rivals of the government and finally into independent local authorities. We will discuss below the resulting problem of "dyarchy."

c) Soldiers Councils at the Front

Soldiers councils in the garrison cities were the general political organs of the revolutionary military masses. Along the same lines soldiers committees were also elected in individual military units.

On March 1, Order No. 1 of the Petrograd Workers and Soldiers Council decreed election of troop committees in the infantry companies, battalions, and regiments, and in equivalent units of other armed services, at military headquarters, and on ships of the navy.[102] Although the order was addressed only to soldiers in the Petrograd military district, and although a few days later the wording of Order No. 2 specifically restricted the first order to the capital,[103] news about formation of independent soldiers committees spread as rapidly as tidings of the revolution itself. Only a few days later frontline units also began to elect their own soviets of soldiers deputies.[104] Though most commanding officers rejected the committees and though some units, especially in the artillery, at first took a waiting position, the spread of the "komitetčina" could not be arrested. After a few weeks the commander-in-chief, General Alekseev, in concert with the Provisional Government and under pressure from the Petrograd soviet, was obliged to sanction the formation of troop committees and to issue a regulation March 30 to the effect that a committee of three soldiers and one officer was to be formed for each company, squadron, or battery.[105] The committee was to: mediate between commanding officer and men, regulate rations and leaves, and oversee cultural and political education of the soldiers. These low-level committees were to provide the foundation for further regimental and army committees. Provisions were also made for delegates congresses of individual armies and fronts and, at the headquarters of the commander-in-chief, a central congress was to elect from its members a central soviet of 11 officers and 22 men. On April 16 the "temporary order" of March 30 was replaced by a final order which introduced minor changes, such as raising the number of members of the company committees to six.[106] In May, finally, formation of division and corps committees was regulated.

These rules systematized the spontaneous formation of soldiers soviets, but also substantially altered their original character. In the first days of the revolution mutinous soldiers in Petrograd and other cities, at the front, and especially in the navy, had used violence against detested officers, independently removing some and electing new ones. Order No. 1 seemed to condone this practice, even though it did not mention election of commanders. The Petrograd soviet had to specify hurriedly in Order No. 2 that "Order No. 1 does not provide that the committees are to elect the officers in each unit."[107] Election of officers by soldiers councils would have meant a radical democratization of the army, but also a total collapse of discipline. The Menshevik-Social Revolutionary majority in the soviets, which endorsed defensive war, therefore stopped short of this final step, although they otherwise vigorously encouraged the broadest possible "self-government of the revolutionary army."

Abolition of soldiers committees in frontline units, as demanded by some commanding officers, was unthinkable. That left one option —to legally determine and limit their competence, as was done through the cited regulations. Though soldiers committees were intended primarily to represent the professional interests of servicemen, they were also meant to educate soldiers to a new civic and political consciousness and to prepare for elections to the constituent assembly. Thus a vast field opened for political propaganda and agitation among the troops; at first this favored the moderate council majority but later it favored Bolshevism.[108]

A close relationship generally existed between soldiers committees in the units and the local soviets. In remote towns soviet deputies elected by soldiers were simultaneously members of the company or regimental committee,[109] and on political matters the committees followed the soviets' guidelines. This dual structure was absent in frontline units; large army and frontline congresses were the equivalent of the soviets in the hinterland. Workers and soldiers councils in the larger cities often maintained direct contact with frontline units through delegations and special emissaries. During the revolution's early weeks the Petrograd soviet had sent to the front its own commissars, who were to inform soldiers about the revolution and place the army under control of the revolutionary capital.[110] Subsequently Kerensky, as minister of war, took over this arrangement. By agreement with the Petrograd soviet's Executive Committee, he sent government commissars to the front to coordinate activities of soldiers councils and duties and rights of the military leadership.[111] The more these commissars supported the preservation of army morale, the more easily they slid into opposition to the committees, in which the "elemental yearning for peace pushed everything else aside."[112]

From the beginning democratic and conservative circles differed as to the role of soldier soviets at the front. While conservatives insisted that major blame for the collapse of military discipline rested with the soldiers committees, democrats pointed out that creation of the soldiers councils, like the soldiers revolution in general, was the consequence, not the cause, of a progressive disintegration of the Russian army. In fact, cause and effect mingled: soldiers soviets, as products of the army's disintegration, undoubtedly contributed in the long run to deterioration of army morale. But during the revolution's first phase, while they were revolutionary but not Bolshevik, the committees functioned more as a brake on the disintegration of the army. Stepun, himself a delegate from the southwestern front and well acquainted with the soldiers committees, wrote "that without the buffer of the committees the military masses would very quickly have refused any kind of obedience and would have moved over into the Bolshevik camp."[113] Only the war which dragged on, the abortive Kerensky offensive of June and July, and the growing disruption in the interior transformed soldiers soviets at the front into Bolshevik strongholds, which eventually swept all frontline troops into the Bolshevik camp, though, as a rule, this happened considerably later than in soviets of the hinterland.

d) Peasants Councils

No peasants took part in the February Revolution, and for the moment the villages remained untouched by events in Petrograd. But soon tidings of the revolutionary risings in the cities stirred the rural masses. In 1917, as in 1905–1906, the peasant movement lagged behind the urban labor movement, both in time and in organization. It peaked in the weeks before and after the October Revolution, and contributed significantly to the revolution's success. The agrarian revolution was motivated by the old demand for the transfer of all land to the "people," the peasants; in other words, for expropriation and distribution of all estates and all land owned by the crown, the state, and the church. The more the peasants lost faith in a quick response to their demands through legal and peaceful channels—the Provisional Government took no drastic action on the agrarian question before the Bolshevik takeover—the more extensive became peasant unrest and independent land seizures.[114] A special role in this was taken by those soldiers on leave, wounded men, and deserters who returned to the villages, and by factory workers in neighboring towns; both groups helped propagandize the agricultural masses.[115]

Before the Revolution of 1917 the Russian peasantry was even less well organized than were the urban workers. The universal desire to organize, which infected all strata, also reached the villages. Instigated by zemstvos, cooperatives, and the rural "intelligentsia" of teachers, agronomists, and the like, elected committees arose under a wide variety of labels (peasants committees, rural committees, committees for people's rule), which replaced old local authorities that had been ousted. On April 21, 1917, the Provisional Government issued regulations for the establishment of a central and many local rural committees (zemel'nye komitety) in the provinces, districts, and volosts, principally to collect the necessary data for land reform, to carry out the government's decrees, and to settle local agrarian problems.[116] Formally speaking, the rural committees were instruments of the Provisional Government. In practice, they increasingly developed into tools of the peasant revolution, and they frequently took radical measures against estate owners (felling the forests; appropriating harvests, inventories, and land).[117]

Compared to the land committees, which were recognized as official institutions, the peasants soviets gained ground very slowly. First impetus came from "peasants in uniform," the soldiers. On March 6, at the instigation of the workers soviet and the soldiers soviet, delegates from nearby villages met in Moscow for a conference, and on March 18 came formal establishment of a soviet of peasants deputies, this time through an appeal of the Moscow association of cooperatives.[118]

In mid-April a council of peasants deputies of the Petrograd garrison was established with 280 deputies elected by the soldiers. As special representative of peasant-soldiers alongside the general soviet, it primarily agitated for expropriation of estate lands without indemnity and arousal of peasants by oral and written propaganda.[119] The soldiers council of Luga, one of the largest near the front, began to organize in the country as early as March. It sent representatives to the villages to help peasants establish land committees, and it issued provisional administrative guidelines. A peasants congress, with 102 participants, resolved to merge with the Luga soviet, which in the meantime had been augmented with workers deputies; the result was one of the first joint soviets of workers, soldiers, and peasants deputies in Russia.[120]

Typically the first peasant councils were formed not at the lowest level in the villages, but in urban centers.[121] Between March and May 1917, 20 provincial councils were established in the respective capitals; they emerged from conferences of peasants deputies, intellectuals, and party people, especially Social Revolutionaries.[122] The First All-Russian Congress of Peasants Deputies, held in Petrograd from March 4 to 28, 1917, represented an important stage in the movement.[123] It was organized and called by the revived All-Russian Peasant Union of 1905,[124] the cooperatives, and the Social Revolutionary Party. All peasants over eighteen years old could elect one deputy for each 150,000 inhabitants in an indirect election. The congress numbered 1,115 members, of whom 537 identified themselves as Social Revolutionaries and only 14 as Bolsheviks.[125] It was a counterpart of the first All-Russian Congress of Workers and Soldiers Soviets, which met shortly thereafter. But while the latter was the root organization of numerous local soviets, the peasants congress met before there were any peasant councils in the villages to speak of.

As proposed by the peasant congress, the next few months saw formation of numerous peasant soviets at the provincial, district, and volost level. The number of village soviets remained small, especially because here the old village assemblies (schody) rendered special soviets unnecessary. By the end of July there were peasants councils in 52 (out of a total of 78) provinces of Russia, and in 371 of 813 districts, but there were comparatively few volost soviets.[126] In Samara province, for example, where organization of rural soviets was relatively advanced, there were only 32 volost and village soviets by the end of July; in Voronezh province there were 64 volost soviets in September.[127] Independent soviets of agricultural workers, which Lenin had strongly advocated, were formed in only a few localities in the Baltic provinces.[128]

Peasants soviets at various levels generally remained independent of workers and soldiers soviets that existed alongside them. Very rarely was a soviet of workers, soldiers, and peasants deputies formed; more frequently the soviets met in joint congresses within the

provinces or their executive committees held joint deliberations.
Social Revolutionaries, who predominated in the peasants councils,
increasingly feared takeovers by more radical workers and soldiers
soviets, and therefore resisted mergers. Not until after the October
Revolution did the Bolsheviks succeed, with difficulty, in combining
the two separate council organizations into one system.

e) The All-Russian Council Organization

In the weeks following the February Revolution the Petrograd
soviet was revolutionary Russia and had significance for the whole
country, far beyond the capital. Workers and soldiers councils in
other cities sent delegates to Petrograd or maintained permanent
observers. Neighboring soviets also began very early to establish
closer ties with each other. In March the first provincial and regional
conferences took place, and later these were changed into periodic
congresses of workers and soldiers soviets, with the necessary executive committees and bureaus.[129] Soldiers councils sent special
delegations to the front; thus, a deputation from the Helsinki soviet
visited the Black Sea fleet and units of the inland front.[130] The sailors,
like their soldier counterparts, collaborated with local soviets in
Kronstadt, Helsinki, and Odessa to establish naval councils;
the Centrobalt especially became important. In June a committee was
founded encompassing representatives from all naval units.[131]

In this way a federation of many local soviets grew from below,
and found its first organizational framework in the First All-Russian
Conference of Workers and Soldiers Soviets which met from March
29 to April 3, 1917.[132] Conceived only as a meeting of the fifty
largest soviets,[133] the conference finally numbered 480 delegates, who
came from the Petrograd soviet, from 138 local workers and soldiers
councils, 7 armies, 13 base units, and 26 special frontline units.[134]
Soldiers predominated among the delegates. In its political resolutions
the conference followed the policies of the majority in the Petrograd
soviet; it supported a Provisional Government under soviet control
and revolutionary defensive war.[135] The conference recommended
organization of soviets throughout the country, the regional federation
of the now separate workers and soldiers councils, and liaison with
peasant organizations. Finally 10 delegates from the country at large
and 6 from the army were taken into the Executive Committee of the

Petrograd soviet, which thereby became a provisional all-Russian soviet.[136]

Further expansion of the soviet movement required creation of a supreme representative organ that would incorporate "revolutionary democracy" and federate under its aegis the existing local soviets. Also, leaders of the soviet's majority parties, who in early May had joined the Provisional Government, strongly desired ratification of their policies by a nationally-based representative body. On May 9, therefore, the Petrograd soviet's expanded Executive Committee called for election and despatch of delegates to the First All-Russian Congress of Workers and Soldiers Soviets in Petrograd. Election procedures were as simple as possible: soviets representing 25,000–50,000 inhabitants were to send 2 delegates; those for 50,000–75,000 inhabitants would have 3, those for 75,000–100,000 inhabitants 4, for 100,000–150,000 5, for 150,000–200,000 6, and for any over 200,000 inhabitants 8. Smaller soviets were to join with others or participate only as advisors. Frontline delegates were to be elected at army congresses.[137] With these ratios, which were not strictly observed, however, an estimated 20 million people were represented at the congress—barely half the number who later voted in elections to the Constituent Assembly.[138] Given the absence of a freely-elected parliament, the Soviet Congress, which opened June 3 and sat until June 24, was certainly the broadest democratic representation in Russia.

The 1,090 delegates represented 305 workers and soldiers soviets, 53 regional soviets, and 21 army organizations, and of the total, 822 had a full vote. Politically there was a decided preponderance of Social Revolutionaries with 285 members and Mensheviks with 248, against 105 Bolsheviks and some members of several smaller socialist groups, and 73 nonaffiliated delegates.[139] The two moderate socialist parties owed their majority at the congress mainly to their domination of provincial soviets and frontline organizations. In Petrograd the Bolsheviks had considerably more adherents by this time.[140] At the congress, however, the socialist majority had no difficulty in prevailing in all political decisions. Lenin's demand for his party's sole assumption of power, publicly articulated for the first time, was overwhelmingly rejected by the congress.[141]

Before closing the congress the delegates elected an All-Russian Central Executive Committee (Vserossijskij Central'nyj Ispolnitel'nyj

Komitet—VCIK) to serve as supreme soviet organ throughout Russia. The Central Executive Committee (CEC), with over 250 members, was itself a miniature congress of soviets. It had the right to decide independently on basic political questions so long as these were within the guidelines established by the All-Russian Congress. Its composition was proportionate to party parities at the congress: 104 Mensheviks, 100 Social Revolutionaries, 35 Bolsheviks, and 18 members of other socialist parties.[142] At its first meeting the CEC elected a 9-man presidium with Chkheidze presiding, and a 50-member bureau also composed according to party parity.[143] Soldier and worker affairs were treated in special sections. In addition, 18 departments were established to deal with different functions, and these in turn were broken down into several commissions,[144] thus creating a huge administrative machine employing hundreds, as the Petrograd soviet had earlier.

As early as June 18 the Executive Committee of the All-Russian Peasant Congress, consisting exclusively of Social Revolutionaries (including Viktor Chernov, Nikolai Avksentiev, and Catherine Breshkovsky), had decided to hold joint sessions with executives of workers and soldiers soviets, to resolve current political problems. Collaboration of the two leading soviet organizations meant a further strengthening of the right wing of "revolutionary democracy." Political composition of both these central soviet organs remained unchanged until the Second Congress of Workers and Soldiers Soviets in October and the Second Peasant Congress in December; but they increasingly lost importance and influence.

The All-Russian Soviet, as it took shape at the First Soviet Congress, was not tightly structured from bottom to top, and its authority was not clearly defined. The Central Executive Committee elected by the congress had no legal or practical power over subordinate soviets. Rather, the soviets, in keeping with revolutionary conditions that loosened ties with the central organization, were completely autonomous in decision and action, though they frequently followed the capital's example. As long as political composition of local soviets conformed to that in the soviet executive, some conformity of action was still possible at both levels. As soon as this changed, however, local soviets could oppose the soviet leadership and exert pressure on it from their provincial stations. This occurred on the eve of the October Revolution.

The CEC's relative unimportance within the All-Russian Soviet was also due to its rivalry with the Petrograd soviet which, as the oldest and largest soviet, continued even after the First All-Russian Congress to command greater prestige in the country than did the CEC. Although the Petrograd soviet relinquished some functions to the all-Russian organization, its decisions elicited more attention and compliance among other soviets than did CEC resolutions, which often remained purely on paper. This was important when the Bolsheviks captured the Petrograd soviet for it resulted in Bolshevization of the provincial soviets.

f) Factory Committees

Concurrent with the establishment of soviets of workers deputies to represent the proletarian class generally, at the beginning of the revolution, factory committees (fabrično-zavodskie komitety) were created at the labor movement's lowest rung—the factory. Indeed, such factory committees were the oldest form of the Russian workers movement, as has been shown. In the 1905 revolution they were one of the soviets' roots. They were never legally recognized, however, except skimpily and briefly in the regulations of 1903 concerning factory elders.[145]

The February Revolution's victory removed the obstacles to factory committees.[146] As early as March 5 the Petrograd soviet called for formation of such committees, and on March 10 the soviet and the employers agreed on introduction of the eight-hour day and formation of "elders councils" (sovety starost) in the factories.[147] On April 23 the Provisional Government issued precise regulations for factory committees. The committees' activities were to be: representation of a plant's workers vis-à-vis management on wages, hours, working conditions; regulation of relations among workers; representation of workers' interests vis-à-vis legal and social institutions; and cultural and educational assistance to workers. Conflicts between management and factory committees were to be settled by boards of arbitration.[148]

In time the Petrograd factory committees achieved a solid organization that to some extent competed with the soviet of workers deputies. They united into borough councils and elected representatives to a central council, headed by an executive committee.[149]

Functions of the soviet and of the central council were not clearly distinguished, though the former dealt predominantly with political problems and the latter concentrated on economic and internal factory matters. Because the committees represented the worker right at his place of work, their revolutionary role grew proportionately as the soviet consolidated into a permanent institution and lost touch with the masses. The limited stability of factory committees, whose membership was constantly changing, proved to the non-Bolshevik soviet majority that Russian workers lacked maturity and were as yet incapable of a "dictatorship of the proletariat."[150] But to the Bolsheviks this instability offered the best chance for their propaganda.

Factory committees therefore became footholds for the Bolshevik Party much sooner than did workers and soldiers councils. This was already evident at elections held in mid-April in the important Putilov Works; 6 of 22 committee members were Bolsheviks, and 7 others were unaffiliated sympathizers.[151] At the first municipal conference of Petrograd factory committees, May 30 to June 3, 1917, 499 delegates met, the strongest group among them being 261 metalworkers from 172 factory committees.[152] The final resolution, introduced by Zinoviev and calling for workers' control in the central economic institutions of the government and in private industry, was passed by 297 votes in favor, 21 against, and 44 abstaining.[153] Bolsheviks also predominated in the central council elected by the conference. At the second municipal conference, August 7–12, approval was given by 213 votes against 26 nays and 22 abstentions to the resolution on workers' control, which had been accepted by the Bolshevik Sixth Party Congress.[154] In Moscow, on the other hand, the Mensheviks were still in the majority at the city-wide conference of factory committees in July; of 682 delegates only 191 voted for the Bolshevik resolution.[155] Sponsored by the Petrograd factory committees, the first and only all-Russian conference of factory committees was held October 17–22, just before the October Revolution. Its composition reflected the victory of left-wing radicalism among metropolitan workers: among 167 delegates, there were 96 Bolsheviks, 24 Social Revolutionaries, 13 anarchists, 7 Mensheviks, 5 Maximalists, one Menshevik-Internationalist, and 21 unaffiliated members.[156]

In the economic struggle, factory committees were the real actors in the confrontation between labor and capital. Trade unions, which also began to organize anew right after the February Revolution, were pushed aside by the factory committees. It took unions a long time to build a solid organization; they never included more than a portion of the workers; and, at first predominantly led by Mensheviks, they were against direct and radical intervention in production.[157] But such intervention came soon by the factory committees, which rarely respected the limits of their functions as determined by law. Workers in numerous factories began to interfere in management and technical administration and even to remove foremen and engineers. If owners wanted to shut down their factories, the committees often took over and ran them. As early as May 1917 it was reported: "The factory committees do not hesitate to engage in economic activities. True, they have been forced to do so, since otherwise many a factory would have had to shut down. Untold numbers of workers would have been thrown out of work to swell the growing ranks of unemployed."[158]

This spontaneous movement—arising from progressive economic disintegration, lack of planning by the government, and radicalization of working masses—was given a slogan by the Bolsheviks in their call for "workers' control," which was a major point in their revolutionary program. With this call, and for tactical reasons to be discussed below, they furthered the syndicalist and anarchist tendencies emerging in factory committees, whose general aim was workers' rule in the plants, without centralized direction from above and without regard to the state of the national economy. While the Mensheviks and the trade unions loyally supported the generally acknowledged socialist principles of controlling production through the state, most factory committees wanted direct control of their work places and self-government in factories. True, these efforts were due much less to a conscious syndicalist program than to the elementary hopes of the workers for tangible improvements, which rule by factory committee seemed to promise. Bolshevik trade unionists themselves admitted that "this primitive home-grown control, exercised from the perspective of the individual factory directed by no one, obviously offers no way out of the given situation."[159] Lenin in 1917 nevertheless counted on factory committees for radicalization and recruitment of the working population. The resulting problems became evident only after the October Revolution, when the Bolsheviks began to build a centralized economy, thus clashing with the interests of factory committees.

4. THE SYSTEM OF "DYARCHY"

a) The Soviets as "Control Organs of Revolutionary Democracy"

The February Revolution defeated czarism with surprising ease, and inaugurated an era of parallel rule by the Provisional Government and the Petrograd Workers and Soldiers Soviet. This "dyarchy" filled the vacuum left by czarist collapse, and reflected the new revolutionary power balance. The Provisional Government, which was sponsored by the Russian bourgeoisie and the liberal nobility, enlisted also the more rightist elements. The Petrograd soviet and those in the provinces represented the urban proletariat and the soldiers, led by the radical petit-bourgeois intelligentsia. Most Russians—the peasantry—were not yet politicized, and occupied a somewhat intermediary position.

After the February Revolution the Petrograd soviet, for all practical purposes, possessed sole power in the capital. By Order No. 1 it controlled the barracks and thus the revolution's armed force. "The Provisional Government has no real power," Minister of War Guchkov wrote on March 9 to the military commander-in-chief, General Alekseev. "Its orders are followed only if endorsed by the Soviet of Workers and Soldiers Deputies. The Soviet possesses the actual power, such as troops, railroads, and postal and telegraphic communications. Stated bluntly, the Provisional Government exists only by the Soviet permission. The military especially can issue only orders that do not openly contradict those from the Soviet."[160]

Only the soviet could terminate the general strike on March 5 by urging workers to return to work; the soviet alone decided that newspapers could resume publication; soviet demands for introduction of the eight-hour day in factories were accepted by employers on March 10.[161] Workers and soldiers recognized the soviet as sole authority, and brought hundreds of problems before the Executive Committee. The soviet was "the true, authoritative organ of the revolution and therefore also the real power in the land."[162]

During early March 1917, however, the Petrograd soviet left government to the duma politicians, a fact which Trotsky called the "paradox of the February Revolution."[163] The soviet's moderate socialist leadership "did not feel called upon when the revolutionary tide was rising to lead the people, only to play left-wing within the bourgeois order."[164]

This had various causes. Since 1905 the Mensheviks had held that the revolution was basically "bourgeois."[165] The workers had to support this revolution unreservedly, try to extend it, utilize democratic liberties to strengthen the working class, and later when economic conditions permitted, advance to socialism. This basic Menshevik theory prevailed even during the First World War. Thus when they had to form a government, its bourgeois character seemed imperative. True to this tenet, Chkheidze refused to be a minister in the Provisional Government. Only a few of the Menshevik "oboroncy" in the soviet Executive Committee then advocated participation of socialists in the Provisional Government.[166]

The Social Revolutionaries, the second-largest majority party in the Petrograd soviet, were less rigid than the Mensheviks. To the Social Revolutionaries the Russian revolution was a democratic rising of workers on all levels, and participation in a revolutionary government was not necessarily ruled out. Kerensky took part in the Provisional Government for personal reasons, with retroactive approval when he joined the Social Revolutionary Party. Beyond that, however, the Social Revolutionaries refused immediate participation in the government.

Soviet party leaders yielded to the bourgeois Provisional Government for practical reasons, too. The old socialist party leaders had emigrated or were still exiled. The "second string" leaders of the revolution in the capital were naturally reluctant to assume government of a gigantic nation in the middle of a war, since they were almost totally unknown to the public. The duma parties, on the other hand, could provide such widely known men as Miliukov and Guchkov. The moderate socialists, inexperienced in government, did not want to put all their eggs in one basket, as the Bolsheviks were later to do, and preferred to leave responsibility to the liberals, who had sat in the zemstvos, the municipal dumas, and the national duma. Thus a keen awareness of the burdens of power affected the socialist belief that government must be left to the bourgeoisie.[167]

On the other hand, leading politicians of "revolutionary democracy"—the designation chosen by the entire socialist camp to distinguish it from the bourgeoisie—were unwilling to cede the real power embodied in the soviets. Rather, the soviets, acting as "control organs of revolutionary democracy," were to supervise the Provisional Government's activities, to influence it along revolutionary lines, and to protect it against "counterrevolutionary" coups. In the critical negotiations between the Soviet Executive Committee and the Duma Committee to establish the Provisional Government, the duma politicians met the soviet's demands for complete democratization of the state. The chief items were: political freedom of every kind, including for soldiers; removal of all class, ethnic, and religious restrictions; immediate preparations for convoking the constituent assembly and retention of the Petrograd garrison within the city.[168] The agreements carried not a word about the status of the Petrograd soviet. It was taken for granted as the acknowledged revolutionary power, and it never asked for formal recognition by the government or a legal definition of its authority.[169] A five-man "liaison commission" was established however, to "convey to the Provisional Government the revolutionary demands, to pressure the government to fulfill these demands, and to control government actions."[170]

During late March the Petrograd soviet's Executive Committee responded to numerous queries from provincial soviets by issuing an "Instruction to All Soviets of Workers and Soldiers Deputies," containing the program of the current soviet majority. The Instruction stated in part: "As long as the agreement between the Petrograd Workers and Soldiers Soviet and the Provisional Government is not breached, the Provisional Government must be regarded as the sole legal government for all Russia. All its decisions, unless protested by the soviet, must be carried out; all its government organs and commissars must be considered as legal authorities, unless they personally or politically endanger the cause of freedom." Provincial soviets were to cooperate with legal authorities and "in no way solely assume government functions." The principal task of the soviets, according to the Instruction, was to "struggle against remnants of the old regime and all counterrevolutionary attempts, while organizing the population."[171] The All-Russian Conference of Soviets held in March-April 1917 once more advocated support of the Provisional Government, with simultaneous control by the soviets.[172] In the discussions, Steklov, who later joined the Bolshevik Party, rejected criticism from bourgeois newspapers that the soviet was to blame for the "dyarchy": "There is no dyarchy—there is only the influence of revolutionary democracy on the bourgeois government, to submit to the latter the demands of the revolutionary people."[173]

In practice, however, this soviet policy of conditional support of the bourgeois government was under constant stress from the unstable balance of power. The Provisional Government nominally possessed supreme power in the state and was thus also ultimately responsible, but continued to depend on the Petrograd soviet, which held real power but was not accountable. For workers and soldiers, the soviet was "the institutionalized expression of their mistrust toward all those who had oppressed them."[174] Therefore they were all too ready to exceed mere control over the government whenever they doubted the government's revolutionary inclinations and goodwill. As early as the first days of March, the Petrograd soviet mobilized workers and soldiers to prevent the rumored departure of the czar and his family, which the Provisional Government had allegedly approved.[175] Especially during the revolution's first weeks, before conditions stabilized, the Petrograd soviet acted as ruling power, in spite of its theoretical self-limitation, and the Provisional Government borrowed the soviet's authority to settle conflicts between soldiers and officers or to enforce government regulations. Thus the relationship between Soviet Executive and Provisional Government was an odd one at best. They watched each other distrustfully and yet were interdependent—the soviet leaders had renounced sole power, but the Provisional Government ministers could not rule without soviet sanction.

The first phase of "dyarchy" lasted a bare two months and ended with the "April crisis" and the socialists' entry into the government. This first severe crisis arose from a foreign-policy conflict between the Petrograd Soviet's Executive Committee and the Provisional Government. Opposing positions on peace and war unspoken during the revolution's early weeks, now surfaced abruptly, accompanying radicalization of the urban masses and the spread of Bolshevism.

The soviet majority, Mensheviks and Social Revolutionaries, after the February Revolution found common ground in the Zimmerwald program, declaring themselves in favor of "peace without annexations or indemnities, based on the people's right of self-determination." Both their internationalist concepts and the Russian people's desire for peace were accommodated by repudiating all czarist plans for imperialist conquest and by advocating an early peace conference.[176] The same spirit animated the now famous "Appeal to the Peoples of the Entire World" by the Petrograd Soviet of March 14 (27), 1917,[177] which exhorted the proletariat of all countries to pressure their governments for early negotiations. At the same time, however, "revolutionary democracy" stuck by the principle of "revolutionary national defense" of democratic Russia against the absolutist central powers as long as the war lasted.

This program, which was advocated or at least tolerated by most Bolsheviks until Lenin's return, demanded that its own government initiate negotiations to end the war. The Provisional Government, however, was reluctant to meet the soviet majority's demands. Foreign Minister Miliukov was known to be a nationalistic imperialist, who even after the revolution's success aimed at Russia's postwar territorial expansion. On March 27, under pressure from the Petrograd soviet, the Provisional Government subscribed to the peace demands of "revolutionary democracy," but in a diplomatic note of April 18 Miliukov spoke of struggle "until decisive victory" and of "guarantees and sanctions" for a lasting peace.[178]

Miliukov's note, published in the newspapers, generated a wave of protest among soldiers and workers. The Executive Committee of the Petrograd soviet called a plenary session for April 20. A spontaneous mass movement, using the slogans "Down with Miliukov" and "Down with the Provisional Government" spread from one regiment to others and to workers, and led to bloody clashes and counterdemonstrations.[179]

The Petrograd soviet for the first time found itself in a precarious situation—caught between a mass movement it had neither created nor led and its role as control organ over the Provisional Government. It had to accommodate in some way the revolutionary masses, among whom Lenin's slogan, "All power to the soviets," had gained currency, but because of its previous policy it could not break completely with the bourgeois government. The soviet therefore opted for a compromise: it exhorted the city's people to resume order and the soldiers to return to their barracks, and it prohibited all demonstrations for two days.[180] The soviet won the Provisional Government's agreement to a "statement" on Miliukov's note, interpreting his controversial points as favoring peace.[181] Simultaneously the Executive Committee strengthened its control over the government by

insisting that in future no important political action was to be undertaken without agreement of the soviet's Executive.[182]

The events of April tested the policies of the soviet majority vis-à-
vis the Provisional Government, showing that mere control would
not suffice in a crisis and that actual power lay with the soviet. The
soviet's authority among workers and soldiers was clearly still intact;
the resolutions settling the conflict were approved by a large majority
and were carried out without demur by the masses.[183] Only one of
two solutions could prevail: either sole assumption of power by the
soviet parties, or formation of a coalition government with bourgeois
elements in the Provisional Government who were prepared to collab-
orate with soviet democracy. The moderate socialists, for the reasons
previously mentioned and now strengthened,[184] could not accept the
first solution, which the Bolsheviks preferred. Therefore only the
second solution was available: a bourgeois-socialist coalition government.

This decision was not easy for the soviet leaders. Joining the
government, after all, meant not only a tactical about-face, but also
renunciation of long-held principles. For the Mensheviks especially
participation in a bourgeois government demanded revision of their
previous theory, which they justified primarily by the exigencies of war
and revolution. "The Executive Committee recognized that Russian
revolutionary democracy, which bears on its shoulders the burden of
the revolution, cannot look calmly on while its own work is ruined.
It must assume responsibility for saving the country."[185] Thus external
circumstances dictated the action of the Mensheviks and Social
Revolutionaries, which was to have such fateful consequences for
them.

The night of May 1 the Executive Committee passed by 44 to 19
votes the resolution favoring socialist participation in the government.[186] The outstanding new personalities of the second Provisional
Government, Miliukov and Guchkov having withdrawn, were
Tseretelli, a Menshevik, as postmaster—his prime duty, however,
being maintenance of relations with the soviet—and Chernov, a Social
Revolutionary, as minister of agriculture. Kerensky, war minister in
the new government, became increasingly prominent.

Inclusion of soviet leaders as ministers, however, could not remove
the system of dyarchy. Socialist ministers were explicitly answerable
to the Petrograd soviet and ultimately to the All-Russian Congress of

Soviets or its Central Executive Committee. Nevertheless, the socialists' entry into the Provisional Government meant a certain shift
of power favoring the latter. "They (the socialist ministers) were
convinced that the power of the soviet which they embodied would
now flow to the official government."[187] Tseretelli gave the following
explanation: "Our attitude—that of the democratic organizations—
toward the government has changed. Formerly, we not only controlled the government, but also aided it by often carrying out its
functions. Without such assistance, the government could not operate.
Now all power would be yielded to the Provisional Government. The
organizations of revolutionary democracy . . . retain their right to
criticize the government's actions, but do not meddle in administrative business. We should not hinder national governance, but sound
the alarm in case of mistakes."[188]

Thus the soviets, in Tseretelli's view, retained their controlling
functions but would not directly intervene in government. Russia
was to be led from dyarchy, which was paralyzing the country, into
orderly state rule. "The coalition government proceeded to build a
bridge to a bourgeois-parliamentary republic."[189] The next few months
would reveal whether the soviets had sufficient vitality to retain their
leading role in the revolution.

b) The Soviets as Local Revolutionary Organs

In the Russian provinces the revolution had destroyed the old administration. Czarist officials, from provincial governor down to the
lowliest village policeman, were deposed within a few days or weeks,
and some were arrested. The Provisional Government established a
makeshift order by appointing heads of provincial zemstvos as commissars; beyond that, however, the government had to allow the
people themselves to create their own organizations. Thus the most
diverse public and semipublic organizations arose in cities and towns
in the form of existing self-governmental bodies or on an ad hoc
basis. Often half a dozen or more such committees existed in one
city, competing with each other and overlapping in functions.[190] In
April the Provisional Government ordered new elections by universal
equal suffrage to the municipal self-government organizations, and
in May to the rural ones.[191] At the same time the scope of local self-
government was broadened; for example, local organizations were

given authority over the civil militia which was to replace the police. These measures reflected the liberals' traditional aversion to an overpowering central government and their identification with the self-governing institutions of czarist times.

The public committees and subsequent organs of self-government competed from the first with the soviets. While municipal dumas were regarded by the bourgeoisie as its domain, the soviets were purely proletarian or a mixture of proletarian and military organizations. Until workers formed their own soviet, they sent representatives to the general committees; later the soviets had official delegates in the various public and social organizations and, until the general elections, in municipal dumas as well.[192] Respective spheres of authority were not clear. Most local soviets followed the arrangement in Petrograd, where the soviet functioned as control over the Provisional Government. Local soviets left administrative detail to the respective committee or the duma, and considered it their principal task to supervise these bodies and push them toward democratic reforms. In general, effectiveness of local soviets depended on the strength and cohesion of the workers and on the presence of garrison troops. Thus from the beginning soviets in large industrial cities influenced local politics much more than did those in smaller towns populated mainly by artisans or commercial employees.[193]

As in 1905, the soviets, as proletarian class organizations, aimed primarily to direct and organize the workers' economic struggle so effectively fueled by victory of the February Revolution. At the First All-Russian Congress of Soviets, a report on this point said: "The revolution met a totally unorganized proletariat. The soviets formed at the revolution's outset were naturally the first organizations to which fell performance of numerous trade union, factory committee, and mediation board functions. For these functions, the larger soviets created special labor departments."[194]

The wealth of economic and social tasks facing the soviets can be gathered from various resolutions of the first all-Russian conference of soviets at the beginning of April on general labor policies, the eight-hour day, minimum wages, freedom of association, formation of trade unions, mediation boards, labor exchanges, social security, unemployment.[195] Labor departments of local soviets collaborated actively in establishing trade unions. Their first nationwide conference in July 1917 was arranged by the labor department of the

Petrograd soviet and the central bureaus of the trade unions in Petrograd and Moscow. A major and on the whole beneficial role by the soviets' labor departments also occurred in settlement of disputes in factories. For example, the "dispute commission" of the Kiev soviet settled 25 major and 40 minor labor disputes during the early months of the revolution.[196]

With the gradual growth and stabilization of trade unions and the increased importance of factory committees, the erstwhile mixture of functions was slowly replaced by division of labor. A resolution of the All-Russian Congress of Soviets considered this new development and stated that "during transition, it is essential to coordinate activities of the soviets' labor departments, the unions, and factory committees" until direction of the workers' economic struggle could be transferred to the latter two. The soviets should then confine themselves to fundamental or national functions, such as organizing central and local labor conciliation panels as provided for by law, participating in government planning for industry and transport, and labor legislation.[197]

The soviets were particularly active in the struggle for the eight-hour day. In 1905 the St. Petersburg soviet was forced to suspend this struggle without result, but after the February Revolution employers had to grant the eight-hour day in early March.[198] The example of Petrograd inspired imitation in other cities. In March and April numerous local soviets won the eight-hour day, either by negotiations with manufacturers or, if they refused—as in Moscow—by decreeing it on resolutions of their own.[199] Employers in most instances were helpless to resist and had to allow soviet control commissions to examine internal factory affairs.

Beyond this specifically proletarian struggle, however, some soviets invaded other public affairs even in the revolution's first phase. Theoretically most soviets wanted to restrict activity to controlling the government and administration, but even the Menshevik and Social Revolutionary soviets eventually intervened directly in all sorts of questions. Sukhanov's characterization of the Petrograd soviet, "throughout the revolution the soviet continually extended its functions and eventually became a state within the state,"[200] also applied to many provincial soviets. "The soviets developed from control organs into administrative organs."[201] This process varied depending on time and place, and the earliest, most frequent manifestation of soviet transformation into "nuclei of power" (to use Lenin's phrase of 1906) was in provisioning. The workers were first to suffer from growing urban food shortages and local soviets independently adopted stringent measures of alleviation. In Nizhni Novgorod, for example, exportation of bread was curtailed; in Krasnoyarsk the soviet introduced ration cards; in other places "bourgeois" homes were searched and goods confiscated. These measures, often carried out arbitrarily, were early harbingers of the Bolshevik requisition system during the civil war, used as an element of the "dictatorship of the proletariat." In general, however, soviets were anxious to restrain the radical and extreme demands of individual workers and soldiers groups; thus they often found themselves caught in a conflict between the admittedly necessary maintenance of public order and the impatient, radical wishes of the masses. Lenin's party later exploited this situation in bolshevizing the soviets.

The slackening of centralization made various regions and communities largely independent and also led to frequent clashes between local soviets and commissars appointed by Petrograd. One deputy at the First All-Russian Congress of Soviets described reigning conditions pointedly: "The government delegates power to the commissars, but you know for yourselves that the commissar really has no power at all. In our town, for example, it went like this: the day after he was appointed, the commissar came to the soviet and said, 'Do what you want; I've been chosen—if you support me, I'll carry out my duties; if you don't, I'll resign tomorrow.' We told him, 'If you carry out your duties well, then we'll support you; otherwise we won't.' "[202] In Russian hinterlands, where decrees from the capital arrived only late or not at all, local soviets often exercised unlimited power. The previously mentioned workers and soldiers soviet of Krasnoyarsk granted leaves to soldiers, disregarding the commanding officer's protests, interfered in labor disputes, and even transferred ownership of factories to trade unions.[203] "In the Urals," Trotsky reported in his history, "where Bolshevism had prevailed since 1905, the soviets frequently administered civil and criminal law; created their own militia in numerous factories, paying them out of factory funds; organized workers controls of raw materials and fuel for the factories; supervised marketing; and determined wage scales. In some areas in the Urals the soviets expropriated land for communal cultivation."[204] Broad authority was also claimed from the beginning by soviets in

Ivanovo Voznesensk, Lugansk, Tsaritsyn, Kherson, Tomsk, Vladivostok, and Luga.

The workers, sailors, and soldiers soviet of Kronstadt—the most
radical place in all Russia—went furthest. Here violence and mur-
ders were committed during the February Revolution, with 40 navy
officers as victims; many other officers were held prisoner; the sailors
vigorously carried out the principle of election of all commanding
officers.[205] In the workers, sailors, and soldiers soviet, Social Revolutionaries—mostly left-wing, Bolsheviks, and radical independents
held the majority as early as April. When new elections were held at
the beginning of May, the soviet numbered 93 Bolsheviks, 91 Social
Revolutionaries, 46 Mensheviks, and 68 independents.[206] On May
13 the Executive Committee passed this resolution: "The sole power
in the city of Kronstadt is the Soviet of Workers and Soldiers Deputies, which acts with the Petrograd soviet in government matters."[207]
Three days later the plenary session passed the Executive Committee's resolution by a vote of 211 to 41.[208] The demand for the commissar's dismissal and his replacement with a person directly elected
by the soviet was justified by the Social Revolutionary spokesman by
citing the democratic nature of the soviet, which was trusted by the
workers and sailors. "The central government has no right whatever
to meddle in a specific territorial unit, or to make decisions for the
individual cell rather than for the state as a whole." Except for the
Mensheviks, all speakers favored speedy establishment of soviet
power throughout Russia. Kronstadt, they claimed, must lead and
set an example.[209]

Proclamation of the "Kronstadt Republic" created a nationwide
sensation. The Provisional Government's reaction was typical for
the system of "dyarchy." Lacking authority, it asked leaders of the
Petrograd soviet to caution the rebellious Kronstadt soviet. A delegation from the Petrograd soviet, headed by Tseretelli and Skobelev,
went to negotiate with the Kronstadt soviet. Tseretelli pointed out
that the vast majority of "revolutionary democracy" supported the
government, which must have full power, in Kronstadt as elsewhere,
to avoid anarchy. Skobelev asked whether the Kronstadt people considered themselves a part of Russia and were therefore ready to acknowledge local representatives of the Provisional Government. It was
necessary to know, he went on, where local autonomy ended and the
central government's authority began. In their replies spokesmen for

the Kronstadt soviet explained that the soviet had never thought of seceding from Russia or forcing its opinions on others; but "life itself" had given all power to the Kronstadt soviet, even before the proclamation of May 16.[210]

Since both sides were eager to avoid more acute conflict, they finally compromised on May 24. The Kronstadt soviet acknowledged that, its principle of exclusive soviet rule in Russia notwithstanding, it would comply with the laws and regulations of the Provisional Government.[211] Practically, nothing changed very much in Kronstadt: the Provisional Government's power existed only on paper, and the soviet remained sole master in the city. The naval fortress outside the capital became the arsenal of the approaching second revolution and the symbol of soviet power.

The soviets' development into local revolutionary instruments of power and administration, as shown most clearly in Kronstadt, was a completely natural process during revolutionary upheaval. When the old state order was dissolved, the soviets, as militant revolutionary organizations, were more active than the municipalities, which were designed for stable conditions. The municipal dumas represented all levels and were therefore more democratic, but the soviets, as explicit instruments of the class struggle, were often superior to the dumas. The best minds in the socialist parties were to be found in the soviets; the parties' struggle for influence was decided here, not in the dumas. Nevertheless the outcome of this competition was doubtful after the first months of the revolution. Everything depended on whether Russia's internal conditions could be normalized or whether the social revolution would engulf the beginnings of democratic self-government, with its promise of peace and stability. The question led right into the larger problem of creating nationwide soviet rule.

c) Will the Soviets Take Power?

The system of "dyarchy" could not endure. The Bolsheviks were absolutely correct in demanding a radical solution of the problem: "All power to the soviets."[212] But here a paradox appeared: the soviets did not want sole power. Although they had in fact ruled in some places, the moderate socialist majority firmly turned against the Bolshevik slogan, arguing that:

1) The soviets are class organizations, embracing only part of the

population. Should soviet rule be established, other strata—especially the bourgeoisie, but also sections of the peasantry—would reject the revolution, and the proletariat, the nucleus of soviet power, would be isolated.

2) A soviet government could solve Russia's enormous problems no better than could a broadly based coalition government. Waging war, especially, required union of all national forces.

3) Establishment of soviet power would reinforce centrifugal tendencies inherent in local soviets, and thereby defeat unity.

The conflicting views on soviet power were discussed in all their ramifications at the First All-Russian Congress of Soviets in June 1917, in every speech by Menshevik and Social Revolutionary delegates. The Social Revolutionary leader, Malevskii, argued that soviet power could not guarantee to end the war swiftly or to immediately effect "revolutionary democracy,"—"and in revolutionary times one may not trust gambles."[213] Liber, a Menshevik, admitted that many governmental functions had fallen by default to the soviets, as a result of the central government's weakness. "Evidently the soviet fails to assume power, not because it can't, but because it won't . . . Doing so would obligate it to solve all current revolutionary problems —and alone, without approval by other social strata, even against their wishes."[214] Another Social Revolutionary speaker questioned whether the soviets were a genuinely democratic authority, since they embraced only a minority of the population, while the millions of Russian peasants, who should really determine Russia's fate, were only beginning to organize. Therefore, Liber claimed "the basic Bolshevik tenet, that soviets are absolute and legitimate instruments of revolutionary power, is objectively false."[215]

Aside from the Bolsheviks, only the small group of United Social Democrats supported the demand for soviet power. Their spokesman, Lunacharski (who joined the Bolsheviks in July), proposed a soviet system, to consist of a revolutionary parliament and an executive committee at the top, with provincial, district, and volost soviets at lower levels.[216] Lenin, first to envision a soviet republic and to advocate it at the All-Russian Congress, had not yet thought about details of its structure.

The resolution accepted at the congress by a majority of 543 to 126, with 52 abstentions, concluded "that assumption of power by the soviets now would weaken the revolution, and prematurely repel all the people who can still serve the revolutionary cause."[217] Formation of the coalition government was approved.

By joining the Provisional Government, the Mensheviks and Social Revolutionaries attempted to supply the broad popular base which, in their opinion, a pure soviet government lacked. Their rejection of soviet power hardened during the following months. Especially after the July events[218] laid bare the split within "revolutionary democracy," there prevailed, in Kerensky's words, "the conviction among soviet leaders that the soviets were not and could not be governing organs but that they were merely tools for transition to a new democratic order."[219] Kerensky himself assured the British ambassador, Sir George Buchanan, as early as May: "The soviets will die a natural death."[220]

Even after they entered the government the Mensheviks remained convinced that the Russian revolution was "bourgeois" and that Russia's backwardness could be overcome only during a long phase of capitalist development. Therefore "all those classes which have a future in a capitalist economy" should be "drawn into government"; without their participation, industrial and economic problems could not be solved.[221] According to the Mensheviks' strict Marxist interpretation, the political structure suited to this stage of development was a democratic republic, modeled on the Western European parliamentary democracies. The soviets, on the other hand, as the Mensheviks realized, were not democratic because they excluded much of the population, no matter how democratically they were structured internally. The Mensheviks' reformist socialism required the broadest democratic structure, and their rejection of government by soviet power therefore grew out of Marxism's democratic heritage, even if Russia's difficult wartime conditions forced temporary compromises.

Basically the Mensheviks saw no future for the soviets; they were to be only militant revolutionary organizations. Chkheidze, chairman of the Petrograd soviet, credited the soviets primarily with "organizing and disciplining the masses in the midst of chaos and destruction" and with "pacifying the nation's elemental vigor when centuries-old chains were thrown off."[222] At the Moscow State Conference in July 1917 the Mensheviks and Social Revolutionaries, in the name of "revolutionary democracy," introduced a resolution about the revolution's most urgent problems; the soviets were not even mentioned in it. Instead, the moderate socialists wanted to place most government reconstruction upon the democratic self-administrative organs.[223] Tseretelli assigned the soviets to "watch over the conquered freedom" until the new democratic bodies could function properly; he said: "Whenever in any region democratic organizations replace the soviets, the latter will voluntarily hand over their work. Soviets will exist only before the change. When democratic self-governing bodies are elected by universal suffrage, they will assume the functions of self-government previously exercised by the soviets."[224]

The Social Revolutionaries, unlike the Mensheviks, did believe that the Russian revolution would develop distinctively and that socialism would be based on cooperatives. But politically they advocated not a soviet republic, but rather a parliamentary-democratic republic headed by a constituent national assembly. "From their beginning the soviets did not aim to represent the country as a whole, but only workers, soldiers, and peasant labor; they did not want to replace an all-Russian constituent assembly. . . . On the contrary, leading the country toward a constituent assembly was their primary purpose. . . . The soviets represent neither a state power paralleling the constituent assembly, nor one aligned with the Provisional Government. They are advisers to the people in the struggle for their interests . . . and they know that they represent only part of the country and are trusted only by the masses for whom they fight. Therefore the soviets have always refused to preempt power and form a government."[225] On the eve of the Democratic Conference representing the soviets, unions, cooperatives, and other self-governing organizations, called for mid-September 1917, the newspaper *Delo Naroda* wrote that it must be admitted "that the soviets are not the entire workers democracy." As rural and urban self-governing organizations consolidated, they reflected the masses' will and mood better than the soviets did."[226] Mensheviks and Social Revolutionaries wanted a gradual transfer of soviet functions to the Provisional Government and later to the national constituent assembly, the democratic municipal dumas, and the local zemstvos. During this transfer the soviets would become ineffective or disappear altogether— as happened during the German Revolution of 1918, when the central government stabilized and the national assembly convened.

This peaceful development of the Russian revolution and a concurrent gradual dismantling of the soviets did not occur, however. On the contrary, the internal class struggle (of which the Kornilov putsch in late August was symptomatic) intensified, undermining the moderate soviet majority's belief that only coalition with the bourgeoisie, rather than rule exclusively by the soviets, could save the country. At the Democratic Conference in mid-September adherents and opponents of coalition were more or less evenly balanced,[227] but almost daily the balance in the local soviets shifted to favor the Bolsheviks and their call for sole soviet power.[228] Even the Mensheviks and Social Revolutionaries increasingly favored a soviet-based, purely socialist government. Martov, the Menshevik leader before 1917, from the beginning disapproved of essential points in his party's majority policy. Both Martov and the Menshevik-Internationalists, a small leftist group, rejected the coalition policy and acknowledged the soviets' future prominence. At the Democratic Conference Martov declared: "All political self-government of this great people that has thrown off the shackles of czarist slavery occurred and still occurs through the soviets. Thus the soviets throughout Russia now directly represent the people's power, act for the democratic republic, and throughout the provinces hold supreme power."[229] Martov conceived a combination of constituent assembly and soviets, an idea also espoused in October by some Bolsheviks.[230] The Left Social Revolutionaries, a separate group since June/July 1917, also demanded exclusive soviet power and rejected a coalition with the bourgeoisie. The Social Revolutionaries' Petrograd conference opened on September 10 and approved a resolution by the left wing, demanding formation of a homogeneous soviet-based government.[231] In the weeks before the Bolshevik October rising, the Left Social Revolutionaries all along the line joined in the Leninist cry, "All power to the soviets."

As social and partisan contrasts deepened during fall 1917, the Bolshevik demand for exclusive soviet rule also evoked the first strong response among the Russian masses. Unlike parties which had majorities in earlier soviets, the Bolsheviks proposed specifically that future soviets should seize power in their own name and build a state on their own pattern. The fate of the Russian soviets increasingly became tied to that of Bolshevism.

CHAPTER FOUR

Bolshevism and Councils,
1917

1. LENIN'S PROGRAM FOR REVOLUTION

a) The Bolsheviks and the Councils before Lenin's April Theses

Since 1905 the Bolsheviks had struggled against czarism under the battlecry "revolutionary-democratic dictatorship of the proletariat and peasantry." Thus they made the Russian revolution responsible for removing the country's remnants of feudalism, for overthrowing the monarchy, and for establishing a democratic republic. The Mensheviks' goal was basically the same, but Lenin's was distinguished principally by his denial that the Russian bourgeoisie could carry out its own "bourgeois" revolution, and by calling instead for an alliance of the proletariat and the peasantry, whose leaders were to form the revolutionary government and carry out the necessary political and social reforms.

Lenin himself altered essential details of his program for revolution, gradually during the First World War and then rapidly after the February Revolution broke out, but for the Bolsheviks in Russia the theory outlined above continued to guide their practical politics.

Shliapnikov reports that the Petrograd Bolsheviks, in their deliberations immediately before the revolution erupted, arrived "logically at a government of revolutionary democracy, to be based on an agreement among the existing major revolutionary and socialist parties in the nation (Bolsheviks, Mensheviks, and Social Revolutionaries)."[1] This theoretical concept became confused during the February Revolution, when the Mensheviks and Social Revolutionaries, as members of the workers and soldiers soviets, agreed with the bourgeois politicians to form the Provisional Government. The new "dyarchy" of Petrograd soviet and Provisional Government called for new tactics from the Russian Bolsheviks. To develop and apply them, however, was enormously difficult because of Bolshevik loyalty to the old 1905 theory of revolution and because of Lenin's absence. The time before Lenin's return from emigration, therefore, was one of wavering and disagreement within the party, which weakened the Bolsheviks' general impact,[2] and their policy on the soviets.

The soviets of workers deputies were not central in the Bolshevik revolutionary program before 1917. Lenin's occasional praise for the soviets during the 1905 revolution and his prophetic remarks concerning the soviets as "cells of revolutionary power"[3] had no significant effect on Bolshevik strategy and tactics, which saw soviets merely as "instruments of strikes and insurrection." Leadership of the revolutionary battle was reserved primarily to party organizations in factories, the army, and elsewhere. "We deliberately did not plan for an unaffiliated organ to lead the semi-spontaneous movement," Shliapnikov wrote of the Petrograd Bolsheviks at the beginning of the February Revolution.[4] Accordingly, Bolshevik proclamations through February 28 do not call for a deputies council and soviets are not mentioned in the manifesto "To All Citizens of Russia" which was written by the party's Central Committee, edited by Molotov and released on February 28. Rather, it demanded, entirely in the spirit of the old Bolshevik program, the prompt establishment of a provisional revolutionary government "which must lead the new republican order now arising" and must enact a number of basic laws, calling among other things for a constitutional convention.[5]

The Bolsheviks drew up their manifesto as the Petrograd soviet began to form. Faced with an accomplished fact, the leading party groups sought in vain during the next few days to arrive at an unequivocal and clear attitude toward the soviet. The absence of experienced and authoritative leaders handicapped this endeavor. At first Shliapnikov, who could count on support of the Central Committee Bureau and part of the Petrograd party committee, sought support among the soviet Executive Committee for the formation of a revolutionary government by the soviet parties. Such a government, Shliapnikov felt, was closest to the Bolshevik program, despite differences between the moderate socialists and the Bolsheviks, especially on the war.[6] On March 1 the Vyborg party section, which continued to stand furthest to the left, unequivocally demanded that "The Petrograd soviet is to declare itself the provisional revolutionary government."[7] On the following day the Vyborg borough committee released an appeal that read in part: "Until the constituent assembly can meet, all power must be concentrated in the hands of the workers and soldiers soviet as the sole revolutionary government. The army and the people should merely carry out the resolutions of the soviet. . . . The soviet must convene the constituent assembly, which will settle on a new constitution and end the war."[8] This was the first Bolshevik call for soviet power, though, as Shliapnikov stresses, it was not yet a program for a new constitution patterned on the soviets, but simply the best practical government by "revolutionary democracy." Also on March 1, the small independent Social Democratic group, Meždurajoncy, and the local Social Revolutionary committee, demanded that the workers and soldiers soviet declare itself the provisional revolutionary government and assume power.[9]

But these voices remained isolated; and both appeals were overruled before they could be published, the Meždurajoncy by the soviet Executive Committee, and the Vyborg borough committee's by its superior, the Petrograd Bolshevik Party committee itself. For in the meantime the Petrograd soviet and the Duma Committee had agreed on formation of the Provisional Government, and the soviet renounced assumption of power. The Bolsheviks now had to decide what tactics they would use toward the bourgeois Provisional Government as well as the Menshevik-Social Revolutionary soviet. The few Bolshevik soviet delegates (on March 2 only 19 delegates voted for the Central Committee Bureau's resolution) demanded clear instructions for their activity in the soviet.[10] They waited in vain, however, for during the following days serious disagreements broke out among the Petrograd Bolsheviks which resulted in open rivalry between the Central Committee Bureau, as nominally the highest party authority, and the Petrograd local committee. Even after formation of the Provisional Government the Central Committee Bureau, for which Molotov usually appeared as spokesman, demanded continued Bolshevik agitation for a revolutionary government representing the socialist parties. A resolution of March 4 states: "The present Provisional Government is counterrevolutionary by its nature, since it represents the upper bourgeoisie and nobility, and therefore must not be tolerated. The task of revolutionary democracy is the formation of a provisional revolutionary government of a democratic nature (dictatorship of the proletariat and peasantry)."[11]

In opposition, the majority in the Petrograd soviet advocated toleration of the Provisional Government, in the framework of the resolution adopted by the soviet. Thus a radical challenge to the Provisional Government would be wrong and would lead to the Bolsheviks' isolation. One small group still further to the right rejected the slogan "Down with war" and proposed contact with the Mensheviks.[12] Only two members of the Petrograd party committee explicitly demanded the establishment of soviet power. A resolution they put forward on March 5—which was, however, rejected—came closest to the subsequent Leninist soviet program: "The task now is development of a provisional revolutionary government through federation of local soviets. For total conquest of the central power it is essential a) to secure the power of the workers and soldiers deputies; b) to begin partial conquest of power in the provinces by overthrowing the old authorities and replacing them with soviets; their task is: arming the people, democratizing the army, expropriating the land, and carrying out independently the minimum program."[13]

In mid-March 1917 a group of Bolshevik exiles returned from Siberia, among them Kamenev and Stalin. As senior leaders, they attempted to grasp the reins of the party. Their first act was to take the editorship of *Pravda* away from Molotov and the other members of the CEC Bureau. In his first programmatic article Kamenev committed himself to the policy adopted by the Petrograd soviet. It would be a mistake, he wrote, to discuss now replacement of the Provisional Government. Only when the liberal government had "exhausted" itself would the practical transfer of power to a revolutionary democracy arise.[14] Concerning the war, Kamenev again opposed most Petrograd Bolsheviks by supporting the policy of "revolutionary defense of the fatherland," with simultaneous pressure

on the government to initiate immediate peace negotiations with all
the powers involved.[15] Stalin, who used somewhat more radical
language, was close to Kamenev in substance, and their appearance
increased the confusion in the Bolshevik Party ranks. Lower-level
party organizations protested the change in course, especially on
the war policy, and persuaded *Pravda* to resume a few days later the
old line of opposition to the war.

Pravda's new editorial board basically followed the Bolshevik
resolution of 1906, which had viewed the formation of some soviets
as a task of local party organizations.[16] *Pravda* reprinted Lenin's
entire resolution verbatim, with the telling alteration: the words
"the formation of such organizations *may* be the task of the local
party organizations" now read "*should* be the task."[17] This change,
minor at first glance, indicated a major switch. With soviets springing
up everywhere, the earlier cautious attitude toward them gave way to
the party's active participation in their development. In several articles
Stalin especially pointed out the revolutionary importance of the
soviets and the necessity of their continued growth. He called for an
"all-Russian organ of revolutionary struggle for Russian democracy,
with sufficient authority to weld the capital's democracy to that in the
provinces and at the appropriate moment to change from a militant
revolutionary organ into an instrument of revolutionary government,
which will mobilize all the people's energies against the counterrevolution. Such an organ can only be the all-Russian soviet. That is the
first requirement for the victory of the Russian revolution."[18] Thus
Stalin correctly assessed the soviets' significance before Lenin's first
"Letter from Abroad" had reached Petrograd. These sentences were
the bridge to Lenin's April Theses, which Stalin, unlike Kamenev,
promptly endorsed.

A resolution of the conflicting views within the Bolshevik Party was
expected from the All-Russian Party Conference in the final days of
March, just before and concurrently with the first All-Russian Soviet
Conference.[19] On the day before the conference convened, the
Central Committee Bureau, obviously already influenced by Lenin's
letters from Switzerland, in a resolution concerning the Provisional
Government, referred to the soviets as "the cells of revolutionary power," which would inherit power "at a specific
moment of revolutionary development." In addition to strict control
of the Provisional Government, the local soviets were already urged

to assume governmental and economic functions.[20] At the conference itself Stalin repeated his views from *Pravda*: the soviets were revolutionary leaders of the people and also control organs of the Provisional Government. Nearly all participants were convinced that at a later stage of the revolution "revolutionary democracy," through the soviets, would assume power, but vagueness and differences of opinion remained concerning party tactics. In any case, no one had in mind an uncompromising struggle against the bourgeois Provisional Government and the moderate soviet majority, such as Lenin was demanding, so the concluding resolution of the conference referred to the soviets not as "cells of revolutionary power," but only as a control over the Provisional Government.[21] The Bolsheviks at the All-Russian Soviet Conference even voted for the majority resolution. When their conference ended the Bolsheviks decided to negotiate with the Menshevik groups who endorsed the Zimmerwald Internationalist program. At this juncture Lenin arrived in Petrograd, and at one blow shattered all projects for coalition, denounced his party's wavering attitude toward the moderate socialists, and proclaimed uncompromising struggle against the Provisional Government. His slogan for leading the Bolsheviks to power was "All power to the soviets!"

b) The New Perspective:
Socialist Revolution and Soviet Republic

Lenin's program, as announced to the party in his April Theses on his arrival in Russia, had evolved during the First World War and in adaptation to actual conditions in the early weeks of the revolution. The new goal of the socialist revolution and the new form of the soviet republic were central to his 1917 theory of revolution and state.

Even during the war years Lenin had clung to the plan of a "bourgeois" revolution giving rise to a "democratic dictatorship" of workers and peasants. But the war's convulsions had, in his mind, "inseparably linked the revolutionary crisis in our country with the growing proletarian socialist revolution in the West. . . . The prologue moves closer in time to the epilogue, with an even closer connection between the democratic revolution in Russia and the socialist upheaval in Western Europe."[22] When Lenin left Zurich in March 1917 his general conception was that "Russia is an agricultural country, one of the most backward European nations where socialism *cannot* succeed *immediately* and *directly*. Judging by the experiences of 1905, the country's agricultural character, specifically the immense holdings of the great aristocratic landowners, *can* lend an enormous impetus to the bourgeois-democratic revolution in Russia and serve as the *prologue* to socialist world revolution, a *step* toward this revolution. . . . The Russian proletariat cannot alone successfully *complete* the socialist revolution. But it can give such momentum to the Russian revolution that the optimal conditions are created, and even a beginning of the socialist revolution."[23]

Trotsky called these sentences by Lenin the "connecting link between the old position of Bolshevism, which limited the revolution to democratic goals, and the new position, which Lenin first proclaimed to the party in his theses of April 4."[24] But Lenin had already stated earlier, in 1905, in a rare look into the more distant future: "Immediately after the democratic revolution and with all our power, we shall . . . start the transition to the socialist revolution. We are for the permanent revolution. We will not stop halfway."[25] The defeat of the Revolution of 1905 had eclipsed this perspective; now the February Revolution renewed it.

After the outbreak of war in 1914 Lenin made another about-face, which was also fundamental for the Bolshevik program and tactics in pursuit of the socialist revolution. In 1914 Lenin broke with the other Russian socialists and with the Second International over war policy. Tirelessly he pounded into his followers' heads the idea that no deals could be made with the "fatherland defenders." Lenin held to this position even after the revolution in Russia. When he first heard that the Petrograd Bolsheviks were wavering toward the Provisional Government and the soviet majority parties, he wrote that the party must wage "the most stubborn, most steadfast, most inexorable struggle" against the "social patriots" and "social pacifists"; and he added: "Personally I am ready to declare without the slightest hesitation . . . that I even prefer an immediate break with any member of our party to any concessions to social patriotism . . . or social pacifism."[26] If, then, Lenin unequivocally ruled out the rest of "revolutionary democracy," there was no meaning left in the old slogan, "revolutionary-democratic dictatorship of the proletariat and peasantry," since it represented a coalition of the three socialist parties. By rejecting at once any collaboration with the Mensheviks and Social Revolutionaries, Lenin logically aimed at sole power for the Bolshevik Party. Socialist revolution and Bolshevik power became the same thing to Lenin.

But Lenin never openly and unequivocally articulated this aim during the revolution. It remained concealed behind the new slogan, "All power to the soviets," which dominated Lenin's program beginning in March 1917. During the revolution's early weeks Lenin outlined the basic Bolshevik idea of soviets, which he subsequently elaborated, especially in *State and Revolution.* At the same time he integrated the soviets into his revolutionary strategy and assigned them preeminence in the struggle for power. This dual character of Lenin's program allowed the Bolsheviks to take power in the name of the soviets, thus linking the two groups, although they differed in origin and nature.

In 1905 the Bolsheviks took a very cool and at times hostile attitude toward the formation of soviets.[27] Lenin was suspicious of all spontaneous—and to him formless—attempts at organization by the proletariat, since they could threaten his party's leadership vis-à-vis the backward masses. But he could not avoid acknowledging the great revolutionary significance of the soviets, most evident in St. Petersburg and Moscow. In 1906 he therefore wrote that the soviets would play an important role in the future as "insurrectionary organs"; he even called them "cells of the provisional revolutionary government," and he demanded of his party "the study of these historical nuclei of the new power . . . its condition and its success."[28] In the following decade, however, the soviets disappeared almost entirely from Lenin's field of vision, until in March 1917 they suddenly became central in his theory.

The February Revolution occurred while Lenin, in his Swiss exile, was occupying himself intensively with the theories of Marx, Engels, and contemporary socialists (especially Kautsky and Pannekoek) concerning the future proletarian state. He copied long excerpts from their works and intended to write a contribution of his own concerning the Marxist state. This material formed the basis of *State and Revolution,* written in August and September 1917.[29] Influenced by Bukharin who examined the relationship between the state and the socialist revolution in various articles in 1916,[30] and the Dutch theoretician Pannekoek who as early as 1912 predicted the replacement of parliamentarianism by proletarian organs,[31] Lenin arrived at the basic insight that the revolution must destroy the existing state institutions and create new ones. He "discovered," as it were, the anti-government Marx of the book on the Commune and—the decisive step—he combined Marx with the experiences of the Russian revolution. In this effort he could fall back on ideas voiced by him in 1905 and 1906 concerning the soviets as organs of revolutionary power, and place them in a larger theoretical and historical context. So far Lenin had only tentatively connected the Russian soviets with Marx's interpretation of the Paris Commune of 1871. Before 1917, Lenin's comments on the Paris Commune were predominantly critical of its mistakes, and he never saw it as idealized and absolute, as the Bolsheviks did later. The fundamental idea, that the Commune had smashed the old bourgeois state machinery and replaced it with popular self-government, was not yet applied to the Russian soviets. In 1905 Lenin specifically declared that the Paris Commune had not been an example of the dictatorship of the proletariat, but much more an example of the "revolutionary democratic dictatorship of the proletariat and peasantry" such as he was promoting.[32]

Until the winter of 1916-1917 the Paris Commune was minor in Lenin's thought; now the Commune dominated his studies of the state. Lenin made a note to himself: "Marx's basic idea reads: the conquest of political power by the proletariat does not consist of the seizure of a 'ready-made' state machinery, but its 'smashing,' 'destruction,' and replacement by a new one. . . . The whole matter can be expressed in a nutshell as follows: replacement of the old ('ready-made') state machinery and parliaments by soviets of workers deputies and by persons authorized by them."[32a] It seemed to Lenin that the soviets in 1905 had initiated—if only hesitantly and feebly—the smashing of the old state power demanded by Marx; a future revolution would have to complete this task.

Thus the February Revolution in Russia coincided with Lenin's new theoretical perceptions concerning *State and Revolution*. The Petrograd soviet's establishment and prominence made Lenin apply those new insights to the concrete revolutionary situation, an important conjunction of theory and practice which can be followed step by step in Lenin's first written expressions concerning the soviets in March 1917. As soon as news from Russia reached him he noticed the dual nature of the new power, the parallelism of the Provisional

Government and the Petrograd soviet. The latter seemed to him "a new, unofficial, still undeveloped, still relatively weak workers government."[33] "The Soviet of Workers and Soldiers Deputies is the nucleus of a workers government."[34] These sentences repeat almost word for word the description in 1906 of the soviets during the first Russian revolution. At that time Lenin had said that one must study these "nuclei of the new power . . . its condition and its success"; now he declared unequivocally that the revolution's next task would be "the conquest of power through a workers government"—that is, through the soviets.[35] In his third "Letter from Abroad" of March 11, 1917, Lenin announced a special article about the assessment of the Paris Commune by Marx and Engels and its "distortion" by Kautsky—a reference to *State and Revolution,* written later. In the same letter he also related his previous analysis of the soviets to Marx's interpretation of the Commune and to the new soviets. He wrote: "What should the soviets do? They must be considered as organs of insurrection, as organs of revolutionary state power—as we wrote in Number 47 of the Geneva *Sozialdemokrat* on October 13, 1915. This theoretical statement, based on the experiences of the Commune[36] and the Russian Revolution of 1905, must be elucidated and developed more concretely to reflect the current revolution in Russia."[37] From now on Lenin sees a straight line of development from the Commune of 1871 by way of the 1905 soviets to the soviets of 1917—all were by nature new proletarian states, superior to the bourgeois-democratic republic.

Lenin thought that the 1905 soviets had been only temporary militant organizations but that they could have taken power during the 1917 February Revolution; instead they ceded it voluntarily to the bourgeois government, contenting themselves with control over that government, thus creating the "dyarchy." Therefore, the Bolshevik revolutionary program had to be modified in essential points. "We must try to supplement and correct the old 'formulas' of Bolshevism, for though clearly they were substantially correct, their concrete application was not. Earlier, no one thought of dyarchy, nor could anyone think of it."[38] The phrase concerning "old formulas" of Bolshevism was aimed directly at the "old Bolsheviks," who opposed Lenin's new program of revolution. His April Theses were read at a meeting of leading party functionaries and at a joint Bolshevik-Menshevik conference immediately after his arrival in

Petrograd on April 4, 1917, and the effect on listeners was described by several eye-witnesses as completely surprising, provocative, and controversial.[39] They signified a complete reversal in the life of the party.

Lenin's startling theses were a resumé of his new theory of revolution and of the resultant Bolshevik party tactics. Its basic concepts were:

1) Even under the new Provisional Government the war remains imperialist and therefore forfeits support of the "class-conscious proletariat" and its party.

2) "Russia's present situation is distinctive as a *transition* from the first stage of revolution—which brought the bourgeoisie to power because the proletariat lacked class-consciousness and organization —to the *second* stage, which must empower the proletariat and the poor peasantry." (Second Thesis.)

3) No support for the Provisional Government, but struggle against it for soviet power, a new superior state. "No parliamentary republic—to return to it from the workers soviets would be a step backward—but a republic of the soviets throughout the country, from the bottom to the top." (Fifth Thesis.)

4) The task of the Bolshevik Party, still a minority in the soviets, must be "patient, systematic, persevering clarification of errors and tactics, especially geared to the masses' practical needs . . . at the same time agitation for the indispensable transfer of the total state power to the workers soviets so that the masses may learn through experience." (Fourth Thesis.)[40]

Lenin's theses were published only in his own name, and *Pravda* labeled them "the personal opinion of Comrade Lenin."[41] The majority of the party by no means sided with Lenin. Even the Central Committee Bureau, which in the preceding weeks had defended a "leftist" course, did not share Lenin's radicalism. His theses were rejected by a vote of 13 to 2 (with one abstention) in the Petrograd local committee.[42] The strongest objection was raised by Kamenev, who with Stalin was responsible for the Bolsheviks' tactics before Lenin's return. He objected that Lenin's theses might be suited to the first steps of socialism in England, Germany, or France, but not in Russia. He claimed that they contained not a single practical answer to the everyday questions of Russian policy, and he offered instead a resolution by a conference of factory workers, which welcomed introduction of an internal "factory constitution" giving control and codetermination rights to factory committees but rejecting further steps toward socialism. "These workers understood clearly," Kamenev added, "that the way to socialism lies, not in the seizure of isolated factories, not in isolated independent communes, but in conquest of the central apparatus of government and economic life, in the transfer of the administration of the banks, railroads, supplies, to the proletariat as a class within the national framework."[43] Thus Kamenev exactly pinpointed Lenin's deviation from his earlier views. Until April 1917 the Bolsheviks, like the Mensheviks, followed the Marxist view of revolution, and imagined the transition to socialism as only a series of central nationwide measures by the proletarian government, with "despotic inroads on the rights of property and on the conditions of bourgeois production."[44] On the other hand the anarchist and Maximalist groups agitated as early as 1905 for direct local "socialization" of the factories.[45] Lenin's theses of the soviets' seizure of power represented a decisive step toward the overthrow of capitalism and toward socialism. It sounded to Kamenev and most Bolsheviks like an echo of those slogans, and Lenin was accused of having assumed Bakunin's throne.[46]

Beyond this, Kamenev's criticism questioned the essential nature of the current Russian revolution. "As far as Comrade Lenin's general scheme is concerned," Kamenev wrote in *Pravda* on April 8, 1917, "we consider unacceptable any assumption that the bourgeois-democratic revolution is completed and subject to the immediate transformation into a socialist revolution."[47] The "old Bolsheviks," whom Lenin accused of clinging to the "old formulas," continued to believe that the revolution was still in its first phase, to be logically followed by the "revolutionary-democratic dictatorship of the proletariat and peasantry," which the Bolsheviks had propagandized in 1905. In contrast, Lenin stressed that: "The revolutionary-democratic dictatorship of the proletariat and peasantry has already arrived in Russia [through] . . . the soviet of workers and soldiers deputies. . . . The order of the day already calls for another, a new task: the separation of the proletarian (communist) elements within this dictatorship from the small owners or the petit-bourgeois elements" (Lenin's term for the Mensheviks and Social Revolutionaries).[48]

The vehement discussions concerning the proper "formula" of the Bolshevik revolutionary program concealed a crucial decision about the party's future. For Lenin, the socialist revolution, seizure of power, and Bolshevik dictatorship coalesced into one. The ruthless fight against the other socialist parties required sole rule by the Bolsheviks. But to Kamenev and his followers this aim of Lenin's was dangerous. They wanted to be a "party of the revolutionary proletarian masses" and not a "group of communist propagandists"[49] who, if they seized power, could prevail only through terror. Kamenev's group disagreed with the Mensheviks and Social Revolutionaries, but nevertheless considered them in the socialist camp, while Lenin equated the moderate soviet majority with the bourgeois Provisional Government and wanted to proceed against the socialists, not with them.

Obviously Lenin's new theory of revolution agrees in essential points with the views on "permanent revolution" propounded by Trotsky since 1905. Already Trotsky had labeled as unrealistic the Bolshevik call for a "revolutionary-democratic dictatorship of the proletariat and peasantry" and had explained that the Russian proletariat would be forced to exceed the democratic program toward socialism.[50] In 1905 and later Lenin had often objected to Trotsky's popularized formula, "Down with the czars, up with the workers government." Now in April 1917, he wanted equally to distinguish his new perspective from Trotsky's theory, by pointing to the soviets as an already realized "dictatorship of the proletariat and peasantry," which must now advance to the dictatorship of the proletariat.[51] But in substance he had unquestionably come closer to Trotsky's view. As soon as he heard of the Petrograd revolution on March 6, 1917, Trotsky wrote in a New York newspaper: "Now, immediately, the revolutionary proletariat must pit its revolutionary organs—the soviets of workers, soldiers, and peasants deputies—against the executive organs of the Provisional Government. In this struggle the proletariat must immediately aim at taking power by coalescing the rebelling masses."[52] Trotsky's experiences in the first Russian revolution led him in 1906 to predict a great future for the soviets; the formation of the Petrograd soviet confirmed the correctness of his prognosis.[53] He had no difficulty, therefore, in joining Lenin's soviet program after his return to Russia in early May 1917, and he became one of the most consistent champions of soviet power within the Bolshevik Party.[54]

The party's future and its relationship to the soviets were decided at a series of conferences during April 1917, at which Lenin won over the party to his new revolutionary theory and tactics. He succeeded primarily because of his outstanding personal authority, but also because since 1903 the Bolsheviks had unremittingly warred on the "bourgeoisie" and the "half-measures" of the Mensheviks, and thus shown themselves to be visually ready for exercising hegemony in the revolution.[55] But the conference discussions also showed clearly that it was difficult for the party members to combine the party's practical aims with Lenin's new theories.

The actual nature of the soviets also caused disagreement. At the Petrograd municipal conference of Bolsheviks, Kalinin stated that it was incorrect to assert, as Lenin did, that the soviets represented the only revolutionary form of government.[56] The Moscow party committee generally stood further to the right than did the Petrograd Bolsheviks, and at the district conference of April 19–21 Smidovich explained that the soviets' general structure had made them neither suited for nor capable of government and administration. Before assuming power, the soviets would first have to be strengthened, extended to the villages, and brought under one roof.[57] At the all-Russian party conference of April 24–29, Nogin, another leading Moscow Bolshevik, expressed the opinion that the soviets would gradually cede their most important functions to the trade unions, political parties, and self-governing organs. The constituent assembly would head the state, followed by a parliament.[58]

Many Bolsheviks who recognized the soviets' great revolutionary significance were nevertheless surprised at Lenin's exclusivity, and wished to keep development optional rather than be stuck with a soviet republic. In fact, nowhere in the resolutions of the all-Russian conference is there a clear-cut definition of future soviet power as a form of government totally opposed to parliamentarianism, like that in Lenin's April Theses. The resolutions of the conference concerning the soviets state that during the second stage of the revolution "all government power" would have to pass "to the soviets *or* other organs that directly express the will of the popular majority (organs of local self-government, constituent assembly, etc)."[59] As in the question of the socialist revolution in Russia, which many leading Bolsheviks continued to view with skepticism,[60] the party hesitated to follow Lenin's program for a soviet republic and certainly had no clear idea of its possible consequences. As Sukhanov rightly noted, most Bolsheviks did not visualize the slogan of soviet power as a "most perfect state constitution" but simply as a momentary political demand, that is, the formation of a government with elements responsible to the soviet.[61]

In the meantime, during the weeks and months after his arrival in Russia, Lenin developed into a complete system his ideas concerning the soviets which he had conceived in Switzerland and formulated in the April Theses. He declared in numerous articles and speeches that "mankind has not until now produced . . . a higher, better type of government than the soviets."[62] Taking up Marx's analysis of the Paris Commune of 1871, he listed the fundamental traits of soviet power:

"1. The origin of power is not the law as debated and passed by parliament, but the direct initiative-from-below of the popular masses, direct 'usurpation' . . .

"2. replacement of police and army—institutions cut off from the people and opposed to the people—with direct arming of the entire population, so that the state order is protected by the armed workers and peasants themselves . . .

"3. either replacement of officials and bureaucracy with direct popular rule, or at least their placement under special controls, their transformation into simple agents who are not only elected but can be recalled at the first popular demand; their transformation from a privileged stratum . . . into workers . . . whose compensation is no higher than the usual wages of a qualified worker."[63]

This program of radical democratization of the state aimed at true "self-government of the people," and Lenin never tired of emphasizing its democratic nature. "What is necessary is not only representation on the model of democracy, but also the structuring of the entire state administration from the bottom up through the masses themselves, their active participation in every step of life, their active role in administration. To replace the old oppression by the police, the bureaucracy, the standing army, . . . with a truly universal militia: that is the only way. . . . The soviets as a self-created supreme power, are simply establishments of this democracy."[64]

Simultaneously with his effusive praise for the soviet system, Lenin sharply criticized parliamentarianism. Here, too, Lenin took up almost literally Marx's condemnation of the abuses of parliamentarianism in his work on the Commune. To Lenin, the soviets, like the

Commune, were legislative and executive bodies in one; the deputies had no preferred position, but were directly answerable to the voters.[65] Lenin's low opinion of parliamentary democracy did not originate in his reading of Marx's *Civil War* or in his experiences of the Russian soviets. Even before 1905 constituent assembly and parliamentary regime in Russia were only expedients for him, as indeed for most socialists, such as Plekhanov.[66] Lenin avoided open polemics against the upcoming constituent assembly, and the Bolshevik propaganda called for its prompt convocation, but his criticism of parliamentarianism nevertheless sought to devalue the constituent assembly in favor of the "superior" soviets.[67]

If, then, the soviets were representative bodies of workers, peasants, and soldiers, they were also, according to Lenin, by virtue of excluding propertied classes, organs of the "dictatorship of the proletariat"—or, more correctly, they *could become* such. For in the spring and summer of 1917 the soviets were still dominated by "petit bourgeois," which hindered their development. Just before the Bolsheviks seized power Lenin expounded on the proletarian-dictatorial state in *State and Revolution*, where he also attempted to interpret Marx's and Engel's doctrine.[68] He stressed the violent nature of this dictatorship,[69] but conversely called it a purely transitional stage toward the nonviolent communist society. The dictatorship of the proletariat, it is true, is directed against and forcibly suppresses the minority of the exploiters, but this is done in the name of the majority—the exploited. "Democracy for the huge majority of the people, and forcible suppression of the exploiters, the oppressors of the people—that is, their exclusion from democracy: thus is democracy modified in the transition from capitalism to communism."[70] Such a transitional state is, in Lenin's words, "no longer a state in the ordinary sense of the word."[71] "A special machinery of suppression, a 'state,' though still necessary, is already a transitional state . . . the people . . . may suppress the exploiters without special apparatus, through the simple organization of the armed masses (such as the workers and soldiers soviets)."[72] The "withering away of the state"—that is, the abolition of all classes and all compulsion—occurs during the second phase of the revolutionary reorganization of society, which turns communism into a reality. Lenin explicitly commits himself to the "final destruction of the state, that is, of every organized and systematic power, of every conceivable coercion of human beings,"[73] but on another page of *State and Revolution* he plainly states: "Clearly it is impossible to determine the moment of the forth-coming 'withering away,' especially since by its nature the process will take a long time."[74]

Conditions for the state's withering away will, however, already be created in the proletarian-dictatorship phase. In the section of *State and Revolution* in which Lenin describes conditions under so-cialism, he seems almost obsessed by the vision of a society that "is an office and a factory with equal work and equal pay." "If *all* people actually participate in the administration of the state, capital-ism can no longer maintain itself. . . . Registration and control are the most important requirements for 'starting the machine'. . . . in the first phase of communist society. *All* citizens turn into remunerated employees of a state of armed workers. *All* citizens become employees and workers of a state syndicate encompassing all the people. . . . When all members of society, or at least the overwhelming majority of them, have learned to run the state themselves . . . the necessity of any kind of government begins to wane . . . then the gate will stand wide open for the transition from the first phase of communist society to the higher phase and the complete withering away of the state."[75]

The picture of the socialist soviet state sketched by Lenin in *State and Revolution* was miles apart from real conditions in Russia and the existing soviets in 1917. Nowhere is the utopian nature of Lenin's theory of the future socialist and communist society more clear than in this vision of a state in which "*everyone* becomes a 'bureaucrat' for a time, so that just in this way *no one* can become a 'bureaucrat.' "[76] In Lenin's theory the soviets become the ideal of a state that removes bureaucracy but also carries out bureaucratic func-tions (everything Lenin termed "accounting and control"). The Bol-shevik economic program just before the seizure of power provided for the nationalization of banks and industrial syndicates and for the compulsory organization of the people into producer and consumer associations.[77] Between this forced and monopolistic state economy and self-governing soviets existed an irreconcilable contradiction, re-sulting from Lenin's general attitude toward the soviets. As Martin Buber[78] aptly expressed it, Lenin assimilated "the soviets into an action program, not into a structural idea."[79] With all the idealized glorification of the soviets as a new, higher, and more democratic type of state, Lenin's principal aim was revolutionary-strategic rather than social-structural. "That the soviets might not only exist for the sake of the revolution, but that, in a deeper, more elementary sense, the revolution might also exist for the sake of the soviets did not cross his mind."[80]

Lenin's attitude to the soviets, like Marx's approach to the Paris Commune, was dominated by the politics of revolution; his blueprint of the socialist soviet state in *State and Revolution* was the theoretic justification of the imminent seizure of power, evolved during the actual struggle. The slogan of the soviets was primarily tactical in nature; the soviets were in theory organs of mass democracy, but in practice tools of power for the Bolshevik Party. In 1917 Lenin outlined his transitional utopia without naming the definitive factor: the party. To understand the soviets' true place in Bolshevism, it is not enough, therefore, to accept the idealized picture in Lenin's state theory. Only an examination of the actual give-and-take between Bolsheviks and soviets during the revolution allows a correct understanding of their relationship.

2. "ALL POWER TO THE SOVIETS"— BOLSHEVIK TACTICS IN THE 1917 REVOLUTION

a) *Soviet Power as Tactical Slogan*

The February Revolution created the first framework in Russia for the development of political parties and the organization of the newly awakened masses. Lenin had developed the model of a party of professional revolutionaries around the turn of the century and as late as the Revolution of 1905 had only reluctantly taken advantage of increased freedom of movement. He "threw aside all sectarian inhibitions"[81] when in March 1917 his party had its first opportunity to gain the needed mass basis. He did not, however, sacrifice his old convictions. The party core, which was to make all decisions, was still to be the small circle of experienced revolutionaries, while the novice masses constituted the sounding board for Bolshevik battlecries. Lenin continued to combine tactical flexibility with rigidly directed party policy. This is demonstrated by his first public statements after the revolution in Russia. "We must now extend the party's sphere of action; organize the masses; attract new strata of the disadvantaged, such as agricultural workers and domestic servants; form cells within the army for the systematic, comprehensive unmasking of the new government; and prepare for the conquest of power by the soviets," he wrote on March 4, 1917.[82] On the previous day, however, he had voiced the fear that the new government might legalize the workers party, enhancing the danger of fusion of the Bolsheviks with the other Social Democrats. If the Provisional Government were to legalize the socialist parties (as proved to be the case), "we [i.e., the Bolsheviks]," Lenin wrote, "will continue to form our own party as before, and we will combine legal work with illegal activity."[83] These words do more than reflect the professional revolutionaries' old mistrust and the tendency toward conspiracy; they are basic Bolshevik policy up to October 1917, combining old conspiratorial tactics with overt political activity. Despite rapid numerical growth[84] and the influx of new groups, the Bolshevik Party remained a solid and rigidly directed semimilitary elite organization, in contrast, for example, to the formless, broad, and mass-oriented Social Revolutionary Party.

Even before the Bolshevik Party surfaced from illegality, the soviets sprang up spontaneously all over the country. Lenin stated at the beginning of March, "Organization—that is the slogan of the hour,"[85] and the mushrooming soviets were the natural centers for organization. "Now we must use the freedom of the new order and the soviets of workers and soldiers deputies and first and foremost try to enlighten and organize the masses," wrote Lenin in the first "Letter from Abroad" to his comrades in Russia.[86] The party organizations in the various Russian cities automatically followed this course; they had to help establish and organize the soviets, or stand aside from the mass movement. Lenin understood clearly that workers and soldiers were tied to the soviets, much more closely than to any party. He therefore decided that the Bolshevik Party policy must primarily rely on the soviets. He combined "the class formula of the Bolshevik program, 'All power to the workers and poor peasants,' with the organizational formula, 'All power to the soviets.' "[87] The soviets were the only serious counterpart to the bourgeois Provisional Government, and they alone could mobilize the masses' revolutionary energy. The proletarian and military masses, in ferment and newly active in politics, were barely reached by the emerging political parties. Ignorant of the ground rules of democratic government, they were easy prey for demagogic agitation. Lenin counted on all this, and though the two socialist opposition parties then held an overwhelming majority in the soviets, he believed that Bolshevism had a chance to separate the masses from their elected leaders—Tseretelli, Kerensky, Chernov. By urging the Bolsheviks to a ruthless battle within the soviets against the official soviet policy, he hoped gradually to attract the workers and soldiers now gathered around the soviets. Lenin's strategic plan of April 1917 allied the strictly organized Bolshevik Party with the politically inexperienced, malleable masses.[88] In this plan the soviets served as the "surest indicator of the masses' real activity";[89] they were, in Stalin's subsequent phrase, the "transmission" the party used to activate the masses.[90]

If the soviets were thus expected to spread Bolshevik influence among the people, Lenin also intended a second function. He hoped with soviet help to paralyze the weakened government and to undermine the Provisional Government and the military leaders at the front and behind the lines—in short, to remove as much as possible the obstacles to a Bolshevik takeover. The Bolsheviks therefore encouraged local soviets to usurp government and administrative powers; in the army they advocated election of superiors through the soldiers committees; and they goaded the peasants to expropriate land on their own initiative. At the All-Russian Party Conference in April Lenin eagerly collected news of the revolution's spread and of the role of local soviets. He concluded that in the provinces, unlike the major cities, where the Provisional Government had more power— "the revolution can be directly advanced by accomplishing absolute power of the soviets, by arousing the revolutionary energy of the masses of workers and peasants, and initiating the control of production and distribution."[91] He used the historical model of the French Revolution, which, as he said, had undergone a period of "municipal revolution," while local self-governments carried out the revolution in the provinces.[92] In Russia a similar development would be possible. "To advance the revolution means to realize self-government on our own initiative."[93] Lenin accepted the Menshevik program of "revolutionary self-government" of 1905, using even the same words. At that time he had vehemently refused to promote revolutionary "communes" as long as czarism had not been broken.[94] Now he declared: "The commune is very well suited to the peasantry. Commune means complete self-government, the lack of all regimentation from above. . . . The soviets could create communes everywhere. The only question is whether the proletariat will be sufficiently organized, but that cannot be calculated in advance, it must be learned from practical experience."[95] Accordingly, the resolution of the April conference again stated: "In many provincial towns the revolution moves toward independent organization of the proletariat and peasantry into soviets, disposition of the old authorities, creation of a proletarian and peasant militia, transfer of all lands to the peasantry, introduction of workers control in the factories. . . . This broadening, deepening revolution in the provinces means, on the one hand, an intensified movement toward transfer of state power to the soviets and toward control of production by the workers and peasants themselves. On the other hand, it guarantees for the gathering forces an all-Russian plane for the revolution's second stage, which must place all state power in the soviets *or* other organs that directly express the will of the popular majority (organs of local self-government, constituent assembly, etc.)."[96]

Lenin's program of "municipal" revolution in places followed almost verbatim the demands made by the Social Revolutionaries' Maximalist wing during the first Russian revolution[97] but it did not amount to a recognition of the superiority of local self-government over state centralism. Lenin's concluding speech to the Petrograd municipal conference contains the significant sentence: "We must be centralists, but at times this task will be shifted to the provinces."[98] Here is the tactical core of the slogan for communal self-government and local soviet power. Because of their intellectual origins and the history of their party, the Bolsheviks could never become sincere believers in genuine self-government. At this time, while writing *State and Revolution*, Lenin declared: "The Bolsheviks are centralists by conviction, in their program and in their tactics."[99] The slogan "All power to the soviets," ostensibly favoring local soviet power, was meant to disrupt the order of the state through removal of its organs. Not for nothing did Lenin demand the "smashing" and "destruction" of the bourgeois "state machinery" and its replacement "by a new apparatus of armed workers."[100] The workers, soldiers, and peasants soviets were supposed to prevent a new consolidation of the badly shaken state until the Bolsheviks could win decisively. Lenin hoped that the soviets' position under "dyarchy" could serve as his springboard to power.

The role assigned to the soviets in Lenin's plan depended on the degree of development in any given case. The danger of a "fetishist attitude toward the soviets as an end in themselves of the revolution,"[101] was no problem for the Bolsheviks. "For us the soviets have no importance as a form; what we care about is which classes the soviets represent," Lenin wrote in the spring of 1917.[102] In other words, at heart the Bolsheviks did not seek a better, more democratic soviet republic, though Lenin and the Bolshevik agitators had said they did hundreds of times; rather, they sought leadership in the soviets. "The soviets in themselves do not yet solve the question," Trotsky wrote on the eve of October. "Depending on program and leadership, they can serve various purposes. The program will be given to the soviets by the party."[103] For the Bolsheviks the soviets were never a question of "doctrine" or "principle,"[104] but of expediency. Lenin's theory of the soviets as a radical form of democracy is irrevocably tied to the soviets' practical role as leadership instruments of the Bolshevik Party. Winning the soviets, therefore, was the immediate tactical goal of the Bolsheviks in the spring and summer of 1917.

b) The "Peaceful" Development of the Revolution

Lenin was realistic enough to see that in the spring of 1917 the slogan of soviet power as he meant it—taking power through Bolshevik soviets—was still remote. His party represented only a small minority in all workers and soldiers soviets. It was therefore only logical that Lenin in his April Theses listed as the party's next task not the immediate conquest of power, but gaining a majority in the soviets. The Fourth Thesis therefore reads: "Recognition that in most soviets of workers deputies our party is a minority, for now even a feeble minority, against the bloc of petit bourgeois, opportunistic elements which transmit bourgeois influence to the proletariat. . . . As long as we are a minority, we must criticize and expose errors, at the same time agitating for the indispensable transfer of total state power to the workers soviets so that the masses may learn through experience."[105]

The final sentence juxtaposes the Bolshevik aim of a majority in the soviets and the demand for assumption of power by the existing Menshevik-Social Revolutionary soviets. A little later Lenin explicitly declared that "In principle we advocated and still advocate transfer of all state power to such an organization [the congress of workers and soldiers soviets], although at present it is held by the Mensheviks and Social Revolutionaries, who stand on the plank of national defense and are hostile to the party of the proletariat."[106] After the July rising, Lenin explained that in the spring of 1917 the slogan "All power to the soviets" had been "the slogan of a peaceful advance of the revolution": "Peaceful not only in that no one, no class, no serious power [from February 27 to July 4] could have opposed and prevented the transfer of power to the soviets. . . . Even the struggle between classes and parties could have been peaceable and painless within the soviets, if all state power had been transferred to them."[107]

The Bolsheviks pursued a dual course by waging ruthless war against the Provisional Government and striving to win the majority in the soviets but also demanding the immediate assumption of power by the moderate socialist soviets. Lenin knew that the moderate socialists would continue the war if they took over the government. He further assumed that the war would cause them to postpone solving the agrarian question. At the same time he counted on the soldiers' yearning for peace, the peasants' hunger for land, and the workers' impatience. These psychological factors, he thought, gave Bolshevism a chance to supersede the government's bankrupt socialists by "peaceful" means, that is, by gaining the majority in the soviets. "This plan does not, of course, mean the dictatorship of the proletariat, but it undoubtedly helps create the conditions essential to it, for by giving power to the Mensheviks and Social Revolutionaries and forcing them to enact their antirevolutionary platform, this plan will expedite their unmasking, their isolation, and their separation from the masses."[108]

Lenin's thesis concerning the possible peaceful assumption of power was not a reversal of his fundamental conception of violent revolution; it was formulated and propagated by him only in the specific, unique conditions of the spring of 1917 in Russia.[109] Lenin repeatedly and unequivocally professed his firm belief in civil war as the normal form of socialist revolution, the "peaceful way" being an exception,[110] which would not preclude future violent measures against the "class enemies."

The conditions considered necessary by Lenin for a peaceful development of the revolution did not occur, however. The majority parties in the soviet did not want a pure soviet government, preferring instead coalition with the bourgeoisie within the Provisional Government.[111] Further, Lenin carried on both an overt tactic of winning the soviets over from inside and a semilegal tactic of taking violent measures,[112] in the spirit of his statements after the February Revolution.[113] On April 21, during the foreign-policy crisis between the Petrograd soviet and the Provisional Government, demonstrations broke out in the metropolis, and the Bolsheviks sought to guide these with the slogans "All power to the soviets" and "Down with the Provisional Government." A few weeks later, during the session of the first All-Russian Congress of Soviets, Lenin planned a Bolshevik mass demonstration for June 10, but the congress prohibited it. In both cases the Bolsheviks sought "a reconnaissance of the hostile forces"[114] to determine the mood of the masses toward the Provisional Government and the moderate socialists. A few radical adherents, however, already favored more drastic steps to overthrow the government by a violent coup. Lenin himself adopted a wait-and-see attitude, and when these forays were vigorously rejected by the Petrograd soviet as well as the soviet congress, he was able to shift the responsibility to subordinates.

This semimilitary maneuver, which coincided with Bolshevik agitation for the soviet takeover, climaxed in the unsuccessful July insurrection. The history and the behind-the-scene events of the July crisis still remain among the least explored phases of the Russian Revolution of 1917. Immediately after the insurrection's failure the official Bolshevik version spoke of a spontaneous mass action which forced unwilling concurrence by the party, but most contemporaries believed the Bolsheviks had planned and staged the uprising to achieve power. Apparently Lenin planned an action for a later time, when the failure of the Kerensky offensive would have domestic repercussions, but was forced by the premature action of Petrograd workers and soldiers and Kronstadt sailors to join the movement. Beyond dispute, immediately before the July demonstration Bolshevik agitation in the capital's factories and regiments was in full swing without, however, directly advocating action. At the same time the Bolshevik faction in the workers section of the Petrograd soviet tried to topple the majority and seize the section. There was, however, no agreement in the Bolshevik executive bodies on next steps. As in April and June, the Central Committee and the majority of the Petrograd municipal committee advocated caution, while the party's military organization and the Kronstadt Bolsheviks—partly on their own—sought a more radical solution. The July uprising was undertaken only half-heartedly by the Bolsheviks; it failed partly because of the party's indecisiveness.[115]

The armed demonstration of July 3–5, 1917, occurred under the slogan "All power to the soviets" and demanded that the All-Russian Executive Committee take over the government. True to its fundamental political orientation, however, the Menshevik-Social Revolutionary soviet Executive Committee refused to accept the rule offered it from the streets and instead called in government troops to put down the insurrection. Turning against the rebels and the Bolsheviks, the Executive Committee declared: "whereas they proposed that state power should belong to the soviets, they were the first to attack this power."[116] An editorial in the Petrograd *Izvestija* mentioned the damaging consequences for the entire soviet democracy: "Under the influence of the completely irresponsible agitation of the Bolsheviks who exploit for their own ends the natural discontent and excitement of the proletarian and military masses brought on by the severe economic crisis, a segment of the Petrograd proletariat and army took to the streets with weapons. What did the deluded worker and soldier comrades hope to achieve yesterday? Their banners spoke of transfer of all power to the soviets and of the end of the war. But did they not themselves rise in the first place against the soviets of all Russia? Did they not shake the authority and strength of the soviets? . . . The workers and soldiers who yesterday took to the streets wanted to impose their will on all of revolutionary Russia by armed force. What will happen if this or another attempt is successful? When the recognized minority in our democracy wants to force its will on the whole country, against the people and even against the majority of the Petrograd soldiers? That day will see the downfall of the revolution, for it can develop successfully only if it is supported and led by organizations that execute the will of the democratic majority."[117]

Izvestija's criticism touched the sore spot of the Bolshevik conception of soviet democracy. Lenin openly admitted that even if the existing soviets assumed power ("if they should become a revolutionary parliament with unlimited power"), he would not submit to decisions abridging the freedom of Bolshevik agitation. "In that case we would prefer to become an illegal, officially persecuted party, but we would not renounce our Marxist, internationalist principles."[118] This means that if the revolution developed "peacefully" the Bolsheviks would fight a socialist soviet government with the same means used heretofore against the coalition government. Lenin, who called the soviet republic the highest form of democracy, denied that decisions of the soviet majority bound the minority. Democracy to him was only "a battlefield, the terrain on which Bolshevik power was best able to maneuver because it was not democratic."[119]

c) Tactical Experiments

The July events caused a deep break in the development of the revolution and Bolshevik revolutionary tactics, and more immediately a definite setback for the Bolsheviks. Court proceedings were instituted against the leaders (which Lenin evaded by flight to Finland); the press carried on an intensive campaign against the "German agents"; the activities of their organizations were restricted and kept under surveillance. The highest organs of "revolutionary democracy," the All-Russian Central Executive Committee of Workers and Soldiers Soviets and the Executive Committee of Peasants Soviets, as well as several provincial soviets, condemned the Bolshevik action.[120] Kerensky became leader of the Provisional Government and tried to mend the crumbling coalition between socialists and the bourgeoisie as the "savior of Russia," standing above parties. The following weeks and months would show whether his personality was strong enough to cement the diverging forces and to bridge the steadily increasing class antagonism.

For the Bolsheviks the failure of the July insurrection necessitated revision of their previous tactics. The slogan of "All power to the soviets" seemed to have lost its meaning with the renewed refusal of the moderate soviet majority to assume power. Within a few days, therefore, Lenin set an entirely different tactical course. He declared that "all hope for peaceful development of the Russian revolution" had "finally vanished." "The objective situation is either victory of the military dictatorship, with all its consequences, or victory, in a decisive battle of the workers, which is possible only as a powerful mass rising against the government and the bourgeoisie because of economic collapse and prolongation of the war."[121] With this Lenin formulated the principle underlying Bolshevik tactics until the October Revolution. The words "decisive battle of the workers" were a deliberate euphemism for an armed rising, which Lenin could not proclaim publicly; he did not call for action until several weeks later. The preparations, however, were to begin at once. "Without relinquishing legality, but also without ever overestimating it, the party . . . must combine legal with illegal activity. . . . Immediately and for every purpose establish illegal organizations or cells."[122]

Lenin rejected as no longer timely the slogan "All power to the soviets." In furious attacks he accused the moderate soviet leaders of treason against the revolution and of depriving the soviets of power, transforming them into a "figleaf of counterrevolution."[123] The soviets, he claimed, had become "ciphers, puppets; the real power is not in them."[124] "The slogan of transferring power to the soviets would now sound quixotic or mocking. Objectively this slogan would mean leading the people astray, feeding them the illusion that the soviets could still obtain power merely by deciding to get it, as if there still were parties in the soviets that had not sullied themselves by abetting the executioners, as if what has been done could be undone."[125] The now detrimental slogan must be replaced by the open call for the conquest of power by the proletariat. "The goal of the battle can only be the transfer of power to the proletariat, supported by the poor peasantry, for implementation of our party program."[126] This was the first barely veiled proclamation that the Bolsheviks aimed to win sole power. Lenin aimed to take power for his party with or against the soviets. The moment he no longer believed that he could achieve supremacy through the soviets, he dropped them. Plainly, to him the soviets were only pawns and had no intrinsic value as a superior democratic form of government. Trotsky, who joined the Bolshevik Party in July and became Lenin's most faithful aide in the preparations for insurrection, emphatically stated that "Important as the role and future of the soviets may be, for us it remains altogether subordinate to the struggle of proletarian and semiproletarian masses of the city, the army, and the village for political power, for revolutionary dictatorship."[127]

Lenin's proposal to abandon the old slogan of soviet power evoked an ambivalent response in the Bolshevik Party. While there was general agreement that the soviets' role had diminished after the July events, opinions differed on their future importance. At the second Bolshevik Petrograd municipal conference, which resumed its interrupted sessions on July 16, Stalin sided with Lenin: "To give power to the soviets, which in reality silently work with the bourgeoisie, means to play into the enemy's hands. If we win, we can entrust power only to the working class supported by the poorest people. We must devise another, more appropriate organizational form for the soviets."[128] Molotov seconded him, emphasizing the specific class nature of soviet power, proletarian dictatorship based on the poor peasantry.[129] Other speakers specifically opposed replacing the old slogan of soviet power by dictatorship of the proletariat; they stressed that the class nature of the revolution had not changed in the July days and that "under the given circumstances the dictatorship of the proletariat will be based, not on the majority of the population, but on the power of bayonets."[130] To renounce the soviet slogan would be dangerous, since the majority of "revolutionary democracy" had rallied around the soviets and the Bolsheviks could become isolated.[131] Stalin answered the critics that the party "is, of course, in favor of those soviets in which it commands a majority. The heart of the matter is not the institution, but which class will prevail in the institution."[132]

Among the Moscow Bolsheviks, too, a strong group advocated retaining the old soviet slogan. When Lenin was most harshly attacking the moderate majority in the soviets, the Bolshevik Smidovich stated at a joint session of the Moscow workers and soldiers soviet: "When we speak of transferring power to the soviets, this does not mean that the power passes to the proletariat, since the soviets are composed of workers, soldiers, and peasants; it does not mean that we are now experiencing a socialist revolution, for the present revolution is bourgeois-democratic." His resolution demanded transfer of power to the soviets for execution of the program of the *entire* revolutionary democracy.[133] These and similar statements revive the old conception of the "revolutionary-democratic dictatorship of the proletariat and peasantry" in the soviet, which Lenin in his April Theses had termed superseded. When Lenin after the July events recommended a direct Bolshevik takeover, misgivings repressed in April were restated. If in April they opposed Lenin's slogan "All power to the soviets" because it seemed too advanced, they now defended the soviet slogan against Lenin. While Lenin and his adherents searched for new revolutionary organs with which the Bolsheviks could mobilize the masses (such as the factory committees),[134] followers of the soviet slogan declared that the soviets were the sole basis of the revolution and that they should be conquered only from within, not attacked from without.[135]

Divergent conceptions also dominated deliberations of the Sixth Bolshevik Party Congress, which was held semilegally in Petrograd from July 26 to August 3, 1917.[136] The old party leaders Lenin, Zinoviev, and Kamenev and the newly admitted Trotsky were absent, so Stalin delivered the principal address. He repeated Lenin's arguments that the dyarchy had disappeared and that the soviets no longer represented real power. Asked which militant organization he recommended to replace the soviets, Stalin replied evasively that though the soviets were "the proper organizational form for the struggle for working-class power," they were "not the only type of revolutionary organization" and that perhaps a "revolutionary committee" or the workers section of the Petrograd soviet (where the Bolsheviks were already in the majority) might assume this task.[137] Most important now, he stated, was to overthrow the present government. "Once we have won power, we will know how to organize it."[138]

Several speakers criticized Stalin's resolution. They rejected abolition of the old soviet slogan because no other had taken its place. For example, Jurenev, a member of the Meždurajoncy group that had been incorporated in the party, stated: "Stalin's resolution contains a grave danger for the revolution. . . . The facts demonstrate that the soviets still represent an active revolutionary force. By accepting Stalin's resolution, we will soon isolate the proletariat from the peasantry and the masses. . . . There is no way except the transfer of power to the soviets."[139] Other speakers pointed out that the battlecry of soviet power had become so intimately bound up with Bolshevism that the masses "identify almost the total content of the revolution with it."[140] Nogin, a leading Moscow Bolshevik, also advocated retention of the old slogan, since a new revolutionary upsurge could be expected soon which would strengthen the Bolsheviks' influence in the soviets.[141] Several provincial delegates pointed out that in their areas the soviets, unlike the All-Russian Central Executive Committee, continued to be revolutionary, and that therefore the Bolshevik soviet slogan must be retained for the provinces.[142]

On the other hand a number of delegates thought that the July events had incontrovertibly proved the counterrevolutionary nature of the soviets. Since the soviets had refused to assume power, they could no longer be recommended as organs of power. Sokolnikov declared: "I do not know in what manual of instructions for Marxists it is written that only the soviets can be revolutionary organs. Surely instruments of insurrection may be completely different institutions. . . . The heart of the matter is not the soviets but unification of the masses for insurrection."[143] Bubnov emphasized that differences of opinion within the party ran deep: what was at stake, he said, was either dictatorship of the proletariat supported by the poorer peasantry or dictatorship of both proletariat and peasantry. After the July rising the former was imperative. "At present the soviets have no power whatsoever, they are rotting, one must hold no illusions about this. . . . The slogan of power to the soviets must be discarded; we must not cling to the old formulas, which are valuable only when they reflect the wishes and mood of the revolutionary masses. New forms may emerge that better express the aspirations of the lowest levels— for example, the factory committees. . . . We must once and for all bury the hope for continued peace. As realistic politicians, we will endorse such organs as will emerge from the class struggle itself."[144]

This extreme view, denying any value whatever to the soviets, meant to a third group that "the baby is being thrown out with the bath water. . . . We must not denounce the form of the soviets because their composition has proved unsuitable."[145] This bloc of delegates, Bukharin among them, wanted to retain the soviets but transform them by new elections into Bolshevik organs, and if necessary organize more new soviets."[146] Thus Bukharin forecast actual changes made during the October Revolution and under Bolshevik rule.

Finally adopted almost unanimously, the resolution on the political situation was in some ways a compromise. The slogan "All power to the soviets" was replaced with the less specific formula proposed by Lenin, "Dictatorship of the proletariat and the poorer peasantry." The immediate objective read: "Liquidation of the dictatorship of the counterrevolutionary bourgeoisie." Hidden behind these abstract formulations lay the overthrow of the Provisional Government and Bolshevik claim to sole power. Although the soviet takeover was no longer mentioned, the party was nevertheless advised "to protect from counterrevolutionary attacks all mass organizations (soviets, factory committees, soldiers and peasants committees) and primarily the workers, soldiers, and peasants soviets; to hold and fortify with all available means the positions conquered by the internationalist wing in these organizations; to fight energetically for influence in these organs and to rally all elements who stand for unremitting struggle against counterrevolution."[147] Thus the soviets lost first place in the Bolshevik revolutionary program, held since Lenin's April Theses, but the party did not renounce them altogether, as some delegates urged. From potential power organs they became simply, in Stalin's words, "organs for unification of the masses."[148] The soviets' part in preparing and executing the Bolshevik insurrection remained undecided.

The discussions at the Sixth Party Congress show clearly the Bolsheviks' purely tactical evaluation of the soviets completely outweighing the idea of a rebirth of state and society which had been so important in Lenin's theory. To much of the Bolshevik Party the soviets still represented foreign bodies to be utilized and subjugated if possible, but also to be abandoned with an easy conscience if revolutionary policy required that. Three months before the Bolshevik October Revolution was consummated in the name of the soviets, the party officially diverged with them.

The assertion of Lenin and the Bolshevik Party.Congress that the dyarchy had disappeared and that power had passed to Kerensky's military dictatorship proved unfounded in the following weeks. Kerensky enjoyed neither the full confidence of the socialist soviet parties nor the support of bourgeois circles and the army. He called a "national conference" in Moscow for mid-August 1917, composed of representatives from every possible political and economic organization, but it did nothing but display the ever-increasing antagonism between the socialist left and the bourgeois right.[149] The crisis of top-level government became evident at the end of August through General Kornilov's attempted putsch and Kerensky's ambiguous part in it.[150] Responding to Kerensky's cry for help addressed to "revolutionary democracy," the Bolsheviks joined the Petrograd "Committee to Combat Counterrevolution." They obtained the release of arrested party members, but Lenin remained in his Finnish hideout. With reaction threatening, the Mensheviks and Social Revolutionaries moved further to the left, and contemplated quitting the coalition with the bourgeois groups. The soviets had once again proved themselves effective in halting the advance on Petrograd of Kornilov's troops merely by their appeal to defend the revolution.

Lenin suddenly adopted still another tactic in early September. He declared himself ready to resume the pre-July slogan, that is, to endorse a government of Social Revolutionaries and Mensheviks responsible to the soviets. "Now—and only now, perhaps only for a few days or only one or two weeks—such a government could be formed and consolidated completely peacefully and perhaps even guarantee peaceful growth of the entire Russian revolution."[151] If his proposals were accepted, Lenin demanded complete freedom to agitate for the Bolsheviks. He counted on infighting to destroy the Menshevik and Social Revolutionary parties and ease formation of a Bolshevik majority in the soviets. "In a true democracy we would have nothing to fear, for life is on our side"[152]—a sentence worth noting in view of developments after the Bolshevik October Revolution. As in the spring of 1917, Lenin still refused Bolshevik participation in a coalition government of the soviet parties, since that "would be impossible for an internationalist without actually realizing conditions for the dictatorship of the proletariat and poor peasants."[153]

The Mensheviks and Social Revolutionaries, however, did not agree to the compromise suggested by Lenin. They were not content with "serving as the agent that transfers power from the bourgeoisie to the proletariat."[154] The majority still clung to a coalition with the bourgeoisie, because they were afraid that otherwise mass anarchy furthered by the Bolsheviks would lead to loss of the ideal revolutionary goals. The Democratic Conference called in Petrograd for September 14, 1917, by the central soviets was to serve as a representative assembly of "revolutionary democracy" to find a way out of the impasse created by the Kornilov putsch. The composition of the conference was considerably broader than that of the All-Russian Congress of Workers and Soldiers Soviets of June. With 230 delegates from the workers and soldiers soviets and an equal number of peasants delegates, there were 300 representatives from the municipal dumas, 200 from the zemstvos, 100 from the trade unions, 83 from army organizations, and others from numerous small ethnic and professional groups.[155] Votes on the conference's central question of coalition with bourgeois forces showed continued conflict.[156] After heated debates between moderate socialists and Bolsheviks, during which the latter temporarily walked out of the meeting, the vote finally favored participation in the bourgeois government by 829 to 106, with 69 abstentions.[157] Before the conference adjourned, a "council of the republic" was elected with proportionate representation: 388 representatives of "democracy," and 167 delegates from the bourgeoisie and ethnic groups. This preparliament was to control the Provisional Government until the constituent assembly could be convoked.

Lenin's attitude toward the Democratic Conference was ambiguous. As before the July uprising, he again followed an equivocal tactic. On September 26 he publicly repeated his proposal for a compromise soviet government composed of Mensheviks and Social Revolutionaries ("probably that is the last chance of a peaceful development of the revolution");[158] but earlier, on September 13, he had said in a secret letter to the party's Central Committee: "It would be the greatest mistake to believe that our compromise proposal has not yet been rejected, that the 'Democratic Conference' might still accept it."[159] In the same letter Lenin advocated immediate armed rebellion. "It would be the greatest mistake, the worst kind of parliamentary idiocy [!] on our part to regard the Democratic Conference as a parliament, for even if it had proclaimed itself the sovereign parliament of the revolution, it would have nothing to decide: the power of decision lies elsewhere, in the workers quarters of Petrograd and Moscow."[160] In dramatic elections in these cities during early September, the Bolsheviks for the first time had won a majority in the soviets. Now Lenin's renewed call for soviet power, which after the Kornilov putsch had been a purely tactical maneuver, led directly to preparations for the Bolshevik takeover. "For this reason," Trotsky wrote, "the slogan 'Power to the soviets' was not removed from the agenda a second time, but it was given a new meaning: all power to the *Bolshevik* soviets. In this formulation the slogan finally ceased to be a call for peaceful development. The party approaches armed uprising through the soviets and in the name of the soviets."[161]

d) Bolshevizing the Soviets and Preparing for Insurrection

Until August 1917 the Bolsheviks had the backing of only a small minority of the Russian people and were the smallest among the three major socialist parties in the soviets, the municipal dumas, the rural zemstvos, and the trade unions and cooperatives. Their membership amounted to about 80,000 in April 1917 and at most 240,000 in August.[162] But their influence made itself felt much earlier in the country's industrial centers and in the principal cities, especially among factory workers. Thus, the Conference of Factory Committees in Petrograd at the end of May adopted a Bolshevik resolution by a large majority; demonstrations in Petrograd on June 18 used almost exclusively Bolshevik slogans; and by spring the Bolsheviks held a majority in the soviet and the municipal duma of Ivanovo Voznesensk. But in most provincial towns, at the battlefront, and especially in the countryside, the Bolsheviks gained ground very slowly.

The unsuccessful July rising seemed briefly to slow the advance of Bolshevik influence; but after only a few weeks the party recovered from its setbacks. The Bolshevik help against the Kornilov putsch materially restored their popular prestige. The permanent crisis at the state's apex, the growing economic plight in the cities, the agrarian half-measures, and especially the lack of a firm peace policy rendered large sections of the Russian people receptive to the simple Bolshevik slogans that promised peace, land, and bread. For the first time Bolshevism became a mass movement, beginning in late August and early September 1917. The party, still relatively small in numbers, received the support of millions of embittered and hopeful people. For each party member there were twenty, thirty, or fifty "Bolsheviks" who were not members but sympathizers.[163]

This rapid growth of Bolshevik influence was reflected in the elections to the soviets, unions, factory committees, municipal and rural organs of self-government, etc., which took place almost daily somewhere in Russia, though growth was sporadic and scattered. Naturally the workers organizations showed this influence first. The factory committees in Petrograd and Moscow, in the Ural region, and in the Donets Basin had a Bolshevik majority as early as summer 1917.[164] But the unions, a Menshevik domain during the revolution's early months, also came increasingly under Bolshevik influence in the autumn. At the All-Russian Trade-Union Conference of June 1917 the Bolsheviks had only 36.4 percent of the delegates on their side, but of the 117 trade-union delegates to the Democratic Conference in September, already 58 percent were Bolsheviks, as against 38.4 percent Mensheviks and right-wing Social Revolutionaries.[165] By October all trade unions in the large industrial cities supported Lenin's party, except for the important railroad workers association, the postal and telegraphic union, and the printers.

The change in the masses' outlook is also evident in elections to municipal dumas, which show the proportion of Bolsheviks in the total voting population. At the August elections to the Petrograd duma the Bolsheviks increased their seats from 37 to 67, thus moving to second place behind the Social Revolutionaries, who had 75 members, opposed to 42 Constitutional Democrats (Kadets) and 8 Mensheviks (down from a previous 40!).[166] Most notable were the results of elections to the borough dumas in Moscow at the end of September. Compared with the elections to the Moscow municipal duma in June, the outcome was as follows:[167]

Party	Votes		Percentage	
	June	September	June	September
Social Revolutionaries	374,885	54,374	58	14
Mensheviks	76,407	15,887	12	4
Kadets	168,781	101,106	17	26
Bolsheviks	75,409	198,320	12	51

For the first time in a major city the Bolsheviks were able to amass an absolute voting majority, although the total vote was much smaller than in previous elections, only about 50 percent of qualified voters.[168] Trotsky judged this outcome to be typical of the situation before October: "The erosion of the intermediary groups, the considerable staying power of the bourgeois camp, and the gigantic growth of the hated and persecuted [?] proletarian party—all these were infallible signs of a revolutionary crisis."[169] Newspapers reflecting the previous soviet majority concurred and wrote that the general movement to the left would encourage the Bolsheviks to step up revolutionary activity and provoke civil war.[170]

The shift of popular sentiment was shown most clearly by the composition of the soviets, which had changed fundamentally since August and September. Although the process of radicalizing and Bolshevizing the soviets differed from place to place, so as to make it impossible to speak of a general Bolshevization of the Russian soviets at the time of the October insurrection, the accelerating swing to the left in the soviets was unmistakable. In this, too, the Kornilov putsch was the turning-point. Frightened by the specter of a counter-revolution, for the first time countless soviets appropriated the old Bolshevik slogan and sent telegrams to the All-Russian Central Executive Committee urging it to assume ruling power.[171] Among the soviets represented at the Democratic Conference, a bare majority still held to the old policy of supporting Kerensky's government; 86 delegates voted for, 97 against soviet power.[172] In the following weeks new elections were held throughout the country in the workers and soldiers soviets, in the frontline organizations, and in the superior soviet organs. Almost everywhere the Bolsheviks, the Left Social Revolutionaries, and small anarchist-Maximalist groups were considerably strengthened.

The subsequent success of the Bolshevik October insurrection depended on a preponderance of Bolsheviks in soviets holding key political or strategic positions. In Kronstadt, where the soviet had achieved sole power as early as May,[173] the new elections secured the left's majority: there were 100 Bolshevik deputies, 75 Left Social Revolutionaries, 12 Menshevik Internationalists, and 7 anarchists; the remaining 90-odd unaffiliated delegates mostly sympathized with the extremists.[174] In Finland the Bolsheviks captured a majority in most soviets (representing only the Russian population), especially in Helsinki and Vyborg, and came close to eliminating the Provisional Government's power as early as September. The soviets' regional committee declared in an appeal of September 21 that no order of the coalition government had any validity without the regional committee's endorsement.[175] In Estonia the soviets newly elected in September in Reval (Tallinn), Dorpat (Tartu), and Wenden (Tsesis) also had a strong majority of Bolsheviks and Left Social Revolutionaries; the regional committee, elected in mid-October, included 6 Bolsheviks, 4 Left Social Revolutionaries, one Menshevik Internationalist, and one right-wing Menshevik.[176] The Centrobalt, the organization of Baltic Fleet sailors, ignored all orders from Petrograd and dealt directly with the commanders concerning possible military operations.[177] The Fifth Army, considered the best at the northern front, in mid-October elected a new army committee with a Bolshevik majority.[178]

Thus the most important strategic positions in the environs of the capital were in Bolshevik hands. In early September the Petrograd Workers and Soldiers Soviet itself decided in favor of the Bolsheviks. Still impressed by the repulsion of the Kornilov troops, the Petrograd soviet the night of August 31 passed a Bolshevik resolution expressing distrust of the Provisional Government by a vote of 279 to 115, with 51 abstentions.[179] The existing soviet presidium of Mensheviks and Social Revolutionaries therefore resigned on September 5. The sparse attendance on August 31, a disadvantage for the old soviet majority, caused the existing presidium to schedule a new vote for September 9. *Izvestija* appealed to the soviet deputies to overcome their increasingly evident apathy concerning the soviet's work and to show their political colors in the upcoming vote.[180] While Menshevik speakers at the soviet session emphasized the fundamental importance of the vote, the Bolsheviks proposed merely to vote on the technical question of representation in the presidium—either proportional, as they proposed, or by majority as before. Thus the Bolsheviks also won over Martov's group and even the People's Socialist faction, the furthest to the right. When Tseretelli mentioned that Kerensky too was a member of the presidium, Trotsky vehemently attacked Kerensky. He reminded the deputies that in voting they would be taking a stand for or against Kerensky's policy. Calculated to impress the gray masses of workers and soldiers, and express their new mood, Trotsky's maneuver did not miss its mark: the Bolshevik resolution was passed by 519 to 414, with 67 abstentions.[181] In the following days the workers section and the soldiers section elected their representatives to the Executive Committee and the presidium of the soviet. For the workers section, the result was 13 Bolsheviks, 6 Social Revolutionaries, and 3 Mensheviks in the Executive Committee; for the soldiers section, 10 Social Revolutionaries, 9 Bolsheviks, and 3 Mensheviks. On September 25 Trotsky was elected permanent chairman of the soviet; after the vote on September 9 he took Chkheidze's chair, fully aware of representing the revolutionary heritage of the 1905 soviets.[182]

At the same time as in Petrograd, the Moscow Bolsheviks captured the majority in the soviet of workers deputies and at its joint sessions with the independent soldiers soviet. The Bolsheviks' strong influence among Moscow workers was already evident by the middle of August, during the state conference, when the trade unions, disregarding a resolution of both soviets, successfully called a protest strike.[183] On September 5 the workers and soldiers soviets passed by 355 to 254 the Bolshevik resolution.[184] Thereupon the existing presidium, headed by the Menshevik Khinchuk, resigned. On September 19 new elections to the workers soviet executive committee resulted in 32 seats for the Bolsheviks, 16 for the Mensheviks, 9 for the Social Revolutionaries, and 3 for the United Social Democrats. The well-known Bolshevik Nogin became chairman. In the executive committee of the soldiers soviet the Social Revolutionaries prevailed until the October Revolution, with 26 representatives against 16 Bolsheviks and 9 Mensheviks.[185] Thus at joint sessions of both executive committees the two factions were almost evenly balanced, and the Bolsheviks often remained in the minority. Their resolutions were passed at plenary sessions of both soviets.[186] Since the end of May 1917 the Bolsheviks had been the majority in the Moscow district soviet and in the provincial soviet.

Capturing the majority in Petrograd and Moscow the Bolsheviks won a new and lasting impetus for their campaign for soviet power, which had been temporarily interrupted. Earlier the moderate socialists could rightly point out that the soviets did not even want power, but not now. On September 21 the Petrograd soviet, in a resolution composed by Trotsky, called for consolidation and federation of all soviet organizations and the immediate convocation of the Second All-Russian Soviet Congress.[187] The struggle for and against a new soviet congress filled the next few weeks and in many cases yielded the Bolsheviks additional provincial soviets.

The First Soviet Congress of June 1917 had decided to summon a congress every three months. But now the Menshevik and Social Revolutionary Central Executive Committee hesitated to call a new congress, especially because it feared that the congress itself would respond strongly to the Bolshevik slogan of soviet power. After all, the Bolsheviks openly declared that the soviet congress would form a "genuine revolutionary government."[188] The moderate socialists further believed that the soviet election and meeting would distract the population from elections to the constituent assembly, scheduled for November 12, 1917, and that resolutions of the soviet congress might anticipate assembly decisions. Various resolutions by local and regional soviets emphasized the priority of the constitutional assembly and rejected a soviet congress.[189] When finally at the urging of the Bolsheviks the All-Russian Executive Committee decided to call the Second All-Russian Congress of Workers and Soldiers Soviets for October 20, 1917, the executive committee of the peasants soviets immediately protested. It asked the peasants soviets to send no delegates or observers; the All-Russian Peasants Congress was to take place only after elections to the constituent assembly.[190] In the following weeks the Central Executive Committee received numerous telegrams from the provinces and the front, also rejecting the soviet congress.[191] Conversely, however, the Bolshevik campaign for a "soviet parliament"[192] also gained support, particularly among the most important soviets. When it became clear that the congress would convene in spite of opposition by the higher army committees and the Menshevik and Social Revolutionary press, the Bureau of the Central Executive Committee on October 17 called on all soviets to send delegates to Petrograd, and put off the opening to October 25.[193]

During these weeks the numerous regional soviet congresses meeting reflected the political mood of the masses. The Moscow regional congress held in early October demonstrated a typically rapid Bolshevization and polarization. At the beginning of the deliberations the Social Revolutionaries offered a resolution opposing the transfer of power to the soviets, which carried by 159 votes against 132. But in another vote, three days later, the Bolshevik faction won 116 votes, with 97 opposed. Thereafter the Social Revolutionaries and some peasant delegates abstained, so that the Bolsheviks won by 143 to one (with 26 abstentions).[194] At many later soviet congresses Bolshevik resolutions were also passed, all calling for assumption of power by the All-Russian Soviet Congress and for removal of the Provisional Government. In Ekaterinburg 120 delegates from 56 Ural soviets met on October 13; 86 of them were Bolsheviks.[195] In this area the Bolsheviks had majority backing as early as the end of August.[196] In Saratov the Volga regional congress rejected a Menshevik-Social Revolutionary resolution and adopted a Bolshevik one on October 16. The moderate socialists thereupon left the congress.[197] At the eastern Siberian soviet congress, convoked in Irkutsk on October 11, the right-wing Social Revolutionaries and Mensheviks still held a majority and the Bolsheviks and Left Social Revolutionaries left the meetings precipitately.[198] But a few days later, at the All-Siberian Congress (consisting of 189 delegates from 69 local soviets), 64 Bolsheviks, 35 Left Social Revolutionaries, 10 Internationalists, and 2 anarchists formed a majority against 11 Mensheviks and 50 right-wing Social Revolutionaries.[199] The Bolsheviks and allied left-wing groups also predominated at the regional congresses in Minsk and Armavir (northern Caucasus), the regional conference in Kiev, the district congresses in Reval (Tallinn) and Sarapul, and the provincial congresses in Vladimir, Ryazan, and Tver.[200] The congress of the northern region, convoked in Petrograd on October 11, was especially important; over 100 delegates from soviets in Finland and the environs of Petrograd took part in it. In spite of protests by the All-Russian Central Executive Committee, which called the congress a nonbinding "private assembly," the delegates, who were almost exclusively Bolsheviks and Left Social Revolutionaries, passed Trotsky's resolution containing a barely veiled call to insurrection.[201] Thus Bolsheviks demonstrated their dominance in the strategic positions around the capital.

But the Bolshevik wave on the eve of the October rising had by no means inundated all the workers and soldiers soviets, let alone peasants soviets and frontline organizations. In some larger cities the moderate socialists retained a majority in the soviets, for example, in the workers soviet of Kiev, and in the workers and soldiers soviet in Tiflis, in Rostov, Vitebsk, Novgorod, Nizhni Novgorod, Vologda, Voronezh, Orel, Penza, Tula, Tambov, Perm, Simbirsk, Ekaterinoslav, and Archangel.[202] At the regional conference of the Donets Basin and Krivoi Rog area, representing over 600,000 workers, the Menshevik-Social Revolutionary resolution received 51 votes against 46 for the Bolsheviks.[203] At the provincial congress in Novgorod also the two moderate socialist parties still controlled the majority.[204] The regional committee of the Caucasian soviets in Tiflis on October 17 expressed itself against convocation of the All-Russian Soviet Congress.[205] In most peasant soviets, both on the district and province levels, the Social Revolutionaries continued strongest although the left wing was gaining. In numerous telegrams the peasants soviets rejected participation in the congress of workers and soldiers soviets.[206]

In contrast to the soldiers soviets in the garrison towns of the hinterland, where during recent weeks the Bolsheviks had been progressing rapidly, the central organs of the soldiers frontline soviets were still overwhelmingly held by the old soviet majority. All frontline committees (the highest representations of the fighting troops) were against the upcoming soviet congress. Most army committees also spoke out against soviet assumption of power, although units stationed nearest the capital (such as the Fifth and Twelfth Armies) were already under Bolshevik influence. The army congress in Finland elected an army committee of 24 Bolsheviks, 12 Left Social Revolutionaries, 11 right-wing Social Revolutionaries, 7 unaffiliated members, and 6 Mensheviks. On the next-lower committee level the Bolsheviks were already making themselves much more strongly felt. The congresses of the Sixth Army Corps and the Forty-second Army Corps rejected the Provisional Government and sent delegates to the soviet congress.[207] The Bolsheviks successfully mobilized the lower-level soldiers committees against the higher soldiers soviets, which had not been reelected for months; the lower committees for their part improvised soldiers meetings to elect delegates to the soviet congress. Such steps only deepened the rift throughout soviet organizations and increasingly weakened the authority of regularly elected committees. The soldiers committees, most of which until autumn exerted a disciplinary influence, now became an element in the army's disintegration.

A comprehensive view of the internal forces affecting soviet Bolshevization just before the October insurrection gives the following pictures[208]:

1) The Bolsheviks were in the majority in the workers soviets of most industrial cities and in most soldiers soviets in garrison towns. Their strongholds were:

    a) Finland, Estonia, Petrograd and its environs, parts of the northern front, the fleet;

    b) the central industrial region around Moscow;

    c) the Ural region;

    d) Siberia, where they were more or less evenly balanced with the Social Revolutionaries.

2) The Social Revolutionaries were still dominant in the peasants soviets and the frontline committees. A strong left wing, which finally seceded from the party during October, sided with the Bolsheviks, however, often assuring them of a majority in the soviets. The moderate Social Revolutionaries were strongest:

    a) in the black-soil region and along the middle Volga;

    b) in the Ukraine (with the ethnic socialist parties);

    c) at the western, southwestern, and Rumanian fronts.

3) The Mensheviks had almost everywhere lost the leading position they had during the early months in the workers soviets. Only in the Caucasus, especially in Georgia, where they still held the rural population, did they retain a significant superiority over the Bolsheviks in October 1917.

4) For the first time Maximalist and anarchist groups also played

a larger role in some soviets. In the October days they supported the Bolsheviks and contributed considerably to the radicalization of the masses.

"Now that the Bolsheviks have received a majority in both metropolitan soviets of workers and soldiers deputies, they can and must seize supreme power."[209] This lapidary sentence was the opening of Lenin's letter of September 13 to the Central Committee as well as to the Petrograd and Moscow party committees. It was the first of an increasingly frequent series of letters that Lenin directed from his Finnish hiding place to party leaders, spurring them on to take power. The preparations for the October insurrection show uniquely Lenin's genius as a political strategist, who recognized and utilized a singular chance to seize power, and his enormous drive to power. Almost alone, against opposition in his own party, he forced a decision which radically changed world history.[210]

Lenin considered Russia's internal crisis, and beyond it the international situation, ripe for an immediate Bolshevik takeover. He was clearly aware of the unique historical moment. Convinced of the political necessity for insurrection, he urged its preparation. "The insurrection must be treated like an art"—this sentence by Engels was the theme of all his letters and conversations during these weeks. The proper moment and location must be chosen, forces must be mobilized, weapons must be procured, and so on. Lenin considered and discarded the most diverse possibilities. In his letter of September 13 he named Moscow as the starting point for the insurrection,[211] then he daringly suggested surrounding the Democratic Conference in Petrograd and occupying the capital.[212] At the end of September he planned with Finnish Bolsheviks to start from Finland a march on Petrograd.[213]

Lenin's swing to armed uprising surprised even the Bolshevik Party leaders. The Central Committee decided to destroy his letter of September 13 and to forbid demonstrations in the barracks and factories.[214] Lenin's demand for boycott of the "preparliament" was rejected on September 21 by a vote of 77 to 50 by the Central Committee and the faction in the Democratic Conference.[215] Lenin doubled his efforts to force party support and at the beginning of October he even threatened to resign from the Central Committee in order to be free to agitate directly for the insurrection.[216] Circumventing the cautious Central Committee, he launched in the lower party organizations a vehement campaign for the armed uprising.[217] He finally steamrollered the Bolshevik resignation from the preparliament, but resistance against immediate insurrection continued strong. No one wanted to risk another defeat like that in July; every one believed in peaceful transfer of power to the soviets from the bankrupt Provisional Government. It was not until October 10 that the party Central Committee decided officially, with a vote of 10 to 2, to consider armed uprising.[218] But still powerful forces, such as the Petrograd Committee, were against rebellion, pointing out that organizational and psychological preparations were insufficient and that the masses were not ready to fight.[219] Hesitance prevailed also in many provincial party committees.[220]

The arguments employed by Lenin's opponents are summarized in the declaration by Kamenev and Zinoviev, written the day after the Central Committee's resolution of October 10 and sent to the most important Bolshevik Party organizations.[221] "We are utterly convinced that to declare an armed uprising now is to risk the future, not only of our party, but also of the Russian and international revolution." They denied Lenin's premises—that the majority of the Russian people and of the international proletariat were with the Bolsheviks. A Bolshevik takeover must lead to minority dictatorship and to the ruin of the revolution by the external enemy. The masses' psychological unreadiness to arm must be added to the objective obstacles to an insurrection. Instead of an adventurous uprising on the eve of the soviet congress, the congress must "organize the growing influence of the proletarian party and . . ." become "the rallying point of all proletarian and semiproletarian organizations." Thus the Bolsheviks were not to win as a minority group against the other left-wing groups but to enlist these, and to prepare for important elections to the constituent assembly, hoping for a third or more of the seats. "We will form such a strong opposition party in the constituent assembly that in a country of universal suffrage our opponents will have to yield to us at every turn; or else we will build a coalition bloc with left-wing Social Revolutionaries, unaffiliated peasants, etc., which must essentially carry out our program." The constituent assembly "will proceed in a highly revolutionary atmosphere" and act through the soviets. "The soviets, now rooted in life, cannot be destroyed. . . . The constituent assembly plus soviets are the combination-type state institution that we aim at. On this basis our party's policy has extraordinarily good chances of genuine victory."

Kamenev and Zinoviev clearly wanted transition from the bourgeois-democratic republic to the proletarian-socialist state to proceed by way of an intermediary stage, the workers and peasants republic. For the coalition with the left-wing Social Revolutionaries could have no other meaning. They relied on the objective laws of universal suffrage, which in Russia would give peasants and workers an overwhelming majority in the constituent assembly, and they also counted on the attractiveness of the Bolshevik program for the masses. This formulation modified the revolutionary program Kamenev had advocated before Lenin's April Theses, the "revolutionary-democratic dictatorship of the proletariat and peasantry," rather than the dictatorship of the proletariat that Lenin strove for. The idea of a truly democratic popular revolution was still so potent in Kamenev's mind that he exclaimed in opposition to Lenin: "Two tactics are at war here: the tactic of conspiracy against that of faith in the driving force of the Russian revolution."[222]

Lenin, however, was not bothered by being accused of "Blanquism" and conspiracy. Rather, in his letter of September 13 to the Central Committee concerning "Marxism and Rebellion,"[223] he accused as opportunists all who refused to treat insurrection as an art when objective conditions for it were ripe. Fascinated by the technical aspect of the planned insurrection, and fearing that he might be too late, Lenin was totally indifferent to whether the uprising had any legal cover or not. "It would be naïve to wait for a 'formal' Bolshevik majority. No revolution waits for that," he wrote on September 13 in his first letter to the Central Committee.[224] In this he even partially opposed Trotsky, who wanted the insurrection on the same date that the Second All-Russian Congress of Soviets was to meet. Lenin thought a postponement would be catastrophic. In an unusually vehement letter to the party he called this delay "complete idiocy or complete treason" and continued: "This congress will have no importance, can have no importance. First beat Kerensky, then call the congress."[225] As late as October 24, when the troops of the Red Guard had begun the uprising, Lenin made a last appeal: "I am trying with all my powers to convince the comrades that everything now hangs by a single thread, that there are questions on the agenda that cannot be settled by conferences, by congresses (not even by congresses of soviets) but that must be decided by the people, by the masses, by the struggle of the armed masses. . . . We must not wait!! We stand to lose everything!! . . . The people have the right and the duty to resolve such questions, not by votes, but by force; the people have the right and the duty, in critical moments of the revolution, to direct even their best representatives and not to wait for them."[226] It is clear here that the "people," for Lenin, meant the host of his followers who in their turn were to "direct" the masses. Behind the revolutionary fervor of the great historical hour stood Lenin's absolute will to power.

If, then, Lenin had so little respect for the supreme soviet organ, what role if any had the soviets in his plan for insurrection? The slogan "All power to the soviets" had been revived again in September; at this stage what did it mean? During these weeks Lenin reverted to the concept held during the first Russian revolution. At that time he had spoken of the soviets as instruments of the uprising against czarism. Now, in the autumn of 1917, he referred to the experiences of 1905 and wrote: "The total experience of the 1905 and 1917 revolutions and all Bolshevik resolutions . . . signifies that the soviet exists only as an organ of insurrection, as an instrument of revolutionary power."[227] The slogan "All power to the soviets" had now become identical with the call to insurrection. In 1905 the soviets could act only partially; during the February Revolution they did not need to act because the mass uprising had succeeded before they organized; in October they were to help the Bolsheviks to power.

But Lenin wanted to assign the task of insurrection only conditionally to the soviets. True, in mid-September he wrote that the Petrograd and Moscow soviets, with their Bolshevik majorities, should assume power. But the party should make the actual preparations, for Lenin feared that in the soviets, with their fluid majorities, practical preparation for the fight would be too difficult. The soviets' public deliberations were bound to harm the necessary conspiracy, although the soviets by this time could almost ignore government organs. Once the question arose of combining the Bolshevik insurrection and the soviet congress, Lenin decidedly favored independent action by the Bolshevik Party.[228] "At best October 25 can serve as camouflage," Trotsky wrote concerning Lenin's attitude, "but the insurrection must absolutely be organized beforehand and independent of the soviet congress. The party should seize power by force of arms, then we will have plenty of time to talk about the soviet congress. Immediate action is imperative!"[229] The Bolshevik Party should carry out the insurrection and then the soviets will sanction the successful assumption of power—that was how Lenin saw the October insurrection.

Lenin's determination was the driving force behind the Bolshevik takeover; practical details were handled by Trotsky and the leaders of the second rank. Because they were closer to events than was Lenin, still in hiding, they had to adapt his plan to prevailing conditions. The most important modification shifted practical preparations for the armed rising to the Petrograd soviet and thus combined the Bolshevik insurrection with the slogan "All power to the soviets," making the two almost indistinguishable to the masses. No matter how strongly the Bolshevik battlecries resonated, the majority of workers and soldiers nevertheless looked to the soviets and expected them to give the call to battle. Subsequently Trotsky wrote: "The broad masses were acquainted with the Bolshevik slogans and the soviet organizations. For them, both merged completely during September and October. The people expected the soviets to decide when and how the Bolshevik program would be realized."[230] If Lenin, impatient with fighting fervor, demanded insurrection in the name of the party as well, other Bolsheviks, especially Trotsky, wished power transferred to the Bolsheviks "on the ground of soviet legality."[231]

After they gained the majority in the Petrograd soviet, the Bolsheviks could prepare for insurrection under cover of this "soviet legality." Petrograd was threatened by the German offensive, and rumors spread of intended removal of government offices and dispatch of garrison troops to the front. These rumors created a nervous and explosive mood, especially among the soldiers. On October 9 the Mensheviks in the soviet Executive Committee proposed formation of a "committee of revolutionary defense" against the Germans. A Bolshevik resolution of the same day seized on this project and demanded that all such measures be placed in the hands of the committee.[232] On October 12 the Executive Committee, this time opposed by the Menshevik representatives but endorsed by the left-wing Social Revolutionaries, resolved to establish a military-revolutionary committee (voenno-revoljucionnyj komitet). On October 16 the soviet plenum approved the resolution and on October 20 the new body's first session took place, led by Trotsky, who was assisted by two members of the Bolshevik military organization, Podvoiskii and N. Antonov-Ovseenko.[233]

The military-revolutionary committee, officially created for defense purposes, was transformed under its Bolshevik leadership into the primary organizer of the armed insurrection. In opposing the Kerensky government's ostensible plans for removing the garrison from the city, the committee claimed authority over the troops. Commissars named by the revolutionary committee established liaison with the army barracks. On October 21 an assembly representing all regimental committees in the garrison declared that the soldiers would obey the committee,[234] and next day the revolutionary committee proclaimed that all orders of the district military General Staff (the formal high command in Petrograd) must be countersigned by the committee.[235] On October 24, finally, the revolutionary committee called on the Petrograd inhabitants to follow its orders, which had been issued "to protect the city against counterrevolutionary pogroms" and to defend the All-Russian Congress of Soviets and the constituent assembly. All regimental and company committees were instructed to sit continuously and to send two deputies each to the Smolny, the seat of the soviet and the revolutionary committee.[236] With this action the leaders of the Bolshevik insurrection opened the attack on the Provisional Government. That evening troops of the Red Guard and patrols of soldiers began to occupy the city's strategic points. Twenty-four hours later the Bolsheviks held Petrograd except for the Winter Palace, where the government was meeting without Kerensky, who had fled.[237]

Soviet sponsorship of the military-revolutionary committee assured its acceptance by the soldiers, which was indispensable to the Bolsheviks. Since the early days of the revolution the soviet had exercised rival authority alongside the military command. The Bolsheviks now were continuing this tradition of dyarchy, which crippled the government and reinforced the rebellion. Using a number of channels— soviet deputies, regimental and company committees, commissars, general soldiers assemblies—they allied the masses of soldiers or at least neutralized them. Through all this most soldiers and workers knew nothing about the real aims of the military-revolutionary committee. "The garrison walked into the insurrection, which it regarded not as a rebellion but as the demonstration of the soviets' undisputed right to decide the country's destiny. The party had to carefully adapt to the political temper of the regiments, most of which were waiting to be called by the soviet, and some by the soviet congress."[238] The workers districts, where attitudes toward active participation were mixed, reported that the masses would "act at the instigation of the soviets, but not of the party."[239] On October 16 in the party conference chaired by Lenin, a participant summed up the prevailing mood: "The general impression is that no one is rushing into the streets but that all will come when summoned by the soviet."[240] The Bolshevik tactics primarily aimed at aggravating this situation to the point of open conflict, but their aggressive intentions had to be concealed behind such slogans as "defense of Petrograd" and "struggle against counterrevolution." The military-revolutionary committee clung until October 24 to this fiction of protecting the revolution against enemy attacks,[241] and only later did Trotsky baldly admit that this was a deception.[242]

Another important circumstance favored the Bolshevik tactic of concealment. According to the Bolshevik campaign for the All-Russian Soviet Congress, which was in full swing, the top-level assembly of soviet democracy would decide on the assumption of power by the soviets. The attention of friend and foe was focused on the date of October 25. The people, adherents of the soviet system, and even Bolshevik Party members expected the change of government to take place "legally," by resolution of the soviet congress, to which the Provisional Government would have to yield. To the end Lenin remained vehemently opposed to coupling the insurrection and the soviet congress, wanting action in the name of the party. Trotsky, on the other hand, recognized the advantage for the Bolsheviks in diverting attention to the congress, but he had no "constitutional illusions" on this account. Later he quite properly stressed his fundamental agreement with Lenin, emphasizing that they had merely "two different attitudes toward insurrection on the same basis, in the same situation, in the name of the same goal."[243] But he also pointed out that his tactic of tying the insurrection to the garrison's conflict with the government and to the meeting of the soviet congress offered the smoothest possible assumption of power. Trotsky compared the soviets' role with a gear in a transmission system comprising party, soviets, and masses. "The impatient attempt to directly link the party gear with the gigantic gear of the masses by leaving out the intermediate gear of the soviets risks breaking the cogs of the party gear and moving only too few of the masses."[244]

Lenin and Trotsky both wanted to confront the soviet congress with an accomplished fact. Trotsky declared unequivocally that "Accommodation of the power bid to the Second Congress of Soviets contained no naïve hope that the congress could solve the power issue by itself. We were far from such fetishism of the soviet form." He never tired of deriding opponents who fell into this "trap of legality. . . . These people seriously believed that we were after a new soviet parliamentarianism, a new congress, where a new resolution concerning power would be introduced. . . ."[245] In reality power had to be seized and could not be achieved by a vote: only armed insurrection could decide the issue."[246]

e) The Soviets During the October Revolution

When the Second All-Russian Congress of Soviets met for its opening session on the evening of October 25 (November 7), 1917, the action of the military-revolutionary committee, begun the previous night, went according to plan; the Bolsheviks held the Russian capital. Lenin's party had won power by a surprise attack, before the congress itself could decide. A few hours earlier, at a session of the Petrograd soviet, Trotsky announced the deposition of the Provisional Government and openly declared: "The will of the Second Congress of Soviets has been *predetermined* by the uprising of the Petrograd workers and soldiers. Our immediate task is to enlarge and exploit the victory."[247] And on October 26 he stated at the Soviet Congress: "Openly, in view of all the people, we unfurled the banner of insurrection. The political formula of this insurrection is: all power to the soviets through the Soviet Congress. We are told: you did not wait for the Soviet Congress. . . . We as a party had to make it materially possible for the Congress itself to assume power. If the Congress had been encircled by junkers, how could it have succeeded in taking power? To do so required a party that could snatch power from the counterrevolutionaries and say to you: here it is—and you are duty bound to accept it."[248]

These words encapsulate the problematic nature of the Bolshevik soviet system: the party seized power in Russia in October 1917 and formally handed it to the soviets. The soviets did not initiate the reach for power—as did, for example, the French National Assembly in 1789. The Bolshevik insurrection, cloaked by soviet legality and nominal soviet power, was carried out behind the back of most soviets. Usurpation of power just before convocation of the highest soviet organ implied the Bolsheviks' break with soviet democracy. This fusion of new soviet power and the Bolshevik insurrection proved disastrous for the soviets themselves; after this, they were merely servants of the party and a cover-up for Bolshevik dictatorship—a role they never had contemplated, and for which they were unsuited. On the very day of their greatest triumph the soviets' decline began, and the banner of Red October, "All power to the soviets," soon proved itself a bitter illusion.

According to Lenin's and Trotsky's plans, the Second All-Russian Congress of Soviets was to legalize the Bolshevik insurrection and seizure of power and to provide nationwide support for the Petrograd events. A number of soviets had opposed a soviet congress and therefore had not sent delegates to Petrograd, so it was less representative than its predecessor, the First All-Russian Congress of June 1917.[249] In all, 402 workers and soldiers soviets and other soldiers committees were represented. Among the roughly 650 delegates, the Bolsheviks controlled a bare majority when the congress ended. The next-strongest group was the Left Social Revolutionaries. Disintegration of the previous soviet majority was shown by the weakness of right-wing Social Revolutionaries and right-wing Mensheviks; together they had less than 100 delegates, while left-wing Menshevik groups (around Martov and *Novaja Žizn'*) voted as independent factions.[250] Of the 366 soviet organizations on which records are available, 255 (69.6 percent) favored the slogan "All power to the soviets"; 81 (22.1 percent) were for "All power to democracy" or "Coalition without Kadets"; 30 (8.3 percent) were undecided.[251] The external image of the congress had changed as well. The old soviet leaders did not participate (except Dan, who opened the session in the name of the All-Russian Central Executive Committee). Instead, unknown delegates from factories, barracks, and navy, and the Bolshevik intelligentsia, took the stage.

The congress opening was dominated by the fighting still going on in the city. To avoid further bloodshed, Martov, leader of the Menshevik-Internationalists, demanded immediate establishment of a commission to negotiate a joint socialist government. To gain time, the Bolsheviks pretended to accept the proposal. Then their opponents, the right-wing Social Revolutionaries and the Mensheviks, committed a tactical error: they recited a protest against the Bolshevik insurrection and walked out of the meeting.[252] The night of October 26, with other organizations including the old All-Russian Central Executive Committee and the executive committee of the peasants soviets, they founded an All-Russian Committee to Save the Country and the Revolution to replace the Provisional Government, and issued a proclamation condemning the Bolshevik takeover as an illegitimate coup d'état.[253] The walkout of the right-wing socialists disrupted the congress and handed the Bolsheviks a welcome pretext for breaking with the "conciliators." In a deliberately provocative speech Trotsky now attacked Martov's compromise proposal; the "shabby outsiders and bankrupts" should get themselves "to the rubbish heap of history"; an understanding with them was impossible.[254] At that, Martov's faction and other small groups also walked out of the congress. When the second session opened on the evening of October 26, only the Bolsheviks, the Left Social Revolutionaries, and a few left-wing delegates were present. Lenin, in his first appearance from illegality, announced the peace declaration and the land decree.[255] Before it adjourned, the congress confirmed the new, purely Bolshevik government, the Council of People's Commissars, with Lenin at its head.[256] Sixty-two Bolsheviks, 29 Left Social Revolutionaries, and 10 other socialists (among them six Social Democrat-Internationalists, adherents of *Novaja Žizn'*) were elected to the new Central Executive Committee.[257]

On the day following the soviet congress, Maxim Gorky's newspaper wrote: "The Congress of Soviets was robbed of the chance to decide freely about today's most important issue, since the military conspiracy, cleverly staged at the moment of the congress opening, confronted the latter with the accomplished seizure of power. The new power (the soviet republic) and its political program were likewise predetermined by the appeal of the military-revolutionary committee.[258] As a matter of form it was proposed that the congress accept these same theses without discussion, in the guise of a solemn proclamation to the people. The 'parliament of revolutionary democracy' was transformed into an apparatus that mechanically gave its stamp of universal approval to the directives of the Bolshevik Central Committee."[259]

Although the congress of soviets confirmed the Bolshevik government, there was immediate protest against Lenin's one-party rule. Numerous local soviets, trade unions, and organizations of "revolutionary democracy," which supported the overthrow of Kerensky's government, demanded a broad socialist coalition government, "from Bolsheviks to People's Socialists." The weeks following the October insurrection were filled with negotiations, in which Lenin and Trotsky gradually outmaneuvered their strongest opponent, the All-Russian Union of Railroad Workers (Vikzhel) and a broad opposition within the party.[260] Only the Left Social Revolutionaries, on whose support the Bolsheviks depended, were admitted to the Council of People's Commissars on December 9.[261] The other socialist parties (even right-wing Social Revolutionaries and Mensheviks) were formally seated in the Central Executive Committee, but in practice they stood in increasing opposition to the soviet government.

The Bolshevik victory in Petrograd and the proclamation of soviet power at the Soviet Congress were not yet tantamount to Bolshevik assumption of power throughout Russia. Unlike the February Revolution, which smashed the czarist system within a few days, the Bolshevik October Revolution—which was directed not only against "junkers and capitalists," but also against the opposing "conciliator-socialists"—spread very unevenly. "Red October" in the provinces lasted for weeks and in places turned into civil war. The attitude of local soviets also varied widely; some immediately joined the Petrograd insurrection or temporized, while others were openly anti-Bolshevik. The party historian Yaroslavsky went so far as to assert that the revolution in the provinces (as distinct from Petrograd) had proceeded "not within the framework of soviet legality but against it."[262] Though undoubtedly an exaggeration, the statement nevertheless illuminates the problems raised by the Bolshevik description of the October Revolution as a soviet revolution. To conceal the widespread opposition among the soviets in October 1917, the contrary assertion is now made that the real mood of the popular masses had been far more radical than that of the soviets.[263] Where elections had taken place some time ago, this was occasionally true; in general, however, it was certainly false.

The Second All-Russian Congress of Soviets issued several proclamations which informed the people of the fall of the Provisional Government and urged local soviets to depose government commissars and assume power.[264] On the morning of October 25 the military-revolutionary committee of the Petrograd soviet had already called on all troop committees to support the new revolution and to take power.[265] During the following days the military-revolutionary committee systematically kept all frontline organizations and cities informed by telegram of the resolutions of the soviet congress and the course of events, but most of those telegrams between October 26 and 30 (November 8 and 12), were undelivered because of the postal workers' strike. Some important appeals reached the provinces by radio. The best and most reliable communication between the revolution's center and the provincial localities was furnished by delegates returning home from the soviet congress. In numerous cities the soviet joined the revolution after the delegates had reported. More than 1,000 agitators (primarily sailors, factory workers, and garrison soldiers) sent out by the Petrograd revolutionary committee and later by the All-Russian Central Executive Committee, as well as soldiers returning home from the front, served as emissaries of soviet power.[266]

Unlike the Petrograd situation, the Bolshevik takeover in Moscow created friction.[267] In mid-October militant Bolsheviks formed a center for preparing the insurrection, but made no further moves. The Moscow party committee, led by Nogin, favored a peaceful transfer of power to a socialist coalition government rather than violent action by the Bolsheviks alone. Conflicts between the parties in the Moscow soviet were not as sharp as in Petrograd. On the evening of October 25, a joint session of the workers and soldiers soviets resolved to form a military-revolutionary committee which the Mensheviks, but not the Social Revolutionaries, joined.[268] The latter took the leadership of the "committee of public safety," with which the municipal duma countered the soviet committee. For the time being, both sides were eager to avoid bloodshed. The garrison remained passive. The soldiers soviet was still dominated by Social Revolutionaries, and the Bolsheviks organized a ten-man council from the soldiers committees and advocated new elections to the soviet.[269] Since the anti-Bolshevik committee was indecisive, the Bolsheviks used the vacillating deliberations to rally their forces. By November 14 (new style), with the help of reinforcements from Petrograd and after violent battles, they occupied the city. In the new elections to the soldiers soviet, the Social Revolutionaries refused to participate and the Bolsheviks gained an overwhelming majority. On November 27 the workers and soldiers soviets resolved to merge and Mikhail Pokrovski was elected chairman.[270]

Outside the two principal cities, the soviets' role in the Bolshevik takeover varied from place to place, depending on the social structure of the region or city in question, the strength of the local Bolshevik party organization, and the soviets' political composition. In populous industrial cities the Bolsheviks had frequently prepared for the revolution and could act quickly and decisively. In localities where they held the majority in the soviet, they took power in its name. Elsewhere they formed special revolutionary committees that seized government offices, and forced the soviet to join them or simply bypassed it. The right-wing Social Revolutionaries and Mensheviks, protesting the Bolshevik action, most often left the soviet and joined with the municipal duma and other organizations to found "committees to save the revolution." The Left Social Revolutionaries, on the other hand, supported the Bolsheviks. In the weeks following the October rising new elections to the soviets were often held and usually resulted in a majority for the Bolsheviks and Left Social Revolutionaries. On the whole there was a confusing coexistence of disparate organizations, all fighting for power, while at the front, in the cities, and in the villages the remnants of the old order dissolved and anarchy gained ground.[271]

In the workers and soldiers soviets of Finland and Estonia, which before October had been under Bolshevik influence, the news from Petrograd resulted in immediate proclamations of soviet power on October 25 and 26 (November 7 and 8).[272] At Pskov, near the battle lines of the northern front, a "northwestern military-revolutionary committee" was formed with all socialist parties, also as early as October 25 (November 7).[273] On the other hand, the workers and soldiers soviet of Luga rejected the Bolshevik rising and declared its neutrality. In new elections in mid-November the Bolsheviks won.[274] The workers and soldiers soviets of Vologda and Vyatka were among the few in the northern districts that opposed the Bolshevik revolution, while the Archangel soviet, then dominated by Mensheviks, declared itself neutral.[275] The Bolsheviks' weakness in northern districts later helped the Entente in its intervention. In June 1918, for example, the Murmansk soviet broke with Moscow.

In the central industrial region, where the Bolsheviks most strongly influenced the workers even before October, the October Revolution went smoothly for the most part. In Yaroslavl the Bolsheviks appealed over the heads of the Social Revolutionary soldiers soviet to a general soldiers assembly, which elected a provisional executive committee and proclaimed the new soviet power.[276] In Tula Bolsheviks opposed a committee composed of all socialist parties, the soviet, and other social organizations. In the soviet the Bolsheviks remained a minority until early December, with 104 deputies against 120 Mensheviks and Social Revolutionaries. The soviet spoke out against the Bolshevik insurrection and for a common revolutionary front of socialist parties.[277] In Nizhni Novgorod the soviet was still overwhelmingly moderate-socialist at the moment of the October rising, but on October 26 (November 8) it resolved to hold new elections within three days. In the meantime the Bolsheviks formed a revolutionary committee, which proclaimed its assumption of power on November 10, provoking armed clashes with opposing duma forces. The newly elected soviet confirmed the Bolshevik committee's resolution by 136 to 83 but simultaneously demanded a socialist coalition government in Petrograd. For weeks to come a "dyarchy" of soviet and duma reigned in the city.[278]

In the black-soil region and along the middle Volga the struggle was chiefly for influence over the peasantry. The countryside was the domain of the Social Revolutionaries; the Bolsheviks exerted greater influence over urban workers and soldiers. In Voronezh the workers and soldiers soviet had by a bare majority protested the Petrograd insurrection and rejected the assumption of power. Thereupon the Bolsheviks, with the Left Social Revolutionaries, founded an action committee that seized the town in mid-November (new style). In new elections to the soviet at the beginning of December the Bolsheviks won 52 of 95 seats, and the Left Social Revolutionaries 23.[279] The soviets of Penza and Simbirsk condemned the October events and remained under Menshevik-Social Revolutionary leadership until December.[280] The Bolsheviks in Kazan succeeded as early as mid-October in gaining the majority in the joint workers, soldiers, and peasants soviet. A revolutionary staff directed the revolution, which established the Kazan Workers and Peasants Republic, with its own Council of People's Commissars.[281] In Samara a revolutionary committee from the workers and soldiers soviet proclaimed power the night of October 26 (November 8). The peasants soviet was opposed. By the end of November the newly elected workers and soldiers soviet numbered 350 Bolsheviks, 160 Mensheviks, 60 Social Revolutionaries, 32 Maximalists, 30 Social Democrat-Internationalists, 30 from the Jewish Bund, and 20 unaffiliated deputies.[282] In Saratov and Tsaritsyn the municipal soviets were Bolshevik before October. The change-over proceeded calmly and peaceably in Tsaritsyn, but in Saratov the soviet and the duma clashed, and the Bolsheviks prevailed.[283]

The central Ural region, the old mining center with a strong revolutionary tradition, was even before October 1917 one of the Bolsheviks' most important strongholds. At the time of the October Revolution most urban workers and soldiers soviets had a Bolshevik majority. In several large factories the workers, using their factory committees and soviets, had already placed production under "workers control." In most cases, therefore, power was transferred easily and painlessly within the framework of "soviet legality."[284] Many supporters of soviet power preferred a socialist coalition government to Bolshevik one-party rule; the Ekaterinburg soviet decided to replace the purely Bolshevik revolutionary committee by a "united revolutionary committee of people's power" that included all socialist parties. Even some local Bolsheviks advocated this compromise. In Perm, Nizhni Tagil, and Votkinsk the soviets remained Menshevik-Social Revolutionary until December.[285] In the southern Ural region the non-Bolshevik parties in the soviets were also strong. In Zlatoust, for example, the Social Revolutionaries maintained their slight lead even in the new elections in early December. Orenburg (Chkalov) became the starting point for General Dutov's anti-Bolshevik Cossack movement, which proceeded against the neighboring soviets and could not be put down until January 1918.[286]

In Siberia the controversy concerning soviet power was linked with the Siberian democratic organizations' efforts toward autonomy. After the October Revolution in Petrograd the soviet organizations in Siberia split; the Extraordinary All-Siberian Congress in Tomsk, dominated by the right-wing Social Revolutionaries, was opposed by the All-Siberian Soviet Congress in Irkutsk, led by the Bolsheviks. While the Tomsk group created a Siberian regional duma as provisional supreme organ, with representatives of all democratic organizations, the Irkutsk congress recognized the Council of People's Commissars in Petrograd.[287] The Bolsheviks' strongest support was in Krasnoyarsk, where the workers and soldiers soviet took power immediately after the Petrograd insurrection.[288] In Irkutsk new soviet elections in November gave the majority to the Bolsheviks and Left Social Revolutionaries, but were followed in December by several days of bloody clashes with the officer cadets of local military academies. Not until January 1918 was the new soviet power consolidated.[289] In the Far East, the Vladivostok soviet held power as early as June and in October assumed it officially. Here, too, the soviet demanded a socialist coalition government and constituent assembly.[290] On November 12 the workers and soldiers soviet of Khabarovsk recorded opposition to soviet power in view of the forthcoming constituent assembly; in December the Bolsheviks gained the majority and Mensheviks and Social Revolutionaries resigned from the soviet.[291] The Third Far-Eastern Soviet Congress on December 25 included 39 Bolsheviks, 22 Left Social Revolutionaries, and 11 Mensheviks, and established a Far-Eastern Council of People's Commissars as the highest regional authority.[292]

In the Ukraine the soviets on the whole had not made much headway, being strongest in the industrial cities with a Russian proletariat. Workers soviets and soldiers soviets usually existed separately, and political power lay in the Ukrainian Central Rada in Kiev, led by Ukrainian Social Revolutionaries and Ukrainian Social Democrats.[293] It was not until September that a regional executive committee of the Ukrainian soviets was founded; but compared to the Rada it had hardly any authority over the local soviets. In the weeks before and after the Bolshevik October insurrection, the Ukrainian Bolsheviks and the ethnic socialist Rada parties temporarily joined forces against the Provisional Government. The Bolsheviks, led by Piatakov, formed a revolutionary committee in the Kiev workers soviet on October 26 (November 8); this committee proclaimed union with the new soviet power. In subsequent clashes with troops loyal to the government, the Rada sided with the Bolsheviks. In mid-November the two Kiev soviets combined in a joint workers and soldiers soviet; the Bolsheviks received 14 of 30 seats in its executive committee.[294] In the soviets of Kharkov, Lugansk, and Ekaterinoslav the Bolsheviks were supported by other left-wing socialist parties and created revolutionary committees that assumed local power.[295] In Nikolaev a revolutionary committee, composed equally of representatives from the soviet and from the municipal duma, assumed power; the soviet itself, by a vote of 116 to 96, rejected a Bolshevik request for sole power.[296] The workers and soldiers soviet of Yuzovka in the Donets Basin by a vote of 70 to 46 adopted a Menshevik resolution condemning the Bolshevik revolution in Petrograd.[297] In Kherson a council of people's commissars was formed by representatives of the local soviet, the provincial peasants soviet, the district peasants soviet, and the municipal self-government.[298] The power balance was still entirely unresolved; local soviets, the Rada, municipal dumas, and various committees existed concurrently or concluded temporary coalitions. Only the All-Ukrainian Soviet Congress, which opened on December 18 in Kiev with about 2,500 delegates, many of them elected irregularly and randomly, staked out the boundaries for the future. Influenced by the ultimatum handed to the Rada by the Petrograd Council of People's Commissars, Rada followers gained superiority at the soviet congress, while the Bolsheviks and some Left Social Revolutionaries—150–200 delegates in all—walked out of the congress. They assembled in Kharkov in a new All-Ukrainian Soviet Congress formed jointly with the regional congress of the Donets and Krivoi Rog Basin, which was then meeting in Kharkov. The central executive committee of the new organization declared itself the temporary Ukrainian workers and peasants government. In the following weeks and months the Ukraine became an arena for civil war between the Red Army, which invaded the country, the troops of the central Rada, and the German occupation forces that soon followed.

The frontline troops decided the success and survival of the Bolshevik revolution.[299] At the time of the October insurrection hardly any of the soldiers committees, especially those of the higher ranks, were bolshevized. On the other hand, the military distrusted the Provisional Government; this became clear when Kerensky could not order troops against the Bolsheviks in Petrograd. The frontline soldiers, immediately after the October insurrection, displayed expectant neutrality.[300] "Not a single soldier for Kerensky and not a single one for the Bolsheviks," read a resolution by the Sixth Army committee.[301] Gradually, however, the Bolsheviks, helped by the propagandist decrees concerning peace and land, won over the troop committees, though sometimes only with slim majorities and with the support of Left Social Revolutionaries. The soldiers at the northern front (First, Fifth, and Twelfth Armies) and the western front (Second, Third, and Tenth Armies) were first to join the revolution.

At the congress of the Twelfth Army, which opened on November 9 in Wenden (Tsesis), the leftist bloc, supporting the new soviet government, received 248 votes in the decisive ballot, against 243 for the "socialist" bloc. Only three weeks later the leftist bloc won two-thirds of the votes at an extraordinary congress of the Twelfth Army.[302] By mid-December the Bolsheviks commanded an overwhelming majority at the first congress of the entire northern front.[303] In Minsk, which was the center of the struggle for control of the western front, the Bolshevik municipal soviet and the Social Revolutionary frontline committee were on opposite sides. As early as October 25 (November 7) the workers and soldiers soviet assumed power in Minsk, and with the Bolsheviks who had resigned from the frontline committee, it established a military-revolutionary committee of the western front. During temporizing deliberations with the opposition "committee to save the revolution," the Bolsheviks stopped troop movements to Petrograd. New army committees, with Bolshevik and Left Social Revolutionary majorities, were elected at the congresses of the Second, Third, and Tenth Armies in mid-November. Two-thirds of the delegates supported the Bolsheviks at both the western frontline congress and the regional congress of western soviets, held concurrently in early December. A council of people's commissars of the western region was elected as supreme soviet organ, prevailing against the White Russian autonomous movement and its organ, the Hromada.[304]

At the front far from the revolution's focal points the Bolsheviks had less support. The Ukrainian Rada acted effectively at the southwestern front (Eleventh, Seventh, and Special Armies) and at the Rumanian front (Eighth, Ninth, Fourth, and Sixth Armies), recalling the Ukrainian units from the front and taking command. At the extraordinary congress of the southwestern front, in late November in Berdichev, 267 Bolsheviks, 213 Social Revolutionaries (50 of them Left), 47 United Social Democrats, 73 Ukrainians, and 42 unaffiliated delegates were present. The congress split over the power question; 322 Bolsheviks and Left Social Revolutionaries called for assumption of power by the frontline army committees, while 232 Ukrainians, Social Revolutionaries, and Mensheviks voted against the proposal. The newly elected frontline revolutionary committee, in which the Bolsheviks held 18 of 35 seats, failed against the Rada.[305] At the Rumanian front and its rear lines the "Rumčerod" (Ispolnitel'nyj komitet Rumfronta, Černomorskogo poberež'ja i Odesskoj oblasti) controlled the highest authority before the October Revolution. The non-Bolshevik parties commanded a majority in it, while the Bolsheviks won the new elections in the autumn to the Odessa workers, soldiers, and sailors soviets. On November 10 a revolutionary committee was established as a coalition of the Rumčerod, the Odessa soviets, the socialist parties, and the Ukrainian Rada, but its heterogeneous composition paralyzed it. On December 23 the second congress of soviets of the Rumanian front met, with 854 frontline delegates, 106 from urban soviets, and 87 from the peasantry. The Bolsheviks with 396 delegates and the Social Revolutionaries with 220 were strongest, trailed by 187 right-wing Social Revolutionaries, 76 independents, 74 Ukrainian Social Revolutionaries, 68 Mensheviks, 37 Social Democrat-Internationalists, and various smaller groups. On the first day a hotly contested vote of 509 to 327 rejected the motion to send a welcoming address to the constituent assembly. The congress elected a new Rumčerod, which the Mensheviks and right-wing Social Revolutionaries refused to join. The pro-soviet resolutions of the congress encouraged the united presidium of the Odessa soviets on December 25 to assume power in the city.[306] Around the same time the Bolsheviks also gained a majority at the second congress of the Caucasian Army in Tiflis, which recognized the decrees of the Second All-Russian Congress of Soviets and the authority of the Council of People's Commissars. The elected army soviet opposed the Menshevik-dominated regional executive committee of the Caucasian workers and soldiers soviets (kraevoj centr).[307]

Following the Bolshevik uprising in Petrograd, the highest elected soldiers organ, the All-Army Committee (obščearmejskij komitet) at headquarters in Mogilev, attempted negotiations for a new socialist coalition government under Chernov. It appealed for restitution of all political freedoms, convocation of the constituent assembly at the scheduled time, transfer of land to the land committees, and immediate peace negotiations.[308] Thereupon the Council of People's Commissars sent to Mogilev the newly named supreme commander, Krylenko, who occupied the headquarters and dissolved the army committee. On December 24 an army congress met that represented all fronts except the Caucasus, and was dominated by the Bolsheviks. A central military-revolutionary committee was elected, and Krylenko was confirmed as commander-in-chief.[309]

The central organization of all sailors committees, the Centroflot, also took a neutral position during the October Days and then condemned the Bolshevik insurrection. The two most important fleets—the Baltic Fleet and the Black Sea Fleet, however, were predominantly Bolshevik. On orders of the All-Russian Central Executive Committee, a naval revolutionary committee was formed with Bolshevik sailors; it demanded dissolution of Centroflot, since it no longer reflected the masses' feelings. Some members of Centroflot joined the Bolsheviks, the others were forcibly idled. On December 1 the first All-Russian Sailors Congress met, dominated by the Bolsheviks. Although some delegates advocated formation of a broadly based socialist government and condemned the Bolshevik violation of democratic principles, an overwhelming majority of 160 to 2, with 28 abstentions, expressed full support for the Council of People's Commissars.[310]

The peasants soviets experienced a unique development during the October Revolution. They were independent, coexistent with the workers and soldiers soviets, with their own executive committees and central organs. Therefore only a few random peasant delegates were present at the Second All-Russian Congress of Workers and Soldiers Soviets on October 25. Social Revolutionaries continued to dominate in local and regional peasants soviets, and after the Bolshevik coup d'état, they tried to use this strength against Lenin. Immediately after the Bolshevik uprising the executive committee of the All-Russian Soviet of Peasants issued several appeals against recognition of the new soviet power. "The seizure of power three weeks before the constituent assembly means a usurpation of the rights of the entire people. . . . The Petrograd workers and soldiers soviet has thus started a fratricidal war."[311] To oppose the slogan "All power to the soviets" the peasant soviet proposed "All power to the constituent assembly." The local peasants soviets, the self-governing bodies, and the army were urged to disobey the new government. By a vote of 33 to 26 the Executive Committee adopted a resolution calling for formation of a socialist government without the Bolsheviks. The 26 dissenting votes by Left Social Revolutionaries favored including the Bolsheviks,[312] and urged the Executive Committee to convene an all-Russian peasant congress. This congress was called for November 23 in Petrograd, but its opening session was so poorly attended that it was considered merely an extraordinary congress. Of the 335 voting delegates, 195 were Left Socialist Revolutionaries,

65 right-wing Social Revolutionaries, 37 Bolsheviks, 22 anarchists, with the remainder from smaller groups. At the very beginning the congress refused to listen to Lenin in his capacity as chairman of the Council of People's Commissars. Both times he spoke, Lenin had difficulty making himself heard. The congress adopted a resolution (the Bolsheviks abstaining) demanding participation of all socialist parties in the soviet government, clearly the overwhelming desire of the peasantry. In the meantime, however, Lenin persuaded the Left Social Revolutionaries to participate in the Council of People's Commissars. The peasant congress resolved to amalgamate its executive committee with the All-Russian Central Executive Committee of the Workers and Soldiers Soviets.[313]

With this the Bolsheviks split the united front of the peasants and significantly strengthened their own weak position by enlisting the Left Social Revolutionaries. At the Second All-Russian Peasant Congress, which met from December 9 to 25, immediately following the extraordinary congress, two equally strong groups were facing each other. Of the 789 delegates, there were 305 right-wing Social Revolutionaries, 350 Left Social Revolutionaries, 91 Bolsheviks, and members of lesser socialist parties.[314] Almost 300 delegates came from the army, 300 from the district peasant soviets, 189 from the provincial organizations. The central districts were the best represented of the 53 Russian provinces attending the congress. The strongly debated vote gave a slight lead to the Left Social Revolutionary Maria Spiridonova over Viktor Chernov for the chairmanship, with deliberations concentrating on the constituent assembly. The rightist faction demanded an unequivocal commitment to the assembly, and passed a resolution to this effect by a vote of 359 to 314.[315] Lenin, on the other hand, emphasized the democratic nature of the soviets, which he called "a hundred times higher than the constituent assembly." To flatter the representatives of "peasant democracy," he even declared: "We are told that the revolution of October 25 has given power only to the Bolsheviks. . . . If the people find that their representatives in the soviet are not carrying out their will, they can simply recall their representatives. In this way the soviet will always express the people's will."[316] The reply to this was given to Lenin by a Social Democratic delegate: "Comrade Ulianov knows that, if you do not agree with him, he will scatter you with bayonets. . . . You speak of the power of the soviets, and in the meantime the actions of the commissars undermine the power of the soviets. In the place of soviet power we have the power of Lenin, who is now in the place formerly occupied by Nicholas."[317]

On December 17 the peasant congress split. The right-wing Social Revolutionaries and their followers walked out, elected their own executive committee headed by Chernov, and called a new congress for January 21, 1918, which was to protect the constituent assembly. The left-wing majority for its part elected an executive committee of 81 Left Social Revolutionaries and 20 Bolsheviks, which merged with the All-Russian Central Executive Committee of the workers and soldiers soviets. The delegates were told to agitate for soviet power in their home localities, to remove right-wing parties from the peasants soviets, and to advocate the union of peasants soviets with the workers and soldiers soviets.[318] Nevertheless, months passed before the soviet organizations in the countryside gained in strength and the right-wing socialist parties were ousted from the provincial and district soviets. The class struggle unleashed by the Bolsheviks in the spring of 1918 defeated genuine democratic representation of the peasantry.

The Bolshevik battlecry for the October Revolution was "All power to the soviets." A review of the historical facts, however, reveals that the assumption of power was desired and executed by only some workers, soldiers, and peasants soviets. The majority of soviets and the masses they represented welcomed the overthrow of the Provisional Government, but they rejected sole rule by the Bolsheviks. Nevertheless, Lenin and Trotsky by force and demagogy eliminated this opposition and laid the groundwork for their party dictatorship behind the façade of the soviets. Only six weeks after the Bolshevik October insurrection, Maxim Gorky's newspaper, *Novaja Žizn'*, published a sharp critique of the new rulers: "Power has passed to the soviets only on paper, in fiction, not in reality. The Second All-Russian Congress of Soviets faced the accomplished power seizure by the Bolsheviks, not by the soviets. The sessions of the congress proceeded in an atmosphere of insurrection, the Bolsheviks relied on the force of bayonets and guns. . . . In the provincial cities, where the soviets hesitated, where no Bolshevik majority was assured, the Bolsheviks sought to intimidate the soviets and to confront them with the alternatives of submitting or of causing civil war within the ranks of democracy. The slogan 'All power to the soviets' had actually been transformed into the slogan 'All power to a few Bolsheviks.' . . . The soviets are already losing their effectiveness, the role of the soviets shrinks to nothing. . . . A soviet republic? Empty words! In reality it is an oligarchic republic, a republic of a few People's Commissars. How have the local soviets changed? They are limited passive appendages of the Bolshevik 'military-revolutionary committees' or of commissars appointed from above. And those soviets still independent, that stubbornly refuse to recognize the 'Council of People's Commissars,' are blacklisted as suspect, opportunist, almost counterrevolutionary institutions. . . . The soviets decay, become enervated, and from day to day lose more of their prestige in the ranks of democracy."[319]

CHAPTER FIVE

The Establishment
of Soviet Dictatorship

1. CONSTITUENT ASSEMBLY OR
SOVIET REPUBLIC?

From the beginning of the Russian revolutionary movement the constituent assembly was the highest liberal and socialist aspiration. It was both emblem and fulfillment of the decades-long struggle for liberation from czarist autocracy, the hope for greater justice and freedom, the ideal of generations of revolutionary fighters. In the February Revolution of 1917 convocation of the assembly as the "mistress of Russia" was demanded by all political parties; the Petrograd soviet concluded its first programmatic appeal with a reference to the constituent assembly, and the Provisional Government promised its prompt convening.

One of the most serious and fateful errors of the bourgeois-socialist coalition government was that time and again mainly legal considerations persuaded it to postpone the election and opening of the national assembly.[1] When the election finally took place on November 25, 1917, the political situation had radically altered: barely three weeks earlier the Bolsheviks had seized power in Petrograd and declared soviet rule. Elections to the constituent assembly were therefore strongly contested although the broad masses had little idea of what had happened in the meantime and saw no difference between soviet power and the assembly. The rapid change in the popular mood, bolshevization of the soviets, and growing adherence in the villages to the Left Social Revolutionaries was only partially evident, given the election procedure. Social Revolutionary party lists generally showed left-wing and right-wing Social Revolutionaries amicably side by side, led by the old party leaders. The right-wing Social Revolutionaries still dominated the peasants soviets and land committees, which gave the party important and influential bases. Nevertheless, there is no proof for the later Bolshevik claim that had they appeared on separate slates the Left Social Revolutionaries and Bolsheviks would have topped the right wing and won a majority.[2] On the contrary, the Bolsheviks in the cities made a better showing, with press bans, arrests, and interference with elections, than with entirely free elections.[3]

The elections to the constituent assembly resulted in the following distribution of votes and seats (only the major groups being listed):[4]

Party	Votes
Russian Social Revolutionaries	15,848,004
Ukrainian Social Revolutionaries	1,286,157
Ukrainian Socialist Bloc	3,556,581
Total Social Revolutionaries and adherents	20,690,742
Bolsheviks	9,844,637
Mensheviks	1,364,826
Other Socialists	601,707
Constitutional Democrats	1,986,601
Russian conservative groups	1,262,418
Ethnic groups	2,620,967

Party	Seats
Russian Social Revolutionaries	299
Ukrainian Social Revolutionaries	81
Left Social Revolutionaries	39[5]
Bolsheviks	168
Mensheviks	18

Other socialists	4
Constitutional Democrats	15
Conservatives	2
Ethnic groups	77

In the most notable result of the elections the Bolsheviks, with 23.9 percent of all votes, entered the constituent assembly as the second-strongest party, but without the majority support of the Russian people. On the other hand, the bourgeois middle classes, the conservative landowners and officials, and all earlier monarchic institutions were unequivocally weak. The struggle took place within the socialist camp; with four-fifths of all votes, the revolutionary socialist parties had broad popular support.[6]

If the Bolsheviks could gain barely one-fourth of the nationwide votes, the regional distribution gave a different picture. The Bolsheviks held an absolute or relative majority in big cities, industrial centers, and inland garrisons, and controlled the armies at the northern and western fronts, as well as the Baltic fleet. They were able to win many of the peasants in Central Russia, northwest Russia, and White Russia. Their influence was small in the black-soil region and in the Caucasus. In the latter the Mensheviks retained their lead though they were beaten everywhere else; in the former the Social Revolutionaries prevailed, as they did in Siberia and the central Volga region. Only in Moscow and Petrograd did the bourgeois parties play a role, taking second place to the Bolsheviks. Considered as a whole, local election results for the constituent assembly coincided with the various parties' strength in the respective soviets. The Bolshevik majority in most urban workers and soldiers soviets paralleled the Bolshevik electoral successes, while the predominance of Social Revolutionaries in the peasant organizations corresponded to their agrarian electoral victory.[7] The election results generally anticipated the geographic distribution of forces during the civil war; the Bolsheviks held the center of the country, while their adversaries had to operate from the periphery.

The elections to the constituent assembly, held under extraordinary political conditions in a country engaged in revolution and war, was a political declaration of allegiance which might have come out quite differently a few months later. Nevertheless, even under normal conditions, democratic development of Russia would have come about through the confrontation and interplay of the predominantly agrarian

Social Revolutionaries and the overwhelmingly urban Bolsheviks. In the meantime Lenin had already decided against parliamentary democracy and for the soviet system, and for sole rule by his party within that system. That left the question of what to do with the constituent assembly.[7a]

The Bolsheviks had always been guided entirely by expediency in their attitude toward the constituent assembly and parliamentarianism. At the 1903 party congress of Russian Social Democrats Plekhanov, who was then close to Lenin, declared that during the revolution the interests of the proletariat might make it desirable to restrict universal suffrage and to dissolve a "bad" parliament. Lenin agreed unreservedly with this subordination of democratic principles to party interests.[8] In 1905 the constituent assembly was expected to crown the dictatorship of the proletariat and peasantry emerging from armed popular insurrection. The assembly, Stalin wrote, was "to sanction the transformation that the Provisional Government will have brought about with the help of the rebelling people."[9] "The question of the constituent assembly is subordinate to the course and outcome of the class struggle between the bourgeoisie and the proletariat," Lenin wrote in late July 1917.[10] At the same time Stalin expressed the point still more clearly: "The constituent assembly is of the greatest importance. But the masses outside are even more important. Power does not lie in the constituent assembly itself but in the workers and peasants who will fight for a new revolutionary justice and a constituent assembly."[11] A popular Bolshevik pamphlet put it in altogether unmistakable terms: "The constituent assembly must meet in Petrograd, so that the revolutionary people, and especially the revolutionary garrison, can watch it and direct it."[12]

After Lenin's turn to the soviet system as a "higher form of democracy," the constituent assembly lost even its relative value in his program and inevitably took second place to the new slogan, "All power to the soviets." It is not mentioned in the April Theses, and at the meeting at which they were set forth, Lenin explicitly stated, "Life and the revolution push the constituent assembly into the background."[13] Lenin nevertheless continued later to demand the assembly. Bolshevik agitation even linked the assembly with the soviet slogan, asserting that only strong and triumphant soviets would guarantee convocation of the national assembly.[14] Lenin accused the government and the "bourgeoisie" of deliberately postponing convocation to the end of the war, and he even spoke of "counterrevolutionary" attacks on the assembly. In reality, however, postponement suited him very well; as early as April 1917 he wrote, "The longer Lvov and company [i.e., the Provisional Government] postpone the constituent assembly, the more easily the people will decide in favor of the Republic of Soviets (through the mediation of the constituent assembly, or without it if Lvov postpones its convocation much longer)."[15] Lenin's "revolutionary realism"[16] prompted retention of the rallying cry for a constituent assembly, as propaganda for the masses; he did not want the new slogan of soviet power directly opposed to traditional revolutionary demands. "Outside the soviet dictatorship and until its arrival, the constituent assembly had to appear as the highest achievement of the revolution," Trotsky thought.[17] He had predicted a soviet republic as early as 1906 but had still held also to the idea of a constituent assembly.[18]

Not all Bolsheviks were convinced that the new call for soviet power had supplanted the old demand for a constituent assembly. As in April 1917 the party only slowly and hesitantly assimilated Lenin's new theory, and the constituent assembly was retained in the background of the Bolshevik revolutionary program. Resolutions of the all-Russian conference of April mention transfer of power to the soviets or "other organs," among them the constituent assembly.[19] Lenin himself sometimes advocated the temporary federation of soviets throughout the country, headed by the assembly.[20] He could all the more easily coddle these revolutionary reminiscenses because to him both the constituent assembly and the soviets were only tactics in the struggle for power. For the "old Bolsheviks" of Kamenev's stamp, however, the "combined type" of soviets and constituent assembly, proposed by Kamenev and Zinoviev on the eve of the insurrection as an alternative to Lenin's plan,[21] meant much more. The combination of soviets and assembly was to guarantee the peaceful transition of the ruling power to a socialist coalition government, but also, many Bolsheviks thought, to establish a national authority superseding the soviet congress. The democratic revolution, of which the Bolsheviks considered themselves executors, was to be crowned by the revolutionary assembly. Lenin and Trotsky, on the other hand, already saw the soviets leading to the next phase, toward socialism, with the constituent assembly representing only an obsolete remnant of the "bourgeois" revolution.

Although the Bolshevik October insurrection proclaimed this socialist goal, it was in no way officially directed against the constituent assembly (which did not yet exist). The Council of People's Commissars called itself a "Provisional Workers and Peasants Government" to rule Russia until the assembly could meet. The other resolutions of the soviet congress and the first decrees of the new government also mentioned the constituent assembly as final authority.[22] On November 20 Rykov, answering a question in the Moscow soviet, said that the Bolsheviks guaranteed free elections and would surrender power to the constituent assembly.[23] The Bolshevik newspapers during those days were outraged over their opponents' "slanderous allegations" that the Bolshevik insurrection had killed the assembly.[24]

Lenin and his firmest followers had long been determined not to let any parliament divert them from the road they had chosen. Lenin first considered postponing the election set for November 25 (the very thing of which he had accused the Kerensky government), lowering the voting age, revising the slates of candidates, and banning the bourgeois parties. His proposal was rejected, however, when the majority of the party's Central Committee pointed out the unpopularity of such measures immediately after the Bolshevik seizure of power.[25] Thereupon Lenin pinned his hopes on the heaviest possible vote for the Bolsheviks. But when early returns proved sparse, the Central Executive Committee of the soviets issued a decree concerning the right of recall and new election of deputies.[26] The assembly's opening, originally planned for December 11, was postponed until at least 400 delegates could be in Petrograd. The Council of People's Commissars dissolved the old election commission and transferred its duties to a soviet commission headed by Uritsky.[27] On December 11 an anti-Bolshevik demonstration honoring the assembly caused a ban of the Constitutional Democratic Party and arrest of several of its leaders.[28]

Along with these government interventions the Bolsheviks after mid-November unleashed a bulldozing press and propaganda campaign against the "new idol," the assembly.[29] Even before the election Volodarsky, at a session of the Petrograd party committee, said that if non-Bolsheviks won a majority, the national assembly might have to be dispersed with bayonets.[30] On November 30 *Pravda* wrote that the constituent assembly should proclaim the republic of soviets and then dissolve itself.[31] On December 12, in the Bolshevik Central Committee, Bukharin proposed that the left-wing section of the assembly proclaim itself a revolutionary convention.[32] An increasing number of resolutions by the Bolshevik factions demanded that the assembly either confirm the basic decisions of the Second Congress of Soviets and the Council cf People's Commissars or disband.[33] The Moscow regional conference of Bolsheviks declared that the masses must recognize the assembly's impotence and abandon "constitutional illusions" by force and terrorism if necessary.[34] On December 27 at a soldiers assembly in Petrograd Zinoviev called the constituent assembly a front for counterrevolutionary antisoviet forces, to which the soviets would not bow.[35] Finally, two days before the opening of the assembly, *Pravda* wrote: "If the constituent assembly comes out on the side of the people, then long live the constituent assembly. If it turns against the people, then down with this fraud."[36]

On December 26 Lenin published his *Theses Concerning the Constituent Assembly*, in which he gave final form to the Bolshevik tactics. Starting from the proposition that "revolutionary Social Democracy . . . has repeatedly stressed that the republic of soviets is a higher form of democracy than an ordinary bourgeois republic with a constituent assembly" (Second Thesis), Lenin argued that the election returns did not correspond to the actual will of the people. Since the October Revolution, he claimed, the masses had moved further to the left, a change not expressed in the assembly. The beginning civil war had "aggravated the class struggle and prevented formal democratic decisions" (Thirteenth Thesis). If, therefore, the constituent assembly would not submit to new elections and did not declare that it unreservedly "recognizes soviet policy on peace, land, and workers control," then "the crisis over the constituent assembly can be resolved . . . only by revolutionary means, by the most vigorous, quickest, firmest, and most determined soviet power" (Eighteenth and Nineteenth Theses).[37]

In practical terms this meant that the Bolsheviks were determined to disperse the constituent assembly. On January 4, 1918, the Central Executive Committee of the soviets fixed the opening date of the assembly for January 18, the Third All-Russian Congress of Workers and Soldiers Soviets for January 21, and the Third Congress of Peasants Soviets for January 28.[38] The two highest organs of the revolution were to confront each other. The soviet congress was to replace the doomed assembly and declare Russia a soviet republic.

The mounting battle and the alternative proposed by Lenin—"constituent assembly or soviet power"—forced the non-Bolshevik socialist parties as well to take a clear stand. Their rejection before October of sole power for the soviets[39] became even more rigid after the Bolshevik insurrection, when the right-wing Social Revolutionaries' newspaper, *Delo Naroda*, wrote: "We chiefly stressed that an insurrection nominally for soviet power penalized the working class, and that we face the constituent assembly elected by universal, equal, direct, and secret suffrage. . . . Answering the Bolshevik slogan 'Insurrection for soviet power,' we cry, 'Long live the constituent assembly.' . . . A revolutionary-democratic power must be based on the most important sections of democracy: the workers, peasants, and soldiers soviets, urban and rural self-administration, and the army. Only a state founded equally on these democratic organizations will be strong enough to secure peace, land reform, and convocation of the constituent assembly."[40] The right-wing Social Revolutionaries did not go so far as to deny all justification to the soviets and demand their transformation into pure trade-union-type organizations, as did the People's Socialists, for example.[41] Rather, Chernov said in his speeches and articles, that the conflict between soviets and constituent assembly had been artificially created by the Bolsheviks, while in reality the two were supposed to work hand in hand. Chernov maintained that the soviets, with trade unions, cooperatives, and political parties, were working-class organizations established for specific purposes, with specific functions. They were to unite the working population, safeguard revolutionary gains, and show a revolutionary initiative. On the other hand, the constituent assembly was to legislate and to define the society. All political parties must be represented in the assembly; a genuine democracy should not seek the political monopoly of one group.[42] Chernov thought that the democratic parliament clearly held first place, rather than the class-bound and improvised soviets, which were incapable of public administration. The Social Revolutionaries believed that most administrative functions should be transferred to local self-governing organs, rural and urban, and that these also must cooperate with local soviets.

Among the Mensheviks opinions differed. At the extraordinary party congress that opened on December 13 in Petrograd, a minority centered around Liber and Potresov advocated a tightly knit popular front of all non-Bolshevik forces (including the Constitutional Democrats) under the banner of the constituent assembly. The majority, however, adopted Martov's resolution acclaiming the October Revo-

lution and its demands as correct in principle and advocating a
coalition extending from Bolsheviks to Social Revolutionaries. "All
power of the state belongs to the constituent assembly," read one
point in the Menshevik program. But Martov opposed the demand
by Dan, Liber, and others, that the Mensheviks abstain in the soviets.
His resolution enjoined party members to remain in those soviets
that were not simply instruments of Bolshevik rule and that cooperated with the municipal dumas. Entry into the Bolshevik committees
or the anti-Bolshevik "rescue committees" was forbidden.[43] Thus the
Mensheviks assumed a neutral position between the Bolsheviks and
their complete opponents; basically they were to continue this attitude.

Of the socialist parties, only the Left Social Revolutionaries joined
the Bolshevik fight against the constituent assembly, an ideological
agreement resulting from the two parties' practical collaboration in
the soviets during the October revolt. At the Third All-Russian Congress of Soviets in January 1918, Maria Spiridonova declared that
the Left Social Revolutionaries also had long believed in the assembly
as "the crown of the revolution" and that therefore they were equally
guilty "of deluding the masses by the belief that the constituent
assembly would be their salvation." Only recently had the "illusions"
begun to disperse "that any parliamentary arrangement, with its
lengthy resolutions, endless debates, monotonous roll calls, and so
on . . . could bring about mankind's social freedom."[44] Instead, the
soviets were the unique creation of the working people and the
defenders of their real interests; therefore the soviets had the right
"to confirm a genuine workers constituent assembly that possesses
all executive and legislative power."[45] For this same reason the Left
Social Revolutionaries resolved on December 11 to support the constituent assembly only if it would recognize workers and peasants
power as defined by the Second Congress of Soviets.[46] On the whole
the Left Social Revolutionaries wanted to let the constituent assembly
convene and then discredit itself in the eyes of the people.[47]

In spite of the unmistakable Bolshevik threats to disperse a re-
calcitrant constituent assembly, the majority parties persisted in an
almost fatalistic passivity. On arrival in Petrograd the strongest faction, the right-wing Social Revolutionaries, busied themselves on
various commissions with preparation of legislative prosposals, and
refused to act to safeguard the assembly. Fear of civil war, aversion
to extraparliamentary weapons, and belief in the validity of democratic

principles which even the Bolsheviks would not dare tamper with, allowed the delegates to forget that the Bolsheviks held power. Outside the official party organs, several energetic people agitated in various regiments and factories for protection of the assembly.[48] An armed demonstration planned for the opening day was changed by a Social Revolutionary resolution into an unarmed demonstration that could easily be dispersed by the Bolsheviks. Nevertheless anti-Bolshevism was growing, as shown by the hundreds of workers who supported the appeal for assembly protection and opposed the Bolshevik takeover of the soviets.[49]

The circumstances surrounding dissolution of the constituent assembly after its single session on January 18, 1918, are well known.[50] After the majority refused (by a vote of 237 to 136) to accept the Bolshevik "declaration of the rights of the working and exploited people" and resolved instead to stick to its own agenda, the Bolsheviks and Left Social Revolutionaries left the meeting. Debate and approval of the most important laws for the new order in Russia continued until the small hours of the morning. At about the same time the Central Executive Committee of the soviets decreed dissolution of the assembly. The decree, written by Lenin, named the reasons once more: "The working classes concluded from their own experience that the old bourgeois parliamentarianism has become obsolete and cannot be reconciled with socialism's aims, that only class institutions (such as the soviets), and not national ones, can break the resistance of the propertied classes and lay the foundations for the socialist society."[51]

When the Third All-Russian Congress of Workers and Soldiers Soviets met on January 23, 1918, to be followed three days later by the Third Peasant Congress, it was officially the single supreme organ of power. The Bolsheviks had a large majority; the opposition had melted away.[52] In his opening address Sverdlov stated: "Dissolution of the constituent assembly has to be compensated for by the congress of soviets, the sole sovereign organ that genuinely represents the interests of the workers and peasants."[53] He said the congress was to legalize the definitive break with bourgeois democracy and establish the dictatorship during socialist reconstruction. On January 28, 1918, despite weak opposition from Menshevik-Internationalists led by Martov and other small groups, the soviet congress proclaimed formation of the Russian Socialist Soviet Republic.[54]

Dissolution of the constituent assembly and the Third Congress of Soviets marked the end of the transition from the Bolshevik seizure of power in October 1917 to final formation of the new state. In less than a year, the attempt at parliamentary democracy had failed. The almost total absence of popular protest against the Bolsheviks' violent measures resulted not only from the intellectual and physical Bolshevik terror, still relatively "mild." Equally important, the Bolsheviks had largely anticipated the assembly's resolution of the vital questions of peace and land. The masses of peasants and workers, who never quite ceased to view the constituent assembly as a distant and abstract concept, tended to prefer the practical measures of the new rulers to the paper resolutions of an assembly backed by no real power. The lack of a "formal aspect" of the Russian revolution (unlike revolutions in Western Europe, with their emphasis on constitutional discussions) was not from its proletarian character, as Pokrovski believed,[55] but because conditions needed for a Western-type parliamentary democracy were altogether absent.[56] Russia had little or no tradition of local democratic self-government or of a national parliament, so that the new revolutionary bodies of workers, soldiers, and peasants soviets could easily be established in their place. In spite of the soviets' inept and undemocratic methods, the masses regarded them as "their" organs, and could not have been mobilized against them. Even later, the anti-Bolshevik forces opposed not the soviets as such, but the Bolshevik dictatorship ruling in the name of the soviets. During the 1917 revolution the Bolsheviks for their part exploited the soviets' preeminence against the assembly and the concept of parliamentary representation. Soviet democracy, replacing "bourgeois democracy," remained only a promise, however; and the soviet constitution increasingly masked party dictatorship.

2. THE BOLSHEVIK SOVIET SYSTEM

a) Expansion of the Soviet System and the Soviet Constitution of 1918

The Bolshevik October Revolution turned the Russian soviets from militant revolutionary organs into pillars of the new state power. In some places the soviets' transformation had been under way before the Bolsheviks seized power.[57] Thus the Bolsheviks found some ready-made forms on which to base the new state after dispensing with "dyarchy." "We only needed to issue a few decrees to turn soviet power from its embryonic state early in the revolution into the legally recognized form which is now the Russian state—the Russian soviet republic," Lenin stated at the beginning of March 1918.[58]

The Second All-Russian Congress of Soviets had in general terms transferred authority to the soviets throughout the country.[59] On November 18 Lenin appealed to the workers to take over all government affairs. Their soviets were now all-powerful and would decide everything.[60] In the following weeks further decrees of the Council of People's Commissars were issued, as were regulations of the People's Commissar of the Interior on type of representation, soviet structure (sections for workers, soldiers and peasants; election of a presidium and executive committee; etc.), and internal separation of functions.[61] A circular of January 5, 1918, from the People's Commissar of the Interior states: "In all localities the soviets are the local organs of power and administration, and all agencies with administrative, commercial, financial, and cultural functions must submit to them. . . . All former local organs, such as regional, provincial, and district commissars, the committees of social organization, the volost administrations, etc., must be replaced by the corresponding soviets of workers, soldiers, peasants, and rural laborers deputies. The whole country must be covered with a network of soviets, and they must maintain close relations. Each of these organizations, down to the smallest, is completely autonomous in local matters, but it coordinates its activities with the general decrees and regulations of the centralized supreme soviet. In this way a coherent and fully integrated soviet republic will emerge."[62] These regulations were issued before the constituent assembly convened, and they were incorporated in the constitution of July 1918. In the first few months of 1918 the organizational framework was established on provincial, district, and volost levels, though only slowly, especially in rural areas.[63] In Perm province, for example, about 500 volost councils were established in the first quarter of 1918; in Voronezh province, with eight districts containing 84 volosts, 16 volost soviets were created in January, 46 in February, and 16 in March.[64] The separate peasants soviets and their executive committees on district and provincial levels merged with corresponding workers and soldiers soviets.[65]

In general, the months immediately following the October Revolution presented a jumble of coexisting diverse local administrative bodies, until gradually the old institutions were abolished and replaced by soviets. The rural zemstvos especially, which had extensive rights of local self-government granted by the Provisional Government, and the municipal dumas remained for months alongside the soviets. Bolshevik treatment of the autonomous rural and municipal organs varied, depending on local political attitudes. Where they actively opposed Bolshevism, local bodies were simply dissolved or refurbished by new elections which usually resulted in a pro-Bolshevik majority. In Petrograd the municipal duma, a center of anti-Bolshevik opposition during the October Days and later in charge of municipal maintenance, was dissolved on November 30. The new elections, which excluded the bourgeois parties, produced 188 seats for the Bolsheviks, 10 for the Left Social Revolutionaries, and 2 for minor groups. In February 1918 the municipal duma was eliminated altogether.[66] The dumas and zemstvos with pro-soviet majorities collaborated and merged voluntarily, following a regulation of January 9, 1918, which transferred their funds and inventory to the soviets.[67] Thereafter the local soviets replaced the zemstvos and dumas; in December 1917 the zemstvos were dissolved in 8.1 percent of all volosts, in January 1918 in 45.2 percent, in February in 32.2 percent, and from March to May in the remaining volosts.[68] Some zemstvo personnel shifted to the new soviet adminstration, and in the cities many municipal employees were absorbed too. The collaboration of such administrative and technical personnel helped the soviets suddenly shoulder enormous new tasks, but also greatly accelerated bureaucratization and detachment from the masses.

Transfer of local government to the soviets was only one aspect of the "smashing" of the old public order by the Bolsheviks after the October Revolution. In the army and navy the soviet principle was also thoroughly imposed. Decrees of December 21 and 29, 1917, transferred full power to the soldiers committees in all army units; the committees elected all superiors up to the regimental commander. All naval administration and even the military leadership was given to the central navy committees; the admiralty was abolished.[69] These measures, however, represented merely a half-reluctant Bolshevik recognition of the enormous decay within Russian military forces, rather than conscious application of the principles of soviet democracy as developed by Lenin in *State and Revolution*. Soldiers and sailors no longer tolerated any higher authority, now that the Bolshevik slogans had fueled their hatred of officers and the October Revolution had proclaimed the rule of the masses. Unauthorized demobilization of the Russian army could not be prevented by the soldiers soviets; at most it could be made less chaotic here and there.[70]

An equally elementary movement was the workers' seizure of the factories. Workers' control of management, advocated by the Bolsheviks before their takeover and decreed on November 27, 1917, very frequently turned into direct administration through the factory committees. The decree envisaged special councils of workers as superior authorities within the factories, allied to the general soviets.[71] These plans, however, were seldom enforced; in reality anarchy prevailed in factories, or from another point of view, "a genuine dictatorship of the workers."[72] The factory committees, one of the Bolsheviks' main supports among workers long before the October Revolution,[73] demanded sole decision-making power in all factory affairs, with little consideration for the national economy. After the October Revolution the central councils of factory committees from various cities attempted to form their own national organization to secure actual economic dictatorship. Here the Bolsheviks first faced the self-created danger of radical industrial democracy applying Lenin's formula of soviet rule. To prevent the economy's imminent collapse into many autonomous factory units, the Bolsheviks called on the trade unions, in which they now held a majority and which were already competing with the factory committees. The unions prevented convocation of an all-Russian congress of factory committees and instead absorbed the factory committees at the lowest level.[74] Thus direct rule by factory committees ended after a very few months, but for years relations between trade unions and state power remained a difficult problem for the Bolsheviks.[75]

Perhaps the strongest expression of the soviet principle of direct mass rule and "the most frankly syndicalist measure ever contained in soviet legislation"[76] was the decree of January 23, 1918, on workers' control of the railroads,[77] which specified soviets of railroad deputies with executive committees, to elect the next-higher territorial organs and finally an all-Russian railroad soviet. The Bolsheviks passed this measure to create a counterweight to the Vikzhel (All-Russian Union of Railroad Workers), which was still dominated by Social Revolutionaries; during October it had stayed neutral and later spoke out for the constituent assembly. The chaotic transportation system was only worsened by the new organs' rivalry with the old Vikzhel, and Lenin a bare two months later restored individual management and responsibility in the rail system, limiting the railroad soviets to advisory functions.[78]

The soviet principle was extended to other areas of public life in the months after the October insurrection. A decree of December 14, 1917, established a Supreme Economic Council to manage the entire Russian economy; it was to lead and unify the economic departments of all local soviets, and later formed territorial councils.[79] Other decrees of December 1917 and February 1918 abolished the old courts, replacing them with people's courts; at first judges were elected, but later they, too, were appointed by the local soviets.[80] Thus emerged a widely differentiated system of soviets, whose backbone was the political workers, soldiers, and peasants soviets, to which were added the various economic and military soviets. Their responsibilities, not always clearly defined, consisted equally of liquidating the old political and social order and of preparing—gropingly at first—a new order which the Bolsheviks called "socialist." Soviet rule during the early months did not subdue but increased the political and economic chaos brought about by war and revolution.

The revolution weakened centralization and encouraged local autonomy. The Bolshevik slogan "All power to the soviets" involuntarily contributed to that effect. "Early in the October revolution, reaction against the old bureaucratic state created a tendency to solve all problems through local forces, though with no idea of seceding from soviet Russia. This process led to the formation of semi-independent republics, autonomous regions, etc."[81] The respective "soviet republics" formed their own councils of people's commissars and often paid very little attention to decrees from Petrograd and Moscow. After the Treaty of Brest Litovsk the Siberian Council of People's Commissars even declared itself still at war with the Central Powers.[82] Thus the revolution created many independent and equal "communes," typifying the first phase of soviet rule in Russia.

These anticentralist tendencies within the soviets were held chiefly by the Left Social Revolutionaries, with some support among the Bolsheviks' left-wing communists.[83] They feared that a strong central power with its authority from above might endanger the independence of local soviets and the "commune state" created from below. "The local soviets carry full state power; they have the right to decide all questions, except those voluntarily delegated to the exclusive authority of the central power," a draft constitution of the Left Social Revolutionaries states.[84] Accordingly, the individual soviets were to be autonomous in voting procedures, ratio of representation, internal organization, etc.[85] The Social Revolutionary Maximalists, who had espoused the idea of communes during the first Russian revolution,[86] proposed "a decentralized society with broad autonomy of the various regions and ethnic groups" as the ideal of a "workers republic" (trudovaja respublika).[87] In their view, as in that of the Left Social Revolutionaries, the soviet system was only a transitional step toward the classless society and the "withering away of the state" which—unlike Lenin—they wanted at once. A "federation of economic soviets" was therefore to parallel the political structure, with the smallest cells in the factories and villages, which would gradually absorb the other soviets. In spring 1918 the Left Social Revolutionary Reisner, who for a time was People's Commissar for Justice, drafted a soviet constitution which provided for a "federation of workers" within an "all-Russian workers commune" instead of a territorial structure.[88] Combining Western European syndicalism with the old rural mir constitution, which the Social Revolutionaries interpreted as an early stage of the soviet system,[89] supposedly would bring about a specifically Russian form of socialism, which nevertheless claimed universal recognition.[90]

The anticentralist and syndicalist ideas of the Left Social Revolutionaries were not incorporated in the final constitution of the Union of Soviet Socialist Republics of July 10, 1918. Rather, state centralism (in spite of formal concessions to the autonomy of local soviets) and the territorial principle prevailed, as advocated by the Bolsheviks. The constitution of 1918 institutionalized the soviet principle and transformed the soviets from purely revolutionary organs into pillars of state power, thus determining the entire future development of soviet Russia. Nevertheless the 1918 constitution already masked the true character of the soviet state, which can only "be understood in the dialectical polarity of a formal legal constitution and a total political system; in the dialectical polarity of the soviets as transmission and lever and the party as guiding force in the system of proletarian dictatorship."[91] The definitive role of the Communist Party under Lenin is not revealed in a single word of the constitution, though the party then possessed a political monopoly. The legal particularities of the Russian soviet system, overestimated for a time, therefore play a relatively minor part; here they will be dealt with only insofar as their roots lie in the preceding revolutionary soviet movement.[92]

The Soviet constitution of 1918 essentially only codified the new political forms developed from below since the February Revolution of 1917 and established from above since the October Revolution. The pyramidal structure of indirect elections, the restriction to workers, peasants, and soldiers, and the union of legislative and executive, were revolutionary expedients that became only retrospectively ideological "superstructure." The Declaration of the Rights of the Toiling and Exploited People which prefaced the constitution, having earlier been adopted by the Third Soviet Congress in January 1918, was consciously a counterpart to the Declaration of Human Rights of the French Revolution.[93] Individual civil rights were replaced by the proletariat's class rule, with the aim of "removing any exploitation of man by man" and "completely abolishing society's division into classes." The temporary nature of "dictatorship of the urban and rural proletariat and the poorer peasantry" was specifically reiterated in article 9 of the constitution.

For the duration of the dictatorship of the proletariat in the "decisive battle between the proletariat and its exploiters, the latter were to find no place in any government organ" (article 7). The suffrage regulations limited the franchise and eligibility to "those who earn their living by productive and socially useful labor" (article 64) and excluded all persons who employed wage earners or lived on unearned income, merchants, and clergy (article 65). These regulations were applied with flexibility. The peasantry especially was affected by this to a greater or lesser extent depending on what the tactics were at any one time.

Limitation of the franchise to the urban and rural proletariat (including salaried employees) and the poor peasantry logically resulted from the dictatorship of the proletariat, for which Lenin had laid the theoretical groundwork before October 1917. Lenin, however, did not consider universal suffrage or its limitation very important. After the establishment of soviet dictatorship Lenin explicitly stressed that disfranchisement "is a purely Russian problem, and not a problem of the dictatorship of the proletariat as such."[94] He left open the possibility that in other countries the dictatorship of the proletariat could be reconciled with universal suffrage. The reestablishment of universal suffrage by the Soviet constitution of 1936 and conditions in the Eastern European Communist states prove that a dictatorial regime can maintain itself even with universal suffrage, when it can use all other resources for controlling and dominating public opinion.

But the class franchise of the first Soviet constitution was practical as well as theoretical. From the outset the soviets were restricted class organizations, closed to the bourgeoisie, the big landowners, and the nonsocialist intelligentsia. In practice the soviet system actually embraced only a minority of the class in question, because it lacked a firm organizational structure. Small artisan enterprises were very poorly represented, not to mention the peasantry, which was included effectively only after the October Revolution. Nor did the 1918 constitution change this situation: participation in soviet elections remained small for years, attaining its 99-percent quota only under Stalin.[95]

Another characteristic of the suffrage regulations originated in soviet practices of 1917. Article 25 of the constitution pegged the number of delegates to the All-Russian Soviet Congress at one to each 25,000 voters for the urban soviets and one to each 125,000 inhabitants for the provincial soviet congresses, delegates to the latter being sent by the rural district and municipal soviets. This regulation was based on the election rules of the First All-Russian Congress of Soviets of June 1917 and the corresponding rules of the First Peasants Congress of May 1917, which provided one delegate for each 150,000 inhabitants. After the two soviet bodies merged in January 1918, the two different ratios continued in force. Elections to provincial soviet congresses were also held on the ratio of one deputy to 2,000 voters in the cities and one to 10,000 in the countryside. This unequal ratio clearly favored the industrial proletariat and introduced a quota system within "soviet democracy," to compensate at least partially for the immense numerical superiority of the peasantry and to advertise the historic proletarian mission in establishing socialism.

Internally the soviets on all levels combined the legislative and executive functions. Karl Marx had already applauded unification of powers as a principle of the Paris Commune.[96] Lenin adopted this principle with the concept of the commune state, and saw it realized

in the soviets.[97] The soviets of 1917 were legislative through resolutions of the plenum or the executive committee, and executive in
that soviet members themselves executed the resolutions. The concentration of powers was legally sanctioned in the constitution. The
occasional comparison of the All-Russian Soviet Congress or the
Central Executive Committee with a parliament (as the legislative
branch) and of the Council of People's Commissars with a cabinet
(as the executive) is therefore not justified.[98] Although the constitution called the Council of People's Commissars merely an executive
organ, responsible to the Central Executive Committee, an important
qualification states that "measures requiring immediate execution"
may be "directly undertaken by the Council of People's Commissars"
(article 41). From the first days of Bolshevik rule, the Council of
People's Commissars independently issued decrees of fundamental
importance without prior approval from the Central Executive Committee. Answering complaints on this score by the Left Social Revolutionaries, the Bolshevik majority declared that "The soviet parliament
[meaning the All-Russian Soviet Congress] cannot abrogate the right
of the Council of People's Commissars to issue decrees of extreme ur-
gency without previously submitting its proposal to the Central Executive Committee.[99] Indeed, the constitutional "last resort" of the
soviet republic, the All-Russian Soviet Congress, as early as the Third
Soviet Congress of January 1918 had played out its independent political role and increasingly turned into pure window dressing for
Bolshevik rule, a change probably abetted by the fact that it met only
irregularly for short periods rather than as a permanent institution
with its own committees, definite rules of procedure, etc.

Contrary to suggestions of the Left Social Revolutionaries on the
constitutional commission, functions of local soviets were much more
narrowly defined in the constitution than they were in practice during
the early months of soviet rule. A primary obligation of "local organs
of soviet power" was the "execution of all decrees of the respective
supreme organs of soviet power" (article 61). Though the soviets
could decide purely local questions, they were controlled by the next-
higher organs which could cancel soviet decisions. Financially, local
soviets depended on appropriations from the Central Executive Committee or from corresponding central people's commissariats. The
soviets were increasingly demoted and lost the autonomy enjoyed in
1917.[100]

b) Soviets in the Civil War and the Road
to the One-Party State

From the beginning the constitution of the Russian Soviet Republic was outdated by the political realities of mid-1918, even though the soviets were officially the new state's cornerstone. The establishment of Bolshevik Party dictatorship, civil war, and economic chaos destroyed the rudiments of genuine democracy achieved during the revolution of 1917, and the gulf between official Bolshevik ideology and soviet practice was deepened, not closed. The end of this period saw open conflict between the enduring revolutionary soviet idea and "soviet power," which had become a party dictatorship.

The Bolsheviks' departure from previously-proclaimed principle was forced by the disintegration of Russia into numerous small independent "communes" which contradicted Bolshevik centralist principles. In 1917 Lenin had for tactical reasons advocated "revolutionary self-government" and far-reaching decentralization, but he had not relinquished his fundamental view that only "proletarian centralism" could establish the socialist order.[101] Such practical exigencies as the military threat and economic chaos, added to these theoretical considerations, led to a return to centralism beginning in the spring of 1918. Trotsky became the ruthless defender of so-called "revolutionary" centralism; in his speech of March 28, 1918, under the characteristic title, "Work, Discipline, and Order Will Save the Soviet Republic,"[102] he signaled the end of direct soviet rule and its replacement by centralized Bolshevik party dictatorship.[103] Lenin's work of April 1918, "The Next Tasks of Soviet Power," stated the new program. Russia, he wrote, was beginning the enormous task of erecting a new socialist order. Destruction of the old order, the "immediate expropriation of the expropriators," until now primary, must yield to "the organization of accountability and control," which required the cooperation of bourgeois "specialists," technicians, and administrators. The workers must increase productivity, organize internal competition, and observe strict discipline. None of this would be possible without unified leadership. Lenin bluntly asked "whether appointment of individuals who are given the unlimited authority of dictators" could be "reconciled with fundamental principles of soviet power," and he gave an unequivocal answer: "If we are not anarchists, we must acknowledge need for the state to enforce the transition from capitalism to socialism. . . . Therefore there is not the least contradiction between soviet (i.e., socialist) democracy and the use of dictatorial power by a few persons."[104] The present moment, he claimed, demanded "unconditional subordination of the masses to the unified will of the plant managers in the interest of socialism."[105] The party must educate the masses in this inevitable readjustment during the period "of parliamentary democracy that overflows its banks."[106] What Lenin here disparagingly branded "parliamentary democracy," however, was the essence of the soviets, which in 1917 he had characterized as "the structuring of the entire state administration from the bottom up through the masses themselves, their active participation in every step of life."[107] Insofar as the Bolsheviks disciplined the spontaneous soviet rule, they discouraged soviet democracy. For they were trying not only to shore up the divergent forces that were threatening to degenerate into anarchy, but also to assure absolute Bolshevik preeminence within this centralized soviet power, which necessarily changed the genuinely democratic and representative soviets into extensions of party dictatorship.

The first breach in the soviet system took place by mid-1918 with the creation of the Red Army.[108] Election of officers—this special soviet principle—was abolished, rights of soldiers committees were curtailed, former czarist officers were increasingly given responsibility.[109] According to the Bolshevik justification for these measures: "When power belonged to the great landowners and the bourgeoisie, the officer was the soldiers' enemy. It is perfectly natural that, as soon as czarism was cast off, the soldiers demanded introduction of the elective principle in the army. It is quite another matter in a socialist state. Here the government exists through the will of the proletariat. . . . It is self-evident that the workers, by trusting their government, also grant it the right to appoint officials and various authorities. It is equally self-evident that the government appoints army commanders."[110] These words should be compared with Lenin's demands for popular elections, abolition of the army and police, and their replacement with a universal people's militia—in short, his entire 1917 program—to measure fully the distance between the October Revolution's ideology and its reversal six months later.

The army's reorganization under the war commissariat's central leadership was paralleled in 1918 by the restructuring of Russian industry with leadership from above, instead of through factory committees.[111] Industry-wide associations increased centralized control; workers control in the plants was restricted; and new managers were appointed.[112] Also introduced were piece rates, compulsory overtime, strict control of labor mobility, measures intended to balance the catastrophic decline of the urban work force resulting from military service and a drift back to the villages.[113] These economic measures, later called "war communism," culminated in Trotsky's proposal of 1919–1920 to militarize labor by forcible draft and deployment.[114]

Soviet political development in 1918–1920 was marked by three features: the gradual elimination of non-Bolshevik parties; bound up with this, actual subordination to Communist Party leadership; finally, increasing centralization and bureaucratization.

The old majority parties of the soviets, Mensheviks and right-wing Social Revolutionaries, strongly opposed the soviet government after the Second All-Russian Soviet Congress of October 1917, where they remained a minority. If at first they had still pinned their hopes on the constituent assembly, after its dissolution they saw themselves robbed of all political mobility. True, neither the Mensheviks nor the right-wing Social Revolutionaries were yet officially excluded from the soviets, and they were still represented at the Fourth All-Russian Soviet Congress in March 1918, but their newspapers were suppressed, numerous party members were alternately arrested and released, and their election campaigns for soviet seats were impeded. Conditions during early 1918 varied widely; while in some places the Mensheviks and right-wing Social Revolutionaries themselves refused participation in the soviets, in others the Bolsheviks excluded them. Frequently they appeared in the soviets as "unaffiliated" members.[115] In some localities, as in Tambov and the large industrial settlement of Izhevsk in Vyatka province, the two parties even won a majority in the new soviet elections of April and May 1918.[116]

The Mensheviks won new adherents among urban workers as disappointment over the continuing economic plight and indignation at the Bolsheviks' arbitrary acts grew. In Petrograd and Moscow the Mensheviks organized so-called nonpartisan conferences in the spring of 1918 to elect "spokesmen for factories and workshops." Since the Petrograd soviet was completely dominated by the Bolsheviks, these assemblies of spokesmen were to represent the true interests of the proletariat. In May 1918 the Mensheviks, declaring that for the people the soviets had come to embody unbearable tyranny and political oppression, demanded restoration of true representation to the soviets.[117]

On June 14, 1918, the All-Russian Central Executive Committee excluded Mensheviks and right-wing Social Revolutionaries and instructed the local soviets to do likewise,[118] because of the Social Revolutionaries' participation in the uprising of the Czech legion and the establishment of the "committee of constituent assembly members" in Samara.[119] Thereafter the two socialist parties were squeezed out of the local soviets; their candidacies were forbidden in new elections. In the meantime the relationship between the Bolsheviks and Left Social Revolutionaries had also changed. On March 19, 1918, protesting conclusion of the Treaty of Brest-Litovsk, the Left Social Revolutionaries resigned from the Council of People's Commissars, but continued in the Central Executive Committee.[120] By propaganda in the army and peasantry, they sought to obstruct the peace treaty. Conflicts with the Bolsheviks on agrarian policy and the death penalty further deepened the antagonism. On July 4, 1918, the Fifth All-Russian Soviet Congress, at which the Left Social Revolutionaries had 470 delegates out of 1,425 (868 of them Bolsheviks), opened amid excitement and tension.[121] On July 6 two Left Social Revolutionaries assassinated the German ambassador in Moscow, Graf von Mirbach; at the same time an attempted putsch against Bolshevik rule was quickly put down,[122] and most Social Revolutionary delegates were promptly arrested. The constitution of the Russian Soviet Republic was passed by the congress on July 10 with the second-largest party absent. Earlier a resolution declared that future soviets would exclude those groups of the Left Social Revolutionary Party that were connected with the assassination and the putsch.[123] On July 15 the All-Russian Central Executive Committee ratified this resolution,[124] making the Bolsheviks the only legal party in Russia aside from small impotent leftist groups that were tolerated.[125]

The Social Revolutionary risings and assassinations in July and August 1918, and the Bolshevik countermeasures culminating in the official proclamation of Red terror, also ended what was left of soviet democracy. As late as June and July the Left Social Revolutionaries were quite strong in the local soviets, and in some rural districts even had the majority.[126] Their disbarment left the local soviets under Communist control after autumn 1918. For example, following a Bolshevik motion, the soviet of Vyatka decided in September 1918 that only the Communists (Bolsheviks) and People's Communists (a splinter group that existed for a few months) could be represented in the soviets. "All other parties [among them the Left Social Revolutionaries, anarchists, and Social Revolutionary Maximalists] being counterrevolutionary parties, cannot nominate candidates. In those factories and troops where party cells exist, these will compile the slates; where such cells are not present, the slates of candidates must be approved by the party committees. The party organizations are entitled to send one official party representative with the right to vote to the soviet for each ten deputies."[127] The soviets were constantly admonished to take care lest, under "masks of sympathizers or independents, enemies of the soviet power, most especially kulaks," gain influence.[128]

These direct interventions and a number of other measures maintained Communist control over the soviets. Often election dates were announced on very short notice; delegates out of favor could be removed; the soviets were enlarged by appointing representatives of the trade unions, and the Red Army.[129] Thus the Bolsheviks built a crushing majority in most urban soviets and provincial congresses. Among the more than 1,800 deputies to the Petrograd soviet at the end of 1919, there were 1,500 Communists, 300 independents, 3 Mensheviks, and 10 Social Revolutionaries.[130] In October 1920 the Saratov soviet, of 644 deputies, consisted of 472 Communists (72.9 percent), 172 independents (26.5 percent), and 4 members of other parties (0.6 percent).[131] According to official information, in the first half of 1918 the proportion of Communists in the district soviet congresses of the Russian Soviet Republic was 48.4 percent, against 19.5 percent of other parties and 32.1 percent of independent deputies. In the second half of 1918 the Communists rose to 72.8 percent, and the other parties fell to 8.9 percent, the independents to 18.3 percent. At the provincial congresses the Bolsheviks held an absolute majority as early as mid-1918, with 52.4 percent against 24.5 percent of other parties (16.8 percent being Left Social Revolutionaries) and 23.1 percent independents. After the summer's events the Communist share rose to 90.3 percent; the other parties accounted for only 4 percent and the independents for 5.7 percent of the delegates.[132] In later years, until 1921, the percentage of non-Communist soviet deputies rose or fell by a few points, depending on Bolshevik tactics toward the socialist parties and the peasantry.[133]

The parties that were largely excluded from the soviets led a

semilegal existence until the civil war ended.[134] The Bolshevik attitude toward them was dictated by the general political and military
situation; in crises the loyalty or conditional support of these groups
was valued but when danger diminished, they were ignored. The
socialist parties themselves disagreed: Should priority be given to
defense of the revolutionary soviet republic against the Whites and
foreign intervention, or to the struggle against the Bolshevik dictatorship, if need be even with nonsocialist and foreign support? Except
for the right-wing Social Revolutionaries, the socialists preferred the
first option; the common revolutionary heritage and the idea of
national defense were stronger than opposition to Bolshevism. Even
the growth of scattered popular support for the Mensheviks and
Social Revolutionaries had no political effect.

Among the opposition parties allowed by the Bolsheviks, the Left
Social Revolutionaries unconditionally supported the soviet system
in its "pure" form and accused Lenin and the Bolsheviks of corrupting and discrediting the soviets. In autumn 1918, Maria Spiridonova
wrote in an "open letter" from prison that, because of their cynical
attitude toward the soviets and their disregard of constitutional rights,
the Bolsheviks were "the true rebels against soviet power. . . . The
soviets must be like a sensitive barometer connected to the people;
therefore unconditional freedom of election, the free play of the
people's spontaneous will must prevail; only then will creative energy,
a new life, a living organism come into being. Only then will the people feel that everything that happens in the country is truly its own
business, and not somebody else's. For this reason we fought exclusion of the right-wing socialists from the soviets."[135] In 1920 a group
surrounding former people's commissar Steinberg was allowed to
issue a periodical, *Znamja*; among other matters it proposed a "genuine soviet democracy" that would be a "dictatorship of the working
classes."[136] The Left Social Revolutionaries turned against the Bolshevik Party monopoly and the betrayal of the "socialist principles
of the October Revolution,"[137] and with the left-wing Communists,
were the first internal critics of the Bolshevik soviet system, in a long
evolution that continues to Tito and the Polish events of October
1956.

The attitude of the right-wing Social Revolutionaries toward the
existing soviets was not uniform. Before convocation of the constitutional assembly, Chernov pleaded for harmonious cooperation of
assembly and soviets;[138] after the assembly's dissolution and the

progressive Bolshevik domination of the soviets he became more decidedly antisoviet. In a circular letter of October 24, 1918, Chernov called the civil war "a struggle between soviet Russia and the Russia of the constituent assembly, between ochlocracy and democracy."[139] The anti-Bolshevik governments of Samara, Omsk, and Archangel, which emerged in the summer of 1918 with right-wing Social Revolutionaries as leaders, decreed dissolution of the soviets in their region and reinstated the municipal dumas and zemstvos.[140] A section of the party, however, refused to fight the Bolsheviks, and in February 1919 agreed to a compromise that enabled them to publish briefly the old newspaper *Delo Naroda* and to send several representatives to the next soviet congresses. But the majority persistently resisted the Bolshevik soviet regime and remained outlawed. The right-wing Social Revolutionaries' policy on the soviets remained ambiguous, with primary emphasis on the constituent assembly.[141]

Unlike the Social Revolutionaries, the Mensheviks refused armed struggle against Bolshevik rule. At the party conference of May 1918 the group around Martov (Menshevik-Internationalists) rejoined the general party, which condemned allied intervention and demanded convocation of the constituent assembly and free elections to the soviets.[142] Although they restricted themselves to legal opposition, the Mensheviks were excluded from the soviets on June 14, 1918, by resolution of the All-Russian Central Executive Committee. But the civil war exacerbated party conflicts and a Menshevik move to the left, embodied in the October 1918 theses of their Central Committee, led to reinstatement on November 30. The October theses rescinded the demand for convocation of the constituent assembly or, that failing, for new elections, since "now the rallying cry of the constituent assembly" could be used "as a banner and mask of the counterrevolution." The Menshevik party acknowledged as the basis of its policy "the form of the soviet state as it exists, not the principle."[143] The party was only half-heartedly tolerated thereafter and suffered constant arbitrary interference by the Bolsheviks,[144] in its role as the legal opposition. In July 1919 the Mensheviks published a manifesto under the title *What To Do?*, designed to unite all revolutionary forces against the White movement. They first demanded universal suffrage and free agitation preceding free elections by secret ballot to all municipal and village soviets, periodic new elections of soviets and executive committees, and rescinding of all discriminatory measures. The All-Russian Central Executive Committee was to reassume its old prerogatives of debating and passing all laws; freedom of the press and of assembly was to be restored, with abolition of the death penalty and dissolution of the Cheka.[145] The Bolsheviks themselves had to admit that nearly all Menshevik demands grew out of the articles of the soviet constitution of 1918, but explained that "in a beleaguered fortress" there could be no "developed democracy" and that the Mensheviks were "sabotaging the revolution."[146]

Representing the Mensheviks as legal opposition, Martov and Dan participated in the Seventh All-Russian Soviet Congress in December 1919 and the Eighth Soviet Congress a year later as advisors, as did several Social Revolutionaries (among them Steinberg), anarchists, and Maximalists.[147] Their attendance could not greatly change the "lifeless atmosphere" and "showcase nature" of the congresses;[148] nevertheless, theirs were the last free words spoken in the supreme soviet assembly. In several urban workers soviets the Mensheviks at times elected a relatively sizable number of deputies; in 1920 they won 46 seats (one of them for Martov) in the Moscow soviet elections, in Kharkov they won as many as 205, in Ekaterinoslav 120, in Kremenchug 78, in Tula 50, and in a number of other cities over 30 seats.[149] There can be little doubt that free elections would by the end of the civil war have given the Mensheviks more soviet seats than the Bolsheviks; even the Bolshevik leaders admitted freely that the majority of Russian workers were anti-Communist.[150]

Compared to the two Social Revolutionary parties and the Mensheviks, the smaller leftist socialist groups were minor,[151] though the Social Revolutionary Maximalists, the Revolutionary Communists, and the People's Communists all unconditionally believed in the soviet system and accepted the class nature of the new soviet state. They wanted to "push [the Bolsheviks] leftward, toward immediate realization of socialism and the workers republic,"[152] and favored direct plant management by the workers "under control of the central and local soviets,"[153] agricultural communes, and an economic-political federation of all agrarian and industrial groups.[154] The three leftist-socialist splinter parties were not constrained by the Bolsheviks and most of their members later joined the Communist Party, but open antagonism reigned between Bolshevism and anarchism, and the deep-rooted enmity was only partially masked by Lenin's ideological rapprochement to the anarchist program in *State and Revolution* and by use of some anarchist slogans in 1917. From 1918 to 1920 the fragmented anarchist groups were almost constantly persecuted, with only occasional concessions.[155] Echoing Bakunin's animosity to any organized ruling power, the anarchists fought Bolshevik "dictatorship of the proletariat" and its threatening centralism, commissars, and terror. They considered soviets a first step toward the anarchist commune, but thought existing soviets were flawed and usually refused to cooperate in them. The leading Ukrainian anarchists in Nestor Makhno's partisan movement[156] raised the cry of "Free soviets without ruling power" (vol'nye i bezvlastnye), against the "subservient and partisan Bolshevik soviets."[157] The group of anarcho-syndicalists active in Petrograd and Moscow called soviet power an "exploitation machine for subjugation of most workers by a small clique."[158] Many anarchist slogans and demands subsequently turned up during the Kronstadt revolt.[159]

Aside from the exclusion of non-Bolshevik parties from the soviets there were other ways by which the soviets lost their character as a broad mass organization during the the civil war. Even before the Bolsheviks seized power in October 1917, actual political authority had been shifted to the Executive Committee, while the soviet plenum was left with only approval or rejection of ready-made resolutions and with decisions on basic questions. This trend toward concentration continued. Alongside the Executive Committee, and partly in its place, emerged the presidium which consisted of only a few people and took care of all current business. In provincial and district capitals (except for Moscow and Petrograd), urban executive committees merged with the respective district and provincial executive committees. The borough soviets in the major cities disappeared.[160] In areas near the front and in territories conquered by the Red Army, special revolutionary committees with unrestricted powers replaced constitutionally provided soviet organs.[161] They were frequently identical with the Bolshevik Party committee.

At the Seventh All-Russian Soviet Congress in December 1919, Kamenev painted the following dark picture of the soviets during the civil war: "We know that because of the war the best workers were withdrawn in large numbers from the cities, and that therefore at times it becomes difficult in one or another provincial or district capital to form a soviet and make it function. . . . The soviet plenary sessions as political organizations often waste away, the people busy themselves with purely mechanical chores. . . . General soviet sessions are seldom called, and when the deputies meet, it is only to accept a report, listen to a speech, and the like."[162] In February

1921 the presidium of the All-Russian Central Executive Committee announced in a circular letter that the cessation of hostilities now called for "the training of broad masses of workers for reconstruction based on the constitution," that therefore new elections to the soviets would be scheduled, and that the soviets must meet regularly to deal with all important questions.[163]

Centralization at the expense of the local soviets increased and the new central bodies, especially those dealing with the economy, created their own subordinate organs, which clashed with local soviets.[164] The resulting friction and conflicts could not be cleared away even by a legal determination of competences and by the principle of so-called dual subordination (to the soviet executive committee and to the respective technical central organ).[165] The Red Army and the Cheka, the powerful terrorist instrument, in any case stood outside soviet control for all practical purposes.

The rural soviets continued to occupy a special position. The soviet organization in the villages was poorly developed when the Bolsheviks assumed power.[166] In spite of numerous decrees, constitutional provisions, and party agitation, soviet organizations at the lowest level made slow progress. Instructions for the formation of volost and village soviets deliberately harked back to the old institution of the skhod, the peasant assembly, to help the peasants understand the new soviet form.[167] Nor were the village soviets very different in practice from the former schody, except that wealthy farmers were not admitted. Complaints about disintegration of urban soviets were supplemented by reports of the sad rural situation, such as the following from a member of the district soviet of Iur'evez: "I must note, to my regret, that in some places there are actually no soviets at all; they exist only on paper. And even where they do exist, they have no life, there are no meetings, no resolutions or decisions are arrived at."[168] In general, administrative chaos reigned in the countryside, the several authorities worked without any plan, all issued instructions, the volost executive committees were flooded with paper, and so on. At the congress of chairmen of the volost executive committees of Ivanovo Voznesensk province in May 1919, for example, there were complaints that rural soviets had no qualified employees, that some of the peasants were hostile, and that the commissars behaved rudely.[169] The provincial revolutionary committee of Vyatka described the situation very candidly: "It is fortunate for the village that none of the authorities tries to find out if its orders have been followed. The village therefore becomes completely independent. . . . Hardly anything is known in the countryside of the soviet system, actions, or aims."[170]

Bolshevik agrarian policy did its part to prevent the idea of soviets from taking hold among the peasants. After the first phase of the spontaneous agrarian revolution, which was politically determined by the Left Social Revolutionaries, the Bolsheviks proceeded to bring the "socialist" revolution to the countryside. A decree of June 11, 1918, created special "committees of village poverty," and assigned them and armed detachments of factory workers to confiscate grain from the wealthier peasants, to requisition livestock and tools, to distribute them among the rural poor, and even to redistribute land.[171] The poverty committees—called organs of the "dictatorship of the proletariat" by the Bolsheviks—displaced the existing peasants soviets and established their own arbitrary regime. Often they did not content themselves with excluding from the soviets the kulaks and all other anti-Bolshevik elements, but simply dissolved soviets they considered "antisoviet." After a few months the Bolsheviks themselves spoke of "dyarchy" in the villages. On December 2, 1918, to remedy this situation, the All-Russian Central Executive Committee ordered new elections for the village and volost soviets. The poverty committees were to direct the elections, and could exclude any person out of favor. In this way "revolutionary" soviets were to be elected, representing only the rural poor and the loyal segments of the middle peasants.[172] Even with the abolition of the village poverty committees and new Bolshevik tactics to win the middle peasants, the soviets were rejected by the majority of Russian peasants. The soviet structure, which in its simplicity and originality could hark back to the traditional institutions of peasant "democracy," was compromised by its link to the Bolshevik fight against the peasantry. For years to come the peasantry distrusted the soviets, which it rightly considered instruments of the Communist Party.

c) Soviets and the Dictatorship of the Proletariat

The Bolsheviks had called their state a "dictatorship of the proletariat" and the soviets organs of this dictatorship. The new state's theoretical principles had been originated by Lenin in his writings of

1917, especially *State and Revolution*.[173] In later years Lenin, Trotsky, Bukharin, Zinoviev, Stalin, and others expanded those early principles into a theory of the soviets and of the soviet state which was elaborated in the 1920s and—with Stalinist restrictions—in the 1930s.[174] Although the Bolshevik theory, in its idealized abstraction, diverges widely from reality, it nevertheless explains soviet responsibilities and functions within the system of proletarian dictatorship, as seen by the Bolsheviks themselves. This self-image of the soviet system can also serve as the starting point for its critique. The two main problems are the relationship of the soviets to the Communist Party and the question of soviet democracy. Neither was new; both continued older views and modes of behavior acted upon by Lenin from the beginning of his political career through 1905 and especially during the revolution of 1917. The earlier discussion of the relationship of Bolshevism and soviets in 1905 and 1917 allows us to concentrate here on the most important aspects.

In the spring of 1918 Lenin called soviet power the "Russian form of the dictatorship of the proletariat.[175] Soviet power is nothing but the organizational form of the dictatorship of the proletariat, the dicatorship of that advanced class which lifts millions upon millions of exploited workers to the level of the new democracy and independent participation in the state's administration, and which helps the proletariat understand that the disciplined and class-conscious vanguard is their true dependable leader."[176]

A few months later, in his polemic against Kautsky, Lenin wrote that "The soviets are the direct expression of the working and exploited masses, making it easier for them to organize and manage the state. It is precisely the avant-garde of workers and exploited people, the urban proletariat, which is favored, since it is most closely united in the large factories; it is easiest for this group to vote and to control elections. The soviet organization automatically facilitates the association of all workers and exploited people around their avant-garde, around the proletariat."[177]

Thus Lenin separates soviet power into three steps or components:

1) the mass of working and exploited people, who must be "lifted," "attracted," "unified";
2) the avant-garde of workers, the urban proletariat;
3) the vanguard of the proletariat and the leader of the working masses, the Communist Party.[178]

These are old views of Lenin, antedating the first revolution to *What Is To Be Done?* and expressed, in 1904 for example, as follows: "Surely it would be wrong to confuse the party as the vanguard of the working class with the whole class. . . . We are the class party, and therefore almost the whole class (and in times of war, in the era of civil war, the whole class without exception) must act under the leadership of our party."[179]

During the transition from capitalism to communism (dictatorship of the proletariat), therefore, the soviets of workers, peasants, and soldiers deputies, under communist leadership, must attract, organize, and hold the masses of workers (including the proletariat), who on their own have not yet fully achieved "socialist consciousness." The soviets do not exist to express the "vacillating" political will of the masses, but to establish contact between them and their "vanguard," the Communist Party. Starting from Lenin's concept, Stalin developed his "transmission theory" in the 1920s; it defines the relationship between soviets and party as follows: "The party achieves the dictatorship of the proletariat, not directly, but only with the help of the trade unions, through the soviets and their branches. Without these 'transmissions' any kind of firm dictatorship would be impossible."[180] Other Bolshevik leaders also openly admitted that the dictatorship of one party reigns in Russia, which uses the soviets (and other organizations) as "levers" and "transmissions." Trotsky, for example, when he was still at the height of power, declared unmistakably: "General control is concentrated in the hands of the party. It does not rule directly, because its organization is not geared that way. But it decides all basic questions. More than that—our practice has brought it about that in all disputes of any kind . . . the last word lies with the party's Central Committee. . . . We have often been accused of faking the dictatorship of the soviets and of practicing in reality the dictatorship of our party. On this point it can be truly said that the soviet dictatorship was only made possible by the party dictatorship; thanks to the clarity of its theory and its firm revolutionary organization, the party changed the soviets from amorphous labor parliaments into an apparatus of labor rule."[181] Trotsky did not mention that the "amorphous labor parliaments" were free democratic workers organizations and genuine organs of self-government, while the "apparatus of labor rule" in reality was an instrument of Bolshevik Party rule. Zinoviev admitted quite candidly "that soviet rule in Russia could not have been maintained for three years—not even for three weeks—without the iron dictatorship of the Communist Party. Any class-conscious worker must understand that the dictatorship of the working class can be achieved only by the dictatorship of its vanguard, i.e., by the Communist Party. . . . All questions of economic reconstruction, military organization, education, food supply—all these questions, on which the fate of the proletarian revolution depends absolutely, are decided in Russia before all other matters and mostly in the framework of the party organizations. . . . Control by the party over the soviet organs, over the trade unions, is the single durable guarantee that any measures taken will serve not special interests, but the interests of the entire proletariat."[182]

The workers and soldiers councils of 1917 furnished the springboard for the Bolsheviks' seizure of power, and they were determined to retain it irrespective of any change in the popular political mood. They forestalled any non-Bolshevik majority in the soviets by banning the other socialist parties. The Bolshevik Party could therefore have ruled alone and without the soviets after the summer of 1918. On the eve of the October Revolution Lenin had written that the 240,000 members of the Bolshevik Party were as able to rule Russia as 130,-000 landowners had been.[183] But Lenin did not abolish the soviets, although "from the beginning" they were "a foreign body in Bolshevik Party doctrine."[184] Earlier Bolshevik agitation under the slogan "All power to the soviets" had linked the concept of soviets too closely with Bolshevism; the rulers' need to legitimate their reign democratically through the soviets was too strong. But the Bolshevik victory immediately and fundamentally changed the soviet concept. The Russian soviets turned from organs of proletarian self-administration and bulwarks of radical democracy to organs used by the party elite to guide the masses. The party as "the power pointing the way" and the soviets as "transmissions" are something quite different from the concept of self-government by the masses, with its abolition of difference between "top" and "bottom." Lenin described that self-government in theory in 1917, and agitated for it, but the soviet state never put it into practice.

In the Bolshevik soviet system the soviets exist, in Trotsky's words, not to "reflect the majority statically, but to form it dynamically."[185] This "dynamic formation of a majority" is the task of the Communist Party. According to the basic resolution of the Eighth Party Congress of March 1919 "The Communist Party has undertaken to win definitive influence and unquestioned leadership in all organizations of working people, in the trade unions, cooperatives, village communes, etc. The Communist Party strives especially to carry out its program and to exercise unlimited leadership in the present government organizations, the soviets. . . . By practical daily dedicated work in the soviets and by filling all soviet positions with its best and most loyal members, the Russian Communist Party must win undivided political rule in the soviets and practical control over all of its activities."[186] In the system of "democratic centralism" the Communist Party factions in the soviets were bound by the orders of their superior party authorities. Although independents continued to dominate the lowest levels of the soviet pyramid, the Communists controlled numerical majorities in the executive committees from the volosts upward.[187] The same people directed administration of both soviet and party organs. The day-to-day work repeatedly caused problems of precise distinctions between state and party organs although the highest political control, and the right of immediate intervention by the party in soviet activities, were never affected.[188]

A major thesis of Lenin's soviet theory maintained that the soviets, as democratic labor organizations, are far superior to the corresponding institutions of bourgeois-parliamentary democracy. "Proletarian democracy is a million times more democratic than any bourgeois democracy; soviet power is a million times more democratic than the most democratic bourgeois republic."[189] This "millionfold" superiority of soviet democracy rests, in the Bolshevik view, on the fact "that in ruling, the soviets' constant liaison with the mass organizations of the workers and peasants allows the broadest popular participation in governing the state."[190] According to Bolshevik theory, the methods of primitive democracy in the spontaneously formed revolutionary soviets were to erase the contradiction between people and government. "The soviet system tries always to involve people in government, the economy, culture, etc., by refusing to allow management to become the privilege of a single, closed, bureaucratic group, isolated from the communal life of society."[191] Lenin spoke unceasingly of the need to induce workers and peasants to participate in the administration, and educate them to "do things on their own." The party repeated this in hundreds of resolutions.

The attempt at democratic administration through the soviets nevertheless failed. Very shortly after the "destruction" of the old state apparatus, the Bolsheviks, in order to get their own machinery going, were forced to reinstate the same people it had earlier branded as class enemies. Officials of the previous administration made themselves indispensable in numerous departments of the soviets, and the bureaucracy in the many new central authorities grew by leaps and bounds. Control over the new bureaucracy constantly diminished, partly because no genuine political opposition existed. The alienation between "people" and "officials," which the soviet system was supposed to remove, was back again. Beginning in 1918, complaints about "bureaucratic excesses," lack of contact with voters, and new proletarian bureaucrats grew louder and louder.[192] They are part of the history of the soviet state to this day.

Lenin himself, in the final years of his life, had to admit the failure of the first revolutionary attempt to abolish bureaucracy. In 1922 he wrote, "We took our practical apparatus from the old regime, since it was utterly impossible to reorganize it from scratch in such a short time, especially during war and famine."[193] By expanding the party's Central Committee and establishing the central control commission (at the party level) with workers and peasants inspection (at the government level),[194] would wipe out the flaws which in Lenin's words arose because "the same Russian apparatus which we took over from czarism" had been "only superficially anointed with the holy soviet oil."[195] Lenin thought the bureaucracy survived primarily because Russia's low cultural level which turned "the soviets, which had been planned to be organs of government *by* the workers into organs of government *for* the workers, into a government by the proletarian vanguard, but not by the working masses themselves."[196] Only prolonged education would enable the backward Russian people themselves to govern. Stalin later described the soviets as "schools for the art of government for tens and hundreds of thousands of workers and peasants."[197]

As early as 1919 a keen Western observer wrote: "Perhaps in the last resort the soviets only mean an increase in bureaucracy . . . and are a way station leading to the replenishment of bureaucracy by working-class elements."[198] Future developments in Soviet Russia bore him out. The soviets, designed to prevent bureaucratization through constant control by the voters, their right to recall deputies, and the union of legislative and executive branches, turned into bureaucratic authorities without effective control from below. Achieving their aim required the free play of political forces, which the Bolsheviks had foreclosed by their party monopoly. Lenin's idealization of "soviet democracy," and his utopia of a state without officials and without police, from the outset contradicted his theory of the party's unconditional leadership. The Bolsheviks were caught in a real dilemma. If attracting the masses to administration and government required loosening their tight political rein on the soviets, opposition forces might win the soviets. But with Communist dictatorship, the people, especially the peasantry, participated only minimally in the soviet elections, since no change or improvement resulted. Although the Bolsheviks tried to arouse popular interest by periodic "stimulation campaigns," they would not relinquish their autocracy and reestablish genuine soviet democracy. Thus the Russian soviets never had a chance to prove their viability and capabilities. The "soviets," allegedly ruling in Russia since 1918, are only powerless adjuncts of the party bureaucracy, "silent walk-on players."[199] Removing the ruling Communist Party from power by a democratic soviet decision seems unthinkable.

The cause for the soviets' developing into purely decorative institutions was never revealed more clearly than by a leading member of the Bolshevik Party. During the internal party debates around 1920, Aleksandra Kollontai wrote: "We are afraid to let the masses do things themselves. We are afraid of allowing their creativity. We fear criticism. We no longer trust the masses. Therein . . . lies the origin of our bureaucracy. Initiative wanes, the desire to act dies out. 'If that's the way it is, let the officials take care of us.' In this way a very damaging division grows up: we—that is, the workers—and they—that is, the soviet officials, on whom everything depends. Here is the root of all evil."[200] And no one better foresaw the future degeneration of the soviets, only a few months after their elevation to official state power, than Rosa Luxemburg, who retained her critical sense despite all her admiration and appreciation of the Bolshevik revolution. Her judgment of the Bolshevik soviet system is contained in the following sentences: "Lenin and Trotsky have presented the soviets as the only true representation of the working masses in place of representative bodies elected by universal suffrage. But with nationwide suppression of political activity, soviet activity must also diminish. Without general elections, unlimited freedom of the press and assembly, and open debate, life dies in any public institution, becomes a pseudolife in which only bureaucracy remains. Public life gradually goes to sleep, a few dozen party leaders of inexhaustible energy and boundless idealism control and rule, a dozen outstanding minds among them are in charge, and an elite from among the workers are occasionally bidden to conventions to applaud the leaders' speeches, unanimously to approve resolutions put before them—at bottom, therefore, government by clique. True, a dictatorship; but not the dictatorship of the proletariat, rather the dictatorship of a handful of politicians—dictatorship in the bourgeois sense, in the sense of Jacobin rule."[201]

3. END OF THE COUNCIL MOVEMENT: THE KRONSTADT INSURRECTION OF 1921

During the winter of 1920–1921 the Bolshevik regime suffered a dangerous internal crisis. Russia's catastrophic economic situation at the end of the civil war, and the rigorous centralization, growing bureaucratization, and dictatorship by party leaders, created general discontent among workers and peasants and even within the Bolshevik Party. The "working masses," in whose name the Bolsheviks ruled, had for three years gone hungry, been cold, endured privations of every sort; now they hoped that the end of fighting would bring an improvement in the economy and a loosening of the strict dictatorship—in short, true fulfillment of the revolutionary promises of 1917. The Bolshevik leadership fully recognized the necessity of progressing from "war communism" to peaceful reconstruction, but party members disagreed on methods, particularly in the so-called trade-union discussion that dominated the Communist Party in the winter months of 1920–1921.[202]

The controversy was in essence over the division of power between the trade unions which encompassed the majority of the proletariat, and the party, which represented only a minority. While the leaders of the Workers Opposition (Shliapnikov, Kollontai, and others), who advocated production management by the trade unions, were themselves Communists, and the clash of opinions took place within the party, among its "heads," they also voiced a genuine dissatisfaction among the masses. The Workers Opposition slogan of "production democracy" protested the factory-manager system, the dominant state bureaucracy, and the "supraclass policy which is neither more nor less than 'adaptation' by the leaders to the contradictory interests of a diverse population."[203] The economy was to be organized by an "all-Russian congress of producers, formed by professions or branches of industry. They are to elect a central organ to manage the entire economy of the republic."[204] At the lowest level, in the factories, the factory committees were once again to have the last word.

What the Workers Opposition raised was simply the problem of proletarian democracy within the dictatorship of the proletariat, though in official Bolshevik doctrine the two systems were identical. Reality, however, taught the workers that the soviet state was not a proletarian state in which they could control their own fate. The Workers Opposition wanted self-government through trade union participation in economic management. They gave as yet no thought to democratizing the state—the soviets—or of relinquishing the Communist Party's monopoly. Rather, the group demanded the broadest kind of freedom and open discussion within the party, the consistent application of the suffrage principle, and cleansing from the party of all nonproletarian elements.[205] In this it came close to another opposition group, the Democratic Centralists, who fought the Central Executive Committee's dominance over local soviets and demanded restoration of the soviets' rights that had been granted by the constitution but ignored in practice during the civil war.[206]

Lenin recognized the potential danger from such opposition to the party's unity and leadership. Despite the popular mood he was determined unconditionally to maintain the dictatorship, if necessary through concessions to the peasants. Lenin specifically stated that Russia was not a pure workers state but a workers and peasants republic, and that therefore the trade unions must remain special-interest representatives of the proletariat, even while they served as "schools of communism."[207] Thus he also opposed Trotsky, who wanted the trade unions formally integrated into the state apparatus, entrusted with administrative duties, and incorporated into his militarized labor system.[208] But on the issue of unconditional party monopoly, Trotsky and Lenin were united against the Workers Opposition. "The Workers Opposition has come out with dangerous slogans. They have made a fetish of democratic principles. They have placed the workers' right to elect representatives above the party, as it were, as if the party were not entitled to assert its dictatorship even if that dictatorship temporarily clashed with the passing moods of the workers' democracy." Trotsky invoked the "revolutionary historical birthright of the party," which obliged it "to maintain its dictatorship, regardless of temporary wavering in the spontaneous moods of the masses."[209] At the Tenth Communist Party Congress in March 1921 a resolution written by Lenin stigmatized the Workers Opposition theses as "anarcho-syndicalist deviations," and the party's unity was restored by severe decrees against the formation of factions.[210] The Bolsheviks strengthened their dictatorship at the very time when they were forcibly opposed by the proletarian masses, in whose name they ruled.

While the discussions about trade unions took place internally and the opposition remained legal, "other workers' and peasants' sons in uniform had no such scruples."[211] Discontent and latent unrest among the proletarian-peasant masses erupted in the Kronstadt insurrection. This event rang down the curtain on the Russian revolutionary movement and ended any organized mass rising against Bolshevism. More effectively than anti-Bolshevik criticism from the outside, the Kronstadt uprising illuminated the internal contradiction of the "dictatorship of the proletariat" that supposedly reigned in Russia. The rising therefore became so dangerous for the Bolshevik rulers that to this day they conceal or falsify the facts.[212]

The Kronstadt movement must be seen in the context of the regime's political and economic crisis at the end of the civil war. In the weeks before the Kronstadt rising there were numerous peasant disturbances in the countryside and workers strikes in the cities.[213] In mid-February 1921 dissatisfaction among Petrograd workers reached a climax. The party organization, weakened by factional disputes during the trade-union discussion, lost control over the factories. The workers, embittered by drastic reductions in food rations and the closing of numerous factories, with ensuing unemployment, vented their exasperation in demonstrations. They demanded liberalized trade to improve urban food supplies. When demonstrations were prohibited, a protest strike began in several factories on February 23; it spread quickly, and on February 25 it led to street demonstrations and even a few armed clashes. On February 24 the Bolsheviks had placed the city under martial law. On February 26 the strike movement was harshly condemned by a defense committee formed under

Zinoviev by the Petrograd soviet. The Bolsheviks called in troop reinforcements, since they could not trust units based in the city. The strikes nevertheless continued to spread until February 28; on that day the workers of the famous Putilov Works also downed tools.[214]

The workers' demands, at first limited and purely economic, quickly became political. The semilegal groups of Mensheviks, Social Revolutionaries, and anarchists published leaflets and appeals and sent speakers to the workers meetings. Contrary to subsequent Bolshevik assertions, however, the socialist party groups, which were weak in any case, had no thought of a violent insurrection, since they considered that futile. The Mensheviks, for example, did not share the hope, widely held in Petrograd during those days, for a second "February"—that is, the overthrow of Bolshevik rule. They wanted a partial success of looser party dictatorship, and then a gradual democratization. "Free elections to the soviets as a first step to replacing the dictatorship with the rule of democracy—that was the political slogan of the day," wrote Dan, who was active in Petrograd during the February Days until his arrest on February 26.[215] An appeal issued on February 27 similarly stated: "A complete change in government policy is necessary. First of all the workers and peasants need freedom. They want not to live under Bolshevik decrees but to determine their own fate. . . . Organize and demand relentlessly the release of all jailed socialist and unaffiliated workers; suspension of martial law; freedom of speech, press, and assembly for all workers; free new elections to the factory committees, trade unions, and soviets."[216]

The Bolsheviks were able to settle the Petrograd strikes and disturbances in a few days by threats and material concessions. But the spark jumped to Kronstadt, the naval base outside Petrograd's gates, the old revolutionary center, whose radical sailors had always been counted among Lenin's most loyal followers. Their revolutionary tradition, however, made the workers and sailors especially sensitive to the methods of the Bolshevik dictatorship, which not only opposed the common class enemy, but also restrained the proletarian masses. The radical sense of freedom of the Kronstadters—among whom the Left Social Revolutionaries and anarchists had considerable influence by 1917—also infected the young Ukrainian recruits who had been newly enrolled in the fall of 1920. They had brought with them from home the widespread peasant discontent with Bolshevik agrarian policy, and later they became the revolt's activists. The Communist Party organizations in the Baltic fleet and in the city were half decayed, had little influence among the sailors, and themselves partially opposed their superior party organs. A party conference of February 15 demanded democratization of party activity; some delegates openly opposed the party units in the navy.[217]

News of the Petrograd strikes alarmed the Kronstadt sailors. While Zinoviev and Kalinin, with difficulty, kept the sailors at the Petrograd naval base from joining the workers movement, the Kronstadt sailors made contact with the strikers. On February 28 the sailors on the battleship *Petropavlovsk* formulated a resolution demanding, among other things, free new elections to the Kronstadt soviet, whose term was about to expire. Simultaneously the sailors sent a delegation to Petrograd, to get firsthand information of the situation there. Other ships joined the *Petropavlovsk* resolution, and on March 1 over 10,000 sailors, soldiers, and workers assembled for an outdoor mass demonstration. Kalinin, chairman of the All-Russian Central Executive Committee, took part in the assembly at which was read the sailors delegation report openly denouncing suppression of the workers' legitimate demands. Kalinin and the naval commissar Kuzmin tried and failed to calm the sailors, and the outraged crowd unanimously adopted the *Petropavlovsk* resolution.

The resolution stated, in part: "Because the present-day soviets do not express the will of the workers and peasants, new elections should immediately be held, after a period of free agitation. . . . Freedom of speech and press for workers, peasants, anarchists, and leftist socialist parties; freedom of assembly for the trade unions and peasant associations; release of all socialist political prisoners and of all workers, peasants, soldiers, and sailors arrested on account of their political activity. Abolition of all political units in the army, since no single party should have special rights to propagandize. Equalization of all workers' rations. Peasants' free right to control their soil and to keep livestock as long as they do not employ paid workmen."[218]

The following day, March 2, a spontaneous movement organized. A conference of about 300 delegates of sailors, soldiers, and workers elected a 5-man presidium, headed by the naval clerk Petrichenko of the *Petropavlovsk*; it acted as a provisional revolutionary committee and within a few days was enlarged to 15 members.[219] The assembly further decided to arrest the Bolshevik soviet chairman Vasilev, the naval commander Kuzmin, and the battleship commissar Korsunin. The most important task ahead was the preparation for new elections to the soviet. The revolutionary committee stopped there. Aside from the three named above, no Communist was taken into custody. On the contrary, the sailors tried to attract as many party members as possible from the ranks. And in fact, during the next few days numerous Bolsheviks—776 altogether, almost one-third of the membership—officially resigned from the party.[220] It was not until the uprising's critical days that about 70 Communists were arrested, none of them being harmed.[221]

The higher military echelons, among them former czarist officers appointed by the Bolsheviks themselves, now joined the mutinous sailors, thus providing for the Bolsheviks an excuse to denounce a White Guard and counterrevolutionary conspiracy against soviet power. A wave of slander through the press and radio burst over Kronstadt. On March 4 the Petrograd soviet condemned the movement as a counterrevolutionary crime, and on March 5 Trotsky, in his capacity as commissar of war, addressed an ultimatum to the naval base demanding unconditional surrender.[222] The insurgents refrained from offensive military action. Social Revolutionary leader Viktor Chernov radioed from Reval an offer to come to Kronstadt and to support the city with shipments of essential goods, which was refused by the revolutionary committee.[223] They also rejected proposals by the military to storm the fortress of Oranienbaum across the Gulf. Bloodshed was to be avoided at all costs, and an accommodation with the soviet regime was strongly anticipated. At the same time the Kronstadters vaguely hoped to ignite a general popular revolution against Bolshevism. This belief seemed justified by simultaneous peasant unrest in various regions of Russia, especially in Tambov province, and the strikes in Petrograd. The insurgents' passive behavior, combined with the naval base's isolated strategic location, made a military success for the insurrection impossible. Nevertheless, more than ten days passed before the Bolshevik attack across the ice of the Gulf of Finland conquered the fortress. Most of the participating Red Army troops were politically unreliable, and there were protest meetings and open refusals to fight. It took massive political propaganda—in which 300 delegates to the Tenth Party Congress participated, the activity of military tribunals, and the dispatch of elite troops to conquer the town on March 17, after an earlier attack on March 7 had been unsuccessful. In the early morning hours of March 18 the last defenders had to give up their resistance. Hundreds were shot on the spot, hundreds more were sent to the Petrograd prisons, a few thousand escaped to Finland.[224]

What were the aims of Kronstadt? The movement arose spontaneously out of the masses' discontent with Communist rule. At the beginning it was anything but a deliberate armed action against the regime. Only the inflexible attitude of the Bolshevik government worsened the situation and drove the Kronstadt sailors to call for a "third revolution" to abolish the Communist dictatorship. The fact, for example, that Lenin was never personally criticized is significant; of all the Bolshevik leaders, it was primarily Trotsky and Zinoviev who were attacked and held responsible for the bloody conflict.[225] Events left the insurgents no time to formulate a detailed program. Their demands, as expressed more or less lucidly in issues of the revolutionary *Izvestija*, reflected the most urgent immediate desires of the workers and peasants. Aside from the restoration of political freedom, the demands included the end of Communist agrarian policy, with its forcible interventions in peasants' property, and abolition of unequal food rations in the cities. The prerogatives of the party and state bureaucracy were to be eliminated, and Communist domination of the army was to be abolished.

All these demands were offshoots of the one fundamental: free elections to the soviets. This demand winds like a red thread through all the insurgents' proclamations, from the first appeal of the *Petropavlovsk*. It virtually symbolized the Kronstadt movement, turning the one-time Bolshevik slogan "All power to the soviets" against the Bolsheviks themselves. "Soviet power must express the will of all the workers without the rule of any political party," an article in *Izvestija* stated. "Kronstadt, the avant-garde of the revolution, made the beginning. . . . It is not here that mean intentions toward the soviets are harbored. The Communist rumors that the insurrection is antisoviet are not true. . . . The rule of a single party must not continue. Our soviets must no longer express the will of the party but rather the will of the voters."[226] The Kronstadt sailors were unconditional adherents of the soviet system, but they believed it should be independent, democratic, free of one-party monopoly. The Bolsheviks, having triumphed in October 1917 with the slogan of soviet power, did not effect soviet democracy, and therefore the insurgents' hatred was directed against them. "Down with commissars' rule! In assuming power, the Communist Party promised all goods to the workers. And what do we see? Three years ago we were told, 'Whenever you want, you can recall your delegates, you can have new elections to the soviets.' And when we in Kronstadt demanded new elections without pressure from the party, the newly emerged Trepov-Trotsky gave the order: Don't spare the bullets!"[227]

The Kronstadters stood by the October Revolution of 1917. They were definitely leftist, and expressly rejected a parliamentary republic with a constituent assembly. "The soviets, not the constituent assembly, are the bastions of the workers." They did not demand freedom for former landowners, officers, and capitalists. But they saw themselves cheated of the fruits of the revolution, and its ideals betrayed by the Bolsheviks. The programmatic article, "What We Are Fighting For," in *Izvestija* of March 8, 1921, clearly expressed these feelings: "The working class had hoped for emancipation through the October Revolution, but found only greater enslavement. The police power of the monarchy fell to usurpers—the Communists, who gave the workers not freedom, but constant fear of the Cheka. . . . What is worst and most criminal, however, is the intellectual enslavement, the spiritual subjection when everyone was forced to think as the Communists command. . . . Even death is easier than this life under Communist dictatorship. There is no middle way! Victory or death! Red Kronstadt sets the example. . . . Here the banner of insurrection has been raised for liberation from three years of tyranny and oppression by the Communist autocracy, which puts to shame the three-century yoke of the monarchy. Here in Kronstadt the cornerstone has been laid for the third revolution, which will free the worker from his last chains and will open a new, wide path for socialist creativity."[228]

The visionary realm of freedom was to be achieved by the soviets. "All power to the soviets and not the parties" was the most frequently used slogan in the revolutionary *Izvestija*. Next to it were: "Long live the power of freely elected soviets," "The power of the soviets will free the working peasantry from the yoke of the Communists," "Down with the counterrevolution of the left and the right."[229] The slogan of free soviets, raised by revolutionary Kronstadt, showed the vitality of the soviet concept among the masses. The revolt against Bolshevism was also the clearest possible proof of

the great gap between Bolshevik dictatorship and the original ideals
of soviet rule. The realm of social equality proclaimed by Lenin in
State and Revolution; elimination of the bureaucracy, aimed at by the
first decrees of the soviet government; self-government by the masses,
which seemed embodied in the soviet slogan—all these were undone
by harsh reality during the years of Bolshevik dictatorship. The
Kronstadters thought that the existing soviets incarnated the betrayed
revolution, and that free elections to independent soviets would form
the overture of the "third revolution." All written declarations of the
Kronstadt revolutionaries radiate an irrational faith in the soviet
idea, which was to renew Russia. The soviets that had been per-
verted, eroded, made the cloak of Bolshevik dictatorship, now celebrated their resurrection in beleaguered Kronstadt.

The idea was not enough to set all Russia afire. The insurgents
lacked support by an organized political movement, which no longer
existed in Russia. The echo of the Kronstadt events therefore remained comparatively feeble; only a few anarchist clubs in Moscow
and Petrograd published leaflets advocating support of the Kronstadters,[230] while the official Menshevik position consisted of pious
declarations of sympathy and demands for an amicable settlement.[231]
The Bolsheviks very clearly recognized the danger of the slogan
"Free soviets," which threatened to pull the legitimacy of their power
out from under them. The pure soviet idea irreconcilably contradicted
their party dictatorship. The Bolsheviks therefore tried by every
means to prevent the fire's spreading. The Tenth Party Congress,
which convened on March 8 under the threatening shadow of the
Kronstadt rebellion, restored iron discipline within the ruling
group.[232] At the same time Lenin effected the great internal political
turn from war communism to the New Economic Policy. He had
considered the plan earlier, but the Kronstadt insurrection hastened
his decision. The Bolsheviks hoped to soften the masses' dissatisfaction by relaxing government coercion in the economy, especially in
agriculture. They even introduced a "stimulation campaign" to re-
vitalize the soviets.[233] But this campaign included none of the Kronstadt demands, neither free elections, nor loosening of party control.
The remnants of the non-Bolshevik parties were finally eliminated
without a formal decision: their members either were arrested or
publicly recanted; some leaders were allowed to emigrate; others
were put on political trial.[234]

Since 1921 there has been no organized political opposition to the Bolshevik regime in Russia, only conflicts of power within the Communist Party leadership itself. None has ever shaken the foundations of the dictatorship.

Outlook

The soviet movement from 1905 to 1921 typifies the Russian revolution, but in results transcends it. Because no democratic parliamentary system existed, the spontaneously formed soviets of workers deputies automatically became all-encompassing representative organs of the "working" masses and then revolutionary organs of the state, thus preparing for the "leap over," the "bourgeois-democratic" phase desired by Lenin and the Bolsheviks. The Russian soviets further embody the revolution's focus on the hitherto-disenfranchised workers and peasants, led by an intelligentsia who worshiped radical social theories. Bolshevism incorporated the soviet tendencies toward social revolution and adapted them to the revolutionary currents of 1917. However, Lenin's party also sought to subdue the antistatist and anticentralist forces inherent in the soviets and to subordinate them to the exigencies and aims of dictatorial "socialist" reconstruction. The result was alienation and finally open conflict between Communism and the "pure" soviet principle. Stalinism, with its coercive machinery of police, army, and bureaucracy, was the final denial of the original soviet idea of the October Revolution. In the autumn of 1956 during the struggle against dictatorship in Eastern Europe, a revolutionary rebirth of the soviets occurred, this time directed against the "degenerate" Russian soviets.

The Russian soviet movement was both economic and political, the two facets being closely interwoven. Political freedom bordering on anarchy went hand in hand with economic equality. Self-government by elected factory committees and peasant cooperatives represented an economic democracy within a political framework of decentralized autonomous communes. These inherent tendencies of the Russian soviets were repressed and destroyed by the centralized planned Bolshevik state economy. Was this development inevitable at that stage of early industrial society in Russia, or were great future possibilities simply cut off? The Yugoslav attempt to build a "socialist market economy" based on self-management in the factories, and similar efforts in Poland, may indicate that in Russia after 1917 a "production democracy" was not necessarily doomed from the outset.

For Russian Communism the soviet problem is still very much alive. The Eastern European workers soviets reopened a basic question of Marxism and Leninism, which in the long run Bolshevism cannot ignore. It is the key problem of the Bolshevik soviet system: how can the "dictatorship of the proletariat" be reconciled with workers democracy? That this is not purely an ideological problem which can be resolved "dialectically," but an urgent practical problem of state and economy, is shown by the 1957 economic reorganization and the constant efforts to organize the "participation of workers in the management of production" through existing organizations, such as trade unions. Certainly the Russian workers want industrial codetermination, and if the soviet leadership makes genuine concessions, the soviet question may revive in Russia also, at least in the economic sphere.

Appendixes

Appendix A
The Soviets in the Revolution of 1905

The following list includes only soviets whose existence is unquestionably verified by several sources and references in the literature. Strike committees and other soviet-like organizations are not included. The list does not, therefore, lay any claim to completeness.

I = *Izvestija* (*news*) or Bulletin of the Soviet

1. SOVIETS OF WORKERS DEPUTIES

Alapaevsk (Perm province)
Aleksandrov (Vladimir province)
Aleksandrovsk
   (Ekaterinoslav province)
Baku (I)
Bialystok
Ekaterinburg
Ekaterinoslav (I)
Golutvin (Moscow province)
Ivanovo Voznesensk
Kiev
Kostroma (I)
Kremenchug (I)
Libau
Lugansk
Mariupol
Moscow (I)
Motovilichinskij (Perm province)
Mytišči (Moscow province)
Nadeždinskij (Perm province)
Nikolaev

Nizhni Tagil (Perm province)
Novorossiysk (I)
Odessa (I)
Orechovo-Zuevo (Moscow province)
Perm
Reval (Tallinn)
Rostov
St. Petersburg (I)
Samara
Saratov
Smolensk
Soči
Sulin (Novočerkassk province)
Taganrog (I)
Tver
Voronezh
Votkinsk (Vyatka province)
Vyatka (I)
Yuzovka (Ekaterinoslav province) (I)
Zlatoust (Ufa province)

2. SOVIETS OF SOLDIERS DEPUTIES

Chita	Moscow	Vladivostok
Harbin	Sevastopol	

3. SOVIETS OF WORKERS AND SOLDIERS DEPUTIES

Irkutsk   Krasnoyarsk

Appendix B
The Second All-Russian Soviet Congress of October 1917

No exact count was kept of the delegates to the Second All-Russian Congress of Soviets of Workers and Soldiers Deputies held on October 25 and 26 (November 7 and 8), 1917. Several diverging reports therefore exist.

Column I: Contemporary newspaper reports

Column II: Delegates' questionnaires

Column III: Preliminary count of the credentials commission

Column IV: Statements of the faction offices at the beginning of the congress

Column V: Count at the conclusion of the congress, after several groups had resigned

Party	I	II	III	IV	V
Bolsheviks	250	338	300	390	390
Social Revolutionaries	159	32	193	160	179
Left SRs		98			
Moderate SRs		40			
Right SRs		16			
Ukrainian SRs	6	4	7	7	21
Mensheviks	60	14	68	72	
Menshevik-Internationalists		35		6	
Menshevik-Oboroncy		22			
United Internationalists (*Novaja Žizn'*)	14	16	14	14	35
Bund		11	10		
Trudoviki		1			

Party	I	II	III	IV	V
Anarchists	3		3		
Independent Socialists	3				
Polish Socialist Party (PPS) and Polish Social Democrats			10		
People's Socialists			3		
Lithuanian Socialists			4		
Unaffiliated	22	23	36		
Unknown			22		
Totals	517	650	670	649	625

Vtoroji vserossijskij s-ezd sovetov rabočich i soldatskich deputatov, Moscow and Leningrad, 1928, p. 171, n. 15.

Appendix C
Political and Social Structure of the Soviets, 1918–1922

A. POLITICAL STRUCTURE

I. District Soviets	1918	1919	1920	1921	1922
1. Congresses			*Percentages*		
Communists	60.6	55.4	43.0	44.0	54.4
Other Parties	14.2	4.9	0.7	0.3	0.1
Unaffiliated	25.2	39.7	56.3	55.7	45.5
2. Executive Committees					
Communists	83.5	85.9	79.9	74.4	81.2
Other Parties	{ 16.5	1.0	4.7	0.1	—
Unaffiliated	{	13.1	15.4	25.5	18.8

II. Provincial Soviets	1918	1919	1920	1921	1922
1. Congresses					
Communists	71.4	79.9	78.6	74.8	78.8
Other Parties	14.2	4.7	0.2	0.1	—
Unaffiliated	14.4	15.4	21.2	25.1	21.2
2. Executive Committees					
Communists	83.9	88.9	91.3	83.6	91.0
Other Parties	16.1	0.7	0.8	0.4	0.2
Unaffiliated	—	10.4	7.9	14.0	8.8

B. SOCIAL STRUCTURE

I. District Soviets	*1920*	*1921*	*1922*
		Percentages	
1. Congresses			
Peasants	65.4	63.3	59.1
Workers	16.2	15.0	16.8
White-collar workers	18.4	21.7	24.1
2. Executive Committees			
Peasants	20.8	28.4	24.4
Workers	32.8	28.7	31.5
White-collar workers	46.4	42.9	44.1
II. Provincial Soviets			
1. Congresses			
Peasants	36.7	36.5	34.7
Workers	33.3	31.0	34.0
White-collar workers	30.0	32.5	31.3
2. Executive Committees			
Peasants	8.8	12.5	10.2
Workers	34.1	35.1	43.3
White-collar workers	57.1	52.4	46.5

Sovety, s-ezdy sovetov i ispolkomy, Moscow, 1924, pp. 25–52.

Notes

INTRODUCTION

1. Throughout this book *council* and *soviet* are used as synonyms. Besides their original meaning, the Russian *sovet*, English *council*, German *Rat*, and French *conseil* refer to any political, economic, etc., advisory body and did so in czarist Russia as today in the Soviet Union. In the special historical-political sense the "soviets" began as "Councils of Workers Deputies" (sovety rabočich deputatov), then became "Councils of Workers, Peasants, and Soldiers Deputies" (sovety rabočich, krest'janskich i soldatskich deputatov), and finally "Councils of Working People's Deputies" (sovety deputatov trudjaščhichsja), as they are called in the constitution of 1936. They are often referred to in the text simply as workers councils, peasants councils, etc.
2. See F. Gutmann, *Das Rätesystem, seine Verfechter und seine Probleme*, Munich 1922; *Die Parteien und das Rätesystem*, Charlottenburg 1919; W. Tormin, *Zwischen Rätediktatur und sozialer Demokratie. Die Geschichte der Rätebewegung in der deutschen Revolution 1918–19*, Düsseldorf 1954.
3. See O. Anweiler, "Die Arbeiterselbstverwaltung in Polen," *Osteuropa*, 8 (1958), pp. 224–232; "Die Räte in der ungarischen Revolution 1956," *Osteuropa*, 8 (1958), pp. 393–400.
4. A. Rosenberg, *Geschichte des Bolschewismus von Marx bis zur Gegenwart*, Berlin 1932; Martin Buber, *Pfade in Utopia*, Heidelberg 1950.

CHAPTER ONE
ANTECEDENTS OF THE RUSSIAN COUNCILS

1. See W. Tormin, *Zwischen Rätediktatur und sozialer Demokratie*, Düsseldorf 1954, p. 7.

2. A. Rosenberg, *Geschichte des Bolschewismus von Marx bis zur Gegenwart,* Berlin 1932, p. 92.
3. F. Wersin, *Diktatur des Proletariats,* dissertation, Breslau, n. d., p. 3.
4. Rosenberg, p. 92.
5. See W. Mautner, *Der Bolschewismus,* Stuttgart 1922, pp. 275 f.
6. See E. Bernstein, *Sozialismus und Demokratie in der grossen englischen Revolution,* 3rd ed., Stuttgart 1919; W. Kottler, *Demokratie und Rätegedanke in der grossen englischen Revolution* (Leipziger rechtswissenschaftliche Studien, vol. 15), Leipzig 1925; E. B. Pašukanis, "Cromwells Soldatenräte," in Otto Hoetzsch, ed., *Aus der historischen Wissenschaft der Sovet-Union,* Berlin and Königsberg, 1929, pp. 128–152.
7. Pašukanis, p. 133.
8. K. Korsch, "Revolutionäre Kommune," *Die Aktion,* 1929, p. 176.
9. The literature concerning the history of the Commune from 1789 to 1794 is vast and cannot be cited here. Among the general works on the French Revolution mention may be made of P. Kropotkin, *Die französische Revolution 1789–1793,* Leipzig 1909. See also the older but well documented work by B. Becker, *Geschichte der revolutionären Pariser Kommune in den Jahren 1789 bis 1794,* Braunschweig 1875. Valuable bibliographic and source references are also contained in two contributions to the Festschrift for A. Meusel, *Beiträge zum neuen Geschichtsbild,* Berlin 1956, by A. Soboul, "An den Ursprüngen der Volksdemokratie. Politische Aspekte der Sansculottendemokratie im Jahre II" (pp. 131–151) and by W. Markov, "Uber das Ende der Pariser Sansculottenbewegung" (pp. 152–183).
10. Kropotkin, p. 232.
11. See Mautner, pp. 278 f., where further references are given.
12. K. Marx, *Die Klassenkämfe in Frankreich,* Berlin 1925, p. 32.
13. This view predominates in the previously cited work by Martin Buber, *Pfade in Utopia,* Heidelberg 1950. See also T. Ramm, *Die grossen Sozialisten als Rechts- und Sozialphilosophen,* vol. 1: *Die Vorläufer. Die Theoretiker des Endstadiums,* Stuttgart 1955; G. D. H. Cole, *A History of Socialist Thought,* vol. 1: *The Forerunners, 1789–1850;* vol. 2: *Marxism and Anarchism, 1850–1890,* London 1953–1954; M. Nettlau, *Der Anarchismus von Proudhon zu Kropotkin,* Berlin 1927.
14. O. Seeling, *Der Rätegedanke und seine Verwirklichung in Sowjetrussland,* Berlin 1925, p. 37.
15. P. Heintz, *Die Autoritätsproblematik bei Proudhon,* Cologne 1956; the work also contains a bibliography of Proudhon's writings and of the secondary literature. See also Nettlau; Cole, vol. 1, pp. 201–218; Buber, pp. 46–67; E. Thier, "Marx und Proudhon," in *Marxismusstudien,* 2nd series, Tübingen 1957, pp. 120–150.
16. Heintz, p. 13.
17. Quoted in Nettlau, p. 15.
18. In his work *De la Capacité politique des classes ouvrières* (1864) Proudhon wrote the following prophetic words which define centralist commu-

nism: "A compact democracy, ostensibly based on the dictatorship of the masses, but in which the masses have no more power than is needed to secure universal servitude, according to the following formulas and principles borrowed from established absolutism: indivisibility of public power, absorbing centralization, systematic destruction of all individual, corporate, and local initiative which would foster disruption, and an inquisitorial police." Quoted in Buber, pp. 57–58.

19. The connection between Proudhon's ideas with workers' autonomy in Yugoslavia is mentioned in V. Meier, *Das neue jugoslawische Wirtschaftssystem*, Zurich and St. Gallen 1956, pp. 103–104.

20. Concerning Bakunin, see P. Scheibert, *Von Bakunin zu Lenin*, vol. 1 (Studien zur Geschichte Osteuropas, vol. 3), Leiden 1956. The next two volumes are announced for publication shortly. P. 133, n. 1, contains information about Bakunin's works. For his biography, see E. H. Carr, *Michael Bakunin*, London 1937. A systematic compilation of Bakunin's political ideas drawn from his numerous works was undertaken by G. P. Maximoff, *The Political Philosophy of Bakunin. Scientific Anarchism*, Glencoe, Illinois 1953.

21. In W. Blos, ed., *Karl Marx oder Bakunin? Demokratie oder Diktatur? Neuausgabe der Berichte an die Sozialistische Internationale über M. Bakunin*, Stuttgart 1920, pp. 89 ff.

22. Letter from Bakunin to Albert Richard, April 1, 1870, in Nettlau, pp. 148 ff.

23. Blos, p. 91.

24. Maximoff, p. 410.

25. Maximoff, p. 289.

26. An extensive bibliography for the history of the Commune of 1871 is given by G. del Bo in *Movimento Operaio*, n. s. 4 (1952), pp. 104–153. A selection of sources with connecting texts is found in *Pariser Kommune 1871. Berichte und Dokumente von Zeitgenossen*, Berlin 1931. See also B. Becker, *Geschichte und Theorie der Pariser revolutionären Kommune des Jahres 1871*, Leipzig 1879; P. Lissagaray, *Geschichte der Kommune von 1871*, Stuttgart 1891; F. Jellinek, *The Paris Commune of 1871*, London 1937; H. Koechlin, *Die Pariser Kommune im Bewusstsein ihrer Anhänger*, Basel 1950.

27. See *Pariser Kommune*, pp. 367 ff.

28. See the list of names of members of the Commune, with their professions and political orientation, in *Pariser Kommune*, pp. 439 ff.

29. Lissagaray, p. 145.

30. *Pariser Kommune*, pp. 243 ff.

31. See the declaration to the French people, April 19, 1871, in *Pariser Kommune*, pp. 281–282.

32. *Pariser Kommune*, p. 216.

33. Letter to Kugelmann, April 17, 1871, *Neue Zeit*, 20:1, p. 710; this passage also in Edmund Wilson, *To the Finland Station*, Garden City, New York 1953, p. 284.

34. See T. Ramm, "Die künftige Gesellschaftsordnung nach der Theorie von Marx und Engels," in *Marxismusstudien*, 2nd series, Tübingen 1957, pp. 77–119; *Der Rätegedanke als Staatstheorie und seine Keime in den Schriften von Karl Marx und Friedrich Engels*, n. p., n. d.

35. H. Laski, *The Communist Manifesto, An Introduction Together with the Original Text and Prefaces by Karl Marx and Friedrich Engels*, New York 1967, p. 160.

36. K. Marx, *Ethüllugen über den Kommunistenprozess zu Köln* (Sozialdemokratische Bibliothek, vol. 4), Hottingen-Zurich 1885, p. 78.

37. Laski, p. 160.

38. This is the point from which Trotsky subsequently derived his famous theory of "permanent revolution." In fact, the cited sentence by Marx contains the core of Trotsky's revolutionary program.

39. Marx, *Enthüllungen*, pp. 79–80. Also in *Capital*, p. 362.

40. Marx, *Enthüllungen*, p. 81. Also in *Capital*, p. 365.

41. Karl Marx, *Der Bürgerkrieg in Frankreich*, Berlin 1891, p. 25.

42. Rosenberg, p. 25.

43. Laski, p. 110.

44. Marx, *Bürgerkrieg*, pp. 46–47. Also in *Capital*, pp. 404–405.

45. Marx, *Bürgerkrieg*, pp. 47–48. Also in *Capital*, pp. 404–405.

46. *Neue Zeit*, 9:1, p. 567.

47. Marx, *Bürgerkrieg*, p. 13. Also in *Capital*, p. 381.

48. Marx, *Bürgerkrieg*, p. 49.

49. The problems inherent in Marx's concept of the Commune are explicitly pointed out in K. Korsch, "Revolutionäre Kommune," *Die Aktion*, 1929, issue 5/8; 1931, issue 3/4.

50. Marx, *Bügerkrieg*, pp. 47–48.

51. Among the anti-Bolshevik writing may be mentioned K. Kautsky, *Die Diktatur des Proletariats*, Vienna 1918; *Terrorismus und Kommunismus*, Berlin 1919.

52. L. Trotsky, "Terrorismus und Kommunismus (Anti-Kautsky)," in *Die Grundfragen der Revolution*, Hamburg 1923, p. 105.

53. See W. Mautner, "Zur Geschichte des Begriffs der Diktatur des Proletariats," in *Archiv für die Geschichte des Sozialismus und der Arbeiterbewegung*, 12 (1926), pp. 280–283.

CHAPTER TWO
THE SOVIETS AND THE RUSSIAN REVOLUTION OF 1905

1. See Th. H. von Laue, "Die Revolution von aussen als erste Phase der russischen Revolution 1917," *Jahrbücher für Geschichte Osteuropas*, n. s. 4 (1956), pp. 138–158; "Einige politische Folgen der russischen Wirtschaftsplanung um 1900," in *Forschungen zur osteuropäischen Geschichte*, vol. 1, Berlin 1954, pp. 217–238; R. Portal, "Das Problem einer industriellen Revolution in Russland im 19. Jahrhundert," in *Forschungen*, ibid. pp. 205–216.

2. There were no reliable labor statistics in czarist Russia. Numbers in the

literature, therefore, vary by several hundreds of thousands in both directions. Compare the most recent Soviet researches by K. Pažitnov, "Položenie rabočego klassa v Rossii nakanune revoljucii 1905–07 gg.," *Voprosy ékonomiki 1955*, issue 5, pp. 34–43, and A. G. Rašin, "O čislennosti i territorial'nom razmeščenii rabočich Rossii v period kapitalizma," *Istoričeskie zapiski*, 46 (1954), pp. 127–181.

3. V. Gitermann, *Geschichte Russlands*, vol. 3, Hamburg 1949, p. 436.

4. See R. von Ungern-Sternberg, "Die Struktur der russischen Gesellschaft zu Anfang des 20. Jahrhunderts," *Schmollers Jahrbuch für Gesetzgebung, Verwaltung und Volkswirtschaft*, 76:2 (1956), pp. 41–69.

5. See R. von Ungern-Sternberg, *Über die wirtschaftliche und rechtliche Lage der St. Petersburger Arbeiterschaft*, Berlin 1909, pp. 34–40; J. Goebel, *Der Entwicklungsgang der russischen Industriearbeiter bis zur ersten Revolution*, Leipzig 1920, p. 11; S. Köhler, *Die russische Industriearbeiterschaft von 1905–1917*, Leipzig 1921, pp. 6–7.

6. See K. A. Paschitnow, *Die Lage der arbeitenden Klasse in Russland*, Stuttgart 1907.

7. *Enzyklopädie der UDSSR*, vol. 1, Berlin 1950, pp. 563 ff.

8. See M. Gordon, *Očerk ékonomičeskoj bor'by rabočich v Rossii*, 3rd ed., Leningrad 1925, pp. 60–84; S. P. Turin, *From Peter the Great to Lenin. A History of the Russian Labour Movement*, London 1935, pp. 36 ff.

9. See L. Kulczycki, *Geschichte der russischen Revolution*, vol. 3, Gotha 1914, pp. 399–410; A. S. Roslova, "Pervye massovye političeskie vystuplenija peterburgskich rabočich," *Voprosy istorii* 2 (1956) pp. 88–95.

10. See W. Grinewitsch, *Die Gewerkschaftsbewegung in Russland*, vol. 1: *1905–1914*, Berlin 1927, pp. 20–24.

11. Grinewitsch, pp. 15–16.

12. "Tverskaja zabastovka 1885 g.," *Krasnyj archiv*, 6:79 (1936) pp. 34–51.

13. "Stačka tkačej Ivanovo-Voznesenskoj manufaktury v 1895 g.," *Krasnyj archiv*, 5:72 (1935) pp. 110–119.

14. "Rabočee dviženie na zavodach Peterburga v mae 1901 g.," *Krasnyj archiv*, 3:76 (1936), pp. 49–66.

15. See I. Kh. Ozerov, *Politika po rabočemu voprosu v Rossii za poslednie gody*, St. Petersburg 1906; J. Walkin, "The Attitude of the Tsarist Government Toward the Labour Problem," *The American and East European Review*, 13 (1954) pp. 163–184.

16. See Ozerov, pp. 260–284; Paschitnow, pp. 126 ff.

17. *Proletarij*, 16:14:1 (1905).

18. See "Vseobščaja stačka na juge Rossii v 1903 godu," *Sbornik dokumentov*, Moscow 1938; "K istorii vseobščej stački na juge Rossii v 1903 g.," *Krasnyj archiv*, 3:88 (1938), pp. 76–122.

19. For "Zubatovščina," see Ozerov, pp. 195–254; Turin, pp. 56–67; J. Mavor, *An Economic History of Russia*, vol. 2, Toronto and London 1914, pp. 191–203; R. von Ungern-Sternberg, *Die Erziehung der St. Petersburger Arbeiterschaft zur Revolution*, Berlin 1909, pp. 9–29; B. D. Wolfe, "Gapon and Zubatov," *The Russian Review*, 7 (1948), pp. 53–61.

20. See Ozerov, pp. 205–206.

21. See K. Nötzel, *Die soziale Bewegung in Russland*, Berlin 1923; F. Dan, *Proischoždenie bol'ševizma*, New York 1946; L. Haimson, *The Russian Marxists and the Origins of Bolshevism*, Cambridge, Mass. 1955. Volumes 2 and 3, about to appear, of P. Scheibert, *Von Bakunin zu Lenin*, will be the definitive German study.

22. See W. Hofmann, "Parteigeschichtliche Grundlagen des sowjetischen Stalinismus," *Jahrbücher für Geschichte Osteuropas*, n. s. 2 (1954), pp. 304–314.

23. E. Rosenstock-Huessy, *Die europäischen Revolutionen und der Charakter der Nationen*, Stuttgart 1951, pp. 462–463.

24. L. Trotzki, "Die Entwicklungstendenzen der russischen Sozialdemokratie," *Neue Zeit*, 28:2, p. 860.

25. See Kulczycki, pp. 372 ff.; E. A. Korol'čuk, "Leninskij 'Sojuz bor'by za osvoboždenie rabočego klassa'—začatok boevoj revoljucionnoj rabočej partii," *Voprosy istorii* 1 (1956), pp. 13–30.

26. See J. Martow and T. Dan, *Geschichte der russischen Sozialdemokratie*, Berlin 1926, pp. 33 ff.; L. Trotzki, *Mein Leben*, Berlin 1930, pp. 102–103.

27. See O. Pjatnitzki, *Aufzeichnungen eines Bolschewiks*, Vienna and Berlin 1927.

28. See Kulczycki, pp. 431 ff. The manifesto of the party congress, written by P. B. Struve, is reprinted in G. Sinowjew, *Geschichte der kommunistischen Partei Russlands*, Hamburg 1923, pp. 191–193.

29. For the early days of Lenin, see B. D. Wolfe, *Three Who Made a Revolution*, New York 1948; P. Scheibert, "Über Lenins Anfänge," *Historische Zeitschrift*, 182 (1956), pp. 549–566.

30. The ideas of economism were first represented in the pamphlet *Ob agitacii* (1894) and later primarily in the columns of the newspapers *Rabočaja Mysl'* (Petersburg, 1897–1902) and *Rabočee Delo* (abroad, 1899–1902); See Haimson, pp. 78–91, 120–124.

31. W. I. Lenin, *Ausgewählte Werke*, vol. 1, Moscow 1946, pp. 213 ff.

32. W. Sassulitsch, "Die terroristische Strömung in Russland," *Die Neue Zeit* 1 (1902–1903), pp. 324 ff. and 361 ff.

33. See Martow, p. 76.

34. W. I. Lenin, *Sämtliche Werke*, Berlin and Vienna 1928 ff., vol. 6, p. 262.

35. Lenin, *Sämtliche Werke*, p. 35.

36. Lenin, *Was Tun?* in *Ausgewählte Werke*, vol. 1, p. 241.

37. The decisive break came in connection with elections to the editorial board of *Iskra* and to the Central Committee. Lenin wanted to secure a majority in both for himself and his followers (Plekhanov was still on his side at the time) and ruthlessly exploited his minimal numerical superiority at the party congress. Martov's followers were in a minority and boycotted the elections. See Trotsky's account in [Trotzki,] *Mein Leben*, pp. 154 ff.

38. Lenin, *Sämtliche Werke*, vol. 6, pp. 180 f.

39. "Protokoly s-ezdov i konferencij vsesojuznoj kommunističeskoj partii (b)," *Pjatyj s-ezd RSDRP*. Maj-Ijun' 1907 g., Moscow 1933, p. 511.

40. For this and the following, see Anweiler, "Die russische Revolution von 1905," *Jahrbücher für Geschichte Osteuropas*, n. s. 3 (1955), pp. 161–193.

41. For the events before and during "Bloody Sunday," see the references in Anweiler, "Russische Revolution," notes 10–15.
42. See E. D. Čermenskij, *Buržuazija i carism v revoljucii 1905–1907* gg., Moscow 1939; D. Sverčkov, "Sojuz sojuzov," in *Revoljucija i RKP (b) v materialach i dokumentach*, vol. 3, Moscow 1925, pp. 180–182; E. Maevskij, "Oživlenie zemskoj i gorodskoj oppozicii," in *Revoljucija*, pp. 177–179; A. S. Izgoev, *Russkoe obščestvo i revoljucija*, Moscow 1910; M. Weber, "Zur Lage der bürgerlichen Demokratie in Russland," *Archiv für Sozialwissenschaften und Sozialpolitik*, n. s. 4 (1906), pp. 234–353; M. Weber, "Russlands Übergang zum Scheinkonstitutionalismus, *"Sozialwissenschaften und Sozialpolitik*, 5 (1906), pp. 165–401.
43. See E. I. Kirjuchina, "Vserossijskij Krest'janskij Sojuz v 1905 g.," *Istoričeskie zapiski* 50 (1955), pp. 95–141. For the peasant movement in general, see G. T. Robinson, *Rural Russia under the Old Regime*, London 1932, pp. 138–207.
44. R. Luxemburg, *Massenstreik, Partei und Gewerkschaften*, Hamburg 1906, p. 32.
45. Luxemburg, *Massenstreik*, p. 28.
46. According to the most recent calculations, a total of 2,086,800 workers took part in the strikes in 1905; of these, 640,400 were railroad workers, 473,600 textile workers, and 300,700 metalworkers. The total number of strikers in 1905—that is, workers repeatedly engaged in strikes—was 5,010,100. A. S. Amal'rik, "K voprosu o čislennosti i geografičeskom razmeščenii stačečnikov v Evropejskoj Rossii v 1905 g.," *Istoričeskie zapiski*, 52 (1955), pp. 142–185.
47. See L. S. Kuznecova, "Stačečnaja bor'ba rabočich Peterburga v janvare 1905 goda," *Voprosy istorii* 1 (1955), pp. 11–25.
48. The official statistics of strikers in the plants subject to factory inspection was 414,000 in January and 291,000 in February, while about 420,000 workers struck in the period 1895–1904. Grinewitsch, pp. 231–235.
49. See the compilation *Revoljucija 1905–07 gg. v nacional'nych rajonach Rossii*, ed. Pankratova-Sidorov, Moscow 1949; V. Nevskij, "K voprosu o vlijanii janvarskich sobytij na provinciju," in *Revoljucija i RKP*, pp. 50–53.
50. See *Proletariat v revoljucii 1905–1907 gg.*, Moscow and Leningrad 1930, pp. 86–87, 94–95.
51. Of the total number of strikes among textile workers in 1905, 43 percent had economic causes and 57 percent political origins. Among the metalworkers the proportion was 28 percent to 72 percent. *Proletariat v revoljucii*, pp. 19, 106.
52. See D. Kol'cov, "Vstuplenie v dviženie novych proletarskich grupp," in *Revoljucija i RKP*, pp. 85–91; M. Pokrowski, *Geschichte Russlands von seiner Entstehung bis zur neuesten Zeit*, Leipzig 1929, pp. 392–393.
53. Of the roughly 700,000 railroad workers in 1905, about one-third were section hands—mostly local peasants. Traffic personnel made up a second group. The actual proletarian section (about 130,000 workers) consisted of the locomotive drivers, stokers, shop and yard workers.
54. See *Proletariat v revoljucii*, pp. 124–175.

55. See Kokovcev's report to the czar of January 19, 1905; *Krasnyj archiv* 4/5:11/12 (1925), pp. 1–25.
56. See V. Nevskij, "Vybory v komissiju Senatora Šidlovskogo," in *Revoljucija i RKP*, pp. 74–84.
57. See Martow, pp. 107–109.
58. One delegate to the Bolshevist Party congress of April 1905 declared: "There was no doubt of the workers' efforts to participate in the election. We had to decide whether to stand . . . aside or to prove . . . concretely the government's mendacity. But this could only be done if we took part in the elections . . . and made demands of the commission that it would undoubtedly not meet." Lenin, *Sämtliche Werke*, vol. 7, n. 132, pp. 613–614.
59. *Iskra* 88, February 17, 1905.
60. Nevskij, p. 80.
61. Turin, p. 78; Martow, p. 108.
62. Turin, p. 78.
63. See above, pp. 23 f.
64. Kuznecova, *Voprosy istorii* 1 (1955), pp. 11–25.
65. See V. Nevskij, "Janvarskie dni v Peterburge v 1905 godu," in *Revoljucija i RKP*, pp. 5–43.
66. M. Mitel'man, B. Lebov, A. Ul'janskij, *Istorija Putilovskogo zavoda 1789–1917*, 2nd ed., Moscow and Leningrad 1941, pp. 180–184.
67. Mitel'man, p. 199.
68. See E. I. Šalaeva and I. P. Lejberov, "Profsojuzy Peterburga v 1905 godu," *Voprosy istorii* 10 (1956), pp. 18–30.
69. See correspondents' reports in the Bolshevik newspapers *Vpered* 9 (February 23, 1905), 12 (March 16, 1905), 16 (April 17, 1905), *Proletarij* 9 (July 13, 1905), 10 (July 20, 1905) and 15 (August 23, 1905).
70. See P. M. Šmorgun, "Sovety rabočich deputatov na Ukraine v 1905 godu," *Istoričeskie zapiski* 49 (1954), pp. 21–52.
71. See E. Jaroslavskij, "Sovety rabočich deputatov v 1905 godu," *Proletarskaja revoljucija* 2 (1940), pp. 11–32; P. Murašev, "Stranička revoljucionnogo dviženia na Urale v 1905 godu," in *1905 god v očerkach i vospominanijach učastnikov*, vol. 2, Moscow 1928, pp. 16–40.
72. See Grinewitsch, p. 41.
73. See V. Nevskij, *Sovety i vooružennoe vosstanie v 1905 godu*, Moscow 1931, pp. 29–34; G. Kostomarov, *Moskovskij sovet v 1905 godu*, Moscow 1955, pp. 65–69 (where the highest number of deputies is given as 318).
74. Nevskij, p. 31.
75. See Grinewitsch, pp. 37–38.
76. See Ju. Milonov, *Professional'nye sojuzy SSSR 1905–1917–1927*, Moscow 1927, p. 11.
77. This interpretation was advanced particularly by P. Gorin in his book, *Očerki po istorii sovetov rabočich deputatov v 1905 g.*, 2nd ed., Moscow 1930, especially pp. 8–10. Gorin and Nevskij entered into a lively literary

controversy concerning the origins and nature of the soviets of 1905. Nevskij dismissed "Gorin's overly narrow and doctrinaire interpretation" and declared that seizure of power could not be a definitive criterion for the 1905 soviets; see Nevskij, pp. 22–25. He wrote concerning the origin of the soviets: "The soviets of workers deputies emerged by degrees during the revolutionary movement; they grew out of various revolutionary fighting organizations, which had everywhere been formed well before the October Days for specific goals (especially as concerned strikes and various revolutionary actions)" (p. 38).

78. Soviet historians also became involved in a scholarly debate concerning the priority of the soviet of Ivanovo Voznesensk. See the survey in F. Samojlov, *Pervyj sovet rabočich deputatov*, Leningrad 1931, pp. 5–7. While Gorin (pp. 10–11) called it merely a strike committee, Pokrovskij considered it a thoroughly "genuine" soviet because it was the first instance of an elected, inter-factory, city-wide delegates committee (p. 392).

79. Gorin, pp. 13–14.

80. For the entire course of the strike, see P. I. Galkina, "Vseobščaja stačka ivanovo-voznesenskich tekstil'ščikov letom 1905 goda," *Voprosy istorii* 6 (1955), pp. 87–97. Amal'rik *Istoričeskie zapiski* 52, p. 160, sets the number of strikers at only 28,000.

81. Beside the previously cited work by Samojlov, a participant in the strike and member of the soviet, see also the collection of documents, Samojlov, ed., *Ivanovo-Voznesenskij sovet rabočich deputatov 1905 g. v dokumentach*, Moscow and Leningrad 1935, as well as Samojlov's article, "O pervom sovete rabočich deputatov," *Proletarskaja revoljucija*, (1930) 12: 107, pp. 104–109. See further reports by correspondents in *Proletarij* 4 (June 4, 1905), 5 (June 13, 1905), 9 (July 13, 1905), 10 (July 20, 1905), and 17 (September 1, 1905); Gorin, pp. 10–24; Nevskij, pp. 14–22.

82. In some instances the number of deputies is given as 150.

83. Gorin, pp. 15–16.

84. One female participant, for example, reported: "One lady agitator once called out: 'Down with autocracy!' And what a to-do there was then! Everybody got excited. 'What? Surely we are not against the czar? But we are only against the manufacturers, and the czar does us no harm. That's not how we want it!' " Gorin, p. 20.

85. Samojlov, pp. 86–87.

86. For the Kostroma soviet, see P. M. Bogačev, "Rabočee dviženie v Kostrome v 1905 godu," *Istoričeskie zapiski* 49 (1954), pp. 86–110; Gorin, pp. 24–30; Nevskij, pp. 26–29. Also *Proletarij* 11 (July 27, 1905), 14 (August 16, 1905), 17 (September 1, 1905), and 22 (October 11, 1905).

87. According to official reports, the number of strikers totaled 150,059 in July, 78,343 in August, and 36,629 in September.

88. See above, p. 39.

89. See *Proletariat v revoljucii*, pp. 150–152; Pokrowski, pp. 400–402.

90. Pokrowski, p. 400.

91. See the article by I. F. Ugarov under the misleading title, "Bol'ševiki vo

glave vseobščej političeskoj stački rabočich Moskvy v oktjabre 1905 g.,"
Voprosy istorii 10 (1955), pp. 3–17.

92. See L. K. Erman, "Učastie demokratičeskoj intelligencii vo vserossijskoj oktjabr'skoj političeskoj stačke," *Istoričeskie zapiski* 49 (1954), pp. 352–390.

93. See N. Trotzky, *Russland in der Revolution*, Dresden 1909, pp. 65–76.

94. See the text of the resolution in Pokrowski, p. 460.

95. See Chrustalev-Nosar', "Istorija soveta rabočich deputatov," in the collection *Istorija soveta rabočich deputatov Peterburga*, Petersburg [1907], p. 127.

96. See N. Gilin, "Mestnoe samoupravlenie v god revoljucii," in *Itogi i perspektivy*, Moscow 1906, pp. 173–197.

97. The circumstances are vividly described in S. Witte, *Erinnerungen*, Berlin 1923, pp. 313, 318–322.

98. Complete text of the October Manifesto in *Polnyj sbornik platform vsech russkich političeskich partij*, n. p., 1906, pp. 5–6.

99. See above, pp. 36 ff.

100. See Nevskij, pp. 7–14, 43–45.

101. See below, pp. 67 ff.

102. See Chrustalev-Nosar', p. 61; Gorin, p. 47; Mitel'man, p. 203.

103. See Kozovlev, "Kak voznik sovet," in *Istorija . . . Peterburga*, pp. 22–44.

104. See Trotsky's letter to the "Istpart" of August 25, 1921, in D. Sverčkov, *Na zare revoljucii*, Moscow 1921, p. 6.

105. Chrustalev-Nosar', pp. 6–7.

106. See L. Geller and N. Rovenskaja, eds., *Peterburgskij i moskovskij sovety rabočich deputatov 1905 g. v dokumentach*, Moscow and Leningrad 1926, p. 11.

107. Geller, pp. 12–13; Chrustalev-Nosar', p. 62.

108. Pokrowski, p. 405.

109. See B. Radin, *Pervyj sovet rabočich deputatov*, Petersburg 1906, p. 7.

110. Nosar' was a young leftist intellectual unaffiliated with any party; he was a lawyer by profession. During the elections to the Shidlovsky Commission in February 1905 he borrowed identity papers from a worker by the name of Chrustalev and used this name at the electors assembly. He was very popular among the workers. In November 1905 he joined the Social Democratic Party (Mensheviks). In 1918 he was shot by the Bolsheviks for alleged counterrevolutionary activities.

111. See Chrustalev-Nosar', pp. 66–76.

112. The history of most of the soviets of 1905 has not yet been thoroughly researched. The source material is also very uneven; while extensive documentation exists for the soviets in the larger industrial centers, detailed references are lacking for the smaller and more short-lived ones. Russian historical research itself suffers from this lack. See the editorial article, "Pjatidesjatiletie russkoj revoljucii 1905–1907 gg." in *Istoričeskie zapiski* 49 (1954), pp. 3–20. A survey, to 1930, of all printed and manuscript sources for the history of the soviets is given in V. Nevskij, *Sovety i vooružennoe vosstanie v 1905 g.*, pp. 262–288. See also Nevskij, *1905. Sovetskja pečat' i literatura o sovetach*, Moscow and Leningrad 1925. A

condensed version is given in Gorin, *Očerki,* but it contains many errors and is biased in an orthodox Bolshevik direction.

113. See the compilation in Appendix A.

114. The most recent soviet account in G. Kostomarov, *Moskovskij sovet v 1905 godu,* 2nd ed., Moscow 1955, has been criticized as biased and faulty by Soviet critics themselves. See the review by Z. M. Bograd in *Voprosy istorii* 3 (1956), pp. 158–163. An eyewitness report is given by M. Vasil'ev Južin, "Moskovskij sovet rabočich deputatov v 1905 godu i podgotovka im vooružennogo vosstanija," *Proletarskaja revoljucija* 4:39 (1925), pp. 84–124; 5:40 (1925), pp. 92–133. See also *Izvestija moskovskogo soveta rabočich deputatov 1905 g.,* Moscow 1925, pp. 8–9, 16–17; Gorin, pp. 263–285.

115. See below, p. 79.

116. See Geller, p. 93.

117. See below, pp. 76 f.

118. Some sources and accounts give November 22 as the opening day of the Moscow soviet.

119. See P. M. Šmorgun, "Sovety rabočich deputatov na Ukraine v 1905 godu," *Istoričeskie zapiski* 49 (1954), pp. 21–52; F. E. Los', "Dekabr'skoe vooružennoe vosstanie na Ukraine," *Istoričeskie zapiski* 49 (1954), pp. 53–85; N. R. Donij, "Vooružennoe vosstanie na Ekaterinoslavščine v dekabre 1905 g.," *Voprosy istorii* 12 (1955), pp. 19–32; Gorin, pp. 398–457.

120. See Amal'rik, *Istoričeskie zapiski* 52 (1955), pp. 159 ff.

121. See the listing in Appendix A.

122. See V. E. Poleščuk, "Revoljucionnoe dviženie v man'čžurskoj armii v 1905 godu," *Istoričeskie zapiski* 49 (1954), pp. 301–351.

123. See N. N. Jakovlev, "Krasnojarskoe vooružennoe vosstanie 1905 g.," *Istoričeskie zapiski* 40 (1952), pp. 29–72; A. M. Pankratova, *Pervaja russkaja revoljucija 1905–1907 gg.,* 2nd ed., Moscow 1951, pp. 186–189; E. Jaroslavskij, *Istorija VKP (b),* vol. 2, Moscow and Leningrad 1930, pp. 518–519; Gorin, pp. 458–468.

124. See A. B. Mel'nikov, "Revoljucionnoe dviženie v moskovskom garnizone v period dekabr'skogo vooružennogo vosstanija," *Istoričeskie zapiski* 49 (1954), pp. 265–300; V. Konovalov, "Revoljucionnoe dviženie v vojskach Moskovskogo voenogo okruga v 1905–1907 gg.," *Voprosy istorii* 10 (1951), pp. 89–103; V. Ul'jaminskij, "Vosstanie Rostovskogo polka v dekabre 1905 goda," in *1905 god v očerkach i vospominanijach učastnikov,* vol. 1, Moscow 1928, pp. 28–51; Pokrowski, pp. 427 ff.

125. See Gorin, pp. 221–228; Pankratova, pp. 159–162.

126. Šmorgun, *Istoričeskie zapiski* 49 (1954), p. 40.

127. There are almost no researches into the organizational forms of the revolutionary peasants movement (peasants soviets, peasants committees, etc.) See P. K. Peb'kin and V. N. Firstova, "O literature po istorii krest'janskogo dviženija v revoljucii 1905–1907 godov," *Vopprosy istorii* 11 (1955), pp. 124–128; Gorin, pp. 239–248.

128. See Jaroslavskij, *Proletarskaja revoljucija* 2 (1940), p. 13.

129. See M. V. Cervadze, "Krest'janskoe revoljucionnoe dviženie v Gurii v 1905 godu," *Voprosy istorii* 12 (1955), pp. 87–95.
130. N. Trotzky, *Russland*.
131. Trotzky, *Russland*, p. 82.
132. See Z. Lenskij, "Formy proletarskoj bor'by," in *Itogi i perspektivy*, Moscow 1906, pp. 140–172.
133. See Chrustalev-Nosar', pp. 165–167.
134. See I. S. Topčeev, "Vybory v sovety 1905 g.," *Voprosy istorii* 12 (1955), pp. 104–108.
135. Trotzky, *Russland*, p. 228.
136. Radin, p. 9.
137. Radin, p. 101.
138. See D. Sverčkov, *Na zare revoljucii*, Moscow 1921, pp. 121–126; Radin, pp. 14 ff.
139. See Topčeev; see also Nevskij, pp. 79–81. Concerning the Kostroma soviet, the ratio of one to 50 is also occasionally given.
140. Of these, the majority (351) were metalworkers; 508 deputies came directly from factories, 54 from trade unions. Chrustalev-Nosar', p. 147.
141. See the list in Kostomarov, p. 200.
142. See Radin, p. 11; Gorin, pp. 279–284, 305–310; V. Nevskij, "Sovet rabočich deputatov v Odesse 1905 g.," in *Revoljucija i RKP*, vol. 3, pp. 373–380; Kostomarov, pp. 86–91.
143. See Chrustalev-Nosar', pp. 151–154; Radin, pp. 12 ff; Aksanov, "V Peterburgskom sovete rabočich deputatov 1905 g.," in *1905 god v očerkach i vospominanijach učastnikov*, vol. 1, pp. 19–27.
144. Both the Petersburg and Moscow editions of *Izvestija* were subsequently collected in *Izvestija soveta rabočich deputatov (S. Peterburg, 17 objtabrja–14 dekabrja 1905 g.)*, Leningrad 1925, and *Izvestija moskovskogo soveta rabočich deputatov 1905 g.*, Moscow 1925. Kostomarov, p. 14, lists the following additional soviets that published their own *Izvestija*: Yuzovka, Mariupol, and Vyatka; Los', in *Istoričeskie zapiski* 49 (1954), p. 67, also adds Nikolaev.
145. Jaroslavskij, p. 521.
146. See V. Manilov, *Kievskij sovet rabočich deputatov v 1905 g.*, Kiev 1926.
147. See Chrustalev-Nosar', p. 141; Grinewitsch, pp. 140–141.
148. See Gorin, pp. 251–257.
149. See Grinewitsch, pp. 175–176.
150. Radin, p. iii.
151. Trotzky, *Russland*, p. 83.
152. See V. Černov, "Ot 'Revoljucionnoj Rossii k 'Synu Otečestva,'" in *Letopis' revoljucii*, vol. 1, Berlin 1923, pp. 95–97; Martow, pp. 167–168.
153. Chrustalev-Nosar', p. 103.
154. Trotzky, *Russland*, p. 163.
155. Chrustalev-Nosar', p. 131.
156. See Geller, pp. 63–64.
157. See Geller, p. 67; Chrustalev-Nosar', pp. 142–146.

158. Geller, p. 28.
159. A. Gerassimoff, *Der Kampf gegen die erste russische Revolution*, Frankfurt and Leipzig 1934, pp. 67–74.
160. See Geller, p. 32; Trotzky, *Russland*, pp. 119–120.
161. See Chrustalev-Nosar', pp. 137–142; Gorin, pp. 237–239.
162. See Geller, pp. 45–47; Chrustalev-Nosar', pp. 106–126; Trotzky, *Russland*, pp. 146–159.
163. See Gorin, pp. 219–221.
164. For the question of armed uprising, see Chrustalev-Nosar', pp. 97–98; Trotzky, *Russland*, pp. 287–292; Radin, pp. 19–20; Zvezdin, "Poslednie dni soveta," in *Istorija soveta rabočich deputatov Peterburga*, pp. 174–175. Beginning in the 1920s, the tactics of the St. Petersburg soviet concerning the armed uprising have been increasingly criticized by the Bolsheviks. Trotsky especially was accused of hampering the preparations for an uprising. In answer to this it must be noted that neither Lenin nor the other participants in the Revolution of 1905 blamed the soviet for a "misguided" policy during the events themselves. For an example of Stalinist falsification of history, see *Kurzer Lehrgang der Geschichte der KPSU*, Berlin 1945, pp. 95 ff. After Stalin's death historians treated the St. Petersburg soviet of 1905 more objectively; L. F. Petrova, "Peterburgskij sovet rabočich deputatoc v 1905 godu," *Voprosy istorii* 2 (1955), pp. 25–40.
165. This was obviously an exaggeration, for the militants included no more than several hundred workers.
166. Quoted in Gorin, p. 353.
167. See Radin, p. 21.
168. See Zvezdin, pp. 170–177.
169. See Zvezdin, pp. 188–190; Sverčkov, pp. 155–158.
170. See Sverčkov, pp. 161–168; I. Deutscher, *The Prophet Armed*, London 1954, pp. 142–144.
171. For the second St. Petersburg soviet, see E. Krivošeina, "O vtorom Peterburgskom sovete rabočich deputatov," *Proletarskaja revoljucija* 6:53 (1926), pp. 181–196; "K istorii Peterburgskogo 2-go soveta rabočich deputatov," in *Revoljucija i RKP*, vol. 3, pp. 339 ff.; Parvus, *In der russischen Bastille während der Revolution*, Dresden 1909, p. 21.
172. See Geller, pp. 79–82.
173. For the course of Trotsky's trial, see Trotzky, *Russland*, pp. 251–295; Deutscher, pp. 163–169. The sentences were comparatively light; thirty-four defendants were acquitted, others were sentenced to deportation or imprisonment.
174. See *Moskovskoe vooružennoe vosstanie*, Moscow 1906; S. N. Černomordik, "Dekabr'skoe vooružennoe vosstanie 1905 g.," *Istoričeskie zapiski* 18 (1946), pp. 3–41; V. Maksakov, "Dekabr'skoe vosstanie v Moskve," in *Revoljucija i RKP*, vol. 3, pp. 345–360; N. N. Jakovlev, "Moskovskie bol'ševiki vo glave dekabr'skogo vooružennogo vosstanija 1905 goda," *Voprosy istorii* 12 (1955), pp. 3–18.

175. See Geller, pp. 108–112.

176. Gorin, p. 284.

177. According to official data from the factory inspection, 418,000 workers went on strike in December, as against 481,000 in October.

178. See "Dekabr'skie dni v Donbasse v 1905 g.," *Krasnyj archiv* 6:73 (1935), pp. 91–125; "Chronika vooružennoj bor'by. Reljacija general'nogo štaba samoderžavija o boevych dejstvijach v dekabre 1905 goda," *Krasnyj archiv*, 4/5:11/12 (1925), pp. 159–181.

179. See above, p. 48.

180. See V. Nevskij, "Novorossijskaja respublika," in *Sovety i vooružennoe vosstanie v 1905 godu*, pp. 87–114; V. D. Sokol'skij, "Novorossijskij sovet rabočich deputatov v 1905 godu," *Voprosy istorii* 12 (1955), pp. 76–86; Gorin, pp. 326–329, 434–439.

181. See above, p. 49.

182. See Trotzky, *Russland*, p. 254.

183. See the memoirs of the principal organizer of the council of the unemployed, W. Wojtinski, *Wehe den Besiegten*, Berlin 1933; S. Malyšev, *O Piterskom sovete bezrabotnych*, Moscow 1932.

184. See below, p. 81.

185. See *Protokoly s-ezdov i konferencij vsesojuznoj kommunističeskoj partii (b). Četvertyj (ob-edinitel'nyj) s-ezd RSDRP*, Moscow 1934, pp. 635–636, n. 93.

186. Kostomarov, pp. 179–186.

187. Jaroslavskij, *Proletarskaja revoljucija* 2 (1940), pp. 14–15.

188. See below, pp. 80 ff.

189. See, for example, S. L. Ronin, "Istoričeskoe značenie sovetov 1905 g.," *Sovetskoe Gosudarstvo i Pravo* 4 (1955), pp. 11–20.

190. See A. Pannekoek, *Die taktischen Differenzen in der Arbeiterbewegung*, Hamburg 1909; "Massenaktion und Revolution," *Die Neue Zeit* 30:2 (1912), pp. 541–550, 585–593, 609–616; W. Tormin, *Zwischen Rätediktatur und sozialer Demokratie*, Düsseldorf 1954, pp. 24–25.

191. See A. Rosenberg, *Geschichte des Bolshewismus*, pp. 18–19, 26.

192. Martynov, *Dve diktatury*, Geneva 1905 (written in 1904).

193. Martynov, p. 58.

194. *Iskra* 93 (March 17, 1905).

195. *Načalo* 1 (November 15, 1905).

196. See the resolutions of the Menshevik Party conference of April 1905 in Lenin, *Sämtliche Werke*, vol. 8, pp. 53, 59–60, 66, 105, 109–110.

197. See Martynov; see also *Pis'ma P. B. Aksel'roda i Ju. O. Martova*, Berlin 1924, p. 146. In a letter written at the end of October, Martov stated that the seizure of power seemed almost unavoidable, but that this prospect was far from tempting—rather, it was dangerous. He feared that this turning point of the revolution would result in "Jacobin dictatorship."

198. *Načalo* 1 (November 15, 1905).

199. See Martow, *Geschichte der russischen Sozialdemokratie*, pp. 112–113.

200. See above, pp. 36 f.

201. Kozovlev, *Istorija soveta rabočich deputatov*, pp. 36–37.
202. See F. Savinskij, "Parlamentskaja taktika s.-d. v epochu pervoj russkoj revoljucii," *Proletarskaja revoljucija* 11:106 (1930), pp. 3–20, 12:107 pp. 39–77.
203. See P. Kolokol'nikov and S. Rapoport, eds., *1905–07 gg. v professional'-nom dviženii*, Moscow 1925, pp. 45–46, 112 ff.
204. See *Pis'ma Aksel'roda i Martova*, pp. 119–121.
205. F. Dan in *Iskra* 106 (July 18, 1905); see further *Iskra* 101 (June 1, 1905).
206. Martov in the Vienna *Arbeiter-Zeitung* (August 24, 1905), quoted in Lenin, *Sämtliche Werke*, vol. 8, pp. 236 ff.
207. Quoted in Lenin, *Sämtliche Werke*, vol. 8, p. 105.
208. Lenin, *Sämtliche Werke*, vol. 8, p. 105.
209. *Iskra* 110 (September 10, 1905).
210. See above, p. 45.
211. Kozovlev, p. 42.
212. *Pis'ma Aksel'roda i Martova*, p. 146.
213. *Načalo* 2 (November 15, 1905).
214. *Načalo* 2.
215. Martow, *Geschichte der russischen Sozialdemokratie*, p. 146.
216. See the resolution of the Mensheviks in Kiev; *Načalo* 14 (November 30, 1905).
217. See A. Tscherewanin, *Das Proletariat und die russische Revolution*, Stuttgart 1908, pp. 129–133; J. Martow, "Preussische Diskussion und russische Erfahrung," *Die Neue Zeit* 28:2 (1909/1910), pp. 907–919.
218. See the speech by Axelrod at the Fourth Party Congress of 1906; *Protokoly*, pp. 258–291.
219. See F. Dan, "Gosudarstvennaja Duma i proletariat," in *Gosudarstvennaja Duma i socialdemokratija*, n. p. 1906, pp. 9–32.
220. Dan, "Gosudarstvennaja," p. 21.
221. See "Protokoly s-ezdov i konferencij vsesojuznoj kommunističeskoj partii (b)," *Pjatyj s-ezd RSDRP. Maj-Ijun' 1907 g.*, Moscow 1933, pp. 93–94, 535.
222. *Protokoly*, p. 585.
223. See below, p. 81.
224. See Martow, p. 206; for the deliberations of the Fifth Party Congress of 1907, see *Protokoly*, pp. 501–567.
225. See V. I. Lenin, *Sočinenija*, 4th ed., vol. 12, pp. 350–354.
226. See Lenin, *Sämtliche Werke*, vol. 8, pp. 160–170.
227. Lenin, *Sämtliche Werke*, vol. 8, p. 127.
228. Lenin, *Sämtliche Werke*, vol. 8, p. 572.
229. Lenin, *Sämtliche Werke*, vol. 7, pp. 571–572.
230. Rosenberg, p. 44.
231. Lenin, *Sämtliche Werke*, vol. 8, p. 248.
232. Lenin, *Sämtliche Werke*, vol. 7, p. 496, vol. 8, p. 572.
233. Lenin, *Sämtliche Werke*, vol. 7, pp. 248–250.

234. For the context, see my essay, "Lenin und die Kunst des Aufstandes," *Wehrwissenschaftliche Rundschau* 5 (1955), pp. 459–472.

235. See Lenin, *Sämtliche Werke*, vol. 7, pp. 570–571.

236. Lenin, *Sämtliche Werke*, vol. 7, p. 113.

237. See the resolution of the Bolshevik Party Congress; Lenin, *Sämtliche Werke*, vol. 7, p. 574.

238. Lenin, *Sämtliche Werke*, vol. 7, p. 376.

239. Lenin, *Sämtliche Werke*, vol. 7, p. 160.

240. Lenin, *Sämtliche Werke*, vol. 8, p. 197.

241. J. W. Stalin, *Werke*, vol. 1, Berlin 1950, p. 135.

242. For the period preceding 1917 no official figures are available for party membership. In April 1905 the Bolsheviks had only about 250 members among the workers in the two strongest proletarian districts of St. Petersburg. By the end of 1905 the total number of Mensheviks and Bolsheviks combined in St. Petersburg amounted to about 3,000. At the Fourth Party Congress of 1906 the delegates from all of Russia represented 13,000 Bolsheviks and 18,000 Mensheviks; see "Partija v revoljucii 1905 g.," *Dokumenty k istorii partii v 1905 g.*, 1934, pp. 74–75; Lenin, *Sämtliche Werke*, vol. 10, p. 169.

243. Lenin, *Sämtliche Werke*, vol. 8, p. 508.

244. Lenin, *Sämtliche Werke*, vol. 8, p. 385.

245. See Martow, pp. 144 ff; Gorin, pp. 86–106. Gorin tries to gloss over the attitude of the St. Petersburg Bolsheviks; for a contrary view, see Nevskij, p. 33, n. 1.

246. For the text of the resolution, see Radin, p. 103, n. 1; see also Nevskij, pp. 50–51.

247. See *Novaja Žizn'* 3 (October 29), 4 (October 30), 5 (November 1), 9 (November 10), 13 (November 15, 1905).

248. See Chrustalev-Nosar', pp. 150–151.

249. P. N. Gvozdev, in the article, "Social'demokratija i sovet rabočich deputatov," *Novaja Žizn'* 7 (November 7, 1905).

250. *Novaja Žizn'* 6 (November 2, 1905).

251. *Novaja Žizn'* 5 (November 1, 1905).

252. *Novaja Žizn'* 6.

253. See Nevskij, p. 43.

254. Gvozdev in *Novaja Žizn'* 7 (November 7, 1905).

255. See above, p. 39.

256. M. I. Vasil'ev-Južin, "Moskovskij sovet rabočich deputatov v 1905 godu i podgotovka im vooružennogo vosstanija," *Proletarskaja revoljucija* 4:39 (1925), pp. 85–86. Vasil'ev-Južin was himself the author of the appeal; see Nevskij, p. 33.

257. See above, pp. 47 ff.

258. *Novaja Žizn'* 24 (November 29, 1905).

259. Some Soviet historians acknowledged this "leftist deviation" only reluctantly and strove to diminish its significance. See Gorin, pp. 95–98, 102; Jaroslavskij, *Istorija RKP*, vol. 2, pp. 513–514; in opposition, see Nevskij, p. 33, n. 1.

260. Gorin, pp. 449–454.
261. See Gorin, pp. 285–287.
262. The letter to the editors of *Novaja Zizn'*, "Naši zadači i sovet rabočich deputatov," was first reprinted in *Pravda* 308 (November 5, 1940), and is included in Lenin, *Sočinenija*, vol. 10, pp. 3–11. It was allegedly not brought to light until that time.
263. Lenin, *Sočinenija*, vol. 10, p. 7.
264. Lenin, *Sočinenija*, vol. 10, p. 5.
265. Lenin, *Sämtliche Werke*, vol. 8, pp. 540, 560.
266. See S. M. Levin, "V. I. Lenin v Peterburge v 1905 g.," *Voprosy istorii* 6 (1955), pp. 3–12.
267. A. V. Lunačarskij, "Bol'ševiki v 1905 g.," *Proletarskaja revoljucija* 11:46 (1925), pp. 49–61; quote from p. 56.
268. Lenin, *Sämtliche Werke*, vol. 8, p. 553.
269. Lenin, *Sočinenija*, vol. 10, p. 88.
270. Lenin, *Sočinenija*, vol. 10, p. 136.
271. Lenin, *Sämtliche Werke*, vol. 8, p. 108.
272. Lenin, "Pobeda kadetov i zadači rabočej partii" (March 1906), *Sočinenija*, vol. 10, pp. 177-250, quote from pp. 217–219.
273. Discussion at the Fourth Party Congress; *Protokoly*, p. 136.
274. See above, p. 71.
275. Lenin, *Sočinenija*, vol. 12, p. 295.
276. Lenin, *Sämtliche Werke*, vol. 10, pp. 522–523.
277. Lenin, *Sämtliche Werke*, vol. 18, p. 413.
278. *Leninskij Sbornik*, vol. 2, Moscow 1924, pp. 249–250.
279. K. Radek, *Wege der russischen Revolution*, Hamburg 1922, p. 18.
280. L. Trotsky, *Stalin*, New York and London, 1941, p. 65.
281. See above, p. 73.
282. The definitive biography of Trotsky is Isaac Deutscher, *The Prophet Armed: Trotsky: 1879–1921*, London and New York 1954. (The second volume, *The Prophet Unarmed*, is announced for publication.) Trotsky's autobiography appeared in German as *Mein Leben*, Berlin 1930, and in English as *My Life*, New York 1931. For criticism of Lenin, see *Naši političeskie zadači*, Geneva 1904. A selection of Trotsky's writings is collected in *Our revolution. Essays on Working Class and International Revolution, 1904–1917*, New York 1918.
283. For Parvus, see the detailed analysis by St. Possony, *Jahrhundert des Aufruhrs*, Munich 1956, pp. 37–51.
284. L. Trotzki, *Die russische Revolution 1905*, Berlin 1923, pp. 5–6. Trotsky first developed his theory while in prison in 1906, in the work *Itogi i perspektivy*, and for the rest of his life he repeated it with ever-new variations. See his last recapitulation in his biography of Stalin (German ed.), pp. 551–560; see also Deutscher, pp. 145–163.
285. See R. Amburskij, "Lenin o rev. dem. diktature proletariata i krest'janstva v revoljucii 1905–07 gg.," *Proletarskaja revoljucija* 12:107 (1930), pp. 3–38.
286. Trotsky, *Our revolution*, pp. 42–43.

287. *Iskra* 93 (March 17, 1905).

288. *Iskra* 93.

289. In the previously cited work, Trotzki, *Russland in der Revolution*.

290. Trotzki, *Russland*, p. 82. Lenin, on the other hand, stated: "The soviet of workers deputies is not a workers parliament nor an instrument of proletarian self-government" (see above, p. 81).

291. Trotzki, *Russland in der Revolution*, p. 235.

292. Trotzki, *Russland*, p. 292.

293. Trotzki, *Russland*, p. 234.

294. Trotzki, *Russland*, p. 229.

295. Trotzki, *Russland*, p. 229.

296. Trotzki, *Russland*, p. 232.

297. Trotzki, *Die russische Revolution 1905*, p. 6.

298. Parvus, "Die gegenwärtige Lage Russlands und die Aussichten für die Zukunft," *Die Neue Zeit* 24:2 (1905–1906), p. 111.

299. L. Trotzki, "Der Arbeiterdeputiertenrat und die Revolution," *Die Neue Zeit* 25:2 (1906–1907), p. 85.

300. To this day there is no adequate study of the history of the Social Revolutionary Party, in either Russian or another language. The work by A. I. Spiridovič, *Revoljucionnoe dviženie v Rossii. Vypusk 2-oj. Partija Socialistov-revoljucionerov i eja predšestvenniki*, Petrograd 1916, contains numerous important details but does not convey the broad picture. The early stage of the SR in a larger context is dealt with by D. W. Treadgold in *Lenin and His Rivals*, London 1955. Personal accounts are given in the various works by V. Černov and I. Steinberg, written after emigration from Russia.

301. See the article by D. W. Treadgold, "The Populists Refurbished," *The Russian Review* 10 (1951), pp. 185–196, which was subsequently incorporated in the work cited above.

302. The program adopted at the First Party Congress of the SR in January 1906 is reprinted in *Polnyj sbornik platform vsech russkich političeskich partij*, n. p. 1906, pp. 19–28; in German, Lenin, *Sämtliche Werke*, vol. 7, pp. 550–557, and elsewhere.

303. *Revoljucionnaja Rossija* 16 (January 15, 1903).

304. *Revoljucionnaja Rossija* 50 (June 1, 1904).

305. See *Novaja Žizn'* 4 (October 30, 1905).

306. V. Černov, "Ot 'Revoljucionnoj Rossii' k 'Synu Otečestva,'" in *Letopis' revoljucii*, vol. 1, Berlin 1923, pp. 95–97.

307. See *Protokoly pervago s-ezda partii socialistov-revoljucionerov*, n. p. 1906.

308. Spiridovič, p. 246.

309. *Protokoly vtorogo (èkstrennogo) s-ezda partii socialistov-revoljucionerov*, Petersburg 1907, p. 37.

310. *Kommuna* 1 (December 1905). Published by the Sojuz revoljucionnych socialistov.

311. *Prjamo k celi*, Moscow 1917 (reprint of a pamphlet of 1906), p. 6.

312. As is the case for Social Revolutionaries, there is no general study of the

history of the Russian anarchists. Considering the multiplicity of the different groups, which were often minute and all of which were independent of one another, it is difficult to acquire a general picture. Sources in this area—mostly pamphlets and leaflets—are almost inaccessible.

313. *Russkaja revoljucija i anarchizm. Doklady čitannye na s-ezde Kommunistov-Anarchistov v oktjabre 1906 goda,* London 1907, p. 58.
314. *Russkaja revoljucija i anarchizm,* p. 22.
315. *Russkaja revoljucija i anarchizm,* p. 23.
316. See K. Diehl, "Anarchismus," in *Handwörterbuch der Staatswissenschaften,* vol. 1, Jena 1923, pp. 283–284; Diehl, *Die Diktatur des Proletariats und das Rätesystem,* Jena 1920, pp. 72–76.
317. *Suščnosť maksimalizma;* quoted in Spiridovič, p. 301.
318. *Russkaja revoljucija i anarchizm,* p. 70.
319. Lenin, *Sämtliche Werke,* vol. 8, pp. 552–553.
320. See above, p. 84 f.

CHAPTER THREE
THE SOVIETS AND THE RUSSIAN REVOLUTION OF 1917

1. According to official statistics, in 1910 only 46,625 workers went on strike, as compared with 64,166 in 1909, 176,101 in 1908, and 740,074 in 1907. Grinewitsch, p. 235.
2. In 1911, 105,110 workers went on stike, in 1912 the number was 725,491, in 1913, 861,289, and from January to July, 1914, 1,337,458. Grinewitsch, p. 235.
3. See Grinewitsch, p. 289.
4. For the general picture, see S. M. Balabanov, *Ot 1905 k 1917 godu. Massovoe rabočee dviženie,* Moscow and Leningrad 1927, pp. 328–455.
5. F. A. Golder, *Documents of Russian History 1914–1917,* New York 1927, pp. 186–187.
6. See Merle Fainsod, *International Socialism and the World War,* Cambridge, Mass. 1935; A. Rosmer, *Le mouvement ouvrier pendant la guerre,* Paris 1936.
7. See O. H. Gankin and H. H. Fisher, *The Bolsheviks and the World War,* Stanford 1940; B. Lazitch, *Lenine et la III. Internationale,* Neuchâtel 1951.
8. See "K istorii 'Rabočej gruppy' pri central'nom voenno-promyšlennom komitete," *Krasnyj archiv* 2:57 (1933), pp. 43–84.
9. See Martow, pp. 287–290.
10. Lenin, *Sämtliche Werke,* vol. 18, pp. 412–413.
11. See Mitel'man, Lebov, and Ul'janskij, *Istorija Putilovskogo zavoda,* pp. 437–442.
12. See "K istorii grozdevščiny ('Bjulleteni' Rabočej gruppy central'nogo voenno-promyšlennogo komiteta," *Krasnyj archiv* 6:67 (1937), pp. 28–92.
13. *Rabočija organizacii g. Kieva. Sbornik svedenij,* Kiev 1918, pp. 60–61.
14. E. B. Genkina, "Fevral'skij perevorot," in *Očerki po istorii oktjabr'skoj revoljucii,* vol. 2, Moscow and Leningrad 1927, pp. 84–85.
15. See above, p. 85.

16. See A. R. Šljapnikov, *Semnadcatyj god*, vol. 2, Moscow and Leningrad 1923, p. 160.

17. Šljapnikov, vol. 1, pp. 279–280.

18. Almost all major accounts of the Russian Revolution of 1917 report the course of events during the February Revolution. For eyewitness reports, see N. Suchanov, *Zapiski o revoljucii*, vols. 1 and 2, Berlin, Petrograd, and Moscow 1922; a condensed English translation appeared under the title *The Russian Revolution 1917*, London and New York 1955; M. Smilg-Benario, *Der Zusammenbruch der Zarenmonarchie*, Vienna 1928; Šljapnikov, vol. 1. Selections from the memoirs of non-Bolshevik personalities are contained in the collection S. Alekseev, ed., *Fevral'skaja revoljucija*, Moscow and Leningrad 1925. The exact chronological development is contained in N. Avdeev, "Revoljucija 1917 goda," *Chronika sobytij*, vol. 1, Moscow and Leningrad 1923.

19. F. Brokenau, *Das Jahr 1917*, special issue of *Der Monat* 37 (1952), p. 13.

20. See Smilg-Benario, p. 137; L. Trotzki, *Geschichte der russischen Revolution*, vol. 1, Berlin 1931, pp. 123–124.

21. For an example of the most recent evaluation of the February Revolution by Soviet historians, see E. D. Čermenskij, "Fevral'skaja buržuazno-demokratičeskaja revoljucija 1917 goda," *Voprosy istorii* 2 (1957), pp. 3–18.

22. Trotzki, *Geschichte*, vol. 1, p. 148.

23. Šljapnikov, vol. 1, p. 87.

24. A. Kerenski, *Erinnerungen*, Dresden 1928, pp. 41–42.

25. See below pp. 128 ff.

26. Martow and Dan, *Geschichte der russischen Sozialdemokratie*, p. 293; see further A. Kerensky, "Why the Russian Monarchy Fell," *Slavonic Review* 8 (1929), pp. 496–513; N. O. Lossky, "Reflections on the Origins and Meaning of the Russian Revolution," *Russian Review* 10 (1951), pp. 293–300.

27. See above, p. 100.

28. Trotzki, *Geschichte*, vol. 1, p. 161.

29. See Genkina, pp. 82–89; Suchanov, vol. 1, p. 28; *Istorija Putilovskogo zavoda*, pp. 464–468.

30. See Smilg-Benario, p. 137; Viktor Chernov, *The Great Russian Revolution*, New Haven 1936, pp. 101–102; *Izvestija Petrogradskogo Soveta rabočich i soldatskich deputatov*, issue 155, August 27, 1917 (commemorative article).

31. See "Revoljucija 1917 g.," *Chronika sobytij*, vol. 1, pp. 40–41.

32. Text of the appeal cited in Golder, p. 286, and I. W. Lomonosoff, *Die russische März-Revolution 1917*, Munich 1921, p. 35.

33. See *Chronika sobytij*, vol. 1, pp. 41–44; A. Pešechonov, "Pervye nedeli" (from *Na čužoj storone*, vol. 1, Berlin and Prague 1923), in *Fevral'skaja revoljucija*, pp. 430–465; S. P. Mansyrev, "Moi vospominanija," in *Fevral'skaja revoljucija*, pp. 265–271.

34. *Chronika sobytij*, vol. 1, pp. 44–45; German text given in Gitermann, *Geschichte Russlands*, vol. 3, pp. 632–633.

35. Mansyrev, p. 261.
36. *Chronika sobytij*, vol. 1, p. 46.
37. *Chronika sobytij*, vol. 1, p. 49.
38. For details, see below, p. 000.
39. Šljapnikov, vol. 1, p. 242.
40. But this did not prevent the soviet on the very first day from excluding Chrustalev-Nosar', the one-time chairman of the 1905 soviet, because of his antirevolutionary stance during the war.
41. Trotzki, *Geschichte*, vol. 1, p. 214.
42. Šljapnikov, vol. 3, p. 173.
43. Šljapnikov, vol. 1, pp. 188–194.
44. The origin of Order No. 1 was soon the subject of heated argument. Because military authorities leveled heavy reproaches, the moderate soviet leaders attempted to withdraw from responsibility and to attribute the order to some unresponsible group or other. In fact, however, on March 1 the soviet plenum passed a resolution concerning the rights of soldiers and charged a commission with working out an appeal along these lines. When Colonel Engelhardt—who had been named provisional commander by the Duma committee—refused his cooperation, the soviet members together with a few soldiers themselves composed Order No. 1. See Kerenski, *Erinnerungen*, pp. 221 ff.; Suchanov, vol. 2, pp. 262–267; Šljapnikov, vol. 1, pp. 211–214.
45. The text of the decree can be found in Šljapnikov, vol. 1, pp. 212–213; *Chronika sobytij*, vol. 1, pp. 186–187; German translation of text in Gitermann, vol. 3, pp. 633–634.
46. Šljapnikov, vol. 3, pp. 167–170.
47. *Izvestija*, 22 (March 23, 1917).
48. See Trotzki, *Geschichte*, vol. 1, p. 215.
49. See *Izvestija*, 22; F. P. Matveev, *Iz zapisnoj knižki deputata 176 pechotnogo polka*, Moscow and Leningrad 1932, pp. 46–51, 55–57, 171–179, 227–229; Šljapnikov, vol. 3, pp. 170–173, vol. 4, pp. 98–99.
50. *Delo Naroda*, 25 (April 15, 1917).
51. A picture of the Executive Committee's activities can be found in its minutes: *Petrogradskij sovet rabočich i soldatskich deputatov. Protokoly zasedanij ispolnitel'nogo komiteta i bjuro i.k.*, Moscow and Leningrad 1925. They cover the period from March 3 through August 9, 1917.
52. See *Izvestija*, 155 (August 17, 1917), which contains reports on the various divisions.
53. *Izvestija*, 27 (March 29, 1917).
54. See Golder, pp. 288–290.
55. *Izvestija*, 44 (April 18, 1917).
56. Sljapnikov, vol. 4, pp. 208–209.
57. See Matveev, p. 7; V. B. Stankevič, "Vospominanija," in *Fevral'skaja revoljucija*, pp. 409–415.
58. E. Jaroslavskij, *Istorija V. K. P. (b)*, vol. 4, Moscow and Leningrad 1930, p. 23, n. 2. Unfortunately the author does not indicate the month for

which these data apply. I had no access to material on composition of the workers section by professions; presumably, as in 1905, metalworkers constituted a large majority.

59. See *Chronika sobytij*, vol. 1, pp. 104, 107.
60. See V. Vladimirova, "Revoljucija 1917 goda," *Chronika sobytij*, vol. 4, Leningrad 1924, pp. 84, 93.
61. See Trotzki, *Geschichte*, vol. 1, p. 170.
62. See Matveev, pp. 221–222, n. 24.
63. See *Izvestija*, 41 (April 15), 60 (May 7, 1917); Vladimirova in *Chronika sobytij*, vol. 3, Moscow 1923, pp. 59, 190–191.
64. See *Chronika sobytij*, vol. 4, p. 167; *Istorija Putilovskogo zavoda*, pp. 483–487, 543–544, 553.
65. "Voting for Social Revolutionaries means voting for the revolution as a whole and imposes no kind of obligation," Trotsky noted on this point. Trotzki, *Geschichte*, vol. 1, p. 220.
66. See the memoirs of Šljapnikov, especially volumes 1 and 2; see further *Pervyj legal'nyj peterburgskij komitet bol'ševikov v 1917 g.*, Moscow and Leningrad 1927.
67. Šljapnikov, vol. 2, p. 175.
68. See *Chronika sobytij*, vol. 3, p. 38; *Izvestija*, 68 (May 17, 1917).
69. According to Stalin in his report at the Sixth Party Congress on July 27; *Chronika sobytij*, vol. 3, p. 223. On June 20 Kalinin stated that approximately three-fourths of the soviets were not Bolshevik, that in the workers section about one-half were Bolsheviks, and that there were only 20 Bolshevik deputies in the soldiers section; *Pervyj legal'nyj PK*, p. 188.
70. See below, p. 179.
71. See O. Seeling, *Der Rätegedanke und seine Verwirklichung in Sowjetrussland*, Berlin 1923, pp. 83, 122–123.
72. Chernov, p. 104.
73. M. Farbman, *Bolshevism in Retreat*, London 1922, p. 146.
74. A. Paquet, *Der Geist der russischen Revolution*, Leipzig 1919, p. 13.
75. As noted in the Introduction, this is not the place for a comprehensive comparison of local variations of the soviet movement. Aside from the necessity for extensive documentation, which can only partly be procured outside Russia, I am primarily concerned with the soviets' basic and typical development. Examples are cited, therefore, mainly to illustrate the whole. Some of the numerous histories of local soviets of 1917 are cited in the bibliography, but could not be used here. Taken as a whole, however, scholarship on the soviets' history is in a sad state—as has repeatedly been admitted by Soviet historians themselves. A general survey of the first half of 1917, with numerous details, is provided in M. S. Jugov, "Sovety v pervyj period revoljucii," in Pokrovskij, ed., *Očerki po istorii oktjabr'skoj revolucii*, vol. 2, Moscow and Leningrad 1927, pp. 113–255.
76. *Chronika sobytij*, vol. 1, pp. 124–125.
77. Jugov, p. 124.
78. One point of reference is given by the figures of the soviets represented

at the All-Russian Soviet Congresses; see below in the appropriate context. See Trotzki, *Geschichte*, vol. 2, p. 273; *Delo Naroda*, 224 (December 5, 1917).

79. *1917 god v Moskve (Chronika revoljucii)*, Moscow 1934, p. 16; see E. P. Tret'jakova, "Fevral'skie sobytija 1917 g. v Moskve," *Voprosy istorii* 3 (1957), pp. 72–84.

80. See *Chronika sobytij*, vol. 1, pp. 47–48.

81. *Chronika sobytij*, vol. 1, p. 58. See E. Izrael, "Pervye dni Moskovskogo soveta," *Izvestija Moskovskogo soveta rabočich deputatov*, 148 (August 27, 1917). I did not have access to the books by E. Ignatov, *Moskovskij sovet rabočich deputatov 1917 g.*, Moscow 1927, and N. Angarskij, *Moskovskij sovet v dvuch revoljucijach*, Moscow 1928.

82. See *Chronika sobytij*, vol. 1, pp. 61, 65, 68.

83. *Izvestija Moskovskogo soveta*, 148 (August 27, 1917).

84. See I. Veger (Otec), *K istorii Moskovskogo soveta r. d." Proletarskaja Revoljucija* 1:48 (1926), pp. 217–232.

85. See *Izvestija Moskovskogo soveta*, 92 (June 22, 1917).

86. See *Protokoly s-ezdov i konferencij vsesojuznoj kommunističeskoj partii (b). Šestoj s-ezd RSDRP (b), Avgust 1917 g.*, Moscow 1934, p. 55.

87. *Izvestija Moskovskogo soveta*, 91 (June 21) and 92 (June 22, 1917).

88. See the examples in Šljapnikov, vol. 2, pp. 28–32, and reports of the delegates to the Bolshevik conference of April in *Protokoly s-ezdov i konferencij vsesojuznoj kommunističeskoj partii (b). Sed'maja ("aprel'skaja") vserossijskaja i petrogradskaja obščegorodskaja konferencii RSDRP (b), Aprel' 1917 g.*, Moscow 1934.

89. See *Izvestija Moskovskogo soveta*, 75 (June 2, 1917).

90. Jugov, p. 155.

91. Jugov, pp. 155–156.

92. With reference to the soviet in Kharkov, see *Izvestija*, 138 (August 8, 1917).

93. *Izvestija Moskovskogo soveta*, 50 (May 3, 1917).

94. *Izvestija Moskovskogo soveta*, 51 (May 4, 1917).

95. *Rabočija organizacii g. Kieva*, Kiev 1918, p. 49.

96. Jugov, p. 214.

97. See Jugov, pp. 116, 119, 156.

98. Jugov, p. 166.

99. *Izvestija Moskovskogo soveta*, 56 (May 10, 1917).

100. Jugov, p. 119; *Rabočija organizacii g. Kieva*, p. 49.

101. Jugov, p. 214.

102. See above, p. 106.

103. Text in Šljapnikov, vol. 2, pp. 92–93.

104. See A. I. Denikin, *Očerki russkoj smuty*, vol. 1, Paris and Berlin 1921. Cited in *Fevral'skaja revoljucija*, pp. 197–198. F. Stepun, *Vergangenes und Unvergängliches*, vol. 2, Munich 1948, p. 96.

105. Text in Šljapnikov, vol. 2, pp. 313–317.

106. Šljapnikov, vol. 2, pp. 317–325; see A. von Freytagh-Loringhoven, *Die Gesetzgebung der russischen Revolution*, Halle 1920, pp. 76 ff.

107. Šljapnikov, vol. 2, p. 92.

108. See M. I. Kapustin, "Bol'ševiki severnogo fronta v bor'be za soldatskie massy v 1917 godu," *Voprosy istorii* 11 (1955), pp. 105–113.

109. See *Chronika sobytij*, vol. 1, pp. 180–181.

110. See Šljapnikov, vol. 4, pp. 132–133.

111. See Šljapnikov, vol. 4, pp. 134–146; Kerenski, *Erinnerungen*, pp. 250–251.

112. So phrased in the survey report on the activities of elected organizations of the western front up to September 1, 1917; see Šljapnikov, vol. 4, pp. 375–382.

113. Stepun, vol. 2, p. 147.

114. Officially recorded peasant disturbances amounted to 49 in March, 378 in April, 678 in May, 988 in June, 957 in July, 760 in August, 803 in September, and 1,169 in October; S. Dubrowski, *Die Bauernbewegung in der russischen Revolution 1917*, Berlin 1929, p. 90.

115. See M. Gajsinskij, *Bor'ba bol'ševikov za krest'janstvo v 1917 g.*, Moscow 1933, pp. 17–18.

116. For the Provisional Government's agrarian policy, see M. K. Eroshkin, "The Land Problem in Russia," in *The Soviets in Russia*, New York 1919; pp. 25–35; Gajsinskij, pp. 20–22.

117. See the examples given in Trotzki, *Geschichte*, vol. 1, pp. 375 ff.

118. See Dubrowski, pp. 126–127; *Chronika sobytij*, vol. 1, p. 105.

119. See Dubrowski, p. 127.

120. See N. Voronovič, "Zapiski predsedatela soveta soldatskich deputatov," in *Fevral'skaja revoljucija*, pp. 466–505.

121. For the total context, see T. A. Remezova, "Sovety krest'janskich deputatov v 1917 g.," *Istoričeskie zapiski* 32 (1950), pp. 3–39. I had no access to the fundamental work by A. V. Šestakov, *Sovety krest'janskich deputatov v 1917–1918 gg.*, n. p., n. d.

122. Remezova; pp. 14–15.

123. See Gajsinskij, pp. 44–85; V. Gurevič, *Vserossijskij krest'janskij s-ezd i pervaja koalicija, Letopis' revoljucii*, vol. 1, Berlin 1923, pp. 176–196.

124. The Peasant Union followed a moderate course during the revolution of 1917 and gradually lost its influence; see Dubrowski, pp. 119–126.

125. Chernov, p. 392; Gajsinskij, p. 49.

126. Remezova, pp. 15–19.

127. Remezova, p. 19; Dubrowski, p. 125.

128. See Gajsinskij, pp. 106 ff.; Dubrowski, p. 135; Trotzki, *Geschichte*, vol. 2, p. 335.

129. In Moscow, for example, a first regional conference was held March 25–27, followed by the first regional congress May 28–31. In Helsinki the first Finnish regional congress opened on April 17 and the second on May 19.

130. See P. E. Dybenko, *Die Rebellen. Erinnerungen aus der Revolutionszeit*, Hamburg 1923, pp. 47–50.

131. See Šljapnikov, vol. 4, pp. 119–120, 365–366.

132. For the proceedings of the conference, see *Chronika sobytij*, vol. 1, pp. 138–183; Šljapnikov, vol. 3, pp. 211–249; Jugov, pp. 149–160.

133. *Pravda*, 22 (March 31, 1917).

134. *Chronika sobytij,* vol. 1, p. 165.
135. See the text of the resolution in *Chronika sobytij,* vol. 1, pp. 203–213.
136. *Chronika sobytij,* vol. 1, pp. 173–174.
137. See Golder, p. 360.
138. See Trotzki, *Geschichte,* vol. 1, p. 416.
139. *Pervyj vserossijskij s-ezd sovetov rabočich i soldatskich deputatov 1917. Protokoly I,* Moscow and Leningrad 1930, p. xxvii.
140. The workers section of the Petrograd soviet, for example, passed a Bolshevik resolution by 173 to 144 on May 31—that is, on the eve of the congress.
141. For the proceedings of the congress, see the Proceedings (two volumes), as well as Suchanov, vol. 4, pp. 198–281; Šljapnikov, vol. 4, pp. 147–216; Stepun, vol. 2, pp. 185 ff.
142. *Chronika sobytij,* vol. 3, p. 78.
143. *Chronika sobytij,* vol. 3, pp. 99, 102, 108.
144. *Chronika sobytij,* vol. 3, p. 126; Šljapnikov, vol 4, pp. 116–123, 366–369.
145. See above, pp. 24 ff.
146. For the general context, see D. A. Cejtlin, "Fabrično-zavodskie komitety Petrograda v fevrale-oktjabre 1917 goda," *Voprosy istorii* 2 (1956), pp. 86–97; M. Dewar, *Labour Policy in the USSR 1917–1928,* London and New York 1956, pp. 2–15. I was unable to consult *Oktjabr'skaja revoljucija i fabzavkomy. Materialy po istorii fabrično-zavodskich komitetov,* 2 vols., Moscow 1927; A. M. Pankratova, *Fabzavkomy i profsojuzy v revoljucii 1917 goda,* Moscow and Leningrad 1927.
147. See *Rabočee dviženie v 1917 godu,* Moscow 1926, pp. 40–41; Šljapnikov, vol. 2, pp. 130–131; *Chronika sobytij,* vol. 1, p. 82.
148. See *Rabočee dviženie,* pp. 72 ff.
149. See *Chronika sobytij,* vol. 4, pp. 49–50.
150. See *Izvestija,* 121 (July 19, 1917).
151. See *Istorija Putilovskogo zavoda,* pp. 498–508.
152. See *Rabočee dviženie,* pp. 77–78.
153. See *Chronika sobytij,* vol. 3, pp. 19, 255 ff.; M. Tomski, *Abhandlungen über die Gewerkschaftbewegung in Russland,* Hamburg 1921, pp. 39–47.
154. Cejtlin, pp. 86–97.
155. *Chronika sobytij,* vol. 3, pp. 213, 231.
156. Dewar, p. 12.
157. In June 1917 Petrograd had about fifty trade unions, with a membership of 250,000. The metalworkers union, with 100,000 members, was the strongest. There were 73 Bolshevik delegates out of a total of 221 at the Third All-Russian Conference of Trade Unions in June 1917; *Chronika sobytij,* vol. 3, pp. 97, 109. For the history of the Russian trade unions after 1917, see also Tomski; A. Losowski, *Die Gewerkschaften in Sowjetrussland,* Berlin 1920; W. Koch, *Die bol'ševistischen Gewerkschaften,* Jena 1932; I. Deutscher, *Soviet Trade Unions,* London 1950.
158. Spoken by a delegate to the first Petrograd conference of factory committees; Tomski, p. 41.
159. Tomski, p. 48.

160. Cited in W. H. Chamberlin, *The Russian Revolution 1917–1921*, 2nd ed., vol. 1, New York 1952, p. 435.
161. See *Chronika sobytij*, vol. 1, p. 82; Chernov, pp. 134 ff.
162. Stepun, p. 132.
163. Trotzki, *Geschichte*, vol. 1, p. 156. [See also Trotsky, *The Russian Revolution*, New York 1959, p. 205.]
164. Trotzki, *Geschichte*, vol. 1, p. 173.
165. See above, pp. 65 ff.
166. See Šljapnikov, vol. 1, pp. 216–217.
167. See Chernov, pp. 117 ff.
168. *Izvestija*, 4 (March 3, 1917); *Chronika sobytij*, vol. 1, pp. 50–51.
169. See Freytagh-Loringhoven, p. 29.
170. *Chronika sobytij*, vol. 1, p. 74.
171. Šljapnikov, vol. 3, pp. 177–180.
172. See *Chronika sobytij*, vol. 1, pp. 204–205.
173. *Chronika sobytij*, vol. 1, p. 153.
174. Trotzki, *Geschichte*, vol. 1, p. 196.
175. See Golder, pp. 299 ff.; Chamberlin, vol. 1, pp. 96–97.
176. See D. Geyer, "Die russischen Räte und die Friedensfrage im Frühjahr und Sommer 1917," *Vierteljahrshefte für Zeitgeschichte*, 5 (1957), pp. 220–240.
177. Text in *Chronika sobytij*, vol. 1, pp. 198–199; Golder, pp. 325–326.
178. Golder, pp. 333–334.
179. See Suchanov, vol. 3, pp. 251–300; Trotsky, vol. 1, pp. 326–343; I. Tseretelli, "Reminiscences of the February Revolution; The April Crisis," *Russian Review*, 14 (1955), pp. 93–108, 184–200, 301–321; G. N. Golikov and Ju. S. Tokarev, "Aprel'skij krizis 1917 g.," *Istoričeskie zapiski* 57 (1956), pp. 35–79.
180. See Golder, pp. 335–336.
181. See Golder, p. 336.
182. See Trotzki, *Geschichte*, vol. 1, p. 335.
183. See Trotzki, *Geschichte*, vol. 1, p. 336.
184. See below, pp. 139 ff.
185. *Izvestija*, 56 (May 3, 1917).
186. For the documents pertaining hereto, including the list of ministers, see Golder, pp. 349–358.
187. Trotzki, *Geschichte*, vol. 1, p. 353.
188. J. G. Ceretelli, *Rečy*, Petersburg 1917, p. 161.
189. Trotzki, *Geschichte*, vol. 1, p. 353.
190. See "Obzor položenija Rossii za tri mesjaca revoljucii po dannym otdela snošenij s provinciej Vremennogo Komiteta Gosudarstvennoj Dumy." *Krasnyj archiv* 4:15 (1926), pp. 30–60.
191. See Freytagh-Loringhoven, pp. 56 ff.
192. See Jugov, pp. 125–126.
193. See Jugov, pp. 206–210.
194. *Pervyj vserossijskij s-ezd sovetov*, vol. 2, p. 258.

195. *Chronika sobytij*, vol. 1, pp. 205–210.
196. *Rabočija organizacii g. Kieva*, pp. 48–49.
197. *Pervyj vserossijskij s-ezd sovetov*, vol. 2, p. 259.
198. See *Rabočee dviženie*, pp. 39–41.
199. *Rabočee dviženie*, pp. 42–64; Jugov, pp. 137 ff.
200. Suchanov, vol. 3, p. 154.
201. See Jugov, p. 210; Trotzki, *Geschichte*, vol. 2, pp. 270–271.
202. *Pervyj vserossijskij s-ezd sovetov*, vol. 1, p. 257.
203. Jugov, p. 210.
204. Trotzki, *Geschichte*, vol. 2, p. 270.
205. See I. Flerovskij, "Kronštadtskaja respublika," *Proletarskaja revoljucija* 11:58 (1926), pp. 29–55; 12:59 (1926), pp. 113–143.
206. Flerovskij. Slightly different figures are given in Jugov, p. 214, n.
207. *Isvestija Kronštadtskogo Soveta rabočich i soldatskich deputatov*, 46 (May 14, 1917).
208. *Izvestija Kronštadtskogo Soveta*, 50 (May 19, 1917).
209. The minutes of the soviet session of May 16 are published in the *Izvestija Kronštadtskogo Soveta*, 69 (June 12), 70 (June 13), and 71 (June 14, 1917), and in "Protokoly zasedanij Kronštadtskogo Soveta, na kotorych obsuždalas' rezoljucija Soveta o vlasti," *Proletarskaja revoljucija*, 12:59 (1926), pp. 144–184.
210. *Izvestija Kronštadtskogo Soveta*, 59 (May 31), 60 (June 1), 61 (June 2, 1917).
211. *Izvestija Kronštadtskogo Soveta*, 54 (May 25, 1917).
212. See below, pp. 160 ff.
213. *Pervyj vserossijskij s-ezd sovetov*, vol. 1, p. 216.
214. *Pervyj vserossijskij s-ezd sovetov*, vol. 1, p. 279.
215. *Pervyj vserossijskij*, vol. 1, p. 237.
216. *Pervyj vserossijskij*, vol. 1, pp. 283–284.
217. *Pervyj vserossijskij*, vol. 1, p. 286.
218. See below, pp. 166 ff.
219. Kerenski, *Erinnerungen*, p. 308.
220. G. Buchanan, *My Mission to Russia and Other Diplomatic Memories*, vol. 2, Boston 1923, p. 111.
221. Skobelev at the Democratic Conference in Petersburg, *Chronika sobytij*, vol. 4, pp. 218–219.
222. *Chronika sobytij*, vol. 4, p. 317.
223. *Chronika sobytij*, vol. 4, pp. 322–323.
224. Ceretelli, pp. 172–173.
225. S. Klivanskij (Maksim), *Rol' i značenie Sovetov rabočich, soldatskich i krest'janskich deputatov*, Petrograd, 1917, pp. 5 ff.
226. *Delo Naroda*, 149 (September 8, 1917).
227. The first vote was 766 to 688 in favor of a coalition, but the second vote of 595 to 493 rejected coalition with the Kadets. In the All-Russian Central Executive Committee, 119 were in favor and 101 against a coalition; Trotzki, *Geschichte*, vol. 2, p. 312; *Chronika sobytij*, vol. 4, pp. 203–204.

228. See below, pp. 177 ff.
229. *Chronika sobytij*, vol. 4, p. 386.
230. See below, p. 212.
231. *Chronika sobytij*, vol. 4, pp. 196–197.

CHAPTER FOUR
BOLSHEVISM AND COUNCILS, 1917

1. Šljapnikov, vol. 1, p. 71.
2. See Trotzki, *Geschichte*, vol. 1, pp. 277–283; E. N. Burdžalov, "O taktike bol'ševikov v marte-aprele 1917 goda," *Voprosy istorii*, 4 (1956), pp. 38–56. This article is the first attempt to break dominant Soviet historical legends, especially about Stalin's role, and to describe events objectively. Shortly thereafter the author paid for this effort by expulsion from the journal's editorial committee.
3. See above, pp. 81 ff.
4. Šljapnikov, vol. 1, p. 119.
5. Published in *Pravda* 1 (March 5, 1917); the wording here is taken from Lenin, *Sämtliche Werke*, vol. 20, part 2, pp. 257–258.
6. Šljapnikov, vol. 1, pp. 185–187, 223–224.
7. Šljapnikov, vol. 1, p. 226.
8. Šljapnikov, vol. 1, pp. 235–236.
9. Šljapnikov, vol. 1, pp. 339–340.
10. See *Pervyj legal'nyj peterburgskij komitet bol'ševikov v 1917 g.* (Materials and minutes), Moscow and Leningrad 1927, pp. 2–4.
11. *Pravda*, 4 (March 9, 1917).
12. See Šljapnikov, vol. 2, pp. 186 ff.
13. *Pervyj legal'nyj*, pp. 19–20.
14. *Pravda*, 8 (March 14, 1917).
15. *Pravda*, 9 (March 15, 1917).
16. See Lenin, *Sočinenija*, vol. 10, p. 136.
17. *Pravda*, 11 (March 17, 1917).
18. *Pravda*, 12 (March 18, 1917); also Stalin, *Werke*, vol. 3, p. 12.
19. See F. I. Drabkina, "Vserossijskoe soveščanie bol'ševikov v marte 1917 g.," *Voprosy istorii* 9 (1956), pp. 3–16.
20. *Pravda*, 18 (March 26, 1917).
21. See Šljapnikov, vol. 3, pp. 210–211.
22. Zinov'ev (who was Lenin's spokesman during the war) in the article, "Der Krieg und die revolutionäre Krise in Russland," in N. Lenin and G. Sinowjew, *Gegen den Strom*, Hamburg 1921, p. 276.
23. Lenin, *Sämtliche Werke*, vol. 20, part 1, pp. 90–91.
24. Trotzki, *Geschichte*, vol. 1, p. 307.
25. Lenin, *Sämtliche Werke*, vol. 8, p. 248.
26. Lenin, *Sämtliche Werke*, vol. 20, part 1, p. 71.
27. See above, pp. 76 ff.

28. Lenin, *Sämtliche Werke*, vol. 10, p. 23.
29. See *Leninskij Sbornik*, vol. 14, pp. 199–389, vol. 21, pp. 25–26; Lenin, *Sämtliche Werke*, vol. 21, p. 663, n. 159; R. V. Daniels, "The State and Revolution, a Case Study of the Genesis and Transformation of Communist Ideology," *The American Slavic and East European Review* 12 (1953), pp. 22–43.
30. Especially "Der imperialistische Raubstaat," in *Die Jugendinternationale*, 6 (December 1, 1916).
31. A. Pannekoek, "Massenaktion und Revolution," *Die Neue Zeit* 30 (1911–1912), vol. 2, p. 545.
32. Lenin, *Sämtliche Werke*, vol. 8, pp. 605 ff.
32a. *Leninskij Sbornik*, vol. 14, pp. 310–314.
33. Lenin, *Sämtliche Werke*, vol. 20, part 1, p. 21.
34. Lenin, *Sämtliche Werke*, vol. 20, part 1, p. 22.
35. Lenin, *Sämtliche Werke*, vol. 20, part 1, pp. 4, 12.
36. Lenin made this assertion after the fact, to demonstrate that as early as 1915, or even 1905, he had already seen the connection between the Commune and the Russian soviets. As was shown, this was not the case.
37. Lenin, *Sämtliche Werke*, vol. 20, part 1, p. 43.
38. Lenin, *Sämtliche Werke*, vol. 20, part 1, p. 125.
39. See Trotzki, *Geschichte*, vol. 1, pp. 289–290, 301–302; Šljapnikov, vol. 3, p. 260.
40. Lenin, *Sämtliche Werke*, vol. 20, part 1, pp. 114–118.
41. *Pravda*, 27 (April 8, 1917).
42. *Pervyj legal'nyj*, pp. 83–90.
43. *Pravda*, 30 (April 12, 1917).
44. Marx in the *Communist Manifesto*, Laski edition, p. 160.
45. See above, pp. 94 ff.
46. See Suchanov, vol. 3, p. 40.
47. *Pravda*, 27 (April 8, 1917); also in Lenin, *Sämtliche Werke*, vol. 20, part 2, pp. 260–261.
48. Lenin, *Sämtliche Werke*, vol. 20, part 1, p. 132.
49. *Pravda*, 27 (April 8, 1917).
50. See above, pp. 86 ff.
51. Lenin, *Sämtliche Werke*, vol. 20, part 1, p. 136.
52. Trotzki, *Geschichte*, vol. 1, p. 447.
53. See above, p. 90.
54. Trotsky's speeches and articles of this period are contained in his *Sočinenija*, vol. 3, parts 1 and 2; see further Deutscher, *The Prophet Armed*, pp. 249–269.
55. See Trotzki, *Geschichte*, vol. 1, p. 311.
56. *Sed'maja ("aprel'skaja") vserossijskaja i petrogradskaja konferencii RSDRP (b), Aprel' 1917*, Moscow 1934, p. 14.
57. "Protokoly pervoj moskovskoj oblastnoj konferencii RSDRP (b) 19.-21. aprelja 1917 g.," *Proletarskaja revoljucija*, 10:93 (1929), pp. 127–206; this statement from pp. 137–138.

58. *Sed'maja ("aprel'skaja") vserossijskaja i petrogradskaja obščegorodskaja konferencii*, pp. 88–89.

59. *Sed'maja . . . obščegorodskaja konferencii*, pp. 237–238. Also Lenin, *Sämtliche Werke*, vol. 20, part 2, pp. 298–299.

60. Rykov, for example, states: "Can we rely on the support of the masses if we call for a proletarian revolution? Russia is the most petit-bourgeois country in all Europe. The masses' sympathy cannot be counted on and therefore the party will turn into a propaganda club if it persists in advocating the socialist revolution. The impetus for that revolution must come from the West." *Sed'maja . . . obščegorodskaja konferencii*, p. 93.

61. Suchanov, vol. 3, pp. 58–60.

62. Lenin, *Sämtliche Werke*, vol. 20, part 1, p. 127.

63. Lenin, *Sämtliche Werke*, vol. 20, part 1, p. 126.

64. Lenin, *Sämtliche Werke*, vol. 20, part 1, pp. 269–270.

65. Lenin, *Sämtliche Werke*, vol. 21, p. 507.

66. The question was briefly discussed at the Second Party Congress of the RSDWP in 1903. Plekhanov declared that circumstances might require disenfranchisement of the bourgeoisie and dissolution of a "bad" parliament. Lenin fully agreed with this statement. See his "Ein Schritt vorwärts, zwei Schritte zurück," *Ausgewählte Werke*, vol. 1, pp. 338–339.

67. See below, pp. 211 ff.

68. See W. Mautner, *Der Bolschewismus*, Stuttgart 1922, pp. 127–214; R. Nürnberger, "Lenins Revolutionstheorie. Eine Studie über 'Staat und Revolution,' " in *Marxismusstudien* (Schriften der Studiengemeinschaft der Evangelischen Akademien, vol. 3), Tübingen 1954, pp. 161–172.

69. "It is based, not on the law, not on the official will of the majority, but directly, immediately on force. Force is a tool of power." Lenin, *Sämtliche Werke*, vol. 20, part 1, p. 332.

70. Lenin, *Sämtliche Werke*, vol. 21, p. 544.

71. Lenin, *Sämtliche Werke*, vol. 20, part 1, p. 179.

72. Lenin, *Sämtliche Werke*, vol. 21, pp. 545–546.

73. Lenin, *Sämtliche Werke*, vol. 21, p. 537.

74. Lenin, *Sämtliche Werke*, vol. 21, p. 540. This sentence and similar utterances by Lenin were later used by Stalin and Soviet political theorists to justify the fact that in the Soviet Union the state did not "wither away" even decades after the revolution.

75. Lenin, *Sämtliche Werke*, vol. 21, pp. 556 ff.

76. Lenin, *Sämtliche Werke*, vol. 21, p. 566.

77. See especially Lenin's article, "Die drohende Katastrophe und wie soll man sie bekämpfen," *Sämtliche Werke*, vol. 21, pp. 193–242.

78. M. Buber, *Pfade in Utopia*, Heidelberg 1950.

79. Buber, p. 183.

80. Buber, p. 190.

81. Borkenau, *Das Jahr 1917*, p. 11.

82. Lenin, *Sämtliche Werke*, vol. 20, part 1, p. 6.

83. Lenin, *Sämtliche Werke*, vol. 20, part 1, p. 4.

84. At the April conference the party numbered about 80,000 members; at the Sixth Party Conference in August 1917, the number had risen to 240,000. See *Chronika sobytij*, vol. 3, p. 224.

85. Lenin, *Sämtliche Werke*, vol. 20, part 1, p. 42.

86. Lenin, *Sämtliche Werke*, vol. 20, part 1, p. 24.

87. I. Galkin, *Sovety kak taktičeskaja problema revoljucii*, Moscow and Leningrad n. d. [1928], p. 98.

88. See P. Selznick, *The Organizational Weapon. A Study of Bolshevik Strategy and Tactics*, New York 1952, pp. 254 ff.; H. Seton-Watson, *From Lenin to Malenkov*, 3rd ed. New York 1954, pp. 29–30; W. Gurian, "Lenins Methoden der Machteroberung im Jahre 1917" in *Deutschland und Europa. Festschrift für Hans Rothfels*, Düsseldorf 1951, pp. 271–291.

89. L. Trotzki, "Kann man eine Konterrevolution oder eine Revolution auf einen bestimmten Zeitpunkt ansetzen?" in *Vom Bürgerkrieg* 3, Berlin 1923, pp. 3–7.

90. J. Stalin, *Probleme des Leninismus*, Vienna and Berlin 1926, p. 29.

91. Lenin, *Sämtliche Werke*, vol. 20, part 1, p. 314.

92. See Lenin, *Sämtliche Werke*, vol. 20, part 1, pp. 344–345.

93. Lenin, *Sämtliche Werke*, vol. 20, part 1, p. 240.

94. See above, p. 75.

95. Lenin, *Sämtliche Werke*, vol. 20, part 1, p. 241.

96. Lenin, *Sämtliche Werke*, vol. 20, part 2, p. 298.

97. See above, pp. 94 ff.

98. Lenin, *Sämtliche Werke*, vol. 20, part 1, p. 241.

99. Lenin, *Sämtliche Werke*, vol. 21, p. 341.

100. Lenin, *Sämtliche Werke*, vol. 21, p. 571.

101. L. Trotzki, *Um den Oktober*, Hamburg 1923, p. 42.

102. Lenin, *Sämtliche Werke*, vol. 20, part 1, p. 322.

103. Trotzki, *Geschichte*, vol. 2, pp. 485–486.

104. Trotzki, *Um den Oktober*, p. 42.

105. Lenin, *Sämtliche Werke*, vol. 20, part 1, p. 116.

106. Lenin, *Sämtliche Werke*, vol. 20, part 2, p. 174.

107. Lenin, *Sämtliche Werke*, vol. 21, p. 37.

108, Stalin, *Probleme des Leninismus*, p. 182.

109. The problem of peaceful transition to socialism was again raised—also in historical perspective—by leading Communists at the Twentieth Party Congress of the CPSU in February 1956; see my article, "Lenin und der friedliche Übergang zum Sozialismus," *Osteuropa* 6 (1956), pp. 190–196; M. I. Mišin, "V. I. Lenin o vozmožnosti mirnovo razvitija revoljucii v 1917 godu," *Voprosy istorii* 5 (1957), pp. 17–42.

110. See Lenin, *Sämtliche Werke*, vol. 10, p. 124; vol. 19, p. 280.

111. For the reasons for the Mensheviks' and Social Revolutionaries' position, see above, pp. 129 ff.

112. See F. Borkenau, "Das Problem der Machtergreifung des Kommunismus," *Sowjetstudien* 1 (1956), pp. 5–19.

113. See above, p. 161.

114. Lenin, *Sämtliche Werke*, vol. 20, part 1, p. 337.
115. For the course of events, see Trotzki, *Geschichte*, vol. 2, pp. 1–77; Suchanov, vol. 4, pp. 360–517; *Chronika sobytij*, vol. 3, pp. 133–166, 307–337, 355–371; Šljapnikov, vol. 4, pp. 248–323. The reports of the hearings of the investigation commission established by the Provisional Government after the rising are contained in *Krasnyj archiv*, 4:23 (1927), pp. 1–63; 5:24 (1927), pp. 3–70. The official Bolshevik version was given by Stalin at the Sixth Party Congress in August 1917; see *Protokoly s-ezdov i konferencij vsesojuznoj kommunističeskoj partii (b)*. *Šestoj s-ezd RSDRP (b), Avgust 1917 g.*, Moscow 1934, p. 21; see further V. K. Medvedev, "Kronštadt v ijul'skie dni 1917 goda," *Istoričeskie zapiski* 42 (1953), pp. 262–275.
116. *Chronika sobytij*, vol. 3, p. 316.
117. *Izvestija*, 108 (July 4, 1917).
118. Lenin, *Sämtliche Werke*, vol. 20, part 2, pp. 174–175.
119. J. Monnerot, *Soziologie des Kommunismus*, Cologne and Berlin 1952, p. 67.
120. See *Izvestija*, 117 (July 14, 1917), and 134, 135 ff. (early August 1917); *Chronika sobytij*, vol. 3, pp. 179–180.
121. Lenin, *Sämtliche Werke*, vol. 21, p. 28.
122. Lenin, *Sämtliche Werke*, vol. 21, p. 29.
123. Lenin, *Sämtliche Werke*, vol. 21, p. 28.
124. Lenin, *Sämtliche Werke*, vol. 21, p. 41.
125. Lenin, *Sämtliche Werke*, vol. 21, p. 39.
126. Lenin, *Sämtliche Werke*, vol. 21, p. 29.
127. Trotzki, *Geschichte*, vol. 2, p. 291.
128. Stalin, *Werke*, vol. 3, pp. 114–115.
129. *Vtoraja i tretaja petrogradskie obščegorodskie konferencii bol'ševikov v ijule i oktjabre 1917 goda*, Moscow and Leningrad 1927, p. 84.
130. *Vtoraja i tretaja*, p. 75.
131. *Vtoraja i tretaja*, p. 72.
132. *Vtoraja i tretaja*, p. 77.
133. *Izvestija Moskovskogo soveta r. i s.d.*, issue 109, July 12, 1917.
134. See Trotzki, *Geschichte*, vol. 2, p. 292.
135. See "Protokoly vtoroj Moskovskoj oblastnoj konferencii RSDRP (b) 1917 goda," *Proletarskaja revoljucija* 12:95 (1929), pp. 137–175; this citation from pp. 164 ff.
136. See N. M. Mor, "Šestoj s-ezd RSDRP (b)," *Voprosy istorii* 8 (1957), pp. 3–24.
137. Stalin, *Werke*, vol. 3, p. 165.
138. Stalin, *Werke*, vol. 3, p. 170.
139. *Protokoly . . . Šestoj s-ezd RSDRP (b)*, pp. 114–115.
140. Trotzki, *Geschichte*, vol. 2, p. 291.
141. *Protokoly . . . Šestoj s-ezd RSDRP (b)*, pp. 123 ff.
142. *Protokoly . . . Šestoj s-ezd RSDRP (b)*, pp. 120–121.
143. *Protokoly . . . Šestoj s-ezd RSDRP (b)*, pp. 121–122.

144. *Protokoly . . . Šestoj s-ezd RSDRP (b)*, p. 135.
145. *Protokoly . . . Šestoj s-ezd RSDRP (b)*, p. 116.
146. *Protokoly . . . Šestoj s-ezd RSDRP (b)*, p. 134.
147. Text of the resolution in *Protokoly . . . Šestoj s-ezd RSDRP (b)*, pp. 238–241; Lenin, *Sämtliche Werke*, vol. 21, pp. 585–587.
148. Stalin, *Werke*, vol. 3, p. 170.
149. See Trotzki, *Geschichte*, vol. 2, pp. 148–169.
150. See A. Ascher, "The Kornilov Affair," *The Russian Review* 12 (1953), pp. 235–252; L. Strakhovsky, "Was There a Kornilov Rebellion?," *The Slavonic East European Review* 33 (1955), pp. 372–395.
151. Lenin, *Sämtliche Werke*, vol. 21, p. 164.
152. Lenin, *Sämtliche Werke*, vol. 21, p. 166.
153. Lenin, *Sämtliche Werke*, vol. 21, p. 165.
154. Trotzki, *Geschichte*, vol. 2, p. 296.
155. See *Chronika sobytij*, vol. 4, p. 209.
156. The first vote approved a coalition 766 to 688, but the second (by 595 to 493) was against a coalition with the Constitutional Democratic Party, which was suspected of having participated in the Kornilov putsch; cf. *Chronika sobytij*, vol. 4, p. 240.
157. *Chronika sobytij*, vol. 4, pp. 246–247.
158. Lenin, *Sämtliche Werke*, vol, 21, p. 291.
159. Lenin, *Sämtliche Werke*, vol. 21, p. 248.
160. Lenin, *Sämtliche Werke*, vol. 21, p. 249.
161. Trotzki, *Geschichte*, vol. 2, p. 296.
162. E. Jaroslavskij, *Istoriia VKP (b)*, vol. 4, Moscow and Leningrad 1930, p. 166.
163. See A. R. Williams, *Durch die russische Revolution 1917–1918*, Berlin 1922, p. 153.
164. See *Rabočee dviženie v 1917 godu*, pp. 288 ff.
165. A. Losowski, *Die Gewerkschaften in Sowjetrussland*, Berlin 1920, p. 67.
166. O. H. Radkey, *The Election to the Russian Constituent Assembly of 1917*, Cambridge, Mass. 1950, p. 53.
167. Radkey, p. 53.
168. See *Delo Naroda*, 165 (September 27, 1917).
169. Trotzki, *Geschichte*, vol. 2, p. 262.
170. E.g. *Delo Naroda*, 168 (September 30, 1917).
171. See *Chronika sobytij*, vol. 4, p. 146.
172. *Chronika sobytij*, vol. 4, p. 238.
173. See above, pp. 138 ff.
174. Trotzki, *Geschichte*, vol. 2, p. 275.
175. *Chronika sobytij*, vol. 4, p. 256.
176. K. Rjabinskij, "Revoljucija 1917 goda," *Chronika sobytij*, vol. 5, Moscow and Leningrad 1926, pp. 73, 112.
177. See P. E. Dybenko, *Die Rebellen*, Hamburg 1923, p. 85.
178. Trotzki, *Geschichte*, vol. 2, p. 264.
179. See *Chronika sobytij*, vol. 4, pp. 138–139.

180. *Izvestija*, 164 (September 7, 1917).
181. See *Izvestija*, 166 (September 9), 167 (September 10, 1917); Trockij, *Sočinenija*, vol. 3, part 1, pp. 276–280; *Chronika sobytij*, vol. 4, pp. 186–189.
182. *Chronika sobytij*, vol. 4, pp. 209, 269; Suchanov, vol. 6, pp. 188–190.
183. See *Chronika sobytij*, vol. 4, pp. 43 ff.
184. *Chronika sobytij*, pp. 170 ff.; *Rabočee dviženie*, pp. 291–292.
185. *Chronika sobytij*, vol. 4, p. 245.
186. See *Chronika sobytij*, vol. 4, pp. 286–287, 291–292.
187. *Chronika sobytij*, vol. 4, pp. 254–255.
188. Trockij, *Sočinenija*, vol. 3, part 1, p. 318.
189. See the examples given in Golder, pp. 603 ff. See further *Izvestija*, 204 (October 22, 1917); *Chronika sobytij*, vol. 5, pp. 90, 110, 131.
190. See *Chronika sobytij*, vol. 5, pp. 20, 74.
191. See *Izvestija*, 204 (October 22, 1917).
192. See *Chronika sobytij*, vol. 5, p. 153.
193. *Chronika sobytij*, vol. 5, p. 109.
194. *Chronika sobytij*, vol. 5, pp. 4, 9, 21, 29.
195. *Chronika sobytij*, vol. 5, pp. 79, 130.
196. *Chronika sobytij*, vol. 4, p. 71.
197. *Chronika sobytij*, vol. 5, pp. 102–103.
198. *Chronika sobytij*, vol. 5, pp. 66, 79.
199. *Chronika sobytij*, vol. 5, pp. 104, 162.
200. *Chronika sobytij*, vol 5, pp. 103, 96, 122, 73, 112, 109.
201. See Trockij, *Sočinenija*, vol. 3, part 2, pp. 5–7, 12–14; *Chronika sobytij*, vol. 5, pp. 63, 71–72, 78, 243–244.
202. Facts assembled on the basis of statistics in *Chronika sobytij*, vol 5, and "Vtoroj Vserossijskij S-ezd Sovetov (Ankety bol'ševikov-delegatov II S-ezda Sovetov)," *Krasnyj archiv* 5: 84 (1937), pp. 12–134.
203. *Chronika sobytij*, vol. 5, pp. 66, 74.
204. *Chronika sobytij*, vol. 5, pp. 96–97.
205. *Chronika sobytij*, vol. 5, p. 110.
206. See *Delo Naroda*, 183 (October 18, 1917).
207. *Chronika sobytij*, vol. 5, pp. 16, 21, 28–29, 32, 35, 53, 47, 66, 73, 78, 104, 131.
208. It is not possible to account in exact numbers for the soviets' political position. We do not even know the total number of workers, soldiers, and peasants soviets in 1917; it is estimated there were around 900 in October 1917. An indication is provided by the political composition of the Second Soviet Congress; see below, p. 193.
209. Lenin, *Sämtliche Werke*, vol. 21, p. 243.
210. The most detailed account of the preparation and execution of the October insurrection, using all sources, is S. Mel'gunov, *Kak bol'ševiki zachvatili vlast'. Oktjabr'skij perevorot 1917 goda*, Paris 1953.
211. Lenin, *Sämtliche Werke*, vol. 21, p. 245.
212. Lenin, *Sämtliche Werke*, vol. 21, p. 251.

213. Lenin, *Sämtliche Werke*, vol. 21, pp. 293 ff.
214. See Trotzki, *Geschichte*, vol. 2, pp. 449–450.
215. See Lenin, *Sämtliche Werke*, vol. 21, p. 650, n. 93.
216. Lenin, *Sämtliche Werke*, vol. 21, p. 309.
217. See Lenin's letters and drafts of October 1–8 in *Sämtliche Werke*, vol. 21, pp. 366–416.
218. Lenin, *Sämtliche Werke*, vol. 21, p. 419.
219. See *Pervyj legal'nyj Peterburgskij komitet*, pp. 310–316.
220. See Trotzki, *Geschichte*, vol. 2, pp. 466–467.
221. Published in Lenin, *Sämtliche Werke*, vol. 21, pp. 613–618.
222. Lenin, *Sämtliche Werke*, vol. 21, p. 625.
223. Lenin, *Sämtliche Werke*, vol. 21, pp. 246–252.
224. Lenin, *Sämtliche Werke*, vol. 21, p. 245.
225. Lenin, *Sämtliche Werke*, vol. 21, p. 307.
226. Lenin, *Sämtliche Werke*, vol. 21, pp. 461–462.
227. Lenin, *Sämtliche Werke*, vol. 21, p. 367.
228. See Trotzki, *Geschichte*, vol. 2, p. 592.
229. Trockij, *O Lenine. Materialy dlja biografa*, Moscow, n. d., 2nd ed., p. 70.
230. Trotzki, *Geschichte*, vol. 2, p. 589.
231. Trotzki, *Geschichte*, vol. 2, p. 595.
232. *Chronika sobytij*, vol. 5, pp. 52–53.
233. See *Dokumenty velikoj proletarskoj revoljucii*, vol. 1: *Iz protokolov i perepiski voenno-revoljucionnogo komiteta Petrogradskogo soveta 1917 goda*, Moscow 1938; I. G. Dykov, "Petrogradskij voenno-revoljucionnyj komitet—boevoj bol'ševistskij štab vooružennogo vosstanija v oktjabre 1917 goda," *Voprosy istorii* 7 (1957), pp. 17–35. (In both instances Trotsky's name is omitted.) Trotzki, *Geschichte*, vol. 2, pp. 407–440.
234. *Izvestija*, 204 (October 22, 1917).
235. *Rabočij put'*, 44 (October 24, 1917).
236. *Dokumenty velikoj proletarskoj revoljucii*, vol. 1, pp. 41–46.
237. See the eyewitness reports in Suchanov, vol. 7, pp. 94–174; J. Reed, *Ten Days That Shook the World*, New York 1919; German edition, *10 Tage, die die Welt erschütterten*, Vienna and Berlin 1927. Events of October 24–26 are told hour by hour in *Chronika sobytij*, vol. 5, pp. 163–214.
238. Trotzki, *Geschichte*, vol. 2, p. 422.
239. Lenin, *Sämtliche Werke*, vol. 21, p. 620.
240. Lenin, *Sämtliche Werke*, vol. 21, p. 621.
241. See Trotsky's addresses to the Petrograd soviet on October 18 and 24; Trockij, *Sočinenija*, vol. 3, part 2, pp. 31 ff., 52–53.
242. Trotzki, *Um den Oktober*, pp. 35–43.
243. Trotzki, *Geschichte*, vol. 2, p. 593.
244. Trotzki, *Geschichte*, vol. 2, p. 591.
245. Trotzki, *Um den Oktober*, pp. 38–39.
246. Trotzki, *Geschichte*, vol. 2, p. 406.
247. Trockij, *Sočinenija*, vol. 3, part 2, p. 58.
248. Trockij, *Sočinenija*, vol. 3, part 2, pp. 65–66.

249. See above, pp. 122 ff.
250. See Appendix B.
251. *Vtorj vserossijskij s-ezd sovetov rabočich i soldatskich deputatov*, Moscow and Leningrad 1928, pp. 144–153; See also E. N. Gorodeckij, "Iz istorii oktjabr'skogo vooružennogo vosstanija i II vserossijskogo s-ezda sovetov," *Voprosy istorii* 10 (1957), pp. 23–48.
252. *Vtoroj vserossijskij s-ezd*, p. 37.
253. See Mel'gunov, pp. 178–179.
254. Trotzki, *Geschichte*, vol. 2, p. 616.
255. Lenin, *Sämtliche Werke*, vol. 22, pp. 5–23.
256. See the list of People's Commissars in V. Gitermann, *Geschichte Russlands*, vol. 3, pp. 636–637.
257. I. N. Ljubimov, *Revoljucija 1917 goda. Chronika sobytij*, vol. 6, Moscow and Leningrad 1930, p. 2.
258. On the morning of October 25 the military-revolutionary committee issued an appeal "To the Citizens of Russia" and an order to all troop committees.
259. *Novaja Žizn'*, 164 (October 27 [November 9], 1917).
260. Details in L. Schapiro, *The Origin of the Communist Autocracy*, London 1955, pp. 69–80. The relevant documents are in *Chronika sobytij*, vol. 6, pp. 423–430. See also J. Bunyan and H. H. Fisher, *The Bolshevik Revolution 1917–18*, Stanford, Calif. 1934, pp. 200–207.
261. Dates after the October insurrection (October 25–26) follow the Western calendar.
262. E. Jaroslavskij, *Istorija VKP (b)*, Moscow and Leningrad 1930, p. 227. At this period Bolshevik historians were already anxious to emphasize the Party's leading role.
263. See Jakovlev in the preface to *Vtoroj Vserossijskij s-ezd sovetov*.
264. *Chronika sobytij*, vol. 5, p. 201.
265. *Dokumenty velikoj proletarskoj revoljucii*, vol. 1, p. 49.
266. See E. Genkina, "Pervye dni oktjabr'skoj revoljucii 1917 goda," *Proletarskaja revoljucija*, 3 (1940), pp. 17–35.
267. See Mel'gunov, pp. 277–382; *Sovety v oktjabre. Sbornik dokumentov*, Moscow 1928, pp. 31–87; A. J. Grunt and N. J. Fedoseeva, "Pobeda oktjabr'skogo vooružennogo vosstanija v Moskve," *Voprosy istorii* 11 (1957), pp. 3–26. I was unable to consult D. Kostomarov, *Oktjabr' v Moskve*, Moscow 1932; A. Čebarin, *Oktjabr'skie boi 1917 goda v Moskve*, Moscow 1939.
268. See "Moskovskij voenno-revoljucionnyj komitet," *Krasnyj archiv* 4:23 (1927), pp. 64–148; 4–5: 65–66 (1934), pp. 164–192; 4:71 (1935), pp. 60–115.
269. *1917 god v Moskve. Chronika revoljucii*, Moscow 1934, p. 183.
270. *Izvestija Moskovskogo soveta* 206 (November 15 (28), 1917).
271. Investigation of the roles and activities of the local soviets during the October Revolution is still in its early stages, as is admitted even by Soviet historians. For obvious reasons one can hardly hope for the uncensored publication of source material, such as appeared before ca. 1928. A

bibliography concerning the October Revolution throughout the country is contained in *Chronika sobytij*, vol. 6, pp. 478–479. See also the previously cited compilation, *Sovety v oktjabre*, Moscow 1928; V. Lejkina, "Oktjabr' po Rossii," *Proletarskaja revoljucija* 2:49 (1926), pp. 185–233, 11:58 (1926), pp. 234–255, 12:59 (1926), pp. 238–254; *Ustanovlenie sovetskoj vlasti na mestach v 1917–1918 godach. Sbornik statej*, Moscow 1953.

272. *Chronika sobytij*, vol. 6, pp. 196, 210.

273. Lejkina, *Proletarskaja revoljucija* 2:49, p. 188.

274. Lejkina, p. 197; *Chronika sobytij*, vol. 5, p. 210.

275. Lejkina, p. 199; *Novaja Žizn'*, 170 (November 2 (15), 1917).

276. Lejkina, p. 203.

277. Lejkina, p. 205; *Delo Naroda*, 211 (November 16 (29), 1917).

278. Lejkina, p. 204; *Izvestija Moskovskogo soveta*, 203 (November 12 (25), 1917).

279. Lejkina, p. 208; *Chronika sobytij*, vol. 6, pp. 309, 332.

280. Lejkina, p. 210; *Izvestija Moskovskogo soveta*, 208 (November 16 (29), 1917).

281. Lejkina, p. 211; *Chronika sobytij*, vol. 6, p. 60.

282. Lejkina, p. 214; *Novaja Žizn'*, 182 (November 16 (29), 1917).

283. Lejkina, pp. 217–219; *Chronika sobytij*, vol. 5, p. 213, vol. 6, p. 8.

284. See F. P. Bystrych, "Pobeda Velikoj Oktjabr'skoj socialističeskoj revoljucii na Urale," *Voprosy istorii* 8 (1957), pp. 25–42; Lejkina, pp. 220–222.

285. Bystrych, p. 37.

286. Bystrych, pp. 41–42; *Izvestija Moskovskogo soveta*, 206 (November 15 (28)), 207 (November 16 (29)), 240 (December 30, 1917 (January 12, 1918)).

287. *Chronika sobytij*, vol. 6, pp. 296, 353.

288. *Delo Naroda*, 212 (November 17 (30), 1917).

289. *Sovety v oktjabre*, p. 185; *Izvestija Moskovskogo soveta*, 11 (January 17 (30), 1918); Lejkina, pp. 228–229.

290. *Izvestija Moskovskogo soveta*, 218 (November 30 (December 13), 1917).

291. *Chronika sobytij*, vol. 6, p. 35; Lejkina, p. 231.

292. *Chronika sobytij*, vol. 6, pp. 333, 347.

293. For the course of the 1917 revolution in the Ukraine, see J. S. Reshetar, *The Ukrainian Revolution 1917–1920*, Princeton 1952; R. Pipes, *The Formation of the Soviet Union. Communism and Nationalism 1917–1923*, Cambridge, Mass. 1954; D. Geyer, "Die Ukraine im Jahre 1917," *Geschichte in Wissenschaft und Unterricht* 8 (1957), pp. 670–687; N. J. Suprunenko, "Ustanovlenie sovetskoj vlasti na Ukraine," *Voprosy istorii* 10 (1957), pp. 49–70. Additional literature in the bibliographies of the above works.

294. Lejkina, 12:59, pp. 238–254.

295. *Chronika sobytij*, vol. 6, pp. 9, 18, 27, 271–272.

296. *Chronika sobytij*, vol. 6, pp. 9, 27.

297. *Chronika sobytij*, vol. 6, p. 43.

298. *Izvestija Moskovskogo soveta*, 214 (November 25 (December 8), 1917).

299. See "Armija v period podgotovki i provedenija Velikoj Oktjabr'skoj social-istiĉeskoi revoljucii," *Krasnyj archiv* 5:84 (1937), pp. 135–187.

300. See Mel'gunov, pp. 165–177.

301. *Chronika sobytij*, vol. 6, p. 65.

302. *Chronika sobytij*, vol. 6, p. 45; Lejkina, 2:49, pp. 186 ff.

303. *Izvestija Moskovskogo soveta*, 225 (December 8 (21), 1917).

304. Lejkina, pp. 190–191; see L. S. Gaponenko, "Bor'ba soldat zapadnogo fronta za pobedu sovetskoj vlasti," in *Ustanovlenie sovetskoj vlasti na mestach*, pp. 182–244.

305. *Chronika sobytij*, vol. 6, pp. 172, 185, 202; Lejkina, 11:58, pp. 234–249.

306. *Chronika sobytij*, vol. 6, pp. 320, 334–335; Lejkina, pp. 249–254.

307. *Chronika sobytij*, vol. 6, pp. 321, 393, 398.

308. *Novaja Žizn'*, 177 (November 10 (23), 1917).

309. Lejkina, 2:49, pp. 192–195.

310. See "Flot posle oktjabr'skoj pobedy," *Krasnyj archiv* 4:53 (1932), pp. 63–99.

311. *Izvestija Vserossijskogo soveta krest'janskich deputatov*, 146 (October 26 (November 8), 1917).

312. *Chronika sobytij*, vol. 6, p. 49.

313. See *Rezoljucii črezvyčajnago i vtorogo vserossijskich s-ezdov sovetov krest'janskich deputatov*, Petrograd 1917; M. Gajsinskij, *Bor'ba bol'ševikov za krest'janstvo v 1917 g.*, Moscow 1933, pp. 179–211; P. N. Sobolev, "Rol' vserossijskich s-ezdov sovetov v bor'be proletariata za trudjaščeesja krest'janstvo (oktjabr' 1917 g.—janvar' 1918 g.)," *Voprosy istorii 12* (1957), pp. 3–24; Bunyan and Fisher, pp. 210–219.

314. Gajsinskij, pp. 230–231.

315. Gajsinskij, p. 221.

316. *Chronika sobytij*, vol 6, p. 258.

317. Gajsinskij, p. 240.

318. See Gajsinskij, pp. 247–266.

319. *Novaja Žizn'*, 195 (December 7 (20), 1917).

CHAPTER FIVE
THE ESTABLISHMENT OF SOVIET DICTATORSHIP

1. Suffrage was universal, equal, secret, and direct. Women and military personnel could vote at age 20 (18 for ordinary soldiers.) Apportionment was to be proportional. The elections originally scheduled for September 17 were first postponed to the end of October, then to November 12 (25); the convocation of the Assembly was set for November 27 (December 10). See A. v. Freytagh-Loringhoven, *Die Gesetzgebung der russischen Revolution*, Halle 1920, pp. 32 ff.

2. See Schapiro, p. 81.

3. See A. Tyrkova-Williams, *From Liberty to Brest-Litovsk*, London 1919, p. 336.

4. Based on the most recent calculations by O. H. Radkey, *The Election to the Russian Constituent Assembly of 1917*, Cambridge, Mass. 1950.

5. The Left Social Revolutionaries entered the Constituent Assembly as a separate faction.

6. See Radkey, pp. 14 ff.

7. A comparison of election results to the Assembly with those to the soviets in various localities, based on sources that are for the most part inaccessible today, would lead to further interesting conclusions concerning the strength of the Bolshevik following in the various population groups.

7a. See W. A. Kropat, "Lenin und die Konstituierende Versammlung in Russland," *Jahrbücher für Geschichte Osteuropas*, n. s. 5, 1957, pp. 488–498.

8. See Lenin, *Ausgewählte Werke*, vol. 1, pp. 338–339, vol. 2, p. 459.

9. Stalin, *Werke*, vol. 1, p. 135.

10. Lenin, *Sämtliche Werke*, vol. 21, p. 62.

11. Stalin, *Werke*, vol. 3, p. 142.

12. M. Ol'minskij, *Ob učreditel'nom sobranii*, Petrograd 1917, p. 10.

13. Lenin, *Sämtliche Werke*, vol. 20, part 1, p. 109.

14. See Lenin, *Sämtliche Werke*, vol. 21, p. 61.

15. Lenin, *Sämtliche Werke*, vol. 20, part 1, p. 160.

16. Trotzki, *Geschichte*, vol. 2, p. 318.

17. Trotzki, *Geschichte*, vol. 2, p. 318.

18. See above, p. 90.

19. See *Sed'maja ("aprel'skaja") vserossijskaja i petrogradskaja obščegorodskaja konferencii RSDRP (b), Aprel' 1917*, Moscow 1934, p. 223.

20. See Lenin, *Sämtliche Werke*, vol. 20, part 1, p. 196; vol. 21, p. 399.

21. See above, pp. 186 ff.

22. See Freytagh-Loringhoven, pp. 133–134.

23. *Sovety v oktjabre*, p. 44.

24. See Bunyan and Fisher, p. 341.

25. Bunyan and Fisher, p. 339.

26. Bunyan and Fisher, pp. 348–349.

27. *Chronika sobytij*, vol. 6, pp. 233–234.

28. See Bunyan and Fisher, pp. 350–360.

29. See E. Ignatov, "Taktika bol'ševikov i učreditel'noe sobranie," *Proletarskaja revoljucija* 4:75 (1928), pp. 12–44, 5:76 (1928), pp. 24–55; N. Šaveko, *Oktjabr'skaja revoljucija i učreditel'noe sobranie*, Moscow and Leningrad 1928.

30. *Pervyj legal'nyj peterburgskij komitet*, pp. 348–351.

31. *Pravda* (November 17 (30), 1917).

32. *Chronika sobytij*, vol. 6, pp. 430–431.

33. See *Chronika sobytij*, vol. 6, pp. 200, 314; *Izvestija Moskovskogo soveta*, 236 (December 23, 1917) (January 5, 1918).

34. "Protokoly 3. moskovskoj oblast'noj konferencii RSDRP (b)," *Proletarskaja revoljucija* 10:105 (1930), pp. 94–134.

35. *Chronika sobytij*, vol. 6, p. 346.

36. *Pravda* (January 3 (16), 1918).

37. Lenin, *Ausgewählte Werke*, vol. 2, pp. 279–283.

38. Bunyan and Fisher, pp. 367–368.

39. See above, pp. 139 ff.

40. *Delo Naroda*, 200 (November 5 (18), 1917).

41. See Bramson's statements at the session of the old Central Executive Committee of the soviets on December 16, 1917; "Protokoly CIK sovetov rabočich i soldatskich deputatov 1-go sozyva posle Oktjabrja," *Krasnyj archiv* 3:10 (1925), pp. 98–137, this statement p. 121.

42. *Delo Naroda*, 236 (December 19, 1917) (January 1, 1918), 238 (December 21, 1917) (January 3, 1918), 239 (December 22, 1917) (January 4, 1918).

43. *Chronika sobytij*, vol. 6, pp. 242–243, 252, 265, 284, 294–295.

44. *Tretij vserossijskij s-ezd sovetov rabočich, soldatskich i krest'janskich deputatov*, Petrograd 1918, p. 45.

45. *Tretij*, p. 46.

46. *Chronika sobytij*, vol. 6, p. 225.

47. See *Chronika sobytij*, vol. 6, p. 259.

48. See the eyewitness report of one of the chief participants, B. Sokolov, *Zaščita vserossijskogo Učreditel'nogo Sobranija (Archiv russkoj revoljucii,* vol. 13, Berlin 1924), in *Revoljucija i graždanskaja vojna v opisanijach belogvardejcev,* vol. 2: *Oktjabr'skaja revoljucija,* Moscow and Leningrad 1926, pp. 332–383.

49. Sokolov, pp. 360–361; Ignatov, 5:76, pp. 37–42.

50. See Bunyan and Fisher, pp. 370–388. The undignified scenes in the Tauride Palace are described by Dybenko, pp. 136 ff.

51. Lenin, *Ausgewählte Werke*, vol. 2, pp. 302–303.

52. According to Bunyan and Fisher, p. 389, only 52 of the 942 delegates were of the opposition. Lenin later put the number of delegates at 710, of whom 434 (61 percent) were Bolsheviks; *Ausgewählte Werke*, vol. 2, p. 451.

53. Bunyan and Fisher, p. 389.

54. See Bunyan and Fisher, pp. 396–397.

55. M. N. Pokrovskij, "Načalo proletarskoj revoljucii v Rossii," *Krasnyj archiv* 11/12 (1925), pp. V–XVI.

56. See Chamberlin, vol. 1, pp. 370–371.

57. See above, pp. 136 ff.

58. Lenin, *Ausgewählte Werke*, vol. 2, pp. 332–333.

59. See above, p. 195.

60. Bunyan and Fisher, p. 278.

61. See J. M. Meisel and E. J. Kozera, *Materials for the Study of the Soviet System*, Michigan 1950, pp. 49 ff.; Freytagh-Loringhoven, pp. 142–143; *Sovety v oktjabre*, pp. 297–300.

62. *Chronika sobytij*, vol. 6, pp. 448–450; *Sovety v oktjabre*, pp. 297 ff.

63. See the various organizational charts for district and provincial soviets in *Sovety v oktjabre*, pp. 301–332.

64. E. N. Gorodeckij, "Bor'ba narodnych mass za sozdanie sovetskich gosudarstvennych organov (1917–1918 gg.)," *Voprosy istorii* 8 (1955), pp. 26–39.

65. See the report from the Moscow region in *Izvestija moskovskogo soveta* 3:251 (January 5 (18), 1918).
66. See Freytagh-Loringhoven, pp. 152 ff.; Tyrkova-Williams, pp. 328–331; *Chronika sobytij*, vol. 6, pp. 154–155, 242.
67. *Sovety v oktjabre*, pp. 300–301.
68. Gorodeckij, p. 31.
69. See Freytagh-Loringhoven, pp. 189 ff.; Dybenko, pp. 133 ff.; Bunyan and Fisher, 298–299.
70. For contemporary conditions in the Russian army, see H. Bergmann, J. Smilga, and L. Trotzki, *Die russische sozialistische Rote Armee*, Zurich 1920.
71. See Freytagh-Loringhoven, pp. 227 ff.; Bunyan and Fisher, pp. 308 ff.
72. W. Koch, *Die bol'ševistischen Gewerkschaften*, Jena 1932, p. 152.
73. See above, pp. 125 ff.
74. See Deutscher, *Soviet Trade Unions*, pp. 17–18; Losowski, *Die Gewerkschaften in Sowjetrussland*, pp. 51–52.
75. See below, pp. 244 ff.
76. E. H. Carr, *The Bolshevik Revolution 1917–1923*, vol. 2, London 1952, p. 396.
77. Bunyan and Fisher, pp. 653–654; for the entire context, see Carr, pp. 394–397.
78. Bunyan and Fisher, pp. 655–656.
79. See *Die Organisation der Volkswirtschaft in Sowjetrussland. Gesetze und Verordnungen*, Berlin 1919.
80. See Freytagh-Loringhoven, pp. 170 ff.
81. *Sovety v épochu voennogo kommunizma*, vol. 1, Moscow 1928, p. 95.
82. A. Vyshinsky, *The Law of the Soviet State*, New York 1948, p. 439.
83. See Schapiro, pp. 130–146; the program of the Left Communists is contained in Bunyan and Fisher, p. 562.
84. A. Šrejder, "Federativnaja Sovetskaja Respublika," in *Respublika sovetov (Teorija i praktika sovetskogo stroja. Vypusk 1-yj)*, Berlin and Milan n. d. [1920], p. 53.
85. Srejder, p. 59.
86. See above, pp. 94 ff.
87. *Maksimalist*, 4 (October 7, 1918).
88. See G. Gurvič, *Istorija sovetskoj konstitucii*, Moscow 1923, pp. 102–107, 142; Carr, vol. 1, pp. 124–128.
89. See Šrejder, p. 114.
90. See *Znamja. Organ levych socialistov-revoljucionerov (internacionalistov)*, 1 (April 1920). "The syndicalist-cooperative federation will gradually encompass all of mankind."
91. B. Meissner in the introduction to the chapter on Russia in B. Dennewitz, ed., *Die Verfassungen der modernen Staaten*, vol. 1, Hamburg 1947, p. 126.
92. See M. Eljaschoff, *Die Grundzüge der Sowjetverfassung*, Heidelberg 1925; J. Neuberger, *Die Verfassung der Russischen Föderativen Sowjetrepublik*, Berlin and Bonn 1926. The text of the constitution is contained in Dennewitz, pp. 164–179.

93. See Sverdlov's remarks at the reading of the declaration in the Assembly; Bunyan and Fisher, p. 372.
94. Lenin, *Ausgewählte Werke*, vol. 2, p. 435.
95. See the table of participation in the soviet elections since 1922 in J. Towster, *Political Power in the USSR. 1917–1947*, New York 1948, p. 206, n. 40.
96. See above, p. 16.
97. See Lenin, *Sämtliche Werke*, vol. 21, p. 328.
98. See Freytagh-Loringhoven, pp. 145–146.
99. Bunyan and Fisher, p. 189.
100. See M. Vladimirskij, *Organizacija sovetskoj vlasti na mestach*, Moscow 1919.
101. See above, p. 164.
102. Printed as a pamphlet, Berlin 1919.
103. See W. Huhn, "Trotzkis Bonapartismus," *Aufklärung* 2:2 (1952).
104. Lenin, *Ausgewählte Werke*, vol. 2, p. 384.
105. Lenin, *Ausgewählte Werke*, vol. 2, p. 385.
106. Lenin, *Ausgewählte Werke*, vol. 2, p. 387.
107. Lenin, *Sämtliche Werke*, vol. 20, part 1, p. 269.
108. See Rosenberg, *Geschichte des Bolschewismus*, pp. 119–120.
109. For the establishment of the Red Army, see Antonow-Owsejenko, *Der Aufbau der Roten Armee in der Revolution*, Hamburg 1923, as well as the work cited above (n. 14).
110. Smilga, p. 28.
111. See L. Larin and L. Kritzmann, *Wirtschaftsleben und wirtschaftlicher Aufbau in Sowjetrussland 1917–1920*, Hamburg 1921; S. N. Prokopovicz, *Russlands Volkswirtschaft unter den Sowjets*, Zurich and New York 1944.
112. In December 1920, 2,183 out of 2,483 concerns were headed by appointed directors and only 300 were managed by committees; Th. Dan, *Der Arbeiter in Sowjetrussland*, Berlin and Stuttgart 1923, p. 15.
113. According to official figures, no more than about 900,000 workers were employed in industrial enterprises in 1921; Dan, p. 24.
114. See Chamberlin, vol. 2, pp. 291 ff.; Carr, vol. 2, pp. 211–216.
115. There are hardly any available sources for the numerical strength of opposition parties in the soviets for the period after 1918. Indirect references and inferences, however, allow for an approximate idea.
116. See *Sovety v oktjabre*, pp. 357–363; *Sovety v épochu voennogo kommunizma*, vol. 2, pp. 423–425; J. Bunyan, *Intervention, Civil War and Communism in Russia, April-December, 1918*, Baltimore and Oxford, 1936, p. 559.
117. I. Vardin, "Ot melkoburžuaznoj kontr-revoljucii k restavracii kapitalizma (Partija men'ševikov posle Oktjabrja)," in *Za pjat' let, 1917–1922. Sbornik CK RKP*, Moscow 1922, pp. 34–58; this event from p. 38.
118. Bunyan, p. 191.
119. See Bunyan, p. 283.
120. At the Fourth All-Russian Soviet Congress, which approved the Treaty

of Brest-Litovsk by 784 to 261, 795 Bolsheviks and 284 Left Social Revolutionaries were represented; see Bunyan and Fisher, pp. 519–534; Towster, p. 122, n. 12.

121. These numbers also include the advisory delegates. Among the 1,132 voting delegates 745 were Bolsheviks and 352 Left Social Revolutionaries; *Pjatyj vserossijskij s-ezd sovetov rabočich krest'janskich, soldatskich i kazač-ich deputatov,* Moscow 1918, p. 163.
122. See Bunyan, pp. 197–225.
123. *Pjatyj vserossijskij s-ezd sovetov,* p. 209.
124. *Pjatyj sozyv vserossijskogo central'nogo ispolnitel'nogo komiteta,* Moscow 1919, p. 7.
125. See below, pp. 234 ff.
126. See *Sovety v épochu voennogo kommunizma,* vol. 2, pp. 387–409.
127. *Sovety v épochu voennogo kommunizma,* vol. 1, pp. 258–259.
128. *Sovety v épochu voennogo kommunizma,* vol. 1, p. 200.
129. See P. Miljukow, *Russlands Zusammenbruch,* vol. 1, Leipzig and Berlin 1925, pp. 61–62; Th. Dan, *Gewerkschaften und Politik in Sowjetrussland,* Berlin and Stuttgart 1923, pp. 24–25.
130. *Sovety v épochu voennogo kommunizma,* vol. 1, p. 116.
131. *Sovety v épochu voennogo kommunizma,* vol. 2, p. 84.
132. *Sovety, s-ezdy sovetov i ispolkomy,* Moscow 1924, pp. 30, 46.
133. See Appendix C.
134. For the civil war as a whole, see F. Borkenau, *Der russische Bürgerkrieg 1918–1921,* Berlin 1954. For the fate of the parties, see the previously cited work by Schapiro.
135. Quoted in I. Steinberg, *In the Workshop of the Revolution,* New York 1953, p. 248.
136. See *Znamja,* 1 (April 1920).
137. Steinberg, p. 247.
138. See above, p. 215.
139. Bunyan, p. 362.
140. See Bunyan, pp. 283, 304–307, 331, 355.
141. See Schapiro, pp. 162–169.
142. See Bunyan, pp. 187–188.
143. Vardin, p. 41.
144. See the eyewitness account by F. Dan, *Dva goda skitanij. (1919–1921),* Berlin 1922.
145. Vardin, p. 46.
146. Vardin, p. 47.
147. See the lively account in Dan, pp. 85–100.
148. Dan, p. 89.
149. Martov and Dan, *Geschichte der russischen Sozialdemokratie,* p. 318. The figures cited in this work—which are at times astonishingly high—could not be checked against other sources.
150. See Schapiro, p. 201.
151. See Schapiro, pp. 179–182.

152. *O rabočem kontrole* (Maximalist pamphlet), Moscow 1918, p. 15.
153. *O rabočem kontrole*, p. 11.
154. See *Sbornik dokladov i rezoljucii pervogo vserossijskogo s-ezda Partii Revoljucionnogo Kommunizma (25.–29.9.1918)*, n. p., n. d. [1919].
155. See Schapiro, pp. 182–189. For a Bolshevik view, see J. Jakovlev, *Russkij anarchism v velikoj russkoj revoljucii*, Char'kov 1921.
156. For the Machno movement, see Chamberlin, vol. 2, pp. 232–239.
157. Minutes of a political conference of delegates of the Machno rebels of February 12, 1919, in *Russkaja Mysl'*, Sofia 1921, 1/2, pp. 226 ff.; Jakovlev, p. 24.
158. Jakovlev, p. 65.
159. See below, pp. 249 ff.
160. See *Sovety v épochu voennogo kommunizma*, vol. 1, p. 101.
161. See Vladimirskij, *Organizacija sovetskoj vlasti na mestach*, pp. 60–63.
162. *Sovety v épochu voennogo kommunizma*, vol. 1, p. 31.
163. *Sovety v épochu voennogo kommunizma*, vol. 2, pp. 44–45.
164. See *Sovety v épochu voennogo kommunizma*, vol. 1, p. 32.
165. See Carr, vol. 1, pp. 217–218.
166. See above, p. 121.
167. See *Sovety v épochu voennogo kommunizma*, vol. 1, pp. 198–199.
168. *Sovety v épochu voennogo kommunizma*, vol. 1, p. 189.
169. *Sovety v épochu voennogo kommunizma*, vol. 1, pp. 207–212.
170. *Sovety v épochu voennogo kommunizma*, vol. 1, p. 313.
171. Text of the decree in Bunyan, pp. 472–473. See N. Murachver, "Komitety bednoty i razvertivanie socialističeskoj revoljucii v derevne (1918 g.)," *Proletarskaja revoljucija* 3 (1940), pp. 68–99.
172. *Sovety v épochu voennogo kommunizma*, vol. 1, pp. 82 ff.
173. See above, pp. 158 ff.
174. See A. I. Denisov, *Istorija sovetskogo gosudarstava i prava*, Moscow 1949.
175. Lenin, *Ausgewählte Werke*, vol. 2, p. 437.
176. Lenin, *Ausgewählte Werke*, vol. 2, p. 381.
177. Lenin, *Ausgewählte Werke*, vol. 2, p. 428.
178. See P. Levi, introduction to Rosa Luxemburg, *Die russische Revolution*, Berlin 1922, pp. 24 ff.
179. Lenin, *Ausgewählte Werke*, vol. 1, p. 356.
180. J. Stalin, *Probleme des Leninismus*, Vienna and Berlin 1926, p. 26.
181. L. Trotzki, "Terrorismus und Kommunismus" in *Die Grundfragen der Revolution*, Hamburg 1923, pp. 121–123.
182. G. Sinowjew, "Der Zentralismus," *Kommunistische Rundschau*, 1 (1920), pp. 26–28.
183. Lenin, *Sämtliche Werke*, vol. 21, p. 336.
184. Rosenberg, p. 123.
185. Trotzki, p. 49.
186. *VKP (b) v rezoljucijach i rešenijach s-ezdov, konferencii i plenumov CK*, vol. 1, Moscow 1932, p. 356.
187. See W. R. Batsell, *Soviet Rule in Russia*, New York 1929, p. 675, and Appendix C.

188. See R. Maurach, *Handbuch der Sowjetverfassung*, Munich 1955, pp. 29–31.
189. Lenin, *Ausgewählte Werke*, vol. 2, p. 429.
190. N. Bucharin, *Das Programm der Kommunisten (B)*, Berlin 1919, p. 34.
191. G. Lukacs, *Lenin*, Vienna 1924, p. 59.
192. See the decisions and reports of various soviet organs in *Sovety v épochu voennogo kommunizma*, vol. 1, p. 314, vol. 2, pp. 68–70, 97–99.
193. Notes by Lenin made on December 26, 1922; first published by the U.S. State Department on June 30, 1956; *Ost-Probleme* 28 (1956), p. 965.
194. See Carr, vol. 1, pp. 226–228.
195. Notes by Lenin of December 30, 1922, "Concerning the National Question or 'Autonomy' "; *Ost-Probleme* 28 (1956), p. 968.
196. Lenin, *Ausgewählte Werke*, vol. 2, p. 523.
197. Quoted from Towster, p. 183, n. 22.
198. A. Paquet, *Der Geist der russischen Revolution*, Leipzig 1919, pp. 15, 50.
199. Eljaschoff, p. 69.
200. A. Kollontai, *Die Arbeiteropposition in Russland*, n. p., n. d. [1921], pp. 44–45.
201. R. Luxemburg, *Die russische Revolution*, Hameln, n. d. [1957], pp. 78–79 (reprint of the 1918 work edited by Paul Levi in 1922).
202. For the details, see Schapiro, pp. 221–295; Deutscher, *Soviet Trade Unions*, pp. 25–58; Rosenberg, pp. 151–153.
203. Kollontai, p. 18.
204. Kollontai, p. 28.
205. Kollontai, pp. 47 ff.
206. See Schapiro, p. 223.
207. See the resolution, composed by Lenin, of the Central Committee of the KPR (B) [Communist Party of Russia, Bolsheviks] of January 12, 1922, "Concerning the Role and Tasks of the Trade Unions Under the Conditions of the New Economic Policy," *Ausgewählte Werke*, vol. 2, pp. 900–911.
208. See W. Huhn, "Trotzkis Bonapartismus," *Aufklärung* 2:2 (1952); "Bolschewismus und Rätedemokratie," *Der Funken* 6 (1952).
209. Deutscher, *The Prophet Armed*, pp. 508–509.
210. Text in Lenin, *Ausgewählte Werke*, vol. 2, pp. 802–808.
211. Rosenberg, p. 154.
212. This falsification in the sense of a "White Guard counterrevolutionary" movement already set in during the insurrection. On the other hand, Lenin himself frequently openly admitted the objective causes of the insurrection. Puchov, who gave the most detailed Bolshevik account of the events, also spoke of the "deep-seated social and political causes" of the rising. For the Kronstadt insurrection in general, see the documentary collection, *Pravda o Kronštadte*, Prague 1921, which reprints verbatim the *Izvestija* published by the rebels; A. S. Puchov, *Kronštadtskij mjatež v 1921 g.*, Leningrad 1931; A. Berkman. *The Kronstadt Rebellion*, Berlin 1922. A condensed German translation of this work by an American anarchist, who advocated negotiations in the course of the conflict, appeared as a special publication of *Der Monat* 30 (1951) under the title *Der Aufstand*

von Kronstadt; R. V. Daniels, "The Kronstadt Revolt of 1921. A Study in the Dynamics of Revolution," *American Slavic and East European Review* 10 (1951), pp. 241–254; Schapiro, pp. 296–313. I was unable to consult I. Mett, *La Commune de Cronstadt,* Paris 1949.

213. See Puchov, pp. 12–15.
214. Puchov, pp. 19–37; Dan, *Dva goda skitanij,* pp. 104–108.
215. Dan, p. 113.
216. *Pravda o Kronštadte,* pp. 5–6. Another appeal, written by the Social Revolutionaries, demanded convocation of the Constituent Assembly. But this was the only appeal for an assembly.
217. See Puchov, pp. 38–54.
218. Shortened literal translation. Complete text in *Pravda o Kronštadte,* pp. 9–10; Puchov, p. 59.
219. The list of names appears in *Pravda o Kronštadte,* p. 131.
220. Puchov, pp. 94–102. The names were published in various issues of *Izvestija vremennogo revoljucionnogo komiteta matrosov, krasnoarmejcev i rabočich goroda Kronštadta.*
221. Even Puchov has to admit this in his book.
222. Berkman (German edition), p. 10.
223. Berkman (English edition), p. 16.
224. See Puchov, pp. 137–170.
225. See *Pravda o Kronštadte,* pp. 150–151.
226. *Pravda o Kronštadte,* pp. 141 ff.
227. *Pravda o Kronštadte,* p. 142.
228. *Pravda o Kronštadte,* pp. 82 ff.
229. The slogan "Soviets without Bolsheviks," often attributed to the Kronstadt mutineers, was not raised by them. It was invented by Miliukov abroad to pinpoint the anti-Communist tendency. See Schapiro, p. 304.
230. See Jakovlev, *Russkij anarchizm,* pp. 79–80.
231. See Dan, pp. 109–115.
232. See above, p. 246.
233. See *Sovety v épochu voennogo kommunizma,* vol. 2, pp. 44–45.
234. See Carr, vol. 1, pp. 176–177; Schapiro, pp. 166–169, 188–189, 208–209.

Sources and References

Abbreviations: IZ: Istoričeskie Zapiski
                KA: Krasnyj Archiv
                PR: Proletarskaja Revoljucija
                VI: Voprosy Istorii

1. Sources

A. INDIVIDUAL AUTHORS

Bucharin, N., *Das Programm der Kommunisten (B)*, Berlin, 1919.
Ceretelli, I. G., *Rečy*, Petersburg, 1917.
(Tseretelli), "Reminiscenses of the February Revolution," *The Russian Review* 14 (1955), pp. 93–108, 184–200, 301–321.
Dan, F., *Dva goda skitanii (1919–21)*, Berlin, 1922.
Dybenko, P. E., *Die Rebellen. Erinnerungen aus der Revolutionszeit*, Hamburg, 1923.
Kerenski, A., *Erinnerungen*, Dresden, 1928.
Klivanskij, S., *Rol' i značenie Sovetov rabočich, soldatskich i krest'janskich deputatov*, Petrograd, 1917.
Kollontai, A., *Die Arbeiteropposition in Russland*, n. p., n. d. [1921].
Laski, H., *Einführung in das Kommunistische Manifest*. With the original text of the Manifesto and the introductions by K. Marx and F. Engels, Hamburg, 1949.
Lenin, V. I., *Sočinenija*, 4th ed., 35 vols., Moscow, 1942–50.
———— *Sämtliche Werke* (German translation from the 2nd Russian ed.), incomplete, Vienna, Berlin, and Moscow, 1927–41.

—— *Ausgewählte Werke*, 12 vols., Vienna and Moscow, 1932 ff.

—— *Ausgewählte Werke*, 2 vols., Moscow, 1946–47.

Lenin, N., and G. Sinowjew, *Gegen den Strom* (essays of 1914–16), Hamburg, 1921.

Lunačarskij, A. V., "Bol'ševiki v 1905 godu," PR 11:46 (1925): 49–61.

Luxemburg, R., *Massenstreik, Partei und Gewerkschaften*, Hamburg, 1906.

—— *Die russische Revolution* (based on the first edition by Paul Levi), Hameln, n. d. [1957].

Martow, I., "Preussische Diskussion und russische Erfahrung,"*Die Neue Zeit*, 28:2 (1909–10): 907–919.

Martynov, A. S., *Dve diktatury*, Geneva, 1905.

Marx, K., *Enthüllungen über den Kommunistenprozess zu Köln*, with an introduction by F. Engels, Hottingen-Zurich, 1885.

—— *Der Bürgerkrieg in Frankreich*, with an introduction by F. Engels, Berlin, 1891.

—— *Die Klassenkämpfe in Frankreich*, with an introduction by F. Engels of 1895, Berlin, 1925.

—— *Briefe an Kugelmann*, Berlin, n. d. [1957].

Matveev, F. P., *Iz zapisnoj knižki deputata 176 pechotnogo polka, Mart-maj 1917*, Moscow and Leningrad, 1932.

Ol'minskij, M., *Ob učreditel'nom sobranii*, Petrograd, 1917.

Pannekoek, A., *Die taktischen Differenzen in der Arbeiterbewegung*, Hamburg, 1909.

—— "Massenaktion und Revolution," *Die Neue Zeit*, 30:2 (1912): 541–550, 585–593, 609–616.

Parvus, A., *In der russischen Bastille während der Revolution*, Dresden, 1907.

—— "Die gegenwärtige Lage Russlands und die Aussichten für die Zukunft." *Die Neue Zeit*, 24:2 (1905–06): pp. 108–120.

Pjatnitzki, O., *Aufzeichnungen eines Bolschewiks. Erinnerungen aus den Jahren 1896–1917*, Vienna and Berlin, 1927.

Priamo k celi, Moscow, 1917 (anonymous pamphlet).

Radin, B., *Pervyj sovet rabočich deputatov*, Petersburg, 1906.

Samojlov, F., *Pervyj sovet rabočich deputatov*, Moscow, 1931.

—— "O pervom sovete rabočich deputatov," PR 12:107 (1930): 104–109.

Šljapnikov, A. G., *Semnadcatij god*, 4 vols., Leningrad and Moscow, 1923–1931.

Sinowjew, G., "Der Zentralismus." *Kommunistische Rundschau*, 1:1 (1920): 26–28.

Stalin, J., *Werke*, vols. 1–13, Berlin, 1950–56.

—— *Probleme des Leninismus*, Vienna and Berlin, 1926.

Steinberg, I., *Gewalt und Terror in der Revolution*, Berlin, 1931.

—— *In the Workshop of the Revolution*, New York, 1953.

Stepun, F. *Vergangenes und Unvergängliches. Aus meinem Leben*, 2 vols. Munich, 1947–48.

Suchanov, N., *Zapiski o revoljucii*, 7 vols., Berlin, Petersburg, and Moscow 1922–23.

—————— *The Russian Revolution 1917* (abridged English translation of the above), London and New York, 1955.

Sverčkov, D., *Na zare revoljucii,* Moscow, 1921.

Trotsky, L., *Sočinenija,* vol. 3, Moscow and Leningrad, n. d.

—————— *Naši političeskie zadači,* Geneva, 1904.

(Trotzki), *Russland in der Revolution,* Dresden, 1909 (2nd ed. under the title *Die russische Revolution 1905,* Berlin, 1923).

—————— *Arbeit, Disziplin und Ordnung werden die sozialistische Sowjetrepublik retten,* Berlin, 1919.

—————— *Mein Leben,* Berlin, 1930.

—————— *Die Grundfragen der Revolution,* Hamburg, 1923.

—————— "Der Arbeiterdeputiertenrat und die Revolution," *Die Neue Zeit,* 25:2 (1906–07):76–86.

—————— "Die Entwicklungstendenzen der russischen Sozialdemokratie," *Die Neue Zeit,* 28:2 (1909–10):860–871.

—————— "Kann man eine Konterrevolution oder eine Revolution auf einen bestimmten Zeitpunkt ansetzen?" *Vom Bürgerkrieg* 3, Berlin, 1923.

(Trotski), *Our Revolution. Essays on Working Class and International Revolution, 1904–1917,* New York, 1918.

(Trotzki) and others, *Um den Oktober,* Hamburg, 1925.

Vasil'ev-Južin, M., "Moskovskij sovet rabočich deputatov v 1905 godu i podgotovka im vooružennogo vosstanija," PR 4:39 (1925):84–124, 5:40 (1925):92–133.

Veger, I, "K istorii Moskovskogo soveta rabočich deputatov," PR 1:48 (1926): 217–232.

Witte, S., *Erinnerungen,* Berlin, 1923.

Woytinski, W., *Wehe den Besiegten. Erinnerungen aus der russischen revolutionären Bewegung (1906–1910),* Berlin, 1933.

B. Collections of Documents, etc.

Alekseev, S., ed., *Revoljucija i graždanskaja vojna v opisanijach belogvardejcev,* vol. 1: *Fevral'skaja revoljucija,* vol. 2: *Oktjabr'skaja revoljucija,* Moscow and Leningrad, 1925–1926.

Antonov-Saratovskij, V., ed., *Sovety v épochu voennogo kommunizma,* 2 vols., Moscow, 1928.

"Armija v period podgotovki i provedenija Velikoj Oktjabr'skoj socialističeskoj revoljucii," KA 5:84 (1937): 135–187.

Blos, W., ed., *Karl Marx oder Bakunin? Demokratie oder Diktatur? Neuausgabe der Berichte an die Sozialistische Internationale über Michael Bakunin,* Stuttgart, 1920.

Bunyan, J., *Intervention, Civil War and Communism in Russia, April-December 1918,* Baltimore and Oxford, 1936.

Bunyan, J., and H. H. Fisher, *The Bolshevik Revolution 1917–18,* Stanford, Calif., and Oxford, 1934.

"Chronika vooružennoj bor'by. Reljacija general'nogo štaba samoderžavija o boevych dejstvijach v dekabre 1905 goda," KA 4/5:11/12 (1925):159–181.

"Dekabr'skie dni v Donbasse," KA 6:73 (1935):91–125.

Dennewitz, B., *Die Verfassungen der modernen Staaten*, vol. 1, Hamburg, 1947.

"9 janvarja 1905 g.," KA 4/5:11/12 (1925):1–25.

Die Organisation der Volkswirtschaft in Sowjetrussland. (Gesetze und Verordnungen), Berlin, 1919.

Dokumenty velikoj proletarskoj revoljucii, vol. 1: *Iz protokolov i perepiski voenno-revoljucionnogo komiteta Petrogradskogo soveta 1917 goda*, Moscow, 1938.

"Flot posle oktjabr'skoj pobedy," KA 4:53 (1932):63–99.

Galkin, I., ed., *Sovety kak taktičeskaja problema revoljucii*, Moscow and Leningrad, n. d. [1928].

Gankin, O. H., and H. H. Fisher, *The Bolsheviks and the World War*, Stanford, Calif, 1940.

Geller, L., and N. Rovenskaja, eds., *Peterburgskij i moskovskij sovety rabočich deputatov 1905 goda v dokumentach*, Moscow and Leningrad, 1926.

Golder, F. A., *Documents of Russian History 1914–1917*, New York and London, 1927.

Gosudarstvennaja Duma i socialdemokratija, n. p., 1906.

"Ijul'skie dni v Petrograde," KA 4:23 (1927):1–63, 5:24 (1927):3–70.

"Iskra" za dva goda, Petersburg, 1906.

Istorija soveta rabočich deputatov Peterburga, Petersburg, n. d. [1907].

Itogi i perspektivi. Sbornik statej, Moscow, 1906.

"Iz nakazov delegatam II Vserossijskogo S-ezda Sovetov," KA 3:82 (1937): 6–17.

Izvestija Moskovskogo soveta rabočich deputatov 1905 goda, Moscow, 1925.

"K istorii gvozdevščiny ('Bjulleteni' Rabočej Grupy Central'nogo voenno-promyšlennogo komiteta)," KA 6:67 (1934):28–92.

"K istorii Rabočej Grupy pri Central'nom voenno-promyšlennom komitete," KA 2:57 (1933):43–84.

"K istorii rabočego dviženija 80–90–ch godov," KA 6:91 (1938): 150–198.

"K istorii vseobščej stački na juge Rossii v 1903 g.," KA 3:88 (1938): 76–122.

Kolokol'nikov, P., and S. Rapoport, eds., *1905–1907 gg. v professional'nom dviženii*, Moscow, 1925.

Leninskij Sbornik, vols. 1, 2, 14, and 21, Moscow, 1924 ff.

Letopis' revoljucii, vol. 1, Berlin, Moscow, and Petersburg, 1923.

Meisel, J., and E. Kozera, *Materials for the Study of the Soviet System*, Ann Arbor, Mich., 1950.

Meller, V. L., and A. M. Pankratova, eds., *Rabočee dviženie v 1917 godu*, Moscow and Leningrad, 1926.

"Moskovskij voenno-revoljucionnyj komitet," KA 4:23 (1927): 64–148, 4/5: 65/66 (1934): 164–192, 4:71 (1935): 60–115.

Moskovskoe vooružennoe vosstanie, Moscow, 1906.

Nevskij, V. I., ed., *1905. Sovetskaja pečat' i literatura o sovetach*, Moscow and Leningrad, 1925.

———— ed., *Revoljucija i RKP (b) v materialach i dokumentach*, vol. 3, Moscow, 1925.

"Obzor položenija Rossii za tri mesjaca revoljucii po dannym otdela snošenij s provinciej Vremennogo Komiteta Gosudarstvennoj Dumy," KA 4:15 (1926): 30–60.

Nezlobin, P., ed., *Rabočija organizacii g. Kieva*, Kiev, 1918.

Pariser Kommune 1871. Berichte und Dokumente von Zeitgenossen, Berlin, 1931.

Partija v revoljucii 1905 goda. Dokumenty k istorii partii v 1905 godu, n. p., 1934.

Pis'ma P. B. Aksel'roda i Ju. O. Martova, Berlin, 1924.

Polnyj sbornik platform vsech russkich političeskich partij, 2nd ed., n. p., 1906.

Pravda o Kronštadte, Prague, 1921.

Proletariat v revoljucii 1905–07 goda, Moscow and Leningrad, 1930.

"Rabočee dviženie na zavadach Peterburga v mae 1901 g.," KA 3:76 (1936): 49–66.

Respublika sovetov. (Teorija i praktika sovetskago stroja. Vypusk pervyj), Berlin and Milan, n. d.

Samojlov, F. N., ed., *Ivanovo-Voznesenskij sovet rabočich deputatov 1905 g. v dokumentach*, Moscow and Leningrad, 1935.

Sojuz SR Maksimalistov, *Trudovaja sovetskaja respublika*, Moscow, 1918.

———— *O rabočem kontrole*, Moscow, 1918.

Sovety, s-ezdy sovetov i ispolkomy, Moscow, 1924.

Sovety v oktjabre. Sbornik dokumentov, Moscow, 1928.

"Stačka tkačej Ivanovo-Vozesenskoj manufaktury v 1895 g.," KA 5:72 (1935): 110–119.

Tretij vserossijskij s-ezd sovetov rabočich, soldatskich i krest'janskich deputatov, Petrograd, 1918.

"Tverskaja zabastovka 1885 g.," KA 6:79 (1936): 34–51.

1905 god v očerkach i vospominanijach učastnikov, 2 vols., Moscow, 1927.

1905. Armija v pervoj revoljucii. Materialy i dokumenty, Moscow, 1927.

"Unveröffentlichte Dokumente, verteilt an die Delegierten des XX. Parteitages der KPdSU," *Ost-Probleme* 28 (1956): 963–971.

Vseobščaja stačka na juge Rossii v 1903 godu. Sbornik dokumentov, Moscow, 1938.

Vtoroj vserossijskij s-ezd sovetov rabočich i soldatskich deputatov, Moscow, 1938.

"Vtoroj vserossijskij s-ezd sovetov. (Ankety bol'ševikov-delagatov II s-ezda sovetov)," KA 5:84 (1937): 12–134.

C. MINUTES OF PROCEEDINGS

"Kronštadtskij Sovet r. i s.d. Protokoly zasedanij Kronštadtskogo Soveta, na kotorych obsuždalas' rezoljucija Soveta o vlasti," PR 12:59 (1926): 144–184.

Pervyj legal'nyj peterburgskij komitet bol'ševikov v 1917 g. Sbornik materialov i protokolov zasedanij Peterburgskogo Komiteta RSDRP (b) i ego Ispolnitel'noj Komissii za 1917 g. s rečami V. I. Lenina, Moscow and Leningrad, 1927.

Pervyj vserossijskij s-ezd sovetov rabočich i soldatskich deputatov 1917, 2 vols., Moscow and Leningrad, 1930–31.

Petrogradskij Sovet rabočich i soldatskich deputatov. Protokoly zasedanij ispolnitel'nogo komiteta i bjuro I. K. 1917, Moscow, 1925.

Protokoly s-ezdov i konferencij Vsesojuznoj Kommunističeskoj Partii (b): Četvertyj (ob-edinitel'nyj s-ezd RSDRP. 1906, Moscow, 1934. *Pjatyj s-ezd RSDRP. 1907,* Moscow, 1933. *Sed'maja ("aprel'skaja") vserossijskaja i petrogradskaja obščegorodskaja konferencii RSDRP (b). 1917,* Moscow, 1934. *Šestoj s-ezd RSDRP (b). 1917,* Moscow, 1934.

Protokoly pervago s-ezda partii socialistov-revoljucionerov, n. p., 1906.

Protokoly vtorogo (ekstrennago) s-ezda partii socialistov-revoljucionerov, Petersburg, 1907.

"Protokoly pervoj Moskovskoj oblast'noj konferencii RSDRP (b) 19.–21. aprelja 1917 g.," PR 10:93 (1929): 127–206.

"Protokoly 3. Moskovskoj oblast'noj konferencii RSDRP (b)," PR 10:105 (1930): 94–134.

"Protokoly zasedanij CIK i bjuro CIK soveta rabočich i soldatskich deputatov I sozyva posle oktjabrja," KA 3:10 (1925): 95–137.

Rezoljucii črezvyčajnago i vtorogo vserossijskich s-ezdov sovetov krest'janskich deputatov, 1917, Petrograd, 1917.

Russkaja revoljucija i anarchizm. Doklady čitannye na s-ezde Kommunistov-Anarchistov v oktjabre 1906 goda, London, 1907.

VKP (b) v rezoljucijach i rešenijach s-ezdov, konferencii i plenumov CK, vol. 1: *1898–1924,* Moscow, 1932.

Vtoraja i tret'ja Petrogradskie obščegorodskie konferencii bol'ševikov v ijule i oktjabre 1917 goda. Protokoly i materialy, Moscow and Leningrad, 1927.

D. NEWSPAPERS

Delo Naroda, 1917.
Edinstvo, 1917.
Iskra, 1900–1905.
Izvestija Kronštadtskogo Soveta rabočich i soldatskich deputatov, 1917.
Izvestija Moskovskogo Soveta rabočich (after November 1917: *i soldatskich*) *deputatov,* 1917–18.
Izvestija Petrogradskogo Soveta rabočich i soldatskich deputatov, 1917.
Kommuna, 1905.
Maksimalist, 1918.
Načalo, 1905.
Novaja Žizn', 1905, 1917.
Pravda, 1917.
Proletarij, 1905.
Vpered, 1905.

2. References

A. INDIVIDUAL ACCOUNTS

Antonow-Owsejenko, V. N., *Der Aufbau der Roten Armee in der Revolution,* Hamburg, 1923.

Balabanov, M., *Ot 1905 k 1917 godu. Massovoe rabočee dviženie,* Moscow and Leningrad, 1927.

Batsell, W. R., *Soviet Rule in Russia,* New York, 1929.

Becker, B., *Geschichte der revolutionären Pariser Kommune in den Jahren 1789–1794,* Braunschweig, 1875.

———— *Geschichte und Theorie der Pariser revolutionären Kommune des Jahres 1871.* Leipzig, 1879.

Berkmann, A., *The Kronstadt Rebellion,* Berlin, 1922.

———— *Der Aufstand von Kronstadt (Der Monat,* special issue 30), Berlin, 1951.

Bernstein, E., *Sozialismus und Demokratie in der grossen englischen Revolution,* 3rd ed., Stuttgart, 1919.

Borkenau, F., *Das Jahr 1917. Wirklichkeit und Legende der russischen Revolution (Der Monat,* special issue 37), Berlin, 1952.

———— *Der russische Bürgerkrieg 1918–1921,* Berlin, 1954.

Brailsford, H. N., *How the Soviets Work,* New York, 1927.

Brigl-Matthias, *Das Betriebsräteproblem,* Berlin and Leipzig, 1926.

Buber, M., *Pfade in Utopia,* Heidelberg, 1950.

Carr, E. H. *Michael Bakunin,* London, 1937.

———— *The Bolshevik Revolution 1917–1923,* 3 vols., London, 1950–53.

Chamberlin, W. H., *The Russian Revolution 1917–1921,* 2 vols., 2nd ed., New York, 1952.

Chernov, V., *The Great Russian Revolution,* New Haven, Conn., 1936.

Cole, G. D., *A History of Socialist Thought,* 2 vols., London, 1953–54.

Cunow, H., *Die Marxsche Geschichts-, Gesellschafts- und Staatstheorie,* 3rd ed., Berlin, 1923.

Dan, Th., *Gewerkschaften und Politik in Sowjetrussland,* Berlin and Stuttgart, 1923.

———— *Der Arbeiter in Sowjetrussland,* Berlin and Stuttgart, 1923.

———— *Proischoždenie bol'ševizma,* New York, 1946.

Denisov, A., *Istorija Sovetskogo gosudarstva i prava,* Moscow, 1949.

Der Rätegedanke als Staatstheorie und seine Keime in den Schriften von K. Marx und Fr. Engels, n. p., n. d.

Deutscher, I., *Soviet Trade Unions,* London, 1950.

———— *The Prophet Armed. Trotsky 1879–1921,* London, 1954.

Dewar, M., *Labour Policy in the USSR 1917–1928,* London and New York, 1956.

Diehl, K., *Die Diktatur des Proletariats und das Rätesystem,* Jena, 1920.

Dubrowski, S., *Die Bauernbewegung in der russischen Revolution 1917,* Berlin, 1929.

Eljaschoff, M., *Die Grundzüge der Sowjetverfassung,* Heidelberg, 1925.

Eroshkin, M., *The Soviets in Russia,* New York, 1919.

Fainsod, M., *International Socialism and the World War,* Cambridge, Mass., 1935.

Farbman, M., *Bolshevism in Retreat,* London, 1922.

von Freytagh-Loringhoven, A., *Die Gesetzgebung der russischen Revolution,* Halle, 1920.

Gajsinskij, M., *Bor'ba bol'ševikov za krest'janstvo v 1917 g.,* Moscow, 1933.

Gerassimoff, A., *Der Kampf gegen die erste russische Revolution,* Frauenfeld and Leipzig, 1934.

Geschichte der KPSU (B), Berlin, 1945.

Gitermann, V., *Geschichte Russlands,* vol. 3, Hamburg, 1949.

Goebel, J., *Entwicklungsgang der russischen Industriearbeiter bis zur ersten Revolution,* Leipzig, 1920.

Gordon, M., *Očerk ékonomičeskoj bor'by rabočich v Rossii,* 3rd ed., Leningrad, 1925.

Gorin, P., *Očerki po istorii sovetov rabočich deputatov v 1905 godu,* 2nd ed., Moscow, 1930.

Grinewitsch, W., *Die Gewerkschaftsbewegung in Russland,* vol. 1: *1905–1914,* Berlin, 1927.

Gurvič, G., *Istorija sovetskoj konstitucii,* Moscow, 1923.

Gutmann, F., *Das Rätesystem, seine Verfechter und seine Probleme,* Munich, 1922.

Haimson, L. H., *The Russian Marxists and the Origins of Bolshevism,* Cambridge, Mass., 1955.

Heintz, P., *Die Autoritätsproblematik bei Proudhon,* Cologne, 1957.

Jakovlev, Ja., *Russkij anarchizm v velikoj russkoj revoljucii,* Kharkov, 1921.

Jaroslavskij, E., ed., *Istorija VKP (b),* 4 vols., Moscow and Leningrad, 1926–1930.

(Jaroslawski), *Aus der Geschichte der KPSU (B),* vol. 1, Hamburg and Berlin, 1929.

Jellinek, F., *The Paris Commune of 1871,* London, 1937.

Kautsky, K., *Die Diktatur des Proletariats,* Vienna, 1918.

——— *Terrorismus und Kommunismus,* Berlin, 1919.

Koch, W., *Die bol'ševistischen Gewerkschaften,* Jena, 1932.

Koechlin, H., *Die Pariser Kommune im Bewusstsein ihrer Anhänger,* Basel, 1950.

Köhler, S., *Die russische Industriearbeiterschaft von 1905–1917,* Berlin and Leipzig, 1921.

Kostomarov, G., *Moskovskij Sovet rabočich deputatov v 1905 godu,* 2nd ed., Moscow, 1955.

Kottler, W., *Demokratie und Rätegedanke in der grossen englischen Revolution* (Leipziger rechtswissenschaftliche Studien, vol. 15), Leipzig, 1925.

Kropotkin, P., *Die Französische Revolution 1789–1793,* Leipzig, 1909.

Kulczycki, L., *Geschichte der russischen Revolution,* 3 vols., Gotha, 1910–14.

Larin, L., and L. Kritzmann, *Wirtschaftsleben und wirtschaftlicher Aufbau in Sowjetrussland 1917–1920,* Berlin, 1921.

Lissagary, P. O., *Geschichte der Kommune von 1871*, Stuttgart, 1891.
Lomonossoff, I. W., *Die russische März-Revolution 1917*, Munich, 1921.
Losowski, A., *Die Gewerkschaften in Sowjetrussland*, Berlin, 1920.
Lukacs, G., *Lenin. Studie über den Zusammenhang seiner Gedanken*, Vienna, 1924.
Martow, J., and Th. Dan, *Geschichte der russischen Sozialdemokratie*, Berlin, 1926.
Mason, E., *The Paris Commune*, New York, 1930.
Maurach, R., *Handbuch der Sowjetverfassung*, Munich, 1955.
Mautner, W., *Der Bolschewismus*, Stuttgart, 1922.
Mavor, J., *An Economic History of Russia*, 2 vols., Toronto and London, n. d. [1914].
Maximoff, G. P., *The Political Philosophy of Bakunin: Scientific Anarchism*, New York, 1953.
Mel'gunov, S. P., *Kak bol'ševiki zachvatili vlast'*, Paris, 1953.
Miliukow, P., *Russlands Zusammenbruch*, 2 vols., Leipzig and Berlin, 1925–26.
Mitel'man, M., B. Glebov, and A. Ul'janskij, *Istorija Putilovskogo zavoda 1789–1917*, 2nd ed., Moscow and Leningrad, 1941.
Monnerot, J., *Soziologie des Kommunismus*, Cologne and Berlin, 1952.
Nettlau, M., *Der Anarchismus von Proudhon zu Kropotkin*, Berlin, 1927.
Neuberger, J., *Die Verfassung der Russischen Föderativen Sowjetrepublik*, Berlin and Bonn, 1926.
Nevskij, V. I., *Sovety i vooružennye vosstanija v 1905 godu*, Moscow, 1931.
Nötzel, K., *Die soziale Bewegung in Russland*, Berlin, 1923.
Ozerov, I. K., *Politika po rabočemu voprosu v Rossii za poslednie gody*, Petersburg, 1906.
Pankratova, A. M., *Pervaja russkaja revoljucija 1905-1907 gg.*, 2nd ed., Moscow, 1951.
Paquet, A., *Der Geist der russischen Revolution*, Leipzig, 1921.
Paschitnow, K. A., *Die Lage der arbeitenden Klasse in Russland*, Stuttgart, 1907.
Pipes, R. E., *The Formation of the Soviet Union. Communism and Nationalism 1917–1923*, Cambridge, Mass., 1954.
Pokrowski, M., *Geschichte Russlands von seiner Entstehung bis zur neuesten Zeit*, Leipzig, 1929.
Possony, S., *Jahrhundert des Aufruhrs*, Munich, 1956.
Prokopovicz, S. N., *Russlands Volkswirtschaft unter den Sowjets*, Zurich and New York, 1944.
Puchov, A. S., *Kronštadtskij mjatež v 1921 g.*, Leningrad, 1931.
Pyziur, E., *The Doctrine of Anarchism of Michael Bakunin*, Milwaukee, Wis., 1955.
Radek, K., *Wege der russischen Revolution*, Hamburg, 1922.
Radkey, O. H., *The Election to the Russian Constituent Assembly of 1917*, Cambridge, Mass., 1950.
Ramm, T., *Die grossen Sozialisten als Rechts- und Sozialphilosophen*, vol. 1, Stuttgart, 1955.

von Rauch, G., *Geschichte des bolschewistischen Russland*, Wiesbaden, 1955.
⸺ *Lenin*, Göttingen, 1957.
Reshetar, J. S., *The Ukrainian Revolution 1917–1920*, Princeton, N. J., 1952.
Robinson, G. T., *Rural Russia under the Old Regime*, London, 1932.
Rosenberg, A., *Geschichte des Bolschewismus von Marx bis zur Gegenwart*, Berlin, 1932.
Rosenstock-Huessy, E., *Die europäischen Revolutionen und der Charakter der Nationen*, 2nd ed., Stuttgart, 1951.
Rosmer, A., *Le mouvement ouvrier pendant la guerre*, Paris, 1936.
Schapiro, L., *The Origin of the Communist Autocracy*, London, 1955.
Šaveko, N., *Oktjabr'skaja revoljucija i učreditel'noe sobranie*, Moscow and Leningrad, 1928.
Scheibert, P., *Von Bakunin zu Lenin. Geschichte der russischen revolutionären Ideologien 1840–1895*, vol. 1 (Studien zur Geschichte Osteuropas, vol. 3), Leiden, 1956.
Schljapnikow, A., *Die russischen Gewerkschaften*, Leipzig, 1920.
Seeling, O., *Der Rätegedanke und seine Verwirklichung in Sowjetrussland*, Berlin, 1925.
Selznick, P., *The Organizational Weapon. A Study of Bolshevik Strategy and Tactics*, New York, 1952.
Seton-Watson, H., *From Lenin to Malenkow*, 3rd ed., New York, 1954.
Shub, D., *Lenin*, New York, 1948.
Sinowjew, G., *Geschichte der kommunistischen Partei Russlands*, Hamburg, 1923.
Smilg-Benario, M., *Der Zusammenbruch der Zarenmonarchie*, Vienna, 1928.
⸺ *Von Kerenski zu Lenin*, Vienna, 1929.
Spiridovich, A., *Histoire du terrorisme russe 1886–1917*, Paris, 1930.
Tomski, M., *Abhandlungen über die Gewerkschaftsbewegung in Russland*, Hamburg, 1921.
Tormin, W., *Zwischen Rätediktatur und sozialer Demokratie. Die Geschichte der Rätebewegung in der deutschen Revolution 1918–19*, Düsseldorf, 1954.
Towster, J., *Political Power in the USSR 1917–1947*, New York, 1948.
Treadgold, D. W., *Lenin and His Rivals. The Struggle for Russia's Future, 1898–1906*, London, 1955.
Trockij, L., *O Lenine, Materialy dlja biografa*, 2nd ed., Moscow, n. d. [1924].
⸺ *Trotzki, Die Geburt der Roten Armee*, Vienna, 1924.
⸺ *Geschichte der russischen Revolution*, 2 vols., Berlin, 1931–33.
⸺ *Stalin*, Cologne and Berlin, 1952.
Tscherewanin, A., *Das Proletariat und die russische Revolution*, Stuttgart, 1908.
Turin, S. P., *From Peter the Great to Lenin. A History of the Russian Labour Movement*, London, 1935.
Čermenskij, E. D., *Buržuazija i carizm v revoljucii 1905–07 g.*, Moscow, 1939.
Tyrkova-Williams, A., *From Liberty to Brest Litowsk*, London, 1919.
von Ungern-Sternberg, R., *Über die wirtschaftliche und rechtliche Lage der St. Petersburger Arbeiterschaft*, Berlin, 1909.
⸺ *Die Erziehung der St. Petersburger Arbeiterschaft zur Revolution*, Berlin, 1909.

Vladimirskij, M., *Organizacija sovetskoj vlasti na mestach*, Moscow, 1919.
Valentinov, N., *Vstreči s Leninym*, New York, 1953.
Vyshinsky, A., *The Law of the Soviet State*, New York, 1948.
Wersin, F., *Diktatur des Proletariats*, Breslau, n. d.
Williams, A. R., *Durch die russische Revolution 1917–1918*, Berlin, 1922.
Wolfe, B. D., *Three Who Made a Revolution*, New York, 1948.

B. COLLECTIONS

Achun, M., and V. Petrov, eds., *1917 god v Moskve. Chronika revoljucii*, Moscow, 1934.
Avdeev, N., *Revoljucija 1917 goda. Chronika sobytij*, vol. 1: *Janvar'-Aprel'*; vol. 2: *Aprel'-Maj*, Moscow and Leningrad, 1923.
Bergmann, Smilga, and Trotzki, *Die russische sozialistische Rote Armee*, Zurich, 1920.
Die Parteien und das Rätesystem, Charlottenburg, 1919.
Izgoev, A. S., ed., *Russkoe obščestvo i revoljucija*, Moscow, 1910.
Ljubimov, I. N., *Revoljucija 1917 goda. Chronika sobytij*, vol. 6: *Oktjabr'-Dekabr'*, Moscow and Leningrad, 1930.
Milonov, Ju., ed., *Professional'nye sojuzy SSSR 1905–1917–1927*, Moscow, 1927.
Pankratova, A., and Sidorov, eds., *Revoljucija 1905–07 gg. v nacional'nych raionach Rossii*, Moscow, 1949.
Pokrovskij, M., ed., *Očerki po istorii oktjabr'skoj revoljucii*, 2 vols., Moscow and Leningrad, 1927.
Rjabinskij, K., *Revoljucija 1917 goda. Chronika sobytij*, vol. 5; *Oktjabr'*, Moscow and Leningrad, 1926.
Ustanovlenie sovetskoj vlasti na mestach v 1917–1918 godach, Moscow, 1953.
Vladimirova, V., *Revoljucija 1917 goda. Chronika sobytij*, vol. 3: *Ijun'-Ijul'*, Moscow and Leningrad, 1923; vol. 4: *Avgust-Sentjabr'*, Moscow and Leningrad, 1924.
Za pjat' let, 1917–1922. Sbornik CK RKP, Moscow, 1922.

C. ARTICLES

Amal'rik, A. S., "K voprosu o čislennosti i geografičeskom razmeščenii stačečnikov v Evropejskoj Rossii v 1905 godu," *IZ* 52 (1955):142–185.
Amburskij, R., "Lenin o revoljucionno-demokratičeskoj diktature proletariata i krest'janstva v revoljucii 1905–1907 gg.," *PR* 12:107 (1930):3–38.
Anweiler, O., "Die russische Revolution von 1905," *Jahrbücher für Geschichte Osteuropas*, n. s., 3 (1955): 161–193.
——— "Lenin und die Kunst des Aufstandes," *Wehrwissenschaftliche Rundschau*, 5 (1955):459–472.
——— "Lenin und der friedliche Übergang zum Sozialismus," *Osteuropa*, 6, (1956):190–196.
——— "Lenins Machteroberung 1917," *Geschichte in Wissenschaft und Unterricht*, 8 (1957):653–670.

———"Die Arbeiterselbstverwaltung in Polen," *Osteuropa*, 8 (1958):224–232.
——— "Die Räte in der ungarischen Revolution 1956," *Osteuropa*, 8 (1958):
393–400.
Ascher, A., "The Kornilov Affair," *The Russian Review*, 12 (1953):235–252.
Bogačev, P. M., "Rabočee dviženie v Kostrome v 1905 godu," *IZ* 49 (1954):
86–110.
Borkenau, F., "Das Problem der Machtergreifung des Kommunismus," *Sowjet-studien*, 1 (1956):5–19.
Burdžalov, E. N., "O taktike bol'ševikov v marte-aprele 1917 goda," *VI* 4 (1956):38–56.
Bystrych, F. P., "Pobeda Velikoj Oktjabr'skoj socialističeskoj revoljucii na Urale," *VI* 8 (1957):25–42.
Cejtlin, D. A., "Fabrično-zavodskie komitety Petrograda v fevrale-oktjabre 1917 goda," *VI* 11 (1956):86–97.
Cervadze, M. V., "Krest'janskoe revoljucionnoe dviženie v Gurii v 1905 g." *VI* 12 (1955):87–95.
Daniels, R. V., "The Kronstadt Revolt. A Study in the Dynamics of Revolution," *The American Slavic and East European Review*, 10 (1951):241–254.
——— "The State and Revolution. A Case Study in the Genesis and Transformation of Communist Ideology," *The American Slavic and East European Review*, 12 (1953):22–43.
Donij, N. R., "Vooružennoe vosstanie na Ekaterinoslavščine v dekabre 1905 g.," *VI* 12 (1955):19–32.
Drabkina, F. I., "Vserossijskoe soveščanie bol'ševikov v marte 1917 goda," *VI* 9 (1956):3–16.
Erman, L. E., "Učastie demokratičeskoj intelligencii vo vserossijskoj oktjabr'skoj političeskoj stački," *IZ* 49 (1954):352–390.
Flerovskij, I., "Kronštadtskaja respublika," *PR* 11:58 (1926):29–55; 12:59 (1926):113–143.
Galkina, P. I., "Vseobščaja stačka ivanovo-voznesenskich tekstil'ščikov letom 1905 g.," *VI* 6 (1955):87–97.
Genkina, E., "Pervye dni oktjabr'skoj revoljucii 1917 goda," *PR* 3 (1940): 17–35.
Geyer, D., "Die russischen Räte und die Friedensfrage im Frühjahr und Sommer 1917," *Vierteljahrshefte für Zeitgeschichte*, 5 (1957):220–240.
——— "Die Ukraine im Jahre 1917," *Geschichte in Wissenschaft und Unterricht*, 8 (1957):670–687.
Golikov, G. N., and Ju. S. Tokarev, "Aprel'skij krizis 1917," *IZ* 57 (1956): 35–79.
Gopner, I. S., "Martovskie i aprel'skie dni 1917 goda. (Iz vospominanij učastnika Oktjabr'skoj revoljucii)," *VI* 3 (1957):42–52.
Gorodeckij, E. N., "Bor'ba narodnych mass za sozdanie sovetskich gosudarstvennych organov (1917–18)," *VI* 8 (1955):26–39.
——— "Iz istorii Oktjabr'skogo vooružennogo vosstanija i II Vserossijskogo s-ezda Sovetov," *VI* 10 (1957):23–48.
Grunt, A. J., and N. T. Fedoseeva, "Pobeda Oktjabr'skogo vooružennogo vosstanija v Moskve," *VI* 11 (1957):3–26.

References   321

Gurian, W., "Lenins Methoden der Machteroberung im Jahre 1917," in *Deutschland und Europa*. *Festschrift für Hans Rothfels*, Düsseldorf, 1951, pp. 271–291.
Hofmann, W., "Parteigeschichtliche Grundlagen des sowjetischen Stalinismus," *Jahrbücher für Geschichte Osteuropas*, n. s. 11 (1954), pp. 304–314.
Huhn, W., "Bolschewismus und Rätedemokratie," *Funken* 6 (1952).
——— "Trotzkis Bonapartismus," *Aufklärung*, 2:2 (1952).
Ignatov, E., "Taktika bol'ševikov i učreditel'noe sobranie," PR 4:75 (1928): 12–44; 5:76 (1928):24–55.
Jakovlev, N. N., "Krasnojarskoe vooružennoe vosstanie 1905 g.," IZ 40 (1952): 29–72.
——— "Moskovskie bol'ševiki vo glave dekabr'skogo vooružennogo vosstanija 1905 goda," VI 12 (1955):3–18.
Jaroslavskij, E., "Sovety rabočich deputatov v 1905 godu," PR 2 (1940):11–32.
Kapustin, H. I., "Bol'ševiki severnogo fronta v bor'be za soldatskie massy v 1917 godu," VI II (1955):105–113.
Kerensky, A., "Why the Russian Monarchy Fell," *The Slavonic Review*, 8 (1929):496–513.
Kirjuchina, E. I., "Vserossijskij Krest'janskij sojuz v 1905 g.," IZ 50 (1955): 95–141.
Konovalov, V., "Revoljucionnoe dviženie v vojskach Moskovskogo voennogo okruga v 1905–1907 g.," VI 10 (1951):89–103.
Korol'čuk, E. A., "Leninskij 'Sojuz bor'by za osvoboždenie rabočego klassa'— začatok boevoj revoljucionnoj rabočej partii," VI 1 (1956):13–30.
Korsch, K., "Revolutionäre Kommune," *Die Aktion*, 5–8 (1929); 3–4 (1931).
Krivošeina, E., "O II Peterburgskom Sovetae rabočich deputatov," PR 6:53 (1926):181–196.
Kropat, W. A., "Lenin und die Konstituierende Versammlung in Russland," *Jahrbücher für Geschichte Osteuropas*, n. s. 5 (1957):488–498.
Kuznecova, L. S., "Stačečnaja bor'ba rabočich Peterburga v janvare 1905 g.," VI 1 (1955): 11–25.
von Laue, T., "Einige politische Fragen der russischen Wirtschaftsplanung um 1900," in *Forschungen zur osteuropäischen Geschichte*, vol. 1, Berlin, 1954, pp. 217–238.
——— "Die Revolution von aussen als erste Phase der russischen Revolution 1917," *Jahrbücher für Geschichte Osteuropas*, n. s. 4 (1956):138–158.
Lejkina, V., "Oktjabr' po Rossii," PR 2:49 (1926):185–233; 11:58 (1926):234–255; 12:59 (1926):238–254.
Levin, Š. M., "V. I. Lenin v Peterburge v 1905 g.," VI 6 (1955):3–12.
Lossky, N. O., "Reflections on the Origins and Meaning of the Russian Revolution," *The Russian Review*, 10 (1951):293–300.
Loš, F. E., "Dekabr'skoe vooružennoe vosstanie na Ukraine," IZ 49 (1954): 53–85.
Markov, W., "Uber das Ende der Pariser Sansculottenbewegung," in *Beiträge zum neuen Geschichtsbild. Festschrift für A. Meusel*, Berlin, 1956, pp. 152–183.
Mautner, W., "Zur Geschichte des Begriffs 'Diktatur des Proletariats,'" *Archiv*

für Geschichte des Sozialismus und der Arbeiterbewegung, 12 (1926): 280–285.

Medvedev, V. K., "Kronštadt v ijul'skie dni 1917 goda," IZ 42 (1953):262–275.

Mel'nikov, A. B., "Revoljucionnoe dviženie v moskovskom garnizone v periode dekabr'skogo vooružennogo vosstanija," IZ 49 (1954):265–300.

Mišin, M. I., "V. I. Lenin o vozmožnosti mirnogo razvitija revoljucii v 1917 godu," VI 5 (1957):17–42.

Mor, N. M., "Šestoj s-ezd RSDRP (b)," VI 8 (1957):3–24.

Murachver, N., "Komitety bednoty i razvertyvanie socialističeskoj revoljucii v derevne (1918 g.)," PR 3 (1940):68–99.

Nürnberger, R., "Lenins Revolutionstheorie. Eine Studie über 'Staat und Revolution,'" in *Marxismusstudien*, 1st series, Tübingen, 1954, pp. 161–172.

Pažitnov, K., "Položenie rabočego klassa v Rossii nakanune revoljucii 1905–1907 gg.," *Voprosy Ekonomiki*, 5 (1955):34–43.

Pašukanis, E. B., "Cromwells Soldatenräte," in O. Hoetzsch, ed., *Aus der historischen Wissenschaft der Sovet-Union*, Ostoeuropäische Forschungen, n. s. 6, Berlin and Königsberg, 1929, pp. 128–152.

Petrova, L. F., "Peterburgskij Sovet rabočich deputatov v 1905 godu," VI 11 (1955):25–40.

Pokrovskij, M., "Načalo proletarskoj revoljucii v Rossii," KA 4/5 (11/12) (1925):v–xvi.

Polеščuk, V. E., "Revoljucionnoe dviženie v man'čžurskoj armii v 1905 g.," IZ 49 (1954):301–351.

Portal, R., "Das Problem einer industriellen Revolution in Russland," in *Forschungen zur osteuropäischen Geschichte*, vol. 1, Berlin, 1954, pp. 205–216.

Ramm, T., "Die künftige Gesellschaftsordnung nach der Theorie von Marx und Engels," in *Marxismusstudien*, 2nd series, Tübingen, 1957, pp. 77–119.

Rašin, A. G., "O Čislennosti i territorial'nom razmeščenii rabočich Rossii v period kapitalizma," IZ 46 (1954):127–181.

Remezova, T. A., "Sovety krest'janskich deputatov v 1917 g.," IZ 32 (1950):-3–39.

Ronin, S. L., "Istoričeskoe značenie sovetov 1905 g.," *Sovetskoe Gosudarstvo i pravo*, 4 (1955):11–20.

Rosloba, A. S., "Pervye massovye vystuplenija peterburgskich rabočich," VI 2 (1956):88–95.

Sassulitsch, W., "Die terroristische Strömung in Russland," *Die Neue Zeit* 21:1 (1902–03):324–329, 361–370.

Savinskij, F., "Parlamentskaja taktika social-demokratov v épochu pervoj russkoj revoljucii," PR 11:106 (1930):3–20; 12:107 (1930):39–77.

Šalaeva, E: I., and I. P. Lejberov, "Profsojuzy Peterburga v 1905 godu," VI 10 (1955):18–30.

Scheibert, P., "Über Lenins Anfänge," *Historische Zeitschrift*, 182 (1956):549–566.

Šmorgun, P. M., "Sovety rabočich deputatov na Ukraine v 1905 godu," IZ 49 (1954):21–52.

Sobolev, P. N., "Rol' Vserossijskich s-ezdov Sovetov v bor'be proletariata za trudjaščeesja krest'janstvo (oktjabr' 1917–janvar' 1918 g.)," VI 12 (1957): 3–24.

Soboul, A., "An den Ursprüngen der Volksdemokratie. Politische Aspekte der Sansculottendemokratie im Jahre II," in *Beiträge zum neuen Geschichtsbild. Festschrift für A. Meusel,* Berlin, 1956, pp. 131–151.

Sokol'skij, V. D., "Novorossijskij Sovet rabočich deputatov v 1905 godu," VI 12 (1955):76–86.

Strakhovsky, L., "Was there a Kornilov Rebellion?," *The Slavonic and East European Review,* 33 (1955): 372–395.

Suprunenko, N. I., "Ustanovlenie Sovetskoj vlasti na Ukraine," VI 10 (1957): 49–70.

Thier, E. "Marx und Proudhon," in *Marxismusstudien,* 2nd series, Tübingen, 1957, pp. 120–150.

Topčeev, I. S., "Vybory v sovety 1905 g.," VI 12 (1955):104–108.

Tret'jakova, E. P., "Fevral'skie sobytija v Moskve," VI 3 (1957):72–84.

Čermenskij, E. D., "Fevral'skaja buržuazno-demokratičeskaja revoljucija 1917 goda," VI 2 (1954):3–18.

Černomordik, S. I., "Dekabr'skoe vooružennoe vosstanie 1905 g.," IZ 18 (1946):3–41.

Ugarov, I. F., "Bol'ševiki vo glave vseobščei političeskoj stački rabočich Moskvy v oktjabre 1905 goda," VI 10 (1955):3–17.

von Ungern-Sternberg, R., "Die Struktur der russischen Gesellschaft zu Beginn des XX. Jahrhunderts," *Schmollers Jahrbuch,* 76 (1956):41–69.

Vardin, I., "Ot melkoburžuaznoj kontrrevoljucii k restavracii kapitalizma. (Partija men'ševikov posle Oktjabra)," in *Za pjat' let, 1917–1922,* Moscow, 1922, pp. 34–58.

Walkin, J., "The Attitude of the Tsarist Government towards the Labor Problem," *The American Slavic and East European Review,* 13 (1954):163–184.

Weber, M., "Zur Lage der bürgerlichen Demokratie in Russland," *Archiv für Sozialwissenschaften und Sozialpolitik,* n. s. 4 (1906):234–353.

——— "Russlands Übergang zum Scheinkonstitutionalismus," *Archiv für Sozialwissenschaften und Sozialpolitik,* n. s. 5 (1906):165–401.

Wolfe, B. D., "Gapon and Zubatov. An Experiment in Police Socialism," *The Russian Review,* 7 (1948):53–61.

3. Recent Works

Andreev, A., *Sovety rabočich i soldatskich deputatov nakanune Oktjabrja (Sovety v period Oktjabr'skoj revoljucii i graždanskoj vojny,* Part 1), Moscow, 1967.

——— *Sovety v pervyj god proletarskoj diktatury (Sovety v period Oktjabr'skoj revoljucii i graždanskoj vojny,* Part 2), Moscow 1967.

Anweiler, Oskar, "The Political Ideology of the Leaders of the Petrograd Soviet in the Spring of 1917," in R. E. Pipes, ed., *Revolutionary Russia,* Cambridge, Mass., 1968, pp. 114–128.

——— "Der revolutionsgeschichtliche Zusammenhang des Räteproblems. Ein

324   SOURCES AND REFERENCES

Abriss," *Politische Vierteljahresschrift*, 11:2 (1970) (special issue):56–69.

Demočkin, N. N., *Sovety 1905 goda—organy revoljucionnoj vlasti*, Moscow, 1963.

Ericjan, Ch. A., *Sovety krest'janskich deputatov v Oktjabr'skoj revoljucii*, Moscow, 1960.

Ferro, M., *La révolution de 1917. La chute du tsarisme et les origines d' octobre*, Paris, 1967.

Gimpel'son, E., *Sovety v period inostrannoj intervencii i graždanskoj vojny* (*Sovety v period Oktjabr'skoj revoljucii i graždanskoj vojny*, Part 3), Moscow, 1968.

Gorodeckij, E. N., *Roždenie Sovetskogo gosudarstva, 1917–1918 gg.*, Moscow, 1965.

Kool, F., and E. Oberländer, *Arbeiterdemokratie oder Parteidiktatur*, Olten and Freiburg im Breisgau, 1967.

Lesnoj, V., *Socialističeskaja revoljucija i gosudarstvennyj apparat*, Moscow, 1968.

Lepeškin, A. I., *Sovety—vlast' trudjaščichsja, 1917–1936*, Moscow, 1966.

Meschkat, K., *Die Pariser Kommune von 1871 im Spiegel der sowj. Geschichtsschreibung*, Berlin, 1965.

Moiseeva, O. N., *Sovety krest'janskich deputatov v 1917 godu*, Moscow, 1967.

Morozov, B. M., *Partija i sovety v Oktjabr'skoj revoljucii*, Moscow, 1966.

Pietsch, W., *Revolution und Staat. Institutionen als Träger der Macht in Sowjetrussland 1917–1922*, Cologne, 1969.

Potechin, M. N., *Pervyj Sovet proletarskoj diktatury. Očerki po istorii petrogradskogo Soveta rabočich i soldatskich deputatov 1917–1918 gg.*, Leningrad, 1966.

Čugaev, D. A., ed., *Petrogradskij voenno-revoljucionnyj komitet. Dokumenty i materialy*, Parts 1–3, Moscow, 1966–67.

Wettig, G., *Die Rolle der russischen Armee in revolutionären Machtkampf 1917* (*Forschungen zur osteuropäischen Geschichte*, vol. 12), Berlin, 1967.

Index

About the Author

Oskar Anweiler is a professor at the Institute of Education of the Ruhr-Universitaet Bochum. He has done major research in the fields of comparative education and Soviet history. Among his works are *Geschichte der Schule und Pädagogik in Russland vom Ende des Zarenreiches bis zum Beginn der Stalin-Ära* [History of schools and education in Russia from the end of czarist rule to the Stalin era] (Heidelberg: Quelle und Meyer, 1968) and *Die Sowjetpädagogik in der Welt von heute* [Soviet education today] (Heidelberg: Quelle und Meyer, 1968). He co-edited with Klaus Meyer *Die sowjetische Bildungspolitik seit 1917, Dokumente und Text* [Soviet education policy since 1917] and with K.-H. Ruffmann *Kulturpolitik der Sowjetunion* [Cultural policy of the Soviet Union] (Stuttgart: Kröner, 1973). He also contributed to *Revolutionary Russia*, Richard Pipes, ed. (Cambridge, Mass.: Harvard University Press, 1968); *Russia Enters the Twentieth Century*, George Katkov *et al.*, eds. (London: Temple Smith, 1971); and *Social Change in the Soviet Union*, Boris Meissner, ed. (Notre Dame, Ind.: University of Notre Dame Press, 1972).

Professor Anweiler is a member of the Executive Committee of the Deutsche Gesellschaft für Osteuropakunde [German society for the study of Eastern Europe] and vice-president of the Comparative Education Society.

INVENTORY 1983